Library of
Davidson College

AGE, GENERATION AND TIME

Age, Generation and Time

Some Features of East African Age Organisations

edited by
P.T.W. Baxter and Uri Almagor

ST. MARTIN'S PRESS · NEW YORK

© C. Hurst & Co. (Publishers) Ltd., 1978

All rights reserved. For information, write:
St. Martin's Press, Inc., 175 Fifth Avenue, New York, N.Y. 10010
Printed in Great Britain
Library of Congress Catalog Card Number 78-18952
ISBN 0-312-01172-5
First published in the United States of America in 1978

Library of Congress Cataloging in Publication Data

Main entry under title:

Age, generation, and time.

    Bibliography: p.
    Includes index.
    1. Ethnology--Africa, East--Addresses, essays,
lectures. 2. Age groups--Addresses, essays, lectures.
I. Baxter, Paul Trevor William.
II. Almagor, Uri.
GN658.A35   301.43'0967   78-18952
ISBN 0-312-01172-5

TO
S.N. EISENSTADT
AND
J.G. PERISTIANY

Printed in Great Britain

Contents

		page
I.	Introduction	1
II.	Aspects of Labwor Age and Generation Grouping and Related Systems *R. G. Abrahams (University of Cambridge)*	37
III.	The Ethos of Equality among Dassanetch Age-Peers *Uri Almagor (Hebrew University, Jerusalem)*	69
IV.	Territorial Organisation and Age among the Mursi *David Turton (University of Manchester)*	95
V.	The Jie Generation Paradox *Paul Spencer (School of Oriental and African Studies, University of London)*	131
VI.	Boran Age-Sets and Generation-Sets: *Gada*, a Puzzle or a Maze? *P. T. W. Baxter (University of Manchester)*	151
VII.	Gabra Age Organisation and Ecology *William Torry (University of California, Berkeley)*	183
VIII.	The Guji: *Gada* as a Ritual System *John Hinnant (Michigan State University)*	207
IX.	Continuity and Change in the Shoa Galla *Gada* System *Hector Blackhurst (University of Manchester)*	245
	Index	268

Figures

		page
I.1.	Map showing principal peoples mentioned in the text	viii
II.1.	*Akiriket* arrangements in Katabok area 1967	53
III.1.	A schematic representation of the Dassanetch age-system	74
III.2.	Relationships within one peer clique	81
IV.1.	Map of Mursi and Bodi country	97
IV.2.	Schematic representation of territorial sections cutting across the 'grain' of natural resources	100
V.1.	Age spread of successive generations (Samburu clan census)	138
V.2.	Proportion of underaging at the tail-end of a closing generation set	139
V.3.	Proportion of overaging in the vanguard of a new generation-set	140
V.4.	Proportion of misfits (underaged and overaged) with varying span for generation-sets	141
VI.1.	Movement of Boran generation-sets	157
VII.1.	Distribution of grades and *gada* officers	196
VII.2.	The movement of *luba* through the grades	200
IX.1.	Tulama *gada* hierarchy	256

Tables

V.1.	Age differences between Samburu fathers and sons	137
V.2.	Revised Jie chronology	146
VIII.1.	Duration of ranks	214
VIII.2.	The contemporary *gada* sequence by classes	215
VIII.3.	A prototypical *gada* system	227

Plates

		page
III.1.	Dassanetch boys showing the hairstyle of *nigen*	73
III.2.	Dassanetch age-peers debating after a meat feast	87
IV.1.	Mursi ceremonial duelling: a contestant ready for his bout	110
IV.2.	Mursi ceremonial duelling: a bout in progress	112
VI.1.	A Boran *raaba* with a *guutu* or 'male tuft'	173
VII.1.	A Gabra political elder	192
VIII.1.	Guji: a father cutting his son's hair during *makabasa*	217
VIII.2.	Guji: cutting the *wudessa* pole	218
IX.1.	Shoa *folle* dancing at a *gada* ceremony	250

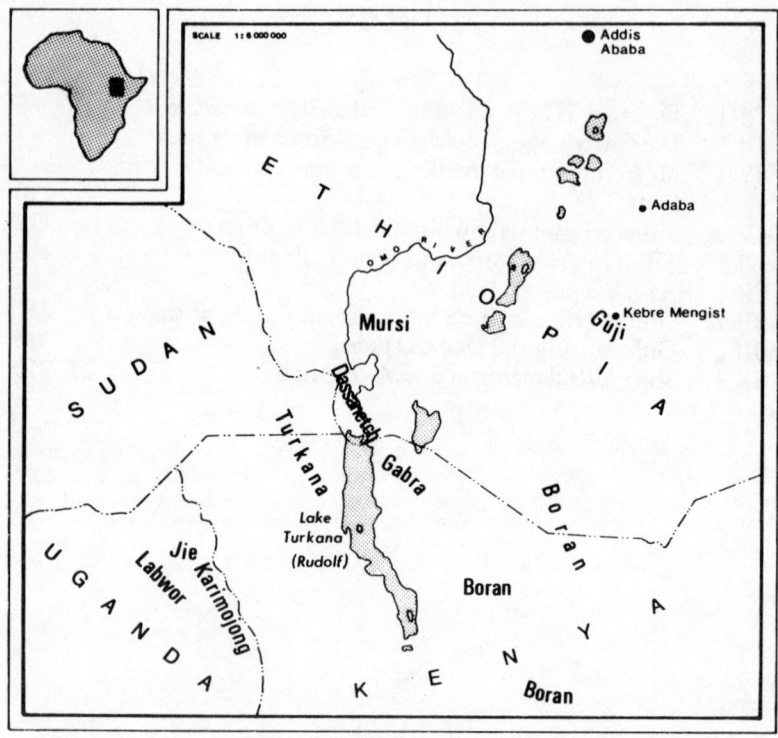

Figure I.1. Map showing principal peoples mentioned in the text

1
Introduction

P.T.W. BAXTER AND URI ALMAGOR

During the academic year 1975-6 four of us (Almagor, Baxter, Blackhurst and Turton) were in Manchester; we had all recently worked in Ethiopia and had studied peoples who had active age and/or generation set systems. We held a small working seminar in July 1975, to which we invited the other contributors who had all recently worked among nearby peoples and shared our interests. We also invited a handful of colleagues whom we knew to be interested in the general problems which arise from the study of age-systems to sit in. With the exceptions of Torry and Spencer, who were not able to attend, each contributor read a first draft of his paper. Each then rewrote his paper in the light of the discussion it had generated.

We consider that the shared interests of the contributors and the selection of peoples give the volume intellectual and ethnographic coherence. Certainly much of the ethnographic data is new. The term 'age-system', or 'age-organisation', is sometimes used as a generic short-hand term for systems and organisations based on age, generation or on mixtures of the two. This is common usage and should not make for any obscurity in context. We assume either some acquaintance with age-systems or access to Gulliver's lucid summary (1968).[1]

Grading by relative age, even between siblings, the grouping of approximate coevals and distinguishing between generations are probably basic modes of social categorisation, like distinctions by sex. Distinctions of age and generation are integral to the etiquette of daily intercourse, to kinship terminology — as Radcliffe-Brown instructed us and as Needham has recently reminded us — and to myth and story. Every culture distinguishes successive stages in the life-cycle from mewling and puking infancy to second childishness. Some indeed, though not usually societies with age-systems, recognise a post-life grade of ancestorhood. Verbal deference to grey hairs and protests about riotous youth have probably been common to all cultures. Elders everywhere must have echoed the shepherd in *The Winters Tale*:

I would there were no age between ten and three-and-twenty, or that youth would sleep out the rest; for there is nothing in the between but getting wenches with child, wronging the ancientry, stealing, fighting.

Likewise many youngsters must have echoed a representative of the Youth Council to the 1969 Ghana Constituent Assembly who complained that 'most Ghanaians still laboured under the impression that knowledge, wisdom and experience are synonomous with age.'[2] Even young anthropologists have been known to mutter against their elders. Age-grading, whether formally marked by a rite of passage or merely tacitly recognised, is probably universal, and gives the process of aging a social impress. But age-setting or generation-setting — the grouping of persons who are either close in age or of the same generation into a structure of hierarchically ordered sets which are vested with a diffuse range of social and ritual responsibilities — is an unwieldy, almost bizarre mode of social organisation.

Age-grading is likely to be incorporated into — or to run in alignment with — age-setting where setting occurs, and to be used as a means of regulating relationships between old and young, simply from convenience and the need for compatibility; as descent groups, where they occur, need to be compatible, or at least not grossly incompatible, with the kinship system and are likely to use the terminology of kinship, age-sets are likely to be compatible with age-grades and use age-grade terminology. But crucially, whereas age-grading does not require setting, setting requires age-grading. Age- and/or generation-setting, which is the limited phenomenon with which we are concerned here, is widespread geographically but, as a mode of social organisation, it is particularly conspicuous in parts of East Africa. An extensive body of publications has been generated, but some confusions still exist. Some of the difficulties which have beset the analysis of age-systems have arisen from attempts to answer misconceived questions or to impose observer classifications on the data, rather than first attempting to elucidate the folk classifications in the social contexts in which they are used. Enquiry may have been obfuscated because of the tendency of some East African ethnographers to treat age-systems as if they formed an isolable class of social phenomena, rather than as institutions which share family resemblances but which, in each society in which they occur, are likely to be enmeshed in different social settings.

Much of the work on age-systems has concentrated on elucidating the rules which regulate the recruitment to sets and the movement of sets within the system, with particular attention to the way in which political offices and authority are vested in sets in acephalous societies. This has frequently led to an emphasis in analysis (*a*) on age-systems as political organisations, (*b*) on historical explanations for the current organisational forms which sets take, (*c*) on age-systems as systems of rules. Whereas in descriptions of age-organisations in societies with centralised political systems, such as Swazi or Zulu, the special terminology which has grown up in the discussion of age-sets has been less used and age-groupings have been set firmly in a military context. Hilda Kuper, for example, writes of 'regimental age-classes' (1963: 62). Oddly where groups of coevals appear to have had what were apparently quite clear military, policing or work tasks they seem to have been less remarked about and less discussed than when their tasks have remained vague, diffuse and concerned with ritual; as if to kill people made more immediate and obvious sense than to meet in order to pray and offer sacrifices. This bias in observers in part springs from colonial obsessions with primitive unruliness and the supposed propensity to raiding and warfare of many African peoples, especially pastoral ones, which was then used to justify their colonisation.

Sets mostly occur in — or at any rate are most conspicuous in — non-centralised political systems and therefore more readily have political tasks attributed to them. When these tasks are discovered to be unperformed, or casually performed, then the set systems are invariably described as less effective organisations than they were in some past time. Analysts have been tempted to suggest that, in some idyllic pre-colonial past, sets were more organised and more active politically, ritually and militarily than they were when the analysts were in the field. Following this ascription of diffuse political, ritual and military authority to sets and their officers in the past, observers have then used that reconstruction to explain the current set activities which they have observed. Age-sets are thereby constantly represented as having fallen away from an earlier more active and effective mode of organisation.[3] So that, in the pre-colonial or pre-market past, age-set systems not only obeyed clearer rules but were much more important social institutions than at the time of their observation. Age-set obligations, like those of kinship (and sometimes with about as much truth), are reported as having been eroded by change; and their martial values, which stressed both individual valour and fortitude and intense group bonding, withered by schooling and wages.

Next we glance at two features of sets which are often considered to be central to them, namely sets as mechanisms for the socialisation of young men and as socially therapeutic channels for the aggressive activities of young men. The existence of sets makes them obvious choices for such purposes, but it does not mean that such activities are then necessary functions of sets. A regular gathering of approximate coevals does not make an age-set system, whether the get-together is to raid for cattle, or to smash up rivals in football stadia. Keiser's study *The Vice-Lords* brings this out clearly and, we suggest, shows most succinctly that many of the traits and socialisation functions frequently attributed to age-sets are performed among urban blacks in Chicago by gangs. Keiser's 'warriors of the streets' form named groups each with a territory, such as the particular gang 'the Vice-Lords', which are sub-divided by age and activities into Seniors, Juniors, and Midgets and down to juvenile Pee-Wees. Expression of loyalty in the face of violence and danger to their sub-group and the maintenance of aggressive encounters with like neighbouring gangs are, according to the rhetoric of members, the primary purposes of gangs. Members flaunt common insignia such as rings and capes. A gang attempts 'to monopolise girls', has officers with flamboyant honorific titles, maintains strict etiquette between members and even pours libations of wine and, above all, explicitly inculcates warrior values and values of mutual help into members. Also, like Maasai or Samburu moran,[4] gang members aim to pass out of warriorhood; as one informant put it 'We are not going to be young savages all our life' (71). But when Vice-Lords move back into mainstream society, or branch of it, they do so as individuals, not as a set where members jointly undergo a change of status. They are, in that respect at any rate, more like Boy Scouts than moran. The cultural comparisons with Samburu, Maasai, Karimojong or Boran junior age-sets are remarkable, but the Vice-Lords, and other gangs, are not a unit in a sequence of similar units and are not an age-set in an age-system. The Vice-Lord traits which are similar to those of moran are of a very general kind, and related to the wide-spread processes of age-grading rather than to age-setting. Gangs are voluntary associations which at best are condoned, but sets are part of the formal social order blessed by tradition and membership is usually ascribed, and is always obligatory.[5]

The unravelling and systematising of the rule complexities which each age-system has evolved has its own fascination, as the recent works of Stewart and Legesse, for example, brilliantly show. Clearly the rules which regulate an age-system must be made explicit in any analysis of it, if those rules have constraining force or influence. The rules of age-sets and generation-sets, because they attempt to regulate for the idiosyncrasies of human behaviour, have to allow for variation and are therefore complex. But too narrow a concern with the study of rules has the danger that the intellectual effort involved can come to provide its own justification; moreover, we are all easily tempted to overestimate the importance of data which have been hard to collect, and to collate and to explain in an ordered way. Excessive concentration on the rules can incur two other risks. On the one hand their very complexity and the possibility for almost infinite variation can result in the analyst playing a sort of mental game equivalent to the old kinship algebra. On the other, he can come to argue that any particular system should have worked in a particular way, because that is what the rules say, so if it does not work in that way it must be because some extraneous event, such as colonial rule, or drought, or labour migration, has interrupted the proper working of the system. What results is an intellectualist view of age-systems, which, to paraphrase Evans-Pritchard, demonstrates that to speak the language of age-sets fluently is very different to understanding them. What a 'rules approach' tends to ignore is the actual behaviour of set-members to each other and to members of other sets, and the ways in which the members of an age-system are enmeshed in other social, economic and ritual relationships. To underemphasise these last is hazardous. On the one hand if the rules themselves become the centre of the analysis, as if they were an isolated compelling force on the actors, the analyst can be led to doubt the statements of informants as recorded by ethnographers of proven reliability. Even as sensitive a commentator as Stewart,[6] for example, suggest that Gulliver's informants 'must certainly have misinformed him' (57), or that 'there is the question of whether to believe Jensen's informants' (80). To do this runs counter to one of the primary rules of analysis, which is that if the data provided by informants seems to contradict one's own assumptions it is time to question those assumptions. On the other hand the explanatory power of the rules, as told by informants, is overweighted if the analyst ignores the distinction (so clearly pointed out by Lévi-Strauss) between conscious models and those unconscious models which, though shrouded, may subtly and firmly constrain behaviour and, indeed, may inhere in those rules.

These essays are concerned with the consequences that being a member of an age-system has for a member and what the inter-active consequences of membership are for his other social relationships. Simply no individual is only a member of his age-system and able to isolate his social position in that system from his other social positions. To paraphrase Meggitt, age-set studies alone are simply not enough, not even for comprehending age-set systems themselves (1972:82). The contributors therefore have endeavoured to limit the description of the rules as far as they could, and bear in mind, as Kuper puts it, that in 'tribal society a person is a meeting point of identities — the identity of siblings, the identity of the lineage, the identity of the age-group' (1963:57).

Age-systems attempt to create cognitive and structural order within and for a population by creating categories based on age and generation; as does a kinship system. They assume demographic regularity and long-run social stability within that population. An age-system implies continuity and replacement of personnel in an orderly and predictable manner through the replacement by birth of new members to replace those who die. Similarly, generation implies begetting, replacement and continuity. When a man's placement within a system is determined by that of his father's an underlying assumption is that fathers will beget sons within a limited time span, and that therefore there will be approximate accord between age and generation. In social reality this assumption is false so that a continuing dilemma in all such systems is the reconciliation of age, generation and the steady flow of time. The biological facts of birth and death must slide out of alignment with the social order with which they should conform. Age-systems which are based on measured units of time are unsuccessful attempts to tame time by chopping it up into manageable slices. So it should be useful, when examining a particular system, to attempt to examine this gap between the cognitive order and the social reality. One is bound to be at least a little out of kilter with the other and to result in 'a degree of built-in malfunctioning' (Dyson-Hudson:202).

Divisions by age and generation must then have an arbitrary quality; as in an examination grading system, the persons on the neighbouring edges of two classes are likely to be more similar to each other than they are to members of their own class at its other extreme. Physical, mental, sexual and social ages do not necessarily correspond, as any teacher of a class recruited strictly by age can testify, and we must all know some pensioners who are more lively minded and physically active than some undergraduates.

In societies in which 'age' is determined by social and/or biological maturation, late or early developers are not anomalous and do not create difficulties. But where 'age' is determined by the calendar or some other arbitrary device, such as the periodic flowering of the *setiot* tree, age and readiness are bound sometimes not to coincide. In our own educational system we have had to invent devices such as remove forms, remedial classes, and mature student entry qualifications; Spencer (1965:308) has suggested illuminating comparisons between Public Schools and the age-system of the Samburu. Only recently has the age of majority been lowered in Britain and the age of consent has always presented difficulties to courts. We speak of persons as 'old' or 'young' for their age or as being 'typical' or 'untypical' of their generation.

Similar difficulties over defining boundaries which coincide with life-stages occur with generation; many people have aunts and uncles, that is members of the generation genealogically senior to them, who are their coevals. In societies in which polygyny is favoured and old men continue to father children on young wives, the likelihood of such anomalous relationships increases with each succeeding generation. If men can father children for a span of fifty years the differences in ages between their grandsons can be greater than the possible life-span of one of those grandsons. There is then a simple difference between a genealogical generation and what might be called a shifting social generation, i.e. persons who cluster in age and share similar social attributes, such as the likelihood of becoming grandfathers, fathers etc. at about the same time. Generation in this social sense, in which similar social behaviour is expected of people who are similar in age measured in years, (as in Shakespeare's seven ages of man), is the basis of all age-grading systems. When genealogical generation and social generation are out of alignment anomalies occur. It is this type of discrepancy which lies at the centre of the so-called '*gada* puzzle', considered here in the essays on the Oromo of Baxter, Blackhurst,

Torry and Hinnant. Not surprisingly, therefore, we find that most age-systems and generation systems, and especially systems which mix both principles, have secondary rules which regulate the legitimate procreation of their members, in an endeavour to control the birth of anomalous persons. These are usually rules which regulate marriage, but they may, as among the Oromo, concern fostering or infanticide. Such rules follow from the logic of the particular systems and, though expressed in the vocabulary of kinship with appropriate moral overtones, they have nothing to do with incest prohibitions which are based on degrees of kinship or affinity.

In any discussion of age and generation systems it is essential to be clear whether what is being discussed is a distinct genealogical generation or a shifting social generation. A genealogical generation is one which consists of men who share the same genealogical level, that is one which consists of men who are all of the generation of fathers and uncles and are followed by their sons and nephews who form the succeeding generation. An uncle and a nephew cannot ever be of the same genealogical generation. What we call here a shifting social generation consists of men who are grouped, in effect, into clusters of similar age, status etc. Uncles and nephews may be members of the same shifting social generation. In our own culture social generations are supposedly separated by a 'gap'. In many generation-systems the larger groupings are genealogical generations and the age-groups into which they are internally segmented are narrow span shifting social generations. Moreover each sort of generation has arbitrary features which create anomalies. Genealogical generations group men of disparate, even contradictory, ages, stages of development and social positions. Social generations must have hazy boundaries because men slide imperceptibly from one into the other. Self-definition of generation is likely to vary with situation, so that the same man may seek at one time the deference due to grey hairs and at another the privileged camaraderie of youth. Also assessment by others is unlikely to be unanimous, to a twenty year old a man of forty is an elder whereas to someone of seventy he is still a youngster.

Rites of passage serve, as Van Gennep pointed out, to mark the passage of time and passing through of boundaries. They separate men out from one category (or generation or set or grade or stage in the life-cycle), pass them through a period of transition, and incorporate them into a new category. Sets seek to diminish differences between members by stressing their equalness and by endeavouring to keep the social development of members in line by exaggerating the differences between sets. Age-systems thereby seek to arrest time for a period, so that it moves forward in jerks. The period between sets (or generations or grades) which are marked by transition rites are periods of liminality, or moments out of time, which allow time to catch up with events or events with time. In extreme instances, such as Boran in the condition of *raaba*, during which men are not allowed to keep their offspring, men are suspended in that one sense out of social life and time altogether. The hands of the clock which had been held back are moved forward again when they leave that condition. Van Gennep's comment on sacredness applies to time also; it 'is not absolute; it is brought into play by the nature of particular situations' (12).

Sometimes the sorts of discrepancies we have indicated above confuse the rules so that sub-rules are created to cope with them; at other times they merely cause uneasy anomalies which are dealt with by the use of social tact or simply endured as among, for example, the Nandi (Huntingford: 73). The essays return to the problem of apparent discrepancies in the rules which are created by the discrepancies between genealogical and shifting social age and generation groupings; for now it is sufficient to point out the problem and the conflict which it must generate between rules which assume regularity and actual life which comprehends irregularity. These discrepancies, of course, more often perplex ethnographers who observe them than they do the people who live them. But not only may men be born out of the time sequence of the system, as it were — usually called under-ageing or over-ageing — but their other social positions within the family or sibling group, or as affines, property holders, or managers may conflict with their age or generation status. In brief, it is an example of the standard conflict between biological and sociological categories, or nature and culture. Age-systems which posit regularity must adapt their rules deliberatively, or develop secondary rules which can regulate anomalies in terms of the system itself, or adapt the rules through an accumulation of *ad hoc* decisions taken to deal with anomalies as they appear, if cultural rules are not to be burst by rampant nature. Indeed some peoples, such as the Boran and Guji described in this volume, in practice and over time, combine the three modes of dealing with the problem.

It is reasonable, therefore, to anticipate a discrepancy between expressed rules, which are based on idealised past experience, and contemporary practise. Any system of rules assumes an underlying set of general principles embedded in a system of thought, but men frequently endeavour to interpret, even to manipulate, rules and principles to their own advantage. One of the classic concerns of the sociology of knowledge is to point to connections between a system of thought and the daily actions of men who operate with it. Because men are members of society and not only members of an age-system, in order to understand the rules of any age-system it is necessary to examine the rules in action, as it were; that is to say in situations in which men are having to reconcile their age-set relationships with a range of other social relationships. Apparent breaches of, or contradictions or discrepancies in, the rules may then become explicable.

Ranks, titles, insignia and privileges are frequently accorded to members of sets by virtue of their membership. Similarly, privileges and rights, such as circumcision and hence the chance to copulate, or permission to drink beer, or the right to carry arms, frequently mark the progress of sets and distinguish set from set. The right to marry and procreate though is often much more than such a privilege because it includes the hope and possibility of producing sons who will, in turn, become members of a later set or later sets. Marriage therefore is an act which may have consequences for the continuance and mechanics of the age-organisation itself so, almost invariably, set systems have rules which attempt to regulate the procreation of legitimate children. Quite specific political, military, legal and ritual responsibilities are often vested in sets on behalf of the community as, for example, those of Samburu fire-stick elders. But a striking feature of sets is that, though they may influence the use of resources and flow of labour, they neither own nor control stock nor any other means of material production. They do not even have the vestigial or residual rights sometimes said to reside ultimately in clans or lineages. At the most sets, as sets, only own things which economically are trivia, such as smoking pipes or songs or drums and the rights in club houses or meeting places.

Social relationships which are neither embedded in property relationships nor run contiguously with them need very, very strong sentiment indeed to maintain them. One of the few generalisations we can make about pastoral societies is that social relationships run close to stock-relationships and that stock have the property of creating and transmitting social relationships. Relationships which require durability and resilience require reinforcement by property sharing or property exchanging. Among the peoples whose age-organisations are described in this volume (and generally throughout the ethnographic area), tools and stock are owned by individuals or families; improved water is usually owned by extended families or some group intermediate between family and tribe (only rarely and recently, as in parts of Somalia, by individuals); and grazing and unimproved water (both of which are God's) are open to responsible exploitation by all members of the largest political unit. Rights of ownership in, and access to, cultivable land vary but we can think of no instance in which they are vested in sets,[7] although (as among Dassanetch) shared set membership may be used by one individual as sentimental or moral reinforcement of a claim he makes through another individual. Reports of incidents in which young men have had to filch stock from stock-owners in order to fulfil an obligation to entertain members of their set abound in the literature. So also do reports of elders who withhold stock from juniors who beg from them so that they may entertain their age-mates. But these appeals are made, for example, by a son to his father and not by a member of a junior set to a member of a senior set. Set rituals often require the slaughter of many animals, indeed set ceremonies may be the major occasion of slaughter, as among Boran and Dassanetch, but the animals are contributed by family herds and their donation requires family approval.

Rights in herds rest in families; sets do not own herds. Even the stock which warrior-sets may acquire on raids, with the exception of the few used for immediate celebratory feasting, are distributed to individuals and absorbed into the family herds of individual members. Among the Boran a warrior who distinguishes himself and brings honour to his age-set (*hariiya*), by cutting off the testicles of an enemy, can only earn acclaim from his age-mates similar to that which is accorded to him by all men and women. For material reward he must go to the cow pen of his mother's brother and claim a heifer by attaching the trophy like a pendant to the beast's horns. This dependence on kin rather than sets or age-mates for gifts of stock seems to apply in mixed farming economies and in centralised states also. Age-regiments, for example, may even be mobilised to labour for the chief or their own support when they are not needed militarily, but for cattle to marry with they must look for family help or chiefly patronage. In Rwanda, for example, the chief either distributed cattle captured by age-companies (*i-torero*) to members who were his clients or stored them in the army herd which, in the end, also made clients for him (Maquet 1954:130-7).

Everything combines against sets having control, even in marginal ways, over such a crucial resource as stock. When a set is junior and its members are young and active their very youth, and hence irresponsibility, rules them out and, as they mature, their domestic and familial obligations and commitments demand all their energies. Almagor's essay shows how set loyalties diminish as members of a set age and become increasingly involved in maintaining the family herd. The ritual authority of elders waxes as their domestic and economic statuses are enlarged and as their family and herd both increase. The extremely old who have relinquished, or been deprived of, the control of economic resources, that is stock, may be listened to but their words are not necessarily heeded. The Samburu age-system serves 'to retain power in the hands of the older men' (Spencer, 1967:140) because the old men control the stock, however dependent they may be on moran labour. Moran own nothing and are dependent on their family seniors for everything from their daily milk to the chance of, in time, becoming elders with homesteads of their own; just as they were harangued by their fathers they will need to harangue, in their turn, their own disgruntled sons.

Opinion and community action may be mobilised by sets and sets may have a moral power, but sets cannot help a man with marriage cattle nor in building up his herd. Family elders control the flow of stock and hence the marriages of their juniors.

Carefree bachelors can share what milk they can obtain in the bush for themselves or what food they can scrounge from their mothers. Most food is controlled by women. Married men are fed by their wives and in that respect depend on them. Men may 'own' all the stock but women control the milking and the milk pots. Men may 'own' the fields but, once grain is in the granary, it is controlled by the woman whose granary it is. Men do not help themselves out of the milk pots or granaries of their wives. Once food has passed into a woman's care it is socialised and domesticated: it ceases to be either a natural product or one which men dispose. (Meat follows different rules — only men slaughter a sacrifice, hence the stress in set-ritual on meat feasts). A man can ask his wife to pour milk or cook porridge for his age-mates but he cannot make her do so, nor can he control her demeanour or make her appear to be truly welcoming. If a wife wants to keep back the food for her family, or even if she just begrudges it to her husband's age-mates, she can make them feel uncomfortable so that they do not call again to share food as age-mates should. (A wife can deal similarly, if she wishes, with her husband's age-mates who presume too far on the wife-sharing of age-mates.) Once a man is married he perforce relinquishes those considerable parts of set activity which are only suitable for bachelors. These same parts, however, as we noted for example of the Vice-Lords, can be features of gangs or informal youth groups or clubs as much as they can be of sets.

Indeed we suggest that it is because women are entangled in domestic cares much earlier and from the start much more tightly than are men — because they are usually married around puberty — that there are no age-systems for women. The transitions from girl, to betrothable maiden, to wife, to mother and to post-menarche old woman may, or may not, be much more dramatically marked than the equivalent stages are for men,[8] but the ceremonies mark individual status changes, of which a number for convenience occur together, rather than group changes (Paulme, 1960). Groupings of women in which social age is a recruitment factor occur, such as the Dassanetch *kob* group of local girls or the Arssi *atete* which is a localised congregation of matrons (Baxter, 1976); but sets of women as part of a system of such sets, do not occur. A woman is usually affiliated to the set of brother or husband for the regulation of her marriage, placement of her children etc.

A man needs kin, affines and stock-associates for help with stock and support in need and in disputes. Men who go in for rituals need stock for consumption and labour help to give them time. Set activities are for recreation and ritual advancement. Recreation is particularly appropriate to careless youth, and leisurely ritual advancement to mature elders who have built up their herds and may, indeed, be ready to relax and retire from the daily struggle; by analogy to play more at Rotary or Masons and rather less at business. Certainly this sort of retirement is institutionalised among the Dassanetch and the Oromo peoples. As Peristiany put it, the comradeship of warriors develops 'into a sort of old boys' community' (1939:41-2).

Moreover the efficient management of a herd requires the assistance of a wife and children. By the cultural definition of the division of labour a man cannot manage a herd on his own and anyone who attempted to do so would become a laughing stock. The paradox that a man must be a husband before he is a full man and must depend on a wife to be independent, is, of course, very general and not specific to pastoral societies or those with age-sets. But that dependence conflicts with the mutual dependence of male on male, which is central to setting, and directs men's practical energies to those on whom they depend for food and care and their posterity. As Monica Wilson noted in her classic study, even among the Nyakusa who reside in villages of age-mates, 'the cultivation of fields requires the co-operation of a wife. Bachelors continue to eat their meals at their parents' village' (1951:44). Sets may influence the direction in which a spouse is sought, they may limit choices and may delay marriage, but they cannot provide bridewealth, nor food, nor a herd which is the source of life, enduring relationships and a man's proper pride.

What is striking about age-systems is that men continue to be members of sets despite their increasing involvement in other social ties which must pull against set ties. Members may not be very enthusiastic and active but they remain members and cannot, like members of a rural Welsh youth group, drop out 'inconspicuously' when they marry or sink into confirmed bachelorhood (Rees 1961, and Peters 1972:110).[9] What varies greatly are; (*a*) the length of time for which a set continues to exist after its inception; (*b*) the amount of activity which sets maintain over time; (*c*) the degree of constraint they continue to maintain over members; (*e*) the extent to which set activities are restricted to members or are open to family or neighbourhood participation; and (*f*), which is a concomitant of (*e*), the extent to which set activities are held at exclusive sites or are held in homesteads and villages. If activities are held in homesteads and villages and do not exclude families and neighbours, which frequently happens as sets advance through time and their members age, then sets are, in part at least, brought into the domestic and neighbourly domains. The bush and separation from the homely village may be appropriate for bachelor warriors but not for elders whose main social roles and activities lie in the family and neighbourhood.

Because sets and age-grading need to be compatible, and sets become manifest agents of age-grades it follows, and is also stated by the folk, that members of a set should progress in step through the life-cycle, ensuring thereby that the passage of time and aging are harmonised. Indeed a common folk explanation for the presence of sets is that they ensure that men of similar age and/or generation move through life in time together. Which is rather like saying that the rules of incest exist to prevent men copulating with their mothers. Nevertheless, though the name of a set of Maasai or Samburu moran or of Boran age-mates continues to endure, a set just seems to fade away as an active body: as they assume the cares thrust on them by their families active members ooze away. (This characteristic, of course, they share with many gangs, sports clubs, etc.). Family exigencies, we suggest, overcome age-set loyalties.[10] For example, if his senior agnates die a man has stock responsibilities thrust on him early, and needs must settle down to social elderhood and become a homestead head, even if by age, temperament and age-set rules he should be living it up as a member of a bachelor set. Of course most men do stock work appropriate to their age and status and hence work which is appropriate to their set. So men in junior sets are likely to be found in the wild performing the roughest herding and most onerous watering, whereas herd management, which is considered suitable work for elders, is likely to be carried out by men in senior sets. But a careful reading of the literature shows that these associations hold only in so far as age-suitability for the task, age-grading and set rules fit in with the labour requirements of the family herd and the need to fill essential familial roles. Family bonds and loyalties, even for the enthusiastic initiates in the most recently formed set, override set bonds and loyalties. Members of a family should help each other without strictly reckoning cost even more than age-mates should, and a family feels dishonour and shame brought on it by a member even more than does a set. (One of us saw a Rendille youth have an epileptic fit as the knife of circumcision was about to nick him. His age-mates, who had just proudly endured the cutting, were outraged and carried the afflicted youth out of the ring and belaboured him while, from a distance, the women jeered. The age-mates returned and carried on; they could brazen out the incident, but the family of the youth crept away ashamedly and hid themselves.)

A family will usually put up with a deal of inconvenience and expense to enable one of its members to enjoy set activities and celebrations; but, when there is a conflict, vital family needs must override set-rules and obligations. Just as an age-system must bend to accommodate men who are born out of sequence with their generation-set, or with the age-set to which they have been allocated by the alternate generation rule, it must also accommodate to family needs by having secondary rules or ignoring or glossing over breaches of rules. Indeed, as we have suggested, it is the control that elders have over stock and wives and management decisions which permit the gerontocratic control which has been remarked as a feature of so many East African pastoral societies.[11] It is gerontocracy which encourages age-setting, rather than age-setting which encourages gerontocracy: age-set rituals provide a platform from which the gerontocrats (however young in years) can exercise their power and harangue the youngsters (however old in years) who are encapsulated in a junior set. They may act thus not just because they are older, or of a senior set, or have accumulated mystical powers which makes their curse feared, but because they are 'the bulls', 'the father of herds', that is the owners of the primary resource.

That sets do not control vital productive resources does not, of course, mean that sets may not constrain the behaviour of members across an extensive range of activities; though many of the constraints may derive from an individual's stage in the life-cycle as much as from his set membership. Most obviously where sets are the basis of recruitment to military units, set membership may affect an individual's chances of life and death. (Army conscripts who share a common birth or entry year, as for example the class of 1950, are not an age-set.) Also, in summary, an individual's position in a set, and the position of his set in a system of sets, may influence his access to one or several of the following: social privileges, marginal economic resources, choice of wife and hence affines, political office and authority, ritual office and general access to ritual benefits (especially blessings) which can affect his whole well-being. Further, and what can be extremely important, a man's age-mates may be not only a source of congenial sociability and moral support, a sort of combination of claque and club, but also, as among the Arusha, a body of practical backers in dispute cases (Gulliver 1963).

Certain consequences follow from the simple fact that relationships between members of sets are not mediated by shared rights in property nor by property transactions of value made between them. (Gifts such as bracelets or stock bells, such as young herders exchange, may have emotional significance for the givers but they are insubstantial, like the beads young lovers exchange compared with the bridewealth their elders negotiate. Such exchanges do not require an age-system. Jean Buxton noted that the Mandari had very recently started 'bead-sets (*rem*), groups of boys who were initiates together wear waist-bands of coloured beads... bead-sets are related to courtship and have no political significance' (95).) A man seeking to extend a set-tie into an enduring and useful relationship is likely to convert it into a stock associateship or affinity, because it is difficult for relationships to flourish if men cannot extend them by passing property along them.

Secondly, though men belong to a set throughout their lives moral compulsions and strong emotional bonding are associated with initiation and with youth, as they were among the Vice-Lords, and fade with maturity. Particularly if they have shared harsh experiences together at initiation, set members stress fraternity and mutual obligation, even as far as allowing sexual access to each others wives. Age-mates share responsibility for each others behaviour, and should discipline their own backsliders. Disputes between age-mates should be settled within the set. These injunctions are usually expressed most vociferously about and between members of junior sets; that is in those sets which are made up of young men who have relatively few rights in stock, are likely to be bachelors, and who are not responsible for managing the family herds. Sharing is urged by and on those who are equal in their juniority and in their limited access to those resources which differentiate men and who, in practice, have little to share but hardships and danger. This slight social responsibility accords both with the casual bravery expected of junior sets when they are called on to act militarily, and with the common association of sets of not long initiated youngsters with the bush and its wild beasts. As men mature they become patently less equal in wealth, wives, influence, office and power; the responsibility property brings divides as it socialises. The ideal of fraternity may remain but it is eroded by cares and responsibilities. Spencer's statement that it is a 'deep-rooted Samburu ideal that each man should have his own herd and ultimately be able to manage independently' (1965:12), could be said of all pastoralists. Both a man's interests in his family herd and his individual ambitions are opposed to, and stronger than, the ideal of sharing all with age-mates. Young Boran age-mates, for example, boast of their solidarity and preparedness to stand together in battle etc., but elders who are celebrating *gaadamoji* boast against each other about the martial exploits of their youth and of the herds which, in their social maturity, so clearly differentiate them. Fraternity becomes more a matter of 'words', and elders become expert at word juggling, and less a matter of actions, as men and their sets are passed by time and as the interests of members of senior sets merge.[12]

Among the Arusha, for example, most disputes between age-mates who were homestead heads should, according to age-set rhetoric, be settled within the set. But Spencer (1976:60-4) has recently suggested that if disputes involve property then they are taken either to modern courts or into the 'patrilineal area', that is that of the property holding corporation. In his essay Abrahams reports similarly from the Labwor. Indeed even disputes over adultery which was an age-set affair, 'since age-mates could claim certain rights in each others' wives', were likely to be moved out of the set for settlement, because such disputes might develop into more serious marital problems of concern to the lineages of the husband and the wife. That is to say that if a dispute was likely to expand and involve property, such as bridewealth, it became too important a matter to be left to age-mates. We can recollect no instances in the literature in which elders, representing the family interests of their dependents, subordinate those interests to the ideal of age-set equality and solidarity.

Thirdly, to expand a point already glanced at, it is the limited rights in property and hence social responsibilities of sets which, at recognised times and in institutionalised ways, makes it permitted and even expected that they will, as sets and not just as a gaggle of lads, act wildly to the edge of delinquency. (In passing, the capacity of sets to encapsulate turbulent youth makes modern youth clubs look feeble.) Boran, for example, anticipate that newly inducted age-sets and men in a generation-set who are in the condition of *raaba* will act like wild bush animals, even if individual members do not want to act so and look and feel silly while they do so. Samburu moran are presumed to require constant harangues and Karimojong juniors to need the threat of the elders' curse to keep them in order.[13] This wildness seems to contrast with their parallel 'predisposition to obedience' to the will of the elders (Dyson-Hudson: 188); but the expected wildness and expected obedience are different presentations of the same role. Members of junior sets, like undergraduates, are maintained in a state of suspended childhood, subdued by the hope that, so long as they only rampage in the ways expected by their elders, that they will, in due course and in turn, move into elderhood and responsibility themselves. Very few undergraduates actually push their misbehaviour so far that they are expelled or, in the appropriately expressive idiom of the older Oxbridge, 'sent down', that is relegated from gentle society. Similarly it is very rare, because it is so drastic, for stock-owning elders to curse junior sets. Juniors may play up their seniors but, in the end, they must be obedient because the elders have temporal control over all the productive assets and are backed by mystical sanctions such as curses.

Fourthly, the only general societal responsibilities usually entrusted to sets, other than ritual ones, are military or similar responsibilities such as, in states, collecting dues for the king. Even these are not restricted to sets in that when a settlement is attacked by surprise everyone turns out, even the women. Indeed stories about demure old ladies who have turned into viragos to confront night raiders are commonplace. But martial activities generally, and stock-raiding in particular, are associated with sets and especially junior sets. This association with junior sets is appropriate because the members of junior sets have little to contribute but their lives and little to lose but those very lives which are not of much social value.

Since the tribal societies were colonised control of force has passed out of local hands and into those of the colonial or post-colonial national governments. But, traditionally, age-sets were often the formations which delivered the force and the age-system was 'the framework for the military organisation'. Among the Kipsigis the offensive military organisation was based on regiments which were organised provincially and the active part of which were 'members of the age-set in the grade of warriors'. The age-system was a prominent structural feature and had military functions among all the Nandi-speaking peoples. (Evans-Pritchard 1940b:69 and 75; Peristiany 1939). But the association between age-sets and military organisation is not invariable: among the Turkana, for example, the age-set system 'provided the core of the primitive military organisation' whereas among the neighbouring Jie 'age-sets are not connected with military or political organisation' (Gulliver 1955:12 and 11). Where the age-system is involved in military activities, sets operate as agents of force, not as the controllers of force. Sets as wielders of the force of society do so, in the last resort, and even if rebelliously, as agents of the wider society. In states age-sets were likely to be converted into age-regiments and then, as among the Zulu, they 'belonged to the king alone' and did his bidding as his strong arm (Gluckman 1940:31). Fifthly, then, age-systems could be the agents of force, but, because they had no base in the property of their society nor control over its productive relationships, they could not be the disposers of that force. Even where, as among the Maasai, the voice of the elders seemed to speak through the senior set, this was so; the age-system could only appear to be the political system, i.e. the controller of force, when there was national consensus. An example is the Maasai rebellion of 1918, when the Purko moran attacked an army camp to demonstrate their opposition to government schooling and the threat of conscription. The elders 'counselled the futility of resistance' to the government, but were ignored and the moran acted in conjunction with the *laibon* Kimurai, son of Olonana.

A frequently reported custom which merits comment here is the one which permits access to (rather than sharing of) the wife of one member of a set by another; or, as it is sometimes more appropriately put, a rule which does not allow adultery actions and payments between set members. Members of a set also protect its wives, that is its members' wives, from members of other sets. Such customs or rules clearly have benefits for sets as military formations. Camaraderie is essential between men who may depend on each other in battle. The maintenance of group morale and solidarity is important and quarrels over sexual rivalries are very likely between young men, so any custom which undervalues exclusive individual rights over a woman's sexuality and stresses group rights can have value for that group's solidarity. Such customs are not restricted to sets nor to licentious soldiery but outbreaks of practices such as gang rape are apposite to both (Huntingford: 75, and innumerable war novels).

Such rules or customs seem to be stressed much more in respect of junior sets than of senior sets. That this should be so is appropriate for a number of reasons; all members of senior sets are likely to be married and may be polygynously so; promiscuity is not considered appropriate for members of senior sets; senior sets are unlikely to be occupied in raiding etc. As a set advances by seniority its members are more likely to be married, but while still only a few are married those few are anomalous in that they cease to be equal with their age-mates by the very fact of having a wife. This inequality is partially evened by permitting sexual access to wives. When the majority of a set is married then the anomaly ceases and the pressure is transferred to the bachelors to get a wife. A consequence is that age-mates prefer to keep their marriages in step. A man who marries too early, usually because his position in his family requires it, (if, for example, his own father is dead) knows that he may have to allow his age-mates access to his wife. Just because sexual access should be free to age-mates does not mean that fond young husbands enjoy honouring the rule. Baxter spent one depressing evening with a very dispirited new Boran husband whose wife was being properly hospitable to one of his age-mates.

Sixthly, just as age-systems do not control the use of force, sets are not formally constituted assemblies to which political powers are delegated. Sets do not compose rudimentary parliaments. Indeed sets seldom meet as a whole and, if they do, it is to perform rituals and not to perform executive, administrative or legislative tasks.[14] We are not arguing that sets perform no political tasks, merely that if they do, those tasks are ancillary ones. Sets are seized on, as it were, to perform the task simply because they are there. For example, among the Karimojong sets have a more than usual political importance, but Dyson-Hudson reports that, though the 'demonstrable *instrument* of political authority is the obedient membership of a sub-senior set', (155) the age-system is not the *source* of authority. Essentially the 'unity of an age-set is a conceptual unity in the minds of the Karimojong, not the observable unity of, say, a company on a drill-square' (174). Or, as Evans-Pritchard noted long ago, Nuer sets 'have no administrative, juridical, or other specific political functions and the country is not handed over to their care... the age-set system ought not to be described as a military organisation' (1940a:253). And again, he wrote: 'sets never act corporately' (259); that is they have no corporate structure, property or power; and: 'it is easy to conceive of the political system existing without an age-set organisation'. Gulliver (1963) has suggested that because there 'is no continuously operating system of public administration outside the ritual sphere' (130), age-systems have had an appearance of political effectiveness thrust on to them. Each of the Oromo essays in this volume attests that, in the four *gada* systems discussed, the functions of the generation-system are primarily ritual.[15]

Age systems, nevertheless, continue to have major political functions attributed to them — however ill-designed they are to perform them and, because they lack corporate resources, however inappropriate political activities would be for them. Where age-systems occur in societies with non-centralised political systems they are especially likely to have political functions ascribed to them. This is the more likely when those societies also lack strong, localised descent groups, as they frequently do, because a strong descent group organisation and a strong age-group organisation tend to incompatability. Age-systems, as it were, get political functions attributed to them just because they are conspicuous and other suitable institutions are not apparent. We would suggest that formal and informal general assemblies rather than sets perform such few political tasks, that is from the point of view of the tribe or nation, as require performing. A residual ethnocentricity still makes it difficult, even for professional observers, to recognise that a society may rub along happily enough without institutions which are obviously political. Yet, everyone has got used to not finding obvious economic institutions. Even Evans-Pritchard felt bound to stress that Nuer age-sets did not have political tasks however hard you looked for them as if that was a bit odd. We labour this point because, it seems to us, that the over-attribution of political tasks to age-systems, as the primary institutions on which the maintenance of social order depends, has been a barrier to our understanding of them.

Age-systems are still often grouped, even if uneasily and with reservations, under a political or life-cycle rubric, as a glance through the International African Institute's Ethnographic Survey of Africa series shows. Middleton and Tait distinguish as a distinctive sub-type of non-centralised political systems that 'in which political relations between local groups are controlled by the holders of statuses in age-set and age-grade systems' (3). In her influential textbook *Primitive Government*, Lucy Mair describes 'the division into age-sets' as 'important primarily as a means of organising government' (80) among many peoples of Kenya. But, we argue, gerontocracy is 'a recurrent theme in the analysis of East African age-systems' (Spencer 1976:55) because it is elderhood which is influential and gives sets their importance. Sets give open expression, cognitive order and ritual respectability to the velvet-gloved hand of the aged with which they wield their control of productive resources.

Out of many recent examples we select one by a distinguished anthropologist who has put together a major collection of ethnographic data. In his most recent book about the Sebei, Walter Goldschmidt (1976) writes:

An orderly social system was maintained through the operation of three sets of institutions: clans, age-sets, and territorial units (55).

And, more generally:

The age-set system in East Africa is a sociological device that is highly adaptive to the function of governance, the maintenance of order, and the protection of property in a predominantly pastoral situation (349).

Yet Sebei age-sets appear to do little as sets, beyond institutionalise age-grading and 'formulate a formal bond' between set-members and, perhaps, give an added strength to 'personal "social ties"' between set members. The fighting organisation was based on territorially organised regiments (63), and was not 'in the domain of the age-set' (67). Indeed Goldschmidt also states that, within memory, sets have not been 'a salient element in the organisation of political, legal and military affairs' (104), and comments on the 'absence of age-set function or structure' (105). But, he presumes that, during some earlier period, age-sets had military importance. In an earlier publication, after quoting Dyson-Hudson on the Karimojong (1966:171), Goldschmidt argues that the socialisation of sub-Saharan pastoralists into collaboration and interdependence 'is frequently based on age-set organisation, as we are all aware' (1972:138). There is little hard evidence to support his assertions. But, as Lawrance observed of the Teso: 'It is not easy to assess the functions of the age-set system ... fifty years after its demise' (173); it is also dangerous.

Age-systems are ancient institutions in East Africa; we have documentary evidence of their existence from the sixteenth century and Ehret conjectures, on the basis of linguistic evidence, that age-sets existed among pre-Southern Nilotic and pre-Southern Cushitic societies from the first millenium B.C., and possibly even earlier. East African age-set and generation-set systems, though not age-grades and age-classes, seem doomed to extinction or, at best, to be preserved, like the elephant and other survivals from less polluted times, in a reserve for tourists to wonder at uncomprehendingly. Why such apparently cumbersome modes of categorising and of organising people should ever have evolved raises unanswerable questions. What can be done however is to ask the sort of 'fundamental' question Monica Wilson set herself about the Nyakusa, 'Why age-villages?' (1951:18). That is, what societal purposes does a particular age-system serve and how does it relate to other social institutions in that particular society? In short, if one dare whisper it, what is the function of a particular age-system? From that one might proceed to a broader discussion about what characteristics societies with age-systems share which are not shared by comparable societies without age-systems. But that question itself raises several problems. One way of phrasing the general question in an answerable way might be: 'Why have some age-systems, or parts of age-systems, continued to flourish even into the 'seventies, whereas others have collapsed at the first colonial puff, missionary whisper or clink of the first pice?' What, then, are the social conditions in which age-systems seem to flourish or decay?

For example, under the same colonial regime in Kenya, according to Tignor, the Maasai 'moran were able to inhibit social change' (85), whereas the Kikuyu 'age-grades lost much of their political and economic importance' (58). Among the Oromo peoples *gada* remains active among the Boran and Gabra of Ethiopia and of Marsabit District in Kenya and also among the Guji, whereas it has faded away among the Arssi of Arussi and Bale Provinces of Ethiopia and among the Boran of Isiolo District of Kenya and among the Orma (Warra' Dai) of the Tana River. Why should there be these variations? Other questions suggest themselves. What, if any, are the relations between age-systems and beliefs about the cosmos? Why should so many age-systems generate rules which are difficult, even impossible, to follow? One might keep on and on. We cannot examine all the questions which suggest themselves about age-systems and social change, but we hope that some suggestions towards some answers are scattered through this Introduction and the essays which follow. Answers to most such question should be available and are the next step.

Despite our caveats, what we have written so far is spotted with testable, if submerged, propositions about age-systems, as well as with suppositions, repetitions and pontifications. Some of the propositions, such as those about the relationships between the control of productive resources and age-systems, should be easily extractable; but some others, which are more embedded, we shall now try to prise into view. Most are exemplified in the Boran *gada* system (see Baxter's essay) in which the generation-system (*luuba*) has a complex and multipurpose organisation, and the age-system (*hariiya*) has a simple organisation and limited purposes. These propositions, which, like most such, look pretty commonplace, are:

1. The more the declared time-rules about the movement of individuals and/or sets run counter to demographic probabilities, *either* the more exceptions will be permitted so that under- or over-aged individuals can qualify, *or* the more likely it is that the rules will be breached to enable such individuals to qualify.

2. The more rigorous the primary rules appear to be, the greater will be the number and complexity of the secondary rules; because it is the secondary rules which allow those exceptions which permit the primary rules to continue apparently unaltered. So, the more complex the rules, the more exceptions they must permit and hence, like canon law, allow a multitude of sinners to slip through their interstices. Wise drafters of University regulations have learned how to appear rigid but be flexible and precede any definite prohibition or injunction with the magic word 'normally'. We suggest that, however categorical informants are about age-system rules, 'normally' is normally understood even if it is unvoiced.

3. The more strictly the rules governing set recruitment are kept, then the more likely it is that members will be heterogeneous in general social status.

4. When a set consists of members of heterogeneous status the more likely it is that the system will be concerned more with ritual affairs and less with practical affairs and, in its age-grading aspects, more concerned with recognition of individual religious development rather than with recognition of individual social development.

5. The more a system is concerned with the allocation of practical tasks, such as raiding or herding, then the more its organisation must be in accord with demographic probabilities. (A military organisation, to survive, must get out on the ground the most men of suitable age, strength, intent and interest that it can mobilise.)

6. The less the similar social attributes and economic dependencies shared by the members of a set the more the system will depend on occult sanctions, such as curses and blessings, to maintain boundaries between sets.

7. Where age and generation are stressed as cognitive categories, to the extent that an age-system is created which is independent of the kinship and descent systems (though there must be terminological agreements), we find that kinship and/or descent groupings which are of much depth or span are unlikely to be foci of political differentiation.[16] When such groups do exist then we find that either: (*a*) age-sets disappear, as they did from the trans-Juban Darood and Rahanwein Somali; or (*b*) the age-system is dove-tailed into the descent system which remains structurally superior to it, as among Samburu and Gabra. Loyalties are not put to strain because the inferior (age-system) is articulated within the superior (descent system). Different ties do not cross cut but run together.

8. When the interests of domestic and familial loyalties diverge from those of set loyalties, set loyalties are likely to be the ones which give.

9. Age-systems go well with (though they are certainly not necessarily concomitant) sharp divisions of labour between junior and senior, such as distant herding and hardship on one hand versus home-herding and comfort on the other.

This division is likely to be paralleled by differential rights in productive resources between senior and junior. This, in turn, is likely to be related, though only as one variable in a cluster, to the durability of age-systems when they are confronted with market forces. In passing we note that these compatibilities help to explain why it is that East African pastoralists, with the possible exception of the Somali, have shown such slight enthusiasm for co-operative, or communal, or government imposed development projects, whereas they have maintained tradition and setting. Age-systems are a conservative feature of conservative societies.

Age-systems are, but not only, a means of holding time past in a steady relation to time present and to time future; a sign of the enduring past which endures through the present and into the future. They place past, present and future in perspective — and provide an individual with hopes for a future similar to the past.

To take two extreme possibilities. If an agriculturalist can see an opportunity to work, and to save, and to acquire his own bridewealth and his own land, which he can then cultivate with the labour of himself and his wife and children, that is if he can hope to become a peasant, then he is likely to discard both his obligations to his set and those to his kin. But, if he is an arid-zone pastoralist who must depend on his seniors for the stock which is the only thing which can give him, eventually, his own independent homestead, and on his peers for reciprocal help, then he is as unlikely to discard his loyalties to his set as he is those to his kin. A modified form of this difference, we suggest, goes some way to explaining the different histories of Kikuyu and Maasai age-systems.[17]

10. In extreme instances the destruction of an age-system may only be explicable by forces external to it. But the durability or disappearance of an age-system can only be understood if, like any other complex of institutions, it is analysed as part of the social system of which it forms a part. Anthropologists have been accused, mostly by other slightly younger anthropologists, of ignoring the impact of colonial changes on indigenous institutions. This they have have often done, but it seems to us an equal danger is to use external forces as explanations of such general efficacy that the organisation of individual systems is devalued. External forces have sometimes been used to avoid analysis.

Age-systems vary greatly in the multiplicity of the tasks they perform and their degree of involvement in other institutions. The degree of involvement of the age-system with other systems, such as those of kinship, has been an important variable in determining the resilience of any specific age-system to change.

11. The presence or absence of an active age-system is not necessarily a sure index of resilience to modernisation, though economic individualism and age-setting are probably incompatible.

12. Age-systems which have had purposes which were primarily military or political have not been likely to endure into colonial and post-colonial times, because their purposes have been usurped. Unlike kings and councillors, because sets contain all of a time based segment of a population, age-systems have been unsuited to survive as emblems once their traditional purposes have been removed.

13. Age-systems are not very adaptable to modern economic or

political institutions. Indeed most administrators have seen them as untidy and obstructive anachronisms which, true enough, cannot be shaped into productive work groups or constituencies. A frequent feature of age-systems is an unruly junior-set which is ill-disciplined at home and aggressive to foreigners. Neither colonial nor post-colonial governments have favoured such carryings on and have endeavoured to disband or divert the moran. Indeed a perennial feature of the East African press has been reports of appeals by officials (in which the elders are reported as having concurred) to the moran to cut their hair, put on trousers and give up stock-raiding, i.e. give up the symbols of moranhood. Such appeals have been going on for so long that the first audience of moran to whom they were addressed must now be ancestors.

14. Age-systems have endured where they have been the vehicles of rituals which the actors have continued to regard as important. Where age-systems have had, as a primary task, the organisation and presentation of individuals for rituals which are beneficial to them, and/or the organisation and presentation by sets of rituals which are beneficial for the nation (or a self-sufficient segment of a nation such as a tribe), then an age-system is likely to have been durable.

15. Where age-systems have faded, rather than suddenly collapsed, we suggest that enquiries may show that ecstatic Islamic cults or Pentecostal sects may have flowered. Cults differ in many ways from sets, but the *Hajj* may offer individuals a culmination to their ritual life which brings blessings and dignity. Certainly folk Islam can adapt to ritual which seeks to promote fertility and rain. Among the Arssi, the Boran of Isiolo and the Tana River Orma cult groups — such as those of the adherents of Shekh Hussen — have insinuated themselves as *gada* declined.

16. The process of aging is a visible physical record of the irrevocable passage of time. Age-systems endeavour to make aging a cultural rather than a physical process. All age-systems seek to arrest the flow of time by setting men together in units and thereby allocating defined segments of time. The aim, as it were, is to mark time rather than to run on the spot.

In so far as age-systems allocate status to named segments of the population who share the same culturally defined segment of time, and that status is incremented through time, age-systems are a device to make the cruel descent through life to decay appear as if it were an ascent to a superior, because senior, condition. It is appropriate that local churches should be ruled by elders and Sangree notes that among the Tiriki some men of 'the elder warrior age grade' had, as their traditional duties declined, come to assume Church leadership (72).

17. To paraphrase Durkheim and Mauss, 'the classification of time

reproduces the classification of men' (11). Just as the modes of animal classification used in each culture have an internal logical consistency, but the modes vary from culture to culture, so do classifications of time. A man may, or may not, perceive a steaming cock in a casserole as he had perceived the same cock crowing on a dunghill in the chilly dawn, but he certainly does not perceive a figurative representation of a cock as either. Age-systems create figurative representations of time as well as being parts of time. The same men may perceive time as it is classified by an age-system variously as lineal, cyclical, parabolic (in both senses), helical, having a trajectory like an arrow or careering like a winged chariot, without confusing the modes. One mode does not exclude the others; men can hold multiple and even contradictory classifications in their heads, just as they can hold polysemous symbols. The Oromo peoples, for example, do so with *gada*.

In summary the key to the understanding of age-systems, or parts of them, lies not so much in what practical societal functions they fulfil but in what ritual benefits they are perceived as endowing individuals, and groups and society.

Obviously no contributor can describe and analyse all the features of one age-system in one paper; each therefore concentrates on some particular features which elucidate the age-system he has selected.

The first essay is about Labwor, a Luo-speaking people of northern Uganda. They live mainly by agriculture, including cotton cash-cropping, and iron working but also keep some cattle and other livestock. They have both an age-system and a generation-system. The generation-sets mainly provide a system of dual classification and differentiation, whereas the age-sets have tasks and members share some mutual responsibilities while the hierarchy of sets forms, in some contexts, a framework for stratification based on relative juniority and seniority of years. Abrahams explains the incompatibilities between the age- and generation-systems and the interesting homologies between those and the organisational principles of the Labwor kinship system. Using the connections which he establishes, and comparative data from the neighbouring Jie, Turkana and Karimojong, he suggests possible explanations for the alterations which have occurred to the age-organisation. Among the other topics he discusses are individual promotion, the timing of age-set closures, the mutual responsibilities of members and 'sacrificial' killings.

The Dassanetch live as herdsmen and cultivators along the banks and hinterland of the Omo River where it flows into Lake Turkana. Almagor considers how the strong ethos of equality, which should hold between age-peers, is contradicted by the increasing differentiation in individual and economic, political and social power and influence as the peers age. He argues, through analyses of specific cases and of rituals, that this contradiction is mediated through a series of ceremonies of transition and through subtle cultural manipulation of etiquette and speech.

North of Dassanetch, and about 60 miles north of Lake Turkana, live another group of herders and cultivators, the Mursi. Turton takes as the starting points of his analysis what he sees as a continuing, if gradual, northward movement of Mursi-speaking people into territory formerly occupied or claimed by their neighbours, the Bodi. Disclaiming any attempt to provide an exhaustive account of the 'form and functions' of the Mursi age 'system', he concentrates on the organisation of local age groups and on the territorial context of age-grade ceremonial. This ceremonial periodically defines the politically significant yet constantly changing (because of northward movement) divisions of Mursi society. Long 'delays' in the staging of certain ceremonies (which the Mursi see as recent departures from normal practice) are explained in the light of this movement and on the assumption that age ceremonies define not only temporal but also spatial divisions of the population. Finally, Turton suggests that, in this context of territorial advance, Mursi age organisation may be the functional equivalent of Nuer segmentary lineage organisation, not because they are both, in Sahlins's phrase, 'organisations of predatory expansion', but because they each serve to camouflage expansion with the appearance of stability and historical continuity.

Unfortunately Spencer was not at the seminar; his paper is a last-minute, but most welcome and relevant, addition to the volume. He focuses on the anomalies which arise when rules are applied continuously and firmly to an actual human population so that there is cumulative mismatch between rules and demographic realities. Among the Jie of northern Uganda the rules which conflict are: (*a*) that only one generation set can be open (i.e. for recruitment) at a time; (*b*) that a man must belong to the set immediately following his father. From the comparative analysis of the Karimojong data and a simulation based on his own Samburu data, Spencer proposes a solution to the problem and develops what he modestly calls 'the notion' of a developmental cycle in the formation of generation-sets.

The other four essays each deal with one of the Oromo (Galla) speaking peoples, each of which has a generation-system of what has come to be known as the *gada* type.* The essays all show that,

―――――――――――
*There are around ten to fifteen million speakers of dialects of Oromo (Galla) in Ethiopia, where it is the most widely spoken language, and getting on for one hundred thousand speakers in Kenya. The dialects vary considerably in pronunciation, vocabulary, grammar and syntax but a lively-minded speaker of any one dialect can learn to make himself understood in another. In Kenya the missions have standardised a convention for Bible translation etc., but it has not been taken up widely. In Ethiopia, until very recently, it was forbidden to publish, preach, teach or broadcast in any Oromo dialect; the language was deliberately oppressed and colonised like the people. Every

whatever may have been the origins of *gada* and whatever its political, legislative, or administrative importance was in the past, at the present it is primarily concerned with the rituals which mediate between man below and God (*Waaka*) above. The dominant concept is that men of the same genealogical generation, and hence all siblings, should proceed through the life-cycle and the ritual cycle approximately in time together. *Gada* aims to acculturate and to control time. This, in nature, is impossible and must create contradictions. The complexities, the rules and the timetabling of *gada*, which make it seem like a revolving and darkened maze, and its variations in different Oromo societies, arise from cultural attempts to bridge or cloak these fundamental contradictions or conflicts. Age-set rituals exaggerate the differences between age groups and generations and, in one sense, it can be argued that it is the very volume and richness of *gada* ritual which differentiates men who are very alike and only slightly differentiated in their secular roles. Oromo societies are classically undifferentiated and egalitarian: where in Oromoland centralised states and petty kingdoms developed, *gada* faded away (see Luling). This accords with Gluckman's proposition: 'The greater multiplicity of undifferentiated and overlapping roles, the more ritual to separate them.'[18] Further we propose tentatively, that the structured contradictions of *gada* have generated further contradictions and complexities which have in turn generated further rituals, as they have also generated secondary rules. Rituals have proliferated and luxuriated and, as it were, taken *gada* over.

Gada provides: (*a*) the categories into which all men can be fitted in a hierarchy of ritual statuses. These statuses are ascribed by generation (and, to some extent, by sibling order) but all men whose life runs its full span should have the opportunity to participate in the ritual activities appropriate to their status. Following from which *gada* provides (*b*) the institutional framework, embodied in rules, for a system of groups (generation-sets) which enable men to perform rituals which they regard as essential for themselves as individuals and for the nation to which they belong. Following from (*a*) and (*b*) *gada* also provides (*c*) a conceptual frame for a uniform mode of ritual

---

Oromo child had to start his studies in school in Amharic which is not even a fellow Cushitic language. Not surprisingly no standard mode of spelling developed and, to further complicate matters each foreign recorder used a different orthography. We hope that the devoted work of B.W. Andrzejewski will bear fruit as did his work for Somali and that soon a standard orthography will be in use. Some of the publications of the Oromo Liberation Front are a hopeful pointer in this direction. But, for the moment we have had to recognize the variations in dialect and in spelling and we have not imposed common spelling because that would have been arbitrary and constricting.

age-grading in which the accent on uniformity is stronger than that on age.

Oromo explain *gada* both as a ritual cycle and as an organisation which performs the rituals in that cycle; that is as an active system and not merely as an inanimate structure. To the participants the rituals of *gada* (*a*) maintain the flow of blessings from God above on which men below depend for their welfare, subsistence, peace and fertility, and (*b*) provide each participant with an endowment of blessings for himself and increments in ritual well-being and ritual status. It is because *gada* embodies the fundamental values of the Oromo that it has proved so adaptive and resilient; it is the organisation of a belief system, that is of a developed faith based in a set of propositions about the nature of man and the Universe. Hinnant's essay brings this out clearly. Blackhurst's essay demonstrates how *gada* has continued to flow like a subterranean river, diverted but not dammed by conquest, colonisation, conversion, migration and cultural isolation.

We have heard reports, though unconfirmed, that, since the near collapse of Amhara domination in Ethiopia, the Oromo traditional rituals including those of *gada*, have undergone a great revival even in Coptic Shoa.

The pastoral Boran of southern Ethiopia and northern Kenya are considered before the other Oromo peoples, because they are generally believed to have the form of *gada* organisation which has been least disturbed by migration and foreign influence over the years, and to approximate most closely to the organisation delineated by Bahrey in his seventeenth century History of the Galla. *Gada* has come to assume an almost mystical aura because of the apparently bewildering complexities of its rules. Baxter attempts to unravel some of the internal contradictions within the generation-system, and to elucidate the principles which underlie both the rules and the performances of sets. He suggests reasons why the rituals of *gada* have been so tenaciously maintained, although its political and military purposes are much less important than they were reputed to have been in the past.

Torry describes the *gada* system of the nomadic camel-herding Gabra who live in the harsh deserts of the Kenya-Ethiopia border country. The Gabra are neighbours of the Boran and speak the same dialect of Oromo but have a variant generation system. He first describes their mode of life, herding strategies and the form of social co-operation which the Gabra have adopted in order to wrest a subsistence from an exceptionally arid environment. He relates these to the formal political organisation and then describes the *gada* organisation, the roles of its officials and its ritual and judicial importance. He examines the connection between the distinctive economic and ecological situation of the Gabra and their version of *gada*. In particular he discusses the difficulties which the harsh environment imposes on the maintenance of the generation system and the ways in which that system is integrated in value orientation and organisationally with their economic pursuits.

Hinnant's essay concerns the *gada* system of the Guji of southern Ethiopia. The Guji have a mixed economy with a strong pastoral bias. Present-day *gada* among the Guji has few political functions but is maintained as a series of elaborate, expensive and time-consuming rituals. Hinnant addresses the problem as to why this ritual system should be maintained but first presents a full account of the organisation of *gada*, the various grades and the ways in which both are related to other aspects of Guji society. He also analyses some of the structural changes that have taken place in the system. He concludes with a detailed analysis of the symbolism and meaning of a number of *gada* rituals, particularly the elaborate ceremony of transition when a new *gada* leader is installed. His analysis demonstrates that the various ceremonies can best be understood as expressions of the fundamental concepts of Guji religion: *kayyo*, loosely destiny or providence, and *woyyu* a sort of mystical strength. The rituals of *gada* affirm and maintain the Guji world view.

Blackhurst worked among peasants who had moved from Shoa to Arussi Province to settle. They formed only a small island of Christians among a sea of Moslem Arssi. The fascinating set of ceremonies he observed and describes were performed by people who, it was generally believed, had given up *gada*. Blackhurst poses two principal questions: why did *gada* change from an intertribal and tribal politico-religious organisation to a largely domestic ritual; and secondly, given these fundamental organisational changes, why did *gada* persist at all? The reduction in the span of *gada* is seen as a response both to pressures within the system itself and to the effects of the incorporation of the Shoa Galla into the Amhara Kingdom of Shoa in the nineteenth century. The persistence of *gada* to the present is accounted for by showing that the central ideas expressed in the rituals of *gada*, peace, fertility of land and cattle and prosperity, have remained the basic concerns of the Shoa Galla, despite the many political, economic and religious changes they have experienced.

We are grateful to a number of people; to Jean La Fontaine, and Virginia Luling for their comments during and after the seminar; to Emrys Peters, Stefan Strelcyn, Jay Close, Nick Mahoney and Richard Werbner for their contributions during our discussions; to Mrs M. Eisenstaedt who drew several of the diagrams and to Mrs Mary Lea, Miss Trudi Armstrong and Miss Cath Byrne for typing uncomplainingly while showing no sign of ageing.

NOTES

1   Our response to two of a number of the dilemmas which have confronted us requires a note of explanation. Firstly we decided not to survey the literature on age-systems. That would have required a longer introduction than it seemed reasonable to expect readers, or publishers, to stand for. This book only aims to add to our data and make some comments and not to be a general assessment of age-system studies. But we are immensely indebted to the many who have wrestled with the recalcitrant data on age-systems, and in particular to the two scholars to whom the volume is dedicated; also to Philip Gulliver (who seems to have thought of every point before us), R. Lowie, D. Paulme, A.H.J. Prins and Frank Stewart. Secondly, we decided not to engage on a discussion of terminology for the same reasons. The importance of such discussion is obvious: we must keep the tools of our trade sharp and agreement on terms precedes comparison; moreover, Radcliffe-Brown's letter of 1929, in which he called for and proposed 'a more exact terminology', has served as a manifesto for age-system studies. But half a loaf seemed likely to cause indigestion and not be better than no bread at all. Our guilt is partially assuaged because Stewart surveys the literature and appraises current terminologies. Common usage and common sense ought to be sufficient for this book. Anyone who is in doubt about terminology could consult Mair (1962: Chapter 3 or 1972:117-22).
2   Luckham: 101.
3   Most peoples also assume that in the past things were better; it is reported of the Ibo that 'deviations from the ideal are attributed to the actions of the Government' or similar extraneous agencies (Jones: 194).
4   Moran is a Maasai word which refers to younger unmarried men, up to the ages of thirty to thirty-five, who are in the warrior age-grade. The word has become part of the vocabulary of anthropology and therefore will not be italicised.
5   Set titles and offices or movement within a set cannot be 'bought' as in West African title societies. Societies such as Poro, concerned with age-grading and involved in mystical and political activities, though in effect obligatory, are not internally age-setted.
6   Stewart, 1972. Unfortunately Stewart's book (1977) was not available in time for reference to be made to it here.
7   At first glance this does not seem to apply to the Nyakusa who lived in age-villages on land allocated to them by members of the age-village of their fathers. But, as Monica Wilson makes clear, the system only worked so long as land was plentiful. As soon as land became scarce, or took on economic value, the system collapsed. Moreover, the 'most valuable land of all... that in old craters', was never redistributed, but was 'retained by an individual until his death and inherited by kinsmen' (174). 'The primary economic units in Nyakusa society are the kinship groups — the elementary family, the cattle-owning lineage, and the group of cognates who co-operate in production and exchange many gifts, and among whom cattle circulate' (44).
8   For example, Richards does not mention sets in her immaculately full analysis of puberty and nubility rites in *Chisungu*, nor in her survey

(1967) of socialisation and contemporary British anthropology. Philip Mayer's stricture, in his Introduction to the A.S.A. survey of socialisation (1967) that anthropologists have ignored age-systems in their role as 'the people's educational system', has some justice: but sets are only sometimes, and secondarily and never exclusively, educational institutions.

Similarly women do not have best-friends in the formal sense that men have, as the Bohannans noted of Tiv (1968:73). Wives are too immersed in family responsibilities and have little time or property to invest in such relationships. As our folk saying has it, 'Men have friends, women have kin.'

9 Peters notes: 'A cardinal feature of the youth group is that most of its members are not youths in terms of physical age' (115). Indeed the range of youths in the Llan group and that which covers moran seems to be much the same. Youths attach themselves to the group in latish adolescence and drop out at thirty to thirty-five, by which time they have either married or given up hope of marriage. (From adolescence to as old as thirty-five seems a frequent age-clustering as, for example, in Wolof 'Companies' [*kompins*].) Llan youths, like moran, are not trusted with 'the burdensome responsibilities of (farm) management'; the small sums of money they have they 'fritter away... on mineral waters and sweets' which they share. Vice-Lords fritter their money on wine which they share from the same bottle. Youths, moran and Vice-Lords all depend for their primary subsistence on their seniors and prefer to consume their tidbits and extras in or by the shop, in the bush or in the street, i.e. they all prefer to meet in neutral places not domestic places. Peters argues that the youth group 'can function successfully only if they have the backing of the adult population' (115). This generalisation also applies to junior sets; indeed in Samburu or Boran, for example, they need the specific blessings of their seniors; but a youth group or a gang is not a set. Gangs may be condoned by their elders and youth groups may even be praised but, unlike sets, they are not institutionalised and approved (though aspects of members' behaviour may not be) and membership is not obligatory.

Gulliver (1963:40) points out that the large majority of Arusha *murran* were married and pre-occupied with consolidating their households. They had adopted the role of junior elders in daily life.

10 Eisenstadt's broad hypothesis B does not appear to tally precisely. He writes: 'Age-homogeneous groups... tend to arise in societies in which the family or kinship unit cannot ensure, or even impedes, the attainment of full social status by its members' (54). We suggest rather that while family and set may seem to be in conflict, as do contiguous generations in the family, sets do not foster an individual's social development in spite of the family.

11 Bonte (1974) starts from an analysis of productive relationships and, as far as we can understand it, his argument on the power of elders does not controvert our own.

12 Cf. L. Bohannan's comments on Tiv sets: 'The age-sets of very old men merge together, but such old men seldom have reason to turn to the age-set' (1958:52 fn) and P. Bohannan writes: 'After its members reach the age of about fifty, their age-set becomes very little more than a sentimental association' (1965:536).

13 Dyson-Hudson:183. On the same page the author notes he has never witnessed such a cursing; we can recollect no one who has reported one.
14 Even among the Arusha, who Mair (1974) takes as the best described example of a society in which age-sets are important: 'An age-set never acts as a unit except in promotion rituals' (140). Ruel writes similarly that Kuria generation classes 'act as clearly defined social groups' only 'on ritual occasions' (28).
15 Hallpike has shown that *gada* stands 'at the centre of Konso life' (221), in a way very similar to that which it does among the Oromo peoples described here.
16 This is similar to Southall's point that many of the attributes of age-organisations 'taken together are incompatible with the development of extensive segmentary lineages' (32). Southall's original insight that 'Eastern Nilotic age-organisation is particularly compatible with elaborate complementary symbolic identifications, usually dichotomous' (32) also applies to *gada* systems.
17 The indication that age-sets have disappeared in Kikuyu may be that Lamb, for example, does not find it necessary to mention either age-sets or Lambert in his discussion of contemporary peasant politics in Murang'a District. But, this may not be sure evidence because clearly Lamb does not perceive the role of the developmental cycle of the domestic group and its relation to land holding (133-5), so perhaps he just did not notice age-sets.
18 1962:34. Interestingly, immediately after this passage Gluckman comments, apparently tangentially but with tentative insight, that his proposition may or may not apply to societies with age-sets.

BIBLIOGRAPHY

Baxter, P.T.W. 1976. 'An Arssi Women's Neighbourhood Festival: *Atete'*. Paper presented to the First World Congress on Cushitic Languages and Cultures. In press, Paris.
Bohannan, Laura. 1958. 'Political Aspects of Tiv Social Organisation' in John Middleton and David Tait (ed.) *Tribes without Rulers*. London
Bohannan, Paul. 1965. 'The Tiv of Nigeria' in J.L. Gibbs (ed.) *Peoples of Africa*. New York.
Bohannan, Paul and Laura. 1968. *Tiv Economy*. London.
Bonte, Pierre. 1974. *Études sur les sociétés de pasteurs nomades II. Organisation économique et sociale des pasteurs d'Afrique Orientale*. Paris.
――――. 1975. 'Cattle for God: An Attempt at a Marxist Analysis of the Religion of East African Herdsmen', *Social Compass*, XXII, 3-4, 381-96.
Buxton, Jean. 1958. 'The Mandari of the Southern Sudan' in John Middleton and David Tait, op. cit. London.
Curley, Richard T. 1973. *Elders, Shades and Women: Ceremonial Change in Lango, Uganda*. Berkeley, Calif.
Durkheim, E. and Mauss, M. 1963. *Primitive Classification*. London.
Dyson-Hudson, Neville. 1966. *Karimojong Politics*. Oxford.
Ehret, Christopher. 1971. *Southern Nilotic History*. Evanston, Ill.
――――. 1974. *Ethiopians and East Africans*. Nairobi.

Eisenstadt, S.N. 1956. *From Generation to Generation: Age Groups and Social Structure*. London.
Evans-Pritchard, E.E. 1940a. *The Nuer*. Oxford: Clarendon Press.
———. 1940b. 'Political Structure of Nandi-Speaking Peoples of Kenya'. *Africa*. Reprinted in E.E. Evans-Pritchard, *The Position of Women in Primitive Societies and other Essays in Social Anthropology*. London (1965).
———. 1965. *Theories of Primitive Religion*. Oxford.
Gamble, David P. 1957. *The Wolof of Senegambia*. London.
Gennep, Arnold van. 1960. *Rites of Passage*, London. Translated from French (*Rites de Passage*, 1909).
Gluckman, Max. 1940. 'The Kingdom of the Zulu of South Africa' in M. Fortes and E.E. Evans-Pritchard (ed.), *African Political Systems*. London.
———. 1962. 'Les Rites de Passage' in Max Gluckman (ed.) *Essays on the Ritual of Social Relations*. Manchester.
Goldschmidt, Walter. 1971. 'Independence as an Element in Pastoral Social Systems'. *Anthropological Quarterly*, 44, 3, 132-42.
———. 1976. *Culture and Behaviour of the Sebei: A Study in Continuity and Adaptation*. Berkeley and Los Angeles, Calif.
Gulliver, P.H. 1953. 'The age-set organisation of the Jie Tribe' *Journal of the Royal Anthropological Institute*, 83: 147-68.
———. 1955. *The Family Herds*. London.
———. 1958. 'The Turkana age organisation'. *American Anthropologist*, 60: 900-22.
———. 1963. *Social Control in an African Society: A Study of the Arusha, Agricultural Masai of northern Tanganyika*. London.
———. 1965. 'The Jie of Uganda' in J.L. Gibbs (ed.) *Peoples of Africa*. New York.
———. 1968. 'Age Differentiation' in *International Encyclopedia of the Social Sciences*, Vol. 1, 157-62. New York.
Hallpike, C.R. 1972. *The Konso of Ethiopia: A Study of the Values of a Cushitic People*. Oxford.
Huntingford, G.W.B. 1953. *The Nandi of Kenya*. London.
Jones, G.I. 1962. 'Ibo Age Organisation, with Special Reference to the Cross River and north-eastern Ibo'. *Journal of the Royal Anthropological Institute*, 92:191-211.
Keiser, R. Lincoln. 1969. *The Vice Lords: Warriors of the Streets*. New York.
Kuper, Hilda. 1963. *The Swazi: A South African Kingdom*. New York.
Lamb, Geoff. 1974. *Peasant Politics*. London.
Lambert, H.E. 1956. *Kikuyu Social and Political Institutions*. London.
Lawrance, J.C.D. 1957. *The Iteso: Fifty Years of Change in a Nilo-Hamitic Tribe of Uganda*. London.
Legesse, Asmaron. 1973. *Gada: Three Approaches to the Study of African Society*. New York.
Lévi-Strauss, Claude. 1963. 'Social Structure', Chapter XV (pp.277-323) of his *Structural Anthropology*. New York. Reprinted with some modifications from A.L. Kroeber (ed.), *Anthropology Today*. Chicago (1953).
Lewis, B.A. 1972. *The Murle*. Oxford.
Lewis, I.M. 1961. *A Pastoral Democracy*. London.
Luckham, Robin and Nkrumah, Stephen. 1975. 'The Constituent Assembly' in Dennis Austin and Robin Luckham (ed.), *Politicians and Soldiers in Ghana 1966-72*. London.

Luling, Virginia. 1965. 'Government and Social Control among some Peoples of the Horn of Africa'. Unpublished M.A. thesis, University of London.

Mair, Lucy. 1962. *Primitive Government*. London.

———. 1972. *An Introduction to Social Anthropology* (2nd ed.) Oxford.

———. 1974. *African Societies*. Cambridge.

Maquet, Jacques J. 1954. *Le Système des Relations sociales dans le Ruanda ancien*. Tervuren. Trans. *The Premise of Inequality in Ruanda*. London (1961).

Mayer, Philip. 1967. 'Introduction' to *Socialisation: The Approach from Anthropology*. London.

Meggit, Mervyn. 1972. 'Understanding Australian Aboriginal Society: Kinship Systems or Cultural Categories' in P. Reining (ed.), *Kinship Studies in the Morgan Centennial Year*. Washington D.C.

Middleton, John and Tait, David. 1958. 'Introduction' to *Tribes without Rulers*. London.

Needham, Rodney. 1971. 'Remarks on the analysis of Kinship and Marriage' in *Rethinking Kinship and Marriage*. A.S.A. Monograph. London.

Paulme, Denise (ed.), 1960. *Femmes d'Afrique Noire*. Paris and The Hague. (See especially the essays; 'Situation de la femme dans une société pastorale' by Marguerite Dupire and 'Le Rôle de la femme dans l'organisation politique des sociétés africaines' by Annie Lebeuf.)

———. 1971. *Classes et associations d'âge en Afrique de l'Ouest*. Paris.

Peristiany, J.G. 1939. *The Social Institutions of the Kipsigis*. London.

———. 1951. 'The age-set system of the pastoral Pokot'. *Africa*, 21;188-206, 279-302.

Peters, E. Lloyd. 1972. 'Aspects of the control of moral ambiguities: a comparative analysis of two culturally disparate modes of social control' in Max Gluckman (ed.), *The Allocation of Responsibility*. Manchester.

Prins, A.H.J. 1953. *East African Age-class Systems*. Groningen.

Radcliffe-Brown, A.R. 1929. 'Age-organisation terminology'. *Man*, 29:21.

———. 1941. 'The Study of Kinship Systems'. *Journal of the Royal Anthropological Institute*. Reprinted as Ch. III of *Structure and Function in Primitive Society*. London (1952).

Rees, A. 1961. *Life in a Welsh Countryside*. Cardiff.

Richards, A.I. 1956. *Chisungu*. London.

———. 1967. 'Socialisation and Contemporary British Anthropology' in Philip Mayer (ed.), *Socialisation: The Approach from Anthropology*. London.

Ruel, M.J. 1962. 'Kuria Generation Classes'. *Africa*, XXXII, 14-37.

Sangree, Walter H. 1965. 'The Bantu-Tiriki of Western Kenya' in J.L. Gibbs (ed.), *Peoples of Africa*. New York.

Southall, Aidan. 1970. 'Rank and Stratification among the Alur and other Nilotic Peoples' in Arthur Tuden and Leonard Plotnicov, *Social Stratification in Africa*. New York.

Spencer, Paul. 1965. *The Samburu*. London.

———. 1967. 'The Function of Ritual in the Socialisation of Samburu Moran' in Philip Mayer (ed.), *Socialisation in the Approach from Anthropology*. A.S.A. Monograph. London.

———. 1976. 'Opposing streams and the gerontocratic ladder: two models of age organisations in East Africa'. *Man* (N.S.) 11, 2, 153-74.

Stewart, Frank H. 1972. 'Fundamentals of Age Set Systems'. Unpublished D.Phil. thesis, University of Oxford.
———. 1977. *Fundamentals of Age-group Systems*. London.
Tignor, Robert L. 1976. *The Colonial Transformation of Kenya*. Princeton.
Wilson, Monica. 1951. *Good Company: A Study of Nyakusa Age-Villages*. London.

II
Aspects of Labwor Age and Generation Grouping and Related Systems [1]

R.G. ABRAHAMS

1

Age and generation are two very widespread if not universal criteria whereby persons in a social system are classed as senior or junior or equal to each other, or more generally as similar to or different from each other. The significance of these principles of ordering in kinship systems has long been clearly recognised, as has the fact that in a number of societies they serve, together or separately, as bases for recruitment into formally structured groups which play a variety of roles in social and political organisation. In the study of such groups, however, and in some contrast to the situation with regard to kinship studies, it has only fairly recently been clearly understood that, as principles for the reckoning of seniority, age and generation are by no means wholly compatible with each other, and in fact their relative priority varies from one system to another. It is possible that some indigenous peoples have themselves at times underestimated or at least underplayed the degree of conflict likely to emerge between the two principles, and certainly the application by such peoples of the same or closely similar terms to both the age and generation groups in their societies has been a ready source of confusion to the outsider. It is of course true that in the most obvious case of parents and their children, and indeed in most cases involving close kin, the two criteria co-exist in harmony with each other. When wider ranges of kin and even non-kin are involved, however, and especially when polygyny and possibly the levirate have worked their full effect, serious discrepancies begin to constitute the rule rather than the exception. Then groups recruited purely on the generation principle become strongly age-heterogeneous, to use Eisenstadt's term, and society-wide age-homogeneous groups cross-cut the boundaries between generations (Eisenstadt 1956: 34-5).

Well-developed systems of age and generation grouping are particularly common in East Africa and the present paper is most immediately concerned with one which operates among the Labwor people of northern Uganda. This Labwor system is closely related historically to that described by Gulliver for the neighbouring Jie people, though it appears to differ from it in a number of important ways. The Jie system similarly relates to others which have been reported at one time or another and with varying degrees of detail for such peoples as the Turkana, Karimojong, Dodoth, Toposa, Teso, Lang'o, northern and eastern Acholi, Didinga, and Pokot (Gulliver 1953, 1958; Dyson-Hudson 1963, 1966: Ch. V.; Thomas 1965: 57-60; Nalder (ed.) 1937: 70-4 and 145; Lawrance 1957: 72-83; Driberg 1922: 213, and 1923: 243-8; Anywar 1954: 210; Peristiany 1951). Structurally comparable systems, which are, however, much less clearly linked historically, have also been described for the Kikuyu, Kuria, Zanaki and Galla (cf. Prins 1953, Ruel 1962, Bischofberger 1972) and these in their turn appear to have some historical connections with the age-set systems of so-called southern Nilo-Hamites, such as the Nandi, Kipsigis and Maasai, in which formal generation groups are absent (cf. Huntingford 1953). The processes of borrowing and intermixture of these various systems in East Africa pose a number of intriguing ethnological and sociological puzzles to which adequate solutions are, with few exceptions, lacking. Nor is there so far any clear understanding of the factors which may lie behind the differences between related systems. In a later section of this paper I suggest that a closer inspection of the relationship between the age and generation system on the one hand and the kinship system on the other may provide a little further insight into variation of this sort.

2

The Labwor people, who call themselves Jo Abwor, number about 9,000 and live in a well-watered hilly area, known as the Labwor Hills, in the far west of Karamoja District in the north of Uganda. Culturally and linguistically the people are more closely linked to the Acholi and the Lang'o, their western neighbours outside Karamoja, than to the major tribes, such as the Jie, Dodoth and Karimojong, who live within the District. Unlike such Karamoja peoples, the Labwor are a Luo-speaking group and their main economic activities are agriculture, including cotton cash-cropping, and iron working, though they also keep some cattle and other livestock. Despite such major differences, however, and indeed to some extent because of them, there exist a number of important economic and other social ties between the Labwor and some of their more pastorally oriented neighbours, especially the Jie. Thus, in times of food shortage the Jie and occasionally other pastoralists have sought grain and even long-term refuge in Labwor, and the area has for a long time been the pastoralists' main source of iron goods including spears which are their principal weapons. Return payments for such goods and services are often in the form of livestock. Again, in the system of inter-tribal opposition and alliance which obtains in the Karamoja region, Labwor and Jie traditionally recognise each other as close allies and there are myths of common origin expressing this.[2] There are also many interpersonal links of friendship between members of the two groups.

Apparently at some time in the course of these connections the Labwor acquired their system of age and generation grouping, and material on age-group names (see Appendix) as well as some explicit statements by informants suggest that relevant Jie influence was particularly intense around the end of the last century. As I have mentioned, however, the Labwor system now differs significantly from that recorded for the Jie. This system, which I now turn to examine, has long formed one of three main frameworks of social organisation in Labwor. The others are today the system of Local Government Administration, which has largely superseded a traditional and relatively weakly developed form of chiefship in the area, and the system of kinship and marriage in which the main structural units are a series of patrilineal clans and their constituent divisions. As with related systems, such as those among the Jie and Turkana, Labwor age and generation groups contain only male members and the whole field of age and generation organisation is a predominantly male concern. Women are only involved to the extent that they are in some minor ways, and decreasingly nowadays, associated with their husband's groups, for example with regards to some forms of dance, song and ornamentation, and secondly to the extent that male age-group assemblies assert the right to deal with some sexual offences and to discipline the unmarried girls of the community, as I shall describe later.

3

Every Labwor male belongs to one of two named major divisions which I term 'generation groups', and these are somewhat similar in structure to the two Turkana groups of 'Stones' and 'Leopards' which Gulliver has labelled 'alternations' (Gulliver 1958: 902 and passim). In the Labwor case the groups are named respectively *Ekothowa* (Buffaloes) and *Ekoria* (Ratels or Honey-Badgers).

Like the Turkana 'Stones' and 'Leopards', Labwor 'Buffaloes' and 'Honey-Badgers' are both fathers and sons to each other, the son of a 'Buffalo' being a 'Honey-Badger', and the son of a 'Honey-Badger' being in his turn a 'Buffalo'. Unlike the Turkana system, however, in situations of widow inheritance, it is a man's own father, rather than the man who originally married his mother, who determines his generation group membership, so that a man whose mother was originally married to a 'Buffalo' may himself also be a 'Buffalo' providing his own father was a 'Honey-Badger'. Also in contrast to the Turkana, who recruit distinct contemporarary age-groups for each alternation, the Labwor operate only a single series of age-groups, each of which contains members of the two generation groups.

The distinction between members of the two groups is, however, significant in certain contexts. Thus, if a 'Honey-Badger' slaughters an animal for a sacrifice or feast, only his fellow 'Honey-Badgers' are allowed to prepare and distribute the bulk of the meat, and a complementary rule applies for 'Buffaloes'. Similarly, when beer is first brewed from a new crop at harvest time, only 'Honey-Badgers' may taste the first calabash of the brew if the head of the household concerned is a 'Honey-Badger', and only 'Buffaloes' can taste it if he is a 'Buffalo'. Again, in some though not all parts of Labwor, members of the two groups sit in order of their age-set seniority on opposite wings of the formal horseshoe-shaped seating arrangement known here and elsewhere in the Karamoja region as *akiriket*. In other parts, only age-set seniority affects the seating order, and members of the two generation groups sit mixed together on each side. Each group also has its own songs, and each group has the right — not often exercised — to wear distinctively coloured feathers and metal ornaments. In addition, there are certain rights and privileges which are held exclusively by one or other of the two groups. Thus, irrespective of a slaughtered animal's provenance, only 'Buffaloes' are entitled to cut up and distribute its tongue, and the meat of the lower back is comparably the sole concern of 'Honey-Badgers' who also have a special role in rituals, known as *akwet*, to purify the killers of certain dangerous wild animals including buffaloes. It is said that formerly the right actually to eat the tongue was only held by one group at a time and was transferred at intervals from one group to the other. In recent years, however, elders of both groups have shared this privilege, following a series of legitimating sacrifices carried out in different parts of Labwor at various times apparently up to the late 1950s and allegedly echoing comparable events among the Jie, though I have not been able to confirm this. Lastly, it should be mentioned that there is a strong taboo for 'Honey-Badgers' against killing and against eating real honey-badger, and they claim the right to impose a fine, such as the payment of a goat for a feast, on any other person whether male or female who has killed one. No such taboo or right exists for 'Buffaloes', however, with respect to their animal name-sakes.

It should be clear from the above that generation grouping in Labwor is more a system of dual social classification and differentiation between complementary and approximately equal groups than a framework for stratification based on relative seniority and juniority. This is, of course, especially consistent with the formal merging of alternate generation in a single group so that each group contains members who are generationally senior and junior to persons in the other group, and it may be noted that such merging would appear also to encourage the already present tendency of such groups to approximate to each other in the range and distribution of the ages of their members.

4

The reckoning of differences in seniority is much more evident and significant in the Labwor system of age-groups. As with many such systems, the designation of such groups simply as 'age-groups' is to some extent misleading since additional principles of seniority are operative, as we shall see, in their organisation and recruitment. Moreover, it is only the younger members of the society, many of whom have had experience of mission and state schooling, who tend to take any interest in actually counting years as a measure of age. But the term is by no means wholly an unsuitable one. For even older and more traditionally oriented informants often assert that co-membership of the groups concerned is based in general on the similarity of age of their members. This is expressed, without recourse to counting years, in terms of the members' having been born at approximately the same time and also, reasonably consistently with this, in terms of their having arrived more or less together at late adolescence which is considered to be the most appropriate time for their initiation (*kwogo*) and formal incorporation as active participants in the age-group system.

Ideally, when a boy is on the verge of manhood, when 'he has grown up' (*odong'o*) as the people put it, his father should provide or pay for the beast which will be killed for his initiation. Such initiation (*kwogo*) takes place every year. Some fathers become clearly aware that their son is old enough when they see similar boys of the community go through the ceremonies or when the boy is caught *amaka* (literally 'a catching') at night at the home of an unmarried girl. Others do not need such obvious or dramatic stimuli. Sometimes a father may delay unduly to agree to the provision of the necessary beast, but it is clearly recognised that it is every young man's right and obligation to go through initiation, and I was told that private and public pressure will quickly produce a resolution of such problems. As one old man put it, 'It is like government tax. It can not be avoided.' In any case, a prospective initiate commonly picks out for himself a beast belonging to another homestead and then lightly spears it, by no means necessarily with its owner's consent, in order to mark it off as his initiation victim. His father will then willy-nilly have to compensate the owner of the beast, and this practice thus provides an avenue of self-help to the son of a reluctant father as well as offering the attraction of adventure to initiates in general. A young man's involvement in formal schooling and possibly subsequent employment outside Labwor are sometimes causes of delay, and delays may also result from the existence of senior full or paternal half-brothers who have prior claims to the provision of initiation beasts. In the case of full brothers, the simple fact that they are older is sufficient reason for their earlier initiation, and in the case of half-brothers, the son of a more senior wife, whose place in the birth order of his mother's sons is the same as or higher than that of a junior wife's son, will have precedence providing that he is not very much younger than the junior wife's child. Similar rules apply to the marriage order among brothers. In this case a breach of the rules is called *odeparet*. Wrong order initiation is said to be 'like *odeparet*', and I was told that a beast sacrificed for such initiation would be found to be unsatisfactory when its intestines were 'read' in divination.

So far we have seen that the time of a person's initiation is significantly though not wholly governed by considerations of age. The further point must now be made that it is the time of initiation, as a social expression of age, rather than age itself which is the main determinant of seniority within the age-group system. This is reflected in the generic name for age-groups which is *wang' kwogo* or *kwogo-*groups. Within an age-group it is order of initiation which determines the relative seniority of members *vis-à-vis* each other and, with some exceptions, discussed below, the members of a senior age-group will normally have been initiated before the members of an age-group junior to theirs.

The exceptions I refer to are as follows. Firstly it is possible in certain circumstances for a person to be promoted into a higher age-group than the one to which he was initially recruited, and a type of situation commonly cited by informants in this context is one in which three brothers are initially recruited into the same age-group. In such cases it is felt that the eldest of the three should move eventually and probably in middle age into the next group above and, although he is likely to have been a fairly senior member of his original group, such promotion can, it seems, occasionally lead to his belonging to a group senior to that of some persons who were initiated before him. I may add that such promotion will also usually mean that the person concerned becomes a relatively junior member of his new group, and some men refuse promotion for this reason. Others refuse or hesitate because of the expense involved, since gifts of beer to the elders, and possibly of meat as well, are usually necessary accompaniments of such advancement. A second small group of exceptions arises out of a rule which prohibits a man from being initiated into the age-group immediately following that of his father. For this may sometimes result in a youth's entering a group junior to that entered by others who are initiated shortly after him but who are not affected by the rule in question. Moreover, such relative advancement of otherwise junior initiates may be further encouraged if the more senior of the two adjacent age-groups whose membership is involved happens to be the next-but-one below that of these initiates' fathers. For there is also a positive preference for a man's eldest son, at least, to be recruited into the alternate junior age-group to his own if it is possible to squeeze him in before the group in question is formally closed to new initiates.

Such closure of groups to new initiates appears to take place at roughly ten to twelve year intervals, but there is no rule to this effect and there appears to be little interest in the number of years, as such, between closures. More directly important is a range of social structural factors, which are themselves influenced by time, such as the immediately senior group's assessment of a group's numerical strength relative to its own and the desire of members of the group itself to assert its identity by closure which in turn marks the formal beginnings of a new group below them. It is also possible, though I lack direct evidence to support this, that the timing of a group's closure is affected by an awareness on the part of the immediately senior group that an increasing number of their own sons have started to grow up. As my earlier discussion implies, however, such sons can be initiated before the formal closure of what will be the group immediately senior to their own so that the members of what will ultimately be two clearly separate groups can be contemporary initiates.

My fullest information on closure relates to proceedings in the Katabok area in the late 1960s when the *Erukojwi* age-group was formally separated from what became the seniormost members of the next junior group, *Eribanya*. There are some gaps in my material, but the situation appears to have been as follows. At an *ameto* gathering (see Section 5) around the end of 1966 a member of the *Erukojwi* age-group, which had not yet been formally closed, was ordered to kill an ox for his adultery with the wife of a member of the next senior age-group, *Bonyo*. His fellow *Erukojwi* were separated from their juniors and ordered to provide honey to mix with the ox's blood to sweeten it for drinking. When, however, only sugar was provided they and the adulterer were further ordered by the *Bonyo* to spend several days in the bush near to the local settlements and they were subjected to a number of prohibitions against washing themselves, combing their hair, smoking, drinking beer and sleeping with women. Afterwards they were ordered to provide beer and tobacco for the *Bonyo*. Then at another *ameto*, in January 1968, they were similarly divided off and told to stay away from the local settlements for a week, and a similar set of prohibitions was imposed upon them, though it is not clear whether a particular offence had been committed in this case. Once more they were ordered to provide tobacco.

Sending a group off in this way is called *ryemo* (to drive or chase) and it is a fairly common way in which an age-group asserts its disciplinary authority over its immediate juniors. What is particularly significant in these two instances is that they, and the preceding fine of honey, were apparently the first occasions on which a clear division between *Erukojwi* and *Eribanya* had been drawn in this area. The time of the young men's initiation and, where relevant, the age-groups of their fathers were the criteria on which the division was based. At the end of the second 'banishment' the various local age-groups assembled at the house of a particular man who has a shrine at which new age-groups should be blessed on such occasions. The *Erukojwi* were told to stand in line in order of initiation and the seniormost *Bonyo* members lightly pricked the heads (*temo tok*) of the most senior *Erukojwi* with a needle used for sewing skins. They also put a pinch of the tobacco which had been collected for them into the nostrils of the *Erukojwi* and also on their foreheads as a blessing. This ceremony marked the completion of the closure of the group though they were told that they would also have to provide a further large drum of beer for the *Bonyo*. Later that year the members of the newly separated group began to assert their own authority over their juniors, the *Eribanya*, and demanded that a feast of chickens be provided for them by the junior group.

Such formal closure of a group to new initiates does not, of course, prevent the subsequent recruitment of new members by promotion, and it may be noted here that, in addition to the sort of case I have described, the most senior members of a group are sometimes promoted into the next group irrespective of their status *vis-à-vis* their siblings. This appears to be especially common in the case of promotion into relatively senior groups whose numbers are becoming depleted by the death of their original members, but further information is required on this topic.

With the various exceptions outlined above, we may say that membership of a particular age-group and seniority within it are dependent upon the time of a youth's initiation, and this in turn is closely related to, though not wholly determined by, his age. Concomitantly, age-groups themselves are ranked in order of their seniority which largely coincides with differences between the times of the initiation of their respective members and this ranking is a major principle, though not the only one as will be seen in the next section, which governs the relations of the age-groups to each other. As old age-groups die away, new ones are formed and the relative status of any particular group within the system thereby rises over time. As has been noted, however, there is some tendency to slow down the disappearance of the more senior groups by the sorts of promotion procedures I have described.

Before turning to examine the activities of age-groups and the form and functions of the system as a whole, it may be useful to say a little more about the rituals of initiation themselves. These commonly take place at the annual age-group gatherings known as *ameto*, but they may sometimes take place at other times of the year in which case they are carried out at the initiate's homestead. Only men attend in either case. As with the Jie and related groups, the central act in a youth's initiation is the killing by spearing of an ox, or sometimes a castrated goat or sheep. There is no rule, as reported for the Jie and Turkana, enjoining the alternate killing of such animals by siblings and other related initiates. Each young man in Labwor will usually offer as good and as big an animal as his father or other guardian seems or feels able to afford. The animal is speared in the right side and one thrust should ideally be sufficient to kill it. The spearing may be done by the initiate himself or it may be done for him by a member of his generation group after he himself has made a token cut. The dead beast is not skinned, but it is cut up into various customary portions which are then distributed. The tongue, lungs, heart, liver, lower ribs, some belly flesh, and a tail piece called *acir* go to the young man's home where they should be placed before an ancestor shrine, *abila*. The chest and head, minus the tongue and lungs may go to the initiate's mother-in-law's home if he is married. Otherwise these parts will go to his own mother's household, or, perhaps, to his mother's mother if his father has not himself provided such meat for her in the past. The two front legs and the whole remaining rear portion, less *acir*, are roasted at the initiation by members of the more junior age-sets present, and the meat along with some of the blood, mixed with sugar provided by the initiate, is distributed among those attending in order of their relative seniority. The smashing of the hindquarters, as is done among the Karimojong (Dyson-Hudson 1966:167), is not customary in Labwor though a comparable custom is said to be found among their Nyakwai neighbours to the south-east. I was told, however, that it is customary for one thigh to be carried to the fire with a large piece of meat dangling from it by a thin strip of skin, and the carrier must himself provide meat for the elders if the skin breaks in transit.

After the beast has been killed, its entrails are read to see if all is well in the ritual itself and for the community's affairs in general. The initiate is annointed by some of the elders with chyme from the beast. Such annointment, typically on the forehead, chest, navel, and some of the major limb joints, is a form of blessing also found in other contexts (cf. Abrahams 1972a:123). The initiate is then spun round three times — there appears to be no rule specifying whether he should be turned clockwise or anti-clockwise — and he is then told to start running. As he does so, elders and others present try to beat him, though not heavily, with switches from the *opobo* tree, the flexible wood of which is used in a number of comparable ritual situations. No special instructions, either ritual or secular, are normally given to an initiate, though the ceremonies are said to mark a youth's transition into manhood and away from the world and status of women and children. Young men whom I have questioned are themselves aware of this, and it is clearly a matter of some pride to them, as is also the provision of food for the elders and others which their initiation brings about. It is sometimes said that the name for initiation, *kwoɛ* derives from a verb, *kwok*, meaning to feel pride. Initiates also express pleasure at the blessing they receive at the ceremonies. That the transition to manhood is dependent on the rituals in only a limited sense can be seen from the fact that a young man can and, according to some informants, always has been able to marry and own and carry weapons prior to his initiation, but it is true and important that initiation brings a young man for the first time into active rightful participation in the world of age-groups and the significant roles they play in the political and ritual life of the community.

A point, which Dyson-Hudson (1966:163ff. and *passim*) notes for the Karimojong but which has not generally received sufficient attention in discussions of related initiation systems, is perhaps worth making in some detail here, though it requires further investigation before its full significance can be properly assessed. I refer to the fact that the killing of an ox or other domestic animal, which forms the central act in the initiation rituals, also commonly occurs in a wide range of ritual situations in Labwor and other societies concerned, and that it is therefore likely to be useful to consider these initiation rituals in the broader context of such 'sacrificial' killings. The failure of some other writers to do this may be partly due to their relative concentration on political and economic as opposed to ritual aspects of the societies in question; and a tacit assumption that 'initiation' and 'sacrifice' are different topics may also have played its part. The situation is, however, further complicated by the fact that it is not always completely clear in Labwor and possibly elsewhere (cf. Dyson-Hudson 1966:95) that such killings, whether at initiation or in other ritual circumstances, are really sacrifices in the generally accepted sense of the term. One problem here, at least in Labwor, is that such killings are not typically preceded by any formal dedication of the beast or invocation, nor are they necessarily accompanied by prayer. Questioned hard enough, Labwor will often state that God (*Rubanga*) drinks the blood of the victim and that his blessing and help are sought, but they often tend to stress more strongly and spontaneously that the killing provides meat for the elders whose blessing is also much desired. This again, however, need not be as straightforwardly secular a statement as it might at first appear, since it makes considerable sense to consider the elders in this area as marginal and mediating between the world of ordinary men and that of 'spirit'. We seem then to be partly operating here with a sort of sacrifice, analogous to tribute to a divine king in a more centralised political context, in which living and, in a sense, sacred persons, who are members of what Dyson-Hudson has interestingly characterised as an authoritative corporation aggregate of elders (Dyson-Hudson 1966: 227), are among the main recipients. However this may be, it is a point which applies equally to initiation and a wide range of other ritual killings in the area; and this leads us to acknowledge that a young man's initiation is, if only in the special sense outlined above, normally the first sacrifice in which he actively participates, and it marks among other things his right to perform and take part in further similar sacrifices which form a regular part of the ritual life of his community. This point is, of course, relatively straightforward in regard to a system like that of the Jie where initiation is in any case of little secular significance, but it may also lead us to pay more attention to the ritual consequences of initiation in apparently more secularly oriented systems which may be rather closer to the Jie system in this context than has been assumed.

A second point also emerges out of a consideration of this pattern of initiation as a sacrificial one. It has often been noted that Central Nilo-Hamitic initiation differs in its form from that among such Southern Nilo-Hamites as the Nandi and Maasai where circumcision is the dominant feature of the rituals. No attempt appears to have been made, however, to go beyond a simple statement of this difference and to seek some logic which might link the systems and their differing forms. Once Central Nilo-Hamitic initiation is seen as 'sacrifice', however, at least one such linking rationale immediately suggests itself. The notion that sacrifice may involve the substitution of the life of a domestic animal for the life of a human being in the course of maintaining satisfactory relationships between the human and the spiritual worlds has become an anthropological commonplace since the work of Evans-Pritchard on the Nuer (Evans-Pritchard 1956: 279-82). But the cutting and removal of the foreskin in circumcision can, of course, also be seen as a comparable act of substitution and as such, akin to sacrifice. In this context, the sacrifice of a domestic animal appears as a fundamentally 'metaphoric' act (Jakobson 1956: 76-82 and *passim*, but see also Lévi-Strauss 1966:227) in which one life is substituted for another, whereas circumcision is perhaps in contrast 'metonymic', involving, as it could be claimed to do, the literal substitution of a part for the whole. The two systems can be looked upon in this light as alternative and contrasting variations on a single theme which is in keeping at least with the cultural and linguistic links between the peoples concerned.

It is unfortunately be no means clear what further differences might be connected with those which I have suggested here, but one possibly promising line of enquiry may be tentatively mentioned. This concerns the fact that the distribution of the two sorts of initiation in question also corresponds quite well, among Nilo-Hamitic and relevant Luo speakers at least, to that of the presence and absence of formal age-grading. Thus it might be argued that such age-grading involves a highly explicit allocation of roles in the male life-process by virtue of initiation into and relative seniority within the age-set system, and that this is matched by the comparably explicit statement of male transformation which the direct mutilation of male initiates through circumcision seems to make. In contrast, in societies such as Labwor, Jie and Turkana without such formal age-grading, the allocation of roles by initiation and seniority is *ex definitione* rather less clear-cut, and this might possibly be matched in turn by the relatively indirect and implicit logic employed in the substitution of a sacrificed domestic animal for a person.[3]

5

At any one time there are likely to be at least six age-groups in formal existence in each of a number of sub-areas of Labwor. It seems that fifty or so years ago age-organisation in the area was considerably more unified than it is today. Until about that time, the population of Labwor was smaller and more residentially compact. Two main districts, known respectively as Wiawer and Morulem were recognised, and in some contexts still are; they lay on either side of a central ridge of hills which divides the country (see Wayland 1931:203). Each of the two districts is said to have recruited its own age-groups and run its own age-group affairs, but there was a constant flow of information between the two. As a result they are said to have kept their groups in line with each other and to have given the same names to contemporaneously recruited groups. Jie influence was also no doubt an important factor for at least part of this earlier period. Today's situation is by no means unrecognisably different from this, but a continuous process of diversification has been taking place. Since the 1920s the population has tended to increase and this, coupled with greater peace and security, has led both to the recognition of new major territorial divisions in the central area and to expansion into outlying areas of the country which were previously not permanently, if at all, occupied. The overall result is that there are today eight local residential districts which organise their own age-group activities, and it seems likely that a ninth will shortly emerge as a fully-fledged and distinct unit. These eight districts are Atung'a, Kano, Kiruu, Awac, Alerek (sometimes called Loyorit), Koya, Katabok, and Aremo. The ninth, Orwamuge, which lies on the south-western edge of Labwor, is said to combine at present in matters of major importance with Kiruu, from which much of its population is drawn, while organising some lesser events on its own. A comparable situation apparently obtained at first for other outlying areas which for a time were closely linked to one or other of the more central districts, these themselves being relatively new 'independent' sub-divisions of the old Wiawer and Morulem areas.

The eight districts organise their age-group affairs independently but not wholly disconnectedly from each other. They arrange their own recruitment and initiation, have their own special shrines concerned with the well-being of their age-groups, and they open new and close old age-groups according to their own convenience. They hold their own *ameto* gatherings in the dry season, and they do not participate in any regular Labwor-wide meetings connected with the age-group system analogous to those reported for the Jie. Nonetheless, the same names tend to be used for age-groups throughout Labwor, though occasionally junior and senior divisions of a large age-group are recognised, and in almost every district they appear in the same order of seniority. Thus in 1967 in most districts most of the men were divided into the following age-groups listed in order of decreasing seniority (see Appendix at the end of this chapter): *Edewa, Enyang'among', Madang'a, Bonyo, Erukojwi, Eribanya.*

The groups operate in more or less identical ways in each district, and they take general note of what age-groups are doing elsewhere in Labwor so that age-group rituals performed in one part of the country, to avert raids for instance, may be taken up and performed in other districts also. Even today the initial warning to perform such rituals sometimes comes from Jie. The groups are everywhere cross-cut by the generation groups of 'Buffaloes' and 'Honey-Badgers', and transfer from one district to another is relatively simple though there is a growing tendency for a person to take the precaution to carry out a special purificatory sacrifice (*ong'et*) upon beginning to participate regularly in the age-group activities of a district other than the one in which he was initiatied. Occasional *ad hoc* participation in other districts' activities presents no problem, and this is apparently true even for Jie visitors though it is of interest that Jie are said to be sometimes rather less hospitable to visiting Labwor in this respect. There is moreover a clear recognition of these common elements by the people themselves, and the unity of the system throughout Labwor is, in fact, occasionally asserted by them almost as a dogma so that inter-district discrepancies are at times only admitted after argument. But the discrepancies are real enough and serious misalignments are beginning to appear, for example in the times of opening and closure of groups of the same name in different districts. Nor is there any sign at present of a halt to this trend.

Owing to the timing of my fieldwork and brief interruption of it due to sickness, I was not able to attend any of the *ameto* meetings mentioned earlier, but it is clear that these annual gatherings are quite the most important and intensive age-group activities which each of the eight Labwor districts organises for itself. The people themselves stress this importance, and although some of the more educated younger men have strong reservations on the subject, it is fair to say that most men still see *ameto* as a key element in Labwor society and culture. They also see it as an institution which they share with many other societies and especially those of the Karimojong cluster. The available literature is, however, rather puzzling on this point and it may be worthwhile to say a little about the distribution of *ameto* before describing its form and functions in Labwor.

The earliest mentions of *ameto* in the literature appear to be brief references by Driberg. In his book *The Lango* (1923:188) he compares the Lang'o ceremony *epet* with those known as *ameto* or *amet* among some Karamoja peoples. Elsewhere (1922:213) he notes that the Didinga have an institution called *nameto* as part of their system of age-organisation which is clearly borrowed from one or other group of Central Nilo-Hamites. Later writers have mentioned institutions of the same or clearly similar names among the Eastern Acholi and the pastoral Pokot (Anywar 1954:210, Peristiany 1951:283, 287). No-one, however, with the exception of the authors of a Government report on security in Karamoja (Uganda Government 1961:6), appears to have mentioned such an institution for the Central Nilo-Hamites themselves. The paradoxical result is that we have descriptions of an institution around the borders of a central area among peoples speaking very diverse languages (Luo, Murle and Kalenjin), and yet next to nothing is known about it for the otherwise rather well-documented central peoples from whom it seems certain to have spread. Labwor informants insist that it is found in Nyakwai, Jie, Turkana, Karimojong and Dodoth, and the few Jie with whom I have discussed the matter lend support to this. Further research into the situation seems desirable, especially if my informants are at all correct when they assert that the significance of the institution in the central area is comparable to its importance in Labwor.

Ameto gatherings in Labwor take place every year, typically around December and January in the heart of the dry season. The proceedings may go on for several days and they may be broken off and resumed again at a later date. Large numbers of men attend and the different age-groups sit as units, separate from each other and ideally each under its own shade tree. The people themselves tend to stress the disciplinary functions of the institution including the 'driving off' of junior groups which takes place there and also the feasting which goes on at the meetings, but other business including initiation and, as we have seen, the occasional formal closure of an age-group is also customarily transacted on these occasions.

The most common response to questions about *ameto* is the statement that it serves to punish wrongdoers and especially those who have shown serious disrespect to their parents or to other senior members of the community. One important exception to this statement seems to be the handling of offences between a man and his parents-in-law since these are dealt with either by the kinship groups concerned themselves or in the courts. According to my records, the commonest offences dealt with at *ameto* are cases of adultery of a man with the wife of a senior kinsman or other local community member of a senior age-group, but many other sorts of offence are also punished. In one case a young man had struck his father, and in another a mother had been struck. In a further case a young man had misused some money which his father had entrusted to him. One youth was punished for playing a trick on his blind father and another was punished for leaving another blind old man behind when he should have guided him to some ceremonies which he needed to attend. Young women may also be punished at *ameto*. Sometimes a whole group of schoolgirls will be harangued and punished for failing to show sufficient respect to their elders and especially their fathers, and sometimes a particular girl will be dealt with, most commonly for refusing to marry an older man whom her father wants as a son-in-law.

The most common penalty for an offence is the provision of a beast and/or beer for the elders of the community, but some offenders, and especially girls, may be beaten and there is also sometimes an attempt to make the punishment particularly appropriate to the offence committed. Thus in the case of the young man who had tricked his blind father, an especially fitting penalty was exacted. The old man had been sitting outside his hut by the side of a skin on which grain had been set out to dry, and the youth had rattled the skin by tapping it with his fingers and had made his father think that chickens were stealing the grain. The father had then rather pitifully tried to chase away the non-existent birds to the amusement of the young man and some of his companions. At the *ameto* gathering it was decreed that the young man and his companions should be forced to tap hard with their fingertips on some nearby rocks until it was decided they could stop, and this decision was only taken when the young men's fingers had become severely bruised and had begun to bleed.

The joint responsibility which was ascribed in this last case to both the blind man's son and his companions turned mainly upon their joint enjoyment of the old man's predicament. But it also fits closely with the Labwor idea that in general age-mates are, or at least should be, mutually responsible for each other; and I was told that although it is common these days that only actual offenders are punished, traditionally more widespread penalties were exacted upon the offenders and their age-mates alike. Even today, moreover, the principle of group responsibility occasionally reveals itself in this way, as is shown in my discussion in the previous section of the joint punishment at the end of 1966 of the Katabok *Erukojwi*, arising from the adultery of one of their number with the wife of a local *Bonyo*.

A further significant aspect of this last case is that the groups concerned were proximal to each other in the order of group seniority. Relationships between such proximal groups are recognised as being marked by opposition and tension in addition to authority and subordination, and it is of interest here that the domination of a junior group by 'driving' them away (*ryemo*) sometimes actually takes the form of more physical attack which can occasionally lead to more serious violence. Thus I was told that at an *ameto* gathering in Kiruu in 1966, the *Erukojwi* whose formal closure there had taken place in the late 1950s (see Appendix) began to dance aggressively and then rushed, brandishing *opobo* switches, at the *Eribanya* who were themselves similarly armed. As is customary in such situations, the *Eribanya* quickly beat a retreat out of respect for the relative seniority of their assailants, and this happened three times. The *Erukojwi* were not, however, satisfied and made a fourth attack, whereupon some *Eribanya* began to lose their patience and exchanged their switches for some rather stouter sticks. As a result five *Erukojwi* had to receive medical attention at the local dispensary and local elders have since considered banning such 'mock' fights.

I was also told that when real fighting broken out on this occasion, some of the local Kiruu *Bonyo*, began to urge on the *Eribanya*, although others in a more statesmanlike manner tried to stop the fray as did the members of the seniormost groups present. Moreover, when the *Erukojwi* later wished to punish the *Eribanya* for the injuries they had inflicted on them, members of the *Bonyo* group interceded on behalf of the *Eribanya* in an attempt to get the penalties reduced. *Bonyo* support here for the *Eribanya* was explained to me as deriving from the more general recognition of a link between alternate age-groups which is expressed, as in a number of East African societies, in terms of father-son relationships. This relates, of course, to the point noted earlier that sons must not be members of the group immediately junior to that of their fathers and that eldest sons at least should, if possible, join the next junior set but one. The support is also clearly seen to derive from the earlier opposition between *Bonyo* and *Erukojwi* which is said to have been similar to that now operating between the *Erukojwi* and *Eribanya* groups and some informants argued that the system is ultimately based upon a self-perpetuating concept of revenge in which those who were dominated and punished earlier by their seniors seek opportunities to do the same to their own juniors.

This opposition and alliance between proximal and alternate age-groups appears to be a major feature of the system and it is, of course, on a formal level, interestingly similar to relationships here and elsewhere between the generations, though in fact it tends to cut across this latter pattern. It must not be forgotten, however, that the system is also fundamentally one of cumulative structural asymmetry based on differential seniority between the groups and individuals concerned and it may be noted that this asymmetry itself has both 'linear' and 'polar' qualities. In 'linear' terms, for instance, there is a chain of authority and respect from the seniormost group down to the most junior and this receives particular expression in the way in which commands are often issued at an age-group gathering. At a recent *ameto* for example, a case was dealt with in which an *Eribanya* youth had committed adultery with the wife of his elder brother who was a *Bonyo*. In this case the *Bonyo* at the gathering gave orders to the

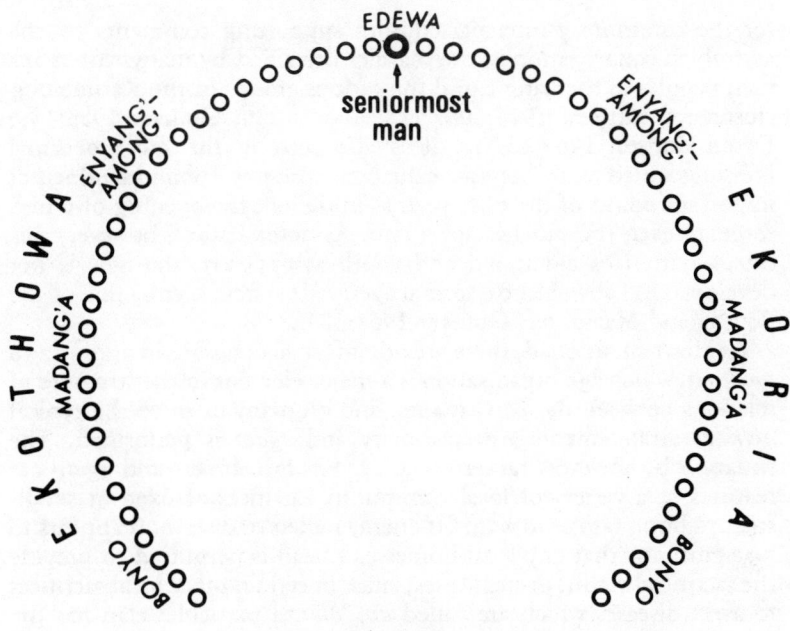

Figure II.1. *Akiriket* arrangements in the Katabok area 1967
(Members of each age-group sit in order of initiation).

Erukojwi who in their turn gave orders to the culprit's fellow *Eribanya* that the culprit should be caught and forced to find a bull to be killed for the assembled age-groups. When such a bull is killed, moreover, it is roasted by the juniormost groups and the meat and blood are given to those present in the order of their seniority within the age-group system. In addition it is common for those attending age-group feasts to sit in this order in the *akiriket* formation mentioned in Section 3. An example of this formation is illustrated in Figure II.1.[4]

The polar aspect of the asymmetry in question lies in a broad opposition between 'elders' and 'young men' in which the old are thought of as, at least ideally, wise and statesmanlike and 'close to God' in contrast to the rash, more secular youth. The role of the seniormost men in trying to bring the fracas, described earlier, to a close fits in with this as does their role in a variety of contexts as intermediaries between their community and the world of God and spirits. This last comes out most clearly at *ameto*, and other formal occasions in the custom of *agato*, in which senior elders make prayers for the community interspersed with supporting comments by the assembled congregation in the manner described by many writers for such peoples as the Lang'o and the various groups of the Karimojong cluster (cf. Driberg 1923:108, 112, 104-5, 250; Gulliver 1953:159; Dyson-Hudson 1966:165-7). It is also seen in the more personal blessings which local elders are called on to bestow upon individuals at important points of their life such as initiation, the opening of a new forge, or even the purchase of a gun. As noted earlier, however, this categorisation of elderhood and youth as opposed 'statuses' is not developed in Labwor into a formal age-grade system such as that of the Arusha and Maasai (cf. Gulliver 1963:364).

As I have mentioned, there are other formal occasions in addition to *ameto* in which age-organisation is a major element in the structure of relations between the participants, and on many of these the typical *akiriket* arrangements are customary and *agato* is performed. The situation is, however, rather complex. Firstly, *akiriket* and *agato* are features of a variety of local community sacrifices of oxen or small-stock to bring rain or to ward off enemy raiders or disease. It appears to be significant that any local homestead head is permitted to provide the sacrificial victim in such cases, since in certain other local sacrifices to avert disease, which are called *ang'olet*, a particular clan has the permanent privilege and duty to provide the victim and organise the affair, and it is apparently consistent with this segmentary emphasis that there is no *agato* or *akiriket* on such occasions. In other cases I was told that the amount of meat available is an important factor in the situation. Thus *akiriket* and *agato* are customary at local gatherings of kin and neighbours to eat part of the meat from an ox paid to a girl's father by a young man who has been caught *amaka*; the rest of the meat is consumed more privately at home. On the other hand, on some other occasions, with a much closer relationship to the age and generation system than is present in *amaka*, there will be no *agato* or *akiriket* because only a small amount of meat is available and relatively few people are likely to attend. This seems to be true, for example, if only a goat is speared for a young man's initiation at his home, though some distinctions between generation groups are likely to be observed in the cooking and distribution of the meat. It is also true when a goat is sacrificed at a ceremony called *ong'et* which takes place when a man is diagnosed as having become ill or liable to a series of mishaps because he has transgressed against another's right to eat or drink before him. Such rights derive from age-group seniority or from the fact that the food or drink in question belongs to a person of another generation group and especially a man's father, who should partake of it first. As was noted earlier, such sacrifice is also sometimes carried out almost prophylactically upon transfer to a new age-group district. It may be added that it is also probably important in these three examples of the significance of the amount of meat available, that each of the occasions has a strong individual and/or domestic focus as opposed to being solely or primarily a matter of concern to the community as a whole. The incidence of *akiriket* and *agato* thus seems in general to embody an interesting expression of difference and articulation between some of the main planes and domains of Labwor social structure.

To close this section, it should be noted that, as the data on *ameto* itself show, age-organisation is clearly geared to exercise more general behavioural constraints on younger persons to respect their seniors, including their senior kin, in addition to its role in structuring more formal situations. It should also be pointed out that, as among the Jie and in contrast to Turkana, the Labwor system seems never to have been used as a basis for military organisation. Again, although junior age-groups are sometimes given the task of helping to enforce decisions at *ameto*, it has not been customary for this policing role to be more generally extended. There is, however, some evidence to suggest that one chief, Aryon, may have started to experiment with something close to this in Wiawer at the beginning of the century.

6

Having set out the main features and functions of age and generation organisation in Labwor, I want in this section to examine some of the ways in which that organisation seems to interlink with the kinship system in the area. Despite some gaps in my data I hope to show, or at least convincingly suggest, that such an investigation may be helpful in understanding a number of aspects of the structure and working of the two systems. One basis for this suggestion is, of course, the point, noted earlier in this paper, that age and generation are regularly used as organisational principles in kinship systems, and this may lead us to consider initially whether there are interesting formal homologies between the two areas of social structure in question. A comparison of the two Labwor systems with those of the Jie and Turkana will help to highlight some possibly significant features here.

Taking age and generation grouping first we find that in Jie there is a well-developed generation-group system in which, at least ideally (Gulliver 1953:148; Lamphear 1972:194-5), all the members of one generation should be initiated before the next generation's members can begin their own initiations. Among the Turkana, on the other hand, we find that there are two more or less permanent generation groups which Gulliver calls 'alternations' and which he plausibly suggests may have developed from the sort of generation groupings found among the Jie (Gulliver 1958:920). Coupled with this contrast we find that Jie 'age-groups' are incorporated within the generation-group and that where the two principles of age and generation clash, e.g. when certain older men belong to a junior generation, then generation is ideally dominant over age and such men may possibly even die before they are initiated. In the Turkana case, however, although the generation principle continues to operate to the extent, for example, that each alternation has its own age-groups, the role of the generations is much attenuated and young men are initiated into age-groups much more clearly according to their age. The Labwor system, as we have seen, is structurally rather closer to the Turkana system than to the Jie system to which it is almost certainly more closely related historically. In Labwor there are two generation groups or alternations but membership in these does not affect the timing of a person's initiation and his right to join an age-group, though the generation principle can exercise some influence upon his allocation to one group rather than another, as I have described. More generally, in contrast to the case among the Jie, age can reasonably be claimed to hold priority over generation in a range of fundamental contexts in the Labwor and Turkana systems.

This similarity between the Turkana and Labwor systems in opposition to the Jie pattern is at first sight rather puzzling. Geographically, Labwor and Turkana lie on opposite sides of Jie and the Jie area is also ecologically intermediate between the Labwor area and Turkanaland. Thus Labwor has better rainfall, greater population density, more intensive agriculture and less involvement in pastoralism than are found among the Jie, while much the same can be said about the Jie in comparing them with the Turkana. Nor can Gulliver's suggestion (1958:921) that military considerations may account for the greater emphasis on age in the Turkana system help us much with the Labwor situation since we have noted that there, as in Jie, military affairs were not apparently organised along age-group lines.

Now it is of course quite possible that totally different historical factors have been responsible for the contrasts I have drawn between these systems in the Labwor and Turkana cases. It is, however, worth noting that the contrasts in question appear to correspond interestingly with further contrasts between the kinship systems of the three societies. Gulliver (1955: Chs. III and IV) has shown how a main feature of the Jie kinship system is the recognition of substantial ties and obligations between men who claim descent from a common grandfather, and how within this group there is a strong emphasis upon the unity of individual 'houses', which consist of a set of full brothers and their wives and children, and which persist as property-owning and property-administering units until the death of the last of the full-brothers who define it. All this is in some contrast to the Turkana situation in which full brothers tend to separate after their father's death and to administer their own 'estates' which are inherited by their own sons. Coupled with this, the Turkana recognise a relatively narrow range of senior agnates to whom they should give precedence, for example with regard to claims on cattle or other livestock for marriage and, most significantly in the present context, for sacrifice at initiation (Gulliver 1955: Chs. V and VI; 1958, 910). Similarly, in Labwor, such seniority is not considered significant outside the sons of one man, and although full-brothers play an important role in each other's affairs and have clear rights to receive portions of the bride-wealth given for the marriage of each other's daughters (Abrahams 1972:205-8 and *passim*), each in due course tends to have his own fund of property which is administered by him and inherited by his own sons.

In short the Labwor and Turkana kinship systems when compared with that of the Jie exhibit a relative weakening of ties between siblings and cousins and a greater emphasis upon the power and rights of individuals. Yet such relationships are, of course, intra-generational relationships *par excellence* and the sibling group can perhaps without undue distortion be considered as the archetypal generation group. The overall result appears to be that 'generation' is a much stronger principle of grouping in both Jie kinship and 'age' organisation than it is in either of the two corresponding systems among the Labwor and Turkana. In each of these latter cases there appears to be a generally greater emphasis upon the individuality of members of the same generation and, concomitantly, more attention is paid to a person's age as a criterion for his right to be initiated and to join an 'age-group'.

A number of questions immediately pose themselves concerning this isomorphism between the kinship and age systems in these three societies. Granted the apparent historical connection for instance between the three forms of age and generation organisation in question, can their link with kinship structure throw any light on the likely direction of the historical change which has resulted in their present diversity? Again, is it possible to make any sensible suggestions about the relative influence, if any, of one of the two structures upon the other in this context?

Two main difficulties beset any attempt to answer these and similar questions. Firstly, there is a shortage of historical data on many of the points in question and it is not clear from Gulliver's and my own research experiences that very much additional reliable historical material can be collected, although recent research by Lamphear among the Jie is encouraging on this score (Lamphear 1972). Secondly, it is as yet by no means wholly clear what the formal isomorphism I have outlined amounts to in real operational terms, though it does seem likely that further research directed closely to this question would be enlightening. A rather more particular difficulty in this context is the fact that Dyson-Hudson's work among the Karimojong shows that there the generation principle is strong on the level of rules if not in practice in the age and generation system, while the pattern of rights in property among agnates, which he has not described in such detail, seems much closer to that of the Turkana (Dyson-Hudson 1966:91-3, 205-6, and Ch. V *passim*). One possible inference from this is that the isomorphism I point to is an operationally insignificant one. Another is that the Karimojong system of age and generation grouping has been in a process of change arising *inter alia* out of the inconsistencies within it between the age and generation principles and those between it and the kinship system. Certainly Dyson-Hudson's work (1966:195-202) makes clear that at the time of his fieldwork the system was in some relevant respects not functioning particularly closely to the ideal model of it which he had constructed. The more general point should perhaps be added here that time and process are, of course, peculiarly intrinsic to and problematic in the working of age systems so that any synchronic picture of them must encapsulate an ideal past and future for them which are by no means always likely to have been or to be realised.

All these are daunting problems, but some comments are perhaps worth making, despite their speculative nature, in the hope that they may stimulate further enquiries. Firstly, with regard to the direction of change, the evidence on the side of age and generation organisation itself seems to point more probably to a shift from Jie-type to Turkana and Labwor forms rather than vice-versa. The vague memories of Turkana of additional, more 'senior' alternations are consistent with this (Gulliver 1958:920 and Lamphear 1972:496-7) and as Gulliver has himself pointed out (1958:919-20) the alternations make relatively little structural sense as they stand. Moreover, some of my Labwor informants would occasionally drift into an elision of some early twentieth century age-groups with the generation-group of 'Buffaloes', though they tended to deny this when it was drawn to their attention, and as I have noted earlier this period appears to have been one of strong Jie influence. It is also of interest in this context that one informant explicitly cited the *Madang'a* age-group, which was formally opened at the beginning of the 1920s, as a source of confusion and change leading to the present system, and it is certainly true that previous close links with Jie age-group names appear to cease with the establishment of this group (see Appendix). Lastly and more generally, in view of the internal strains of trying to run age and generation principles together and the concomitant difficulty of using generation over any significant period as a society or community wide principle of recruitment to groups which will follow on each other in a relatively well-ordered way, it seems easier to imagine the establishment of such a combination and its subsequent modification through an attenuation of the generation principle, than it is to picture any long-term process of change in the opposite direction. This point should not, however, lead us to forget that such combinatory systems seem at one time or another to have attracted a range of peoples outside the immediate limits of the Karimojong cluster.

The evidence from the kinship side also seems to offer some support for the direction of change outlined above. In the Turkana case the shift into their present ecological conditions has been shown by Gulliver to be highly consistent with the development of greater individuation in the kinship system (1955:255-9). In the Labwor case a comparable process has been taking place as agriculture including cotton production has intensified, cash flow in general has increased, and the population has become more widely dispersed. I do not, however, possess clear evidence to show that a 'house' system was at any time as strongly developed in Labwor as Gulliver describes it for the Jie.

So far, then, I have tentatively suggested that not only are kinship and age-organisation interestingly co-variant in Labwor, Jie and Turkana but the present patterns are probably the result of change in both Labwor and Turkana away from the Jie-style forms. It is with comparable hesitation that I turn now to the question of the direction of influence between the two systems and note that the evidence available seems to point more clearly to the 'dominance' of kinship than to the reverse, at least in this particular context. Firstly, whereas it is not hard to conceive how the very different Labwor and Turkana economies and ecologies could foster the development of their comparable kinship systems, it is rather harder to envisage their common direct influence upon an age and generation system. Secondly, one of the most clear points of actual connection between the two systems on which we have good evidence, namely the seniority order for the provision of sacrificial animals for the initiation of new age-group members, seems to be importantly influenced by the rules of the kinship system. For it seems highly probably that the general control of livestock in Jie by a 'house' of full brothers, and the recognition of strong intra-generational kinship ties and livestock obligations beyond this range, will contribute significantly to the maintenance of the priority of generations in initiation whereas such support would be lacking in a more individuating system.[5] On the other hand it must be admitted that another point of direct linkage, namely *ameto* which I will return to shortly, may theoretically be exercising a comparable support of the generation principle in Jie kinship structure though we have no clear evidence for this. Lastly, to the extent that the Karimojong material does not simply contravert the whole argument either by refuting outright the suggestion of significant linkage or by involving a process of change to a more generationally dominated situation, it does seem to support at least the temporal priority of individuation in the kinship system, as does the point noted earlier for Labwor that there is no clear evidence that a Jie house system was ever in full-scale operation there.

The relation between *ameto* and kinship organisation in Labwor forms my second topic for discussion in this section. The relevant material has already been described and it remains here simply to highlight some significant aspects of it. I particularly want to draw attention to the role of *ameto* in the support of norms of behaviour between senior and junior kin and especially between parents and their children. It may be noted that this seems to be consistent with the rule noted earlier that father and son should not be members of proximal age groups but should rather be in alternate groups if that is possible, since, given the pattern of relations between age-groups, this rule should help to avoid conflict and foster co-operation between fathers and their sons. However this may be, it is clear that a major function of *ameto*, which has been seen to be a central institution in the age-group system, is the maintenance of the internal structure of the kinship units which participate in that system. Partly, of course, because the domestic domain of kinship serves to produce and rear the members of the wider society it is subject to considerable external interference. I shall return to this point later, but it should not be forgotten that in this case descent and clan organisation provide an important mediating structure and that wider Labwor society can to some extent be considered as a congeries of intermarrying clans. While not wishing to exaggerate the 'segmentary' features of this system, it is arguable that its political structure has been, at least traditionally, not far from Mair's conception of 'minimal government' (Mair 1962: Ch. 2) and a picture emerges of age organisation in this and comparable societies as a relatively undemanding form of unification between descent groups. The lack of jurisdiction of *ameto* gatherings over affinal disputes can perhaps be looked at in this light as an expression of the rights of descent groups to operate as relatively free agents in this important sphere of relationships between them.

One is tempted to ask in this context whether this aspect of the character of age-organisation as incipient 'civitas' and as a kind of minimal social contract between lineages and clans might help to account for its relative rarity as a well-developed social structural sub-system in as much as it may not be well-equipped in itself to resist the opposition of forces for lesser or for greater unity or for a less symmetrical division of power. Yet it would be clearly mistaken to overemphasise this element of relative weakness and dependence in Labwor (and indeed elsewhere) and in so doing underplay the way in which the age and generation system continues to flourish there despite the impact of so many new forces for change as the people become more involved in wider Ugandan society and beyond. Partly, of course, this depends upon continued support from the participating kin groups and especially their more senior members. But many other functions of the system need to be remembered here, and especially its varied ritual roles and its more general ordering of local community and, to a lesser extent, society-wide relationships. Nor should one forget that the pattern of relations between succeeding age groups, in which those dominated from above in turn enjoy their power over those below them, contains its own dynamic for continuity and acts as a force for the unity of the groups concerned. Lastly, one needs to take into account the fact, noted earlier, that the age-group system must in itself, at least to some extent, be considered as a major agency of wider Labwor society operating upon and influencing the domain of kinship. Perhaps the most important symbol of this is the inescapability of a father's obligation to pay for the initiation of his sons into the system, and the comparison of this obligation to 'government tax' seems to be a peculiarly apt recognition of this.

7

To close this paper I would like to say a little more about the generation principle and particularly about the fact that so many of the societies to which I have referred have at some time been attracted to the idea of running a system of generation groups in diachronic series despite the very serious difficulties which this involves. Given this, and also the presence of 'synchronic' generation groupings in Labwor and elsewhere as well as the existence of well-developed generation rules in the age organisation of such peoples as the Maasai, it seems worthwhile to ask what makes the generation principle so attractive.

I have mentioned how time is peculiarly intrinsic to age and generation systems so that they may be seen at any point in time to project an ideal past and future for themselves, and it can be argued that this point may be reasonably expanded into a statement that, in addition to their many more practical functions, such systems typically constitute a sort of prophecy of the ordered unfolding and development of the societies in which they are found. Looked at in this context, some contrasting features of generation and age as principles of social organisation are perhaps relevant to the point in question. Firstly, it may be noted that a system of generation groups has a certain predictable, prescriptive and 'elementary' quality analogous to that classically ascribed by Lévi-Strauss to certain marriage systems, so that it is possible, for example, to picture quite clearly and well in advance the exact place of real or hypothetical individuals in a system of preordained and well defined groups. An age-group system on the other hand appears to be essentially a more statistical and 'complex' phenomenon in which the numbers of and boundaries between groups tend to have to be decided somewhat arbitrarily without reference to clear social structural rules such as those determining generational placing.[6] In addition to such formal qualities, a further and possibly more significant feature of the generation principle and groups based upon it must also be mentioned. This is, of course, the fact that whereas age in many ways asserts human mortality, generation much more clearly implies the possibility of its transcendence through the processes of physical and social reproduction and such wide-spread notions as the unity of alternate groups. All in all, I would suggest then that, notwithstanding the many difficulties involved in actual operation, the model of a system of generation groups succeeding one another has certain formal and substantive properties which make it well-nigh ideal as a conception of the well-ordered progression of a society through time. It seems at least possible that it is these qualities which have attracted so many adherents to such systems and to related forms of generational rules and grouping.

APPENDIX

SOME NOTES ON LABWOR GENERATION AND AGE GROUP NAMES AND APPROXIMATE DATES OF AGE-GROUP OPENING AND CLOSURE

The purpose of this appendix is to present further detailed ethnographic data which may be of use to anthropologists and historians with special interests in the Karamoja area.

A. *Generation Groups*

It has been noted that the Labwor generation groups are called *Ekothowa* (Buffaloes) and *Ekoria* (Honey-Badgers). According to one informant *Ekothowa* are sometimes also called *Ng'itome* (Elephants). *Ekoria* are fairly often referred to by the alternative name *Ereng'elem* which I understood to refer to a link with red hornless cattle (cf. Gulliver 1953:151) but which Dyson-Hudson (1966:158) and Lamphear (1972:91) associate more directly with red head-dresses for the Karimojong and Jie respectively. A less common name for *Ekoria* is, I was told *Emugeto* (Topi antelopes). It seems clear that all these names are derived from Jie and it may be noted that they are used despite the fact that there are perfectly good Luo words in ordinary use for all of them except the cattle-name *Ereng'elem*. It is significant in this context that Buffaloes (*Ng'kothowa*) was the name of the senior Jie generation at the time of Gulliver's study in 1951 and that Gulliver (loc. cit.) reports Topi (*Ng'mugeto*) as the name of the junior generation at that time which contained a fairly senior *Ng'iringilim* age-group. Gulliver does not mention Honey-Badgers, but Lamphear (1972:97-9) says that *Ngikoria* (Honey-Badgers) and *Ngitome* (Elephants) are a cyclically recurring pair of names for alternate Jie generation groups to which other more specific names, e.g. *Ngimugeto* (Topi) and *Ngikosowa* (Buffaloes) respectively, are also attached.

Differences in the spelling of Jie terms here arise out of differences between Gulliver's and Lamphear's orthography. Lamphear (1972: 525-7) also describes a Jie ritual to expiate the killing of a honey-badger.

B. *Age-group names and dates*

Little difficulty was encountered in collecting the age-group names of living Labwor men though the differences between localities were not always easy to sort out and problems were encountered due to changes over time in the names of some of the more senior groups.

With the possibility of one or two exceptions, living males belonged to the following groups in the three areas of Katabok, Kiruu and Alerek in 1967. Katabok is part of the old Morulem division, Kiruu part of the Wiawer division, and Alerek a relatively modern offshoot from Wiawer but nowadays linked administratively to Katabok. As far as I am aware, other areas (cf. Atung'a below) are organised more similarly to Katabok and Kiruu than to Alerek. The groups are listed in order of decreasing seniority with the seniormost at the top.

Katabok:	Kiruu:		Alerek:
Edewa (Snakes)	*Edewa*		*Edewa*
Enyang'among' (Tan coloured oxen)	*Enyang'among'*		*Enyang'among'*
Madang'a (Ticks)	*Abwor* (Elands) *Eling'akan* (Ringed Hands) } Senior and Junior *Madang'a*		*Abwor* or *Madang'a*
Bonyo (Locusts)	*Bonyo*		*Bonyo* *Eling'akan*
Erukojwi (Proud ones)	*Erukojwi*		*Erukojwi* or
Eribanya (Short grass)	*Eribanya*		*Eribanya*

I was told in Alerek that *Erukojwi* and *Eribanya* were simply alternate names for the most junior group, but some informants from other areas argued plausibly that a separation into distinct *Erukojwi* and *Eribanya* groups would take place there as elsewhere in due course.

The alternative name *Eritai* (Leopards) is sometimes used to refer to the *Enyang'among'* group in these areas. With the exception of the local Luo names *Abwor, Bonyo, Erukojwi* and, possibly, *Eribanya*, all the above names seem to be Jie in origin as are most if not all the names of earlier groups. There is expectably more variation in the information obtainable about the names of such earlier groups and about the order in which they were recruited.

The following is a list with approximate dates of the main recruiting periods of the last ten age-groups in the central area of the old Waiwer division (present-day Atuṅg'a *ameto* district).

Oluga (Green pigeon)	1855-65
Ng'atunyo (Lions) also called *Eyeramong'* (?)	1866-76
Ekwein (Jackals)	1877-87
Eruda (Bush-buck) also called *Ng'imoru* (Rocks) and *Emukura* (Hills)	1888-99
Edewa	1900-12
Enyang'among'	1913-21
Madang'a	1922-32
Bonyo	1933-45
Erukojwi	1946-56
Eribanya	1957-

The names and order of seniority of the four earliest groups on this list were collected from an *Edewa* elder, Stefan Oyolo, who was generally my most knowledgeable and reliable informant on historical matters in that area. With the exceptions of the name *Oluga* and the relative seniority of *Ng'imoru* in both of which he was supported by a number of other informants, his list fits well with the available Jie data (Gulliver loc. cit. and Lamphear 1972:90-1) as too does his list of yet earlier groups given in the following order: *Etiro* (Dik-dik), *Ekorkol* (Black-spotted oxen according to Lamphear but also associated with thunder by some Labwor informants), *Emuria* (Duiker), and *Ebereng'e* (small children) said to be the same as *Etuko* (Zebra).

I have hesitated to attach dates to these last four groups, and the most reliable of the dates I have ascribed to groups are those for the period back to about 1900 since these can be based upon or checked against a variety of political and economic events which can be independently dated and documented. These include an important battle between Jie and Acholi at the turn of the century (cf. Lamphear and Webster's 1971 discussion of this), the subsequent establishment of peace (*Etilo*) between Labwor and Eastern Acholi, Leeke's operations in the area (see Leeke 1917:202 and *passim*), the beginnings of British Administration from Kitgum in 1913 (see Barber 1965:36; and Wayland 1931:190), the establishment of administration from Moroto in the early 1920s and a range of more recent events. The nineteenth century dates are based simply upon an extension of eleven year periods back from 1900. The resultant figures for this earlier period tally reasonably well with information concerning the known age-group membership and other biographical details of some of the deceased kin of present day informants. They are, however, slightly earlier than Lamphear's estimates for Jie, which are mainly based upon a projection back of a forty- to forty-five-year generation cycle from 1920-3 (Lamphear, loc. cit.). As it is quite unlikely that Jie borrowed their age-group names from Labwor rather than vice-versa, some adjustment of this discrepancy seems necessary, though it is hard to say in which direction it should be made since no mechanical mode of calculation is very satisfactory for data of this sort. It is, however, clear from both my own and Lamphear's material on more recent groups that Gulliver (1953:148, 157) has tended to underestimate the longevity of Jie and the antiquity of their more senior age-groups.

As has been noted, the names of the most recent Labwor age-groups are mostly, if not all, Luo and they appear, in fact, to have nothing to do with recent age-group names in Jie. This fits well with present-day differences between the structure of the two systems as documented in the main body of the paper, where it was also pointed out that some discrepancies were developing, e.g. in the naming and ordering of groups and the timing of their formal opening and closure even within Labwor itself. Data on some of this variation have already been presented here and it remains only to recall, with respect to timing, that whereas *Eribanya* was apparently formally opened in most areas of Wiawer during the late 1950s, this only began to happen in Katabok in 1966-7 and had not yet begun by that time in Alerek.

NOTES

1 The fieldwork data upon which this paper is mainly based were collected in Labwor during the greater part of 1967. I wish to thank the British Academy, the Makerere Institute of Social Research and the University of Cambridge for generous financial and other aid in support of this work. I have been able to supplement my original material on some topics with the help of two Labwor visitors to Britain, Mr P. Kotol, and Mr C. Obonyo-Jabwor. I am extremely grateful to them and also to Mr C. Kotol and the very many people in Rac-Koko (Katabok) and other parts of Labwor who helped me during fieldwork.
2 Such myths are much more political charters than historical texts (see Dyson-Hudson 1966:263).
3 The fact that the sacrificial animals in question are castrated males is also possibly of some significance here. Beidelman (1966) has proposed for the Nuer that the sacrifice of such beasts asserts the value of socially inhibited male sexuality, oriented towards the maintenance of a system of solidary groups, as opposed to less controlled and more disruptive forms. If sacrifice and circumcision are transformations of each other in the present context, as I have suggested, it could perhaps be argued that this adds to the plausibility of Beidelman's insistence upon the importance of the sexual component in sacrifice though the form of such an argument would depend heavily upon as assessment of the sexual significance of circumcision in societies like that of the Maasai. One problem is that the

period of moranhood which immediately follows circumcision is typically one of relatively wild male sexuality. If one focuses upon this fact, it appears to be necessary to argue that circumcision is the opposite, rather than simply a more explicit version, of sacrifice in order to exploit it in support of Beidelman's more detailed thesis. On the other hand, it can reasonably be argued that the wild stage of moranhood is unintelligible except as the subordinate presager of the more disciplined and society-oriented stage of elderhood and that circumcision essentially marks the beginning of the process which includes them both and transforms the first into the second. This would fit more straightforwardly with Beidelman's ideas and it would also fit sensibly with my suggestion of the greater explicitness both of circumcision as ritual and of the age-grades as stages in the male life-process. It should be borne in mind, however, that a rather different interpretation of the nature of the ox-man connection in the Nuer case has been made by Burton (1974) and, more generally, Firth (1973:181) has noted the shortage of empirical data proferred in support of Beidelman's and comparable speculations. I am very conscious of this last point in the case of my own speculative discussion here.

4 It is perhaps worth noting that, despite the major cultural differences of table, tableware and gowns, the structural arrangement is not unduly unlike that of the seating orders at some Oxbridge College high tables in which seniority by initiation into fellowship comparably overrides simple age differences.

5 It is of interest here that Lamphear (1972:94) reports pressure from potential Jie initiates to begin their generation group's initiation as soon as possible.

6 Looked at from this point of view, the cyclical age-group systems of the Nandi and others seem to be rather comparable to the quasi-elementary Crow and Omaha systems in Lévi-Strauss's formulation.

BIBLIOGRAPHY

Abrahams, R.G. 1972a. 'Spirit, twins and ashes in Labwor', in La Fontaine J. (ed.) *The Interpretation of Ritual*, London.

―――――. 1972b. 'Reaching an agreement over bridewealth in Labwor', in Richards, A.I. and Kuper, A. (eds.) *Councils in Action*. Cambridge Papers in Social Anthropology No. 6, Cambridge.

Anywar, Reuben S. 1954. *Acoli ki ker megi* (Acholi and their Kingships). Kampala.

Barber, J.P. 1965. 'The Moving Frontier of British Imperialism in Northern Uganda'. *Uganda Journal*, Vol. 29, No. 1, pp.27-43.

Beidelman, T.O. 1966. 'The Ox and Nuer Sacrifice: Some Freudian Hypotheses about Nuer Symbolism'. *Man* (new series), Vol. I, No. 4, pp.453-67.

Bischofberger, O. 1972. 'The Generation Classes of the Zanaki'. *Studia Ethnographica Friburgensia No. 1*. Fribourg.

Burton, J.W. 1974. 'Some Nuer Notions of Purity and Danger'. *Anthropos*, Vol. 69, pp.517-36.

Driberg, J.H. 1922. 'A Preliminary Account of the Didinga'. *Sudan Notes and Records*, Vol. V, pp.208-22.

Driberg, J.H. 1923. *The Lango, A Nilotic Tribe of Uganda*. London
Dyson-Hudson, N. 1963. 'The Karimojong Age System'. *Ethnology*, Vol. II, No. 3, pp.353-401.
_____. 1966. *Karimojong Politics*. Oxford.
Eisenstadt, S.N. 1956. *From Generation to Generation*. Glencoe, Ill.
Evans-Pritchard, E.E. 1956. *Nuer Religion*. Oxford.
Firth, R. 1973. *Symbols: Public and Private*. London
Gulliver, P.H. 1953. 'The Age-set Organization of the Jie Tribe'. *Journal of the Royal Anthropological Institute*, Vol. 83, pp.147-68.
_____. 1955. *The Family Herds*, London.
_____. 1958. 'The Turkana Age-Organization'. *American Anthropologist*, Vol. 60, pp.900-22.
_____. 1963. *Social Control in an African Society*. London.
Huntingford, G.W.B. 1953. 'The Southern Nilo-Hamites'. *Ethnographic Survey of Africa*. I.A.I. London.
Jakobson, R. 1956. 'Two Aspects of Language and Two Types of Aphasic Disturbances', in Jakobson, R. and Halle, M. *Janua Linguarum:* 'Fundamentals of Language', No. 1. The Hague.
Lamphear, J.E. 1972. 'The Traditional History of the Jie of Uganda'. Ph.D. dissertation, University of London.
Lamphear, J.E. and Webster, J.B. 1971. 'The Jie-Acholi War'. *Uganda Journal*, Vol. 35, Part 1, pp.23-42.
Lawrance, J.C.D. 1957. *The Iteso*. London.
Leeke, R.H. 1917. 'Northern Territories of the Uganda Protectorate'. *Geographical Journal*, Vol. 49, pp.201-8.
Lévi-Strauss, C. 1966. *The Savage Mind*. London.
Mair, L. 1962. *Primitive Government*. Harmondsworth.
Nalder, L.F. (ed.), 1937. *A Tribal Survey of Mongalla Province*. I.A.I. London.
Peristiany, J.G. 1951. 'The Age-set System of the Pastoral Pokot'. *Africa*, Vol. XXI, pp.188-206, 279-302.
Prins, A.H.J. 1955. *East African Age-class Systems*. Groningen.
Ruel, M.J. 1962. 'Kuria Generation Classes'. *Africa*, Vol. XXXII, pp.14-26.
Thomas, Elizabeth Marshall. 1965. *Warrior Herdsmen*. New York.
Uganda Government. 1961. *Report of the Karamoja Security Committee*. Entebbe.
Wayland, E.J. 1931. 'Preliminary Study of the Tribes of Karamoja'. *Journal of the Royal Anthropological Institute*, Vol. 6, pp.187-230.

III
The Ethos of Equality among Dassanetch Age-Peers [1]

URI ALMAGOR

1

The enduring equality of age-mates has been a central assumption in almost all the literature on age-systems. A few quotations will be sufficient to point out that the equality of age-mates has simply been assumed: 'The essential character of the age system, as opposed to the secret society, is that the former is equalitarian: every man is a member of his age set, and as the set rises in rank, he passes through every grade of seniority in his own tribe simultaneously with all its other members' (*Notes and Queries*, 1961:68). Evans-Pritchard writes of the Nuer: 'Within the age-set system the position of every male Nuer is structurally defined in relation to every other male Nuer and his status to them is one of seniority, equality or juniority.... Members of the same age-set are on terms of entire equality' (1940:257). Bernardi states of the Turkana that 'the age-system emphasises the unity (the 'brotherhood') of all members of the society and, being the only system that is co-extensive with the whole society, provides a general and equal basis for their structural status' (1952:326). Finally, Spencer, on the age-system of the Samburu, writes: 'The basic relationships which characterise the age-set system are equality between members of one age-set and inequality between members of different age-sets.... Members of one age-set, or age-mates, are not merely equals, they are expected to observe certain norms of behaviour which derive from and express their joint membership...' (1965: 81-2).

In some societies with age-systems relative age may be an important determinant of individual access to resources and social power, but it would be simplistic to proceed from this fact to a view of age-systems which stresses either that relatively similar shared age provides a premise of equality, or that differentiation of age produces inequality.[2] Certainly, any analysis of age-systems as a separate entity would have to show that age is an organising principle which stresses equality within any group, and inequalities in power between age-groups. But such an analysis is likely to be partial and artificial because an age-system does not stand separate from other social institutions and because age relationships are not simply a further category of social relationships which can be set beside political, economic and social relationships. To say that relationships are based on age and, therefore, are equal in nature tells us little about their content. The very emphasis placed on the equivalence of age with status indicates that the reference is to norms rather than to actual behaviour. I hope to show why I am sceptical about status homogeneity based on age.

My primary concern is with the interplay of inequality as an idea in juxtaposition to equality; that is, on the one hand the differences in the quality and quantity of social ties that individual members of an age-group maintain and, on the other hand, the ethos of equality which they preserve and manipulate. It is the relationship and the feedback between the idea and the social context which concern me here. In his daily activities, every Dassanetch is involved in what appear to be two, sometimes opposed, situations. He is a member of an age-group and he is also an individual who interacts with other individuals in other contexts. As an age-peer, a man is to some extent constrained by loyalties and obligations, and above all by the emotional unity, which derive from being a member of a recognised age-group. As an individual a man establishes ties and engages in reciprocal co-operation with many people.

I shall deal with these two aspects in the following order: the image of the equality of peers, the solidarity of equals as an element in the manipulation of social relationships and, finally, equality in debates. But, first, I describe briefly such features of Dassanetch society as are necessary to present a schematic outline of the Dassanetch age-system.

2

The Dassanetch are a small tribe of about 15,000 people which inhabits the Lower Omo Valley in southwest Ethiopia, north of Lake Turkana (Rudolf). Their mixed economy is based on pastoralism and flood retreat cultivation. Cultivation is crucial in their economic life but their overt values are pastoral and livestock transactions are central to all their social relationships. They are grouped into several tribal sections each of which is made up of exogamous patrilineal clans. Each clan is an amalgam of a number of named descent groups of diverse origins. Clans do not have genealogical structure, common territory, shared ritual or political organisation. Each tribal section has an age-organisation which is its central political institution.

The household, consisting of a husband, his wives and their unmarried children, is the basic unit of production and consumption, and each follows a transhumant pattern of herding and cultivating. The inundations of the Omo River, on which cultivation is based, are irregular and the areas flooded vary from year to year. A complex method of allocating strips of land along the river banks has been developed through which no one can acquire permanent exclusive rights, and which enables the maximum number of people to cultivate land at any one time. The eldest married son usually remains with his father until the latter's death, but the other sons leave and establish independent households.

Affinal relationships are a crucial means of creating economic and social independence and they are established and maintained through a long, gradual process of bridewealth allocation and transfer. Rights to claim bridewealth are obtained through genealogical ties or bond partnership to the bride or her father.

A man starts to build up his social and economic position as a young herder by creating his own bond partnerships and continues to do so until he reaches elderhood. There are five basic types of bond partnership: 'lips' (*afo*), 'gift' (*shisho*), 'smearing' (*uru*), 'holding' (*kerno*) and 'name-giving' (*meto*). The bond of 'lips' is usually established between teenage youngsters, carries no enduring rights and obligations and stems from natural affection and seeks to secure reciprocal assistance in herding camps. The bond of 'gifts' is usually established between men in their twenties and thirties by the exchange of simple gifts, and merely formalises relationships between persons who are already engaged in economic co-operation. It fades away once the boys become men. If the economic interests of the partners change the bond is ignored. The bonds of 'smearing', 'holding' and 'name-giving' are considered to be 'strong' since they carry rights to bridewealth. The bond of 'smearing' is established at the ceremony of physical maturity for a boy, at which he is ritually 'smeared' with the contents of the stomachs of small stock by an adult partner. The bond of 'holding' is established at the circumcision ceremony when the circumcised is 'held' by someone who thereby becomes his partner. The bond of 'name-giving' is established whenever a man's name is given to a new born boy. In the strong bond partnership there is always a junior and a senior partner.[3] Each partner acquires potential rights and obligations according to his status in the partnership which only become effective if fostered by continuing co-operation. A bond partnership is a common way of strengthening existing co-operation and also a means of opening up new fields of potential co-operation with persons who are related to one's partner. Thus, a person can mediate access to the resources of others for a partner by utilising his own genealogical position or social network to accumulate brokerage power and social credit.[4]

A man builds up his economic and social position by his own endeavours so that his social standing thus depends on events which provide him with possibilities of accumulating further credit and brokerage power. These include a man's first bonds, his marriage and those of his brothers and sisters and opportunities to make people indebted to him when he is an active herdsman. How successful a man has been at exploiting these possibilities becomes apparent at the *dimi* ceremony, which a man undergoes when he has fathered a daughter, and is a crucial point in his life. After 'going to *dimi*', a man usually retires into social elderhood and settles down in one settlement. For now I merely note that the time at which a man undergoes the *dimi* ceremony is not connected in any way to his position in the age-system, nor to his membership of a particular age-group. The *dimi* ceremony is an annual and collective event which is performed by, and on behalf of, those men who have fathered a daughter some seven or eight years previously and has nothing to do with age-grading. So a man acquires recognition as an elder in one important social context independent of his position in the formal age-system. *Dimi* makes age-peers unequal in status.

The Dassanetch view their age-system as their main political institution. It is divided into six named generation-sets which may be ordered by seniority as follows:

A1	A2	A3
B1	B2	B3
A1	A2	A3
B1	B2	B3

A man always joins the alternate generation-set to his father. The six generation-sets are divided into three pairs, each of which pairs form one line through which a man and his male descendants pass. So, for example, the sons of a member of A1 will all be members of B1 and B1's sons are members of A1. Similarly, the sons of A2 will be members of B2, and B2's sons members of A2 and so on. Sets follow each other in the order A1, A2, A3, B1, B2, B3, A1 and so on. My surveys showed a considerable overlap of age across generation-sets but also some clustering. Although persons belonging to different generation-sets can be of the same age, the hierarchy of the generation-set system is based on age-differences. This is particularly evident when comparing the ages of the oldest or youngest in adjacent generation-sets, i.e. the oldest members of one generation-set are approximately eight to ten years older than the oldest members of the generation-set immediately junior to them. Similarly, the younger persons of each generation-set are older than the young persons of the generation-set below them by approximately the same number of years.

Entry into a generation-set depends on when its alternate one starts to beget children.[5] Each set holds four circumcision ceremonies (*ha idi mita*) at approximately four to six year intervals, and recruitment to it stops after the fourth ceremony. Each set holds its own series of ceremonies independently of other sets, and in each ceremony members of various 'annuals' (youngsters who share a hair-dressing ceremony, see below) are circumcised together. The rules make for complexity in operation, but this summary is sufficient for my present purposes. It should be noted that owing to the long period of recruitment to each generation-set, the age differences between the

Plate III.1. Dassanetch boys showing the hairstyle of *nigen*

oldest and the youngest members in that generation-set may be up to forty years, so each generation-set is not a set of coevals. Thus, men of similar age may join quite different generation-sets and different sets, therefore, which are ranked in an order of seniority, may in fact contain men of similar age.

All young men of a set who change their hairstyle from that worn by boys (*nigen*) to that worn by men (*kabana*) in the same year I call an 'annual' (*chad*). 'Annuals' are ranked in order of their formation. Each new annual is like a new course added to the structure of the set. Each is composed of a number of cliques of close friends, usually numbering ten to fifteen boys and called *shele*, a term which is difficult to translate but is near in meaning to 'close-friends'. The members of a clique may share other social connections and may develop reciprocal relations, but these are only formalised and institutionalised within the framework of the set at the hairdressing ceremony. Each clique holds its own hairdressing ceremony separately and independently and in any one year many such ceremonies will be performed. An 'annual' then is made up of all the *shele* cliques of the same generation-set which are initiated at the hairdressing ceremonies held in the same year. An 'annual' is a loose structure of independent cliques but 'annuals' are clearly structured in the hierarchy of age within a generation-set.

Dassanetch notions of equality are not derived from any general principles of equality of opportunity or equality of status, but from the age-system and are limited to the small clique of age-peers. The

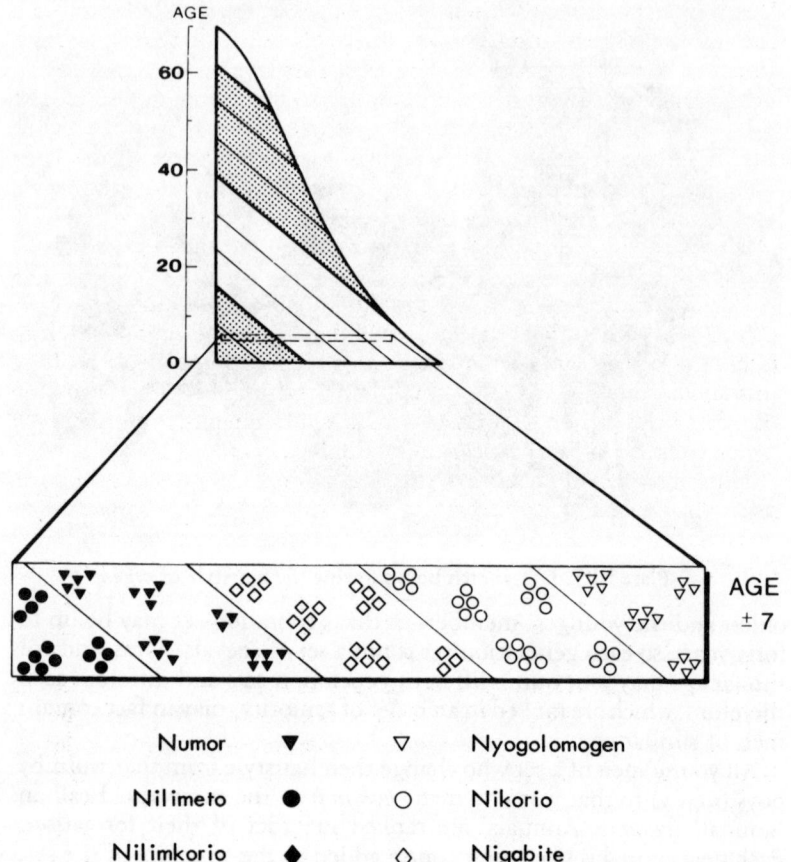

Figure III.1. A schematic representation of the Dassanetch age-system

Each of the slanting rungs represents a generation-set. The shaded and the light generation-sets correspond to the division into alternations of the six named sets A1 A2 A3 and B1 B2 B3. The large rectangle below the distribution curve is an extension of the smaller rectangle which cuts across five sets and which encloses those boys around the age of seven years. Members of sets are represented by triangles, by spots and by diamonds and each cluster of these symbols indicates a peer clique.

Dassanetch perceive themselves to be hierarchically stratified in a continuum of generation-sets and 'annuals' and, in that sense, the structure of social ranking is rigid. Men of the same age but who belong to various generation-sets may regard themselves as equals, but they do so largely in terms of a very generalised continuum of relative age in which all are relatively seniors or juniors, but this does little more than regulate the ordinary decencies of daily life. I shall analyse the much more emotionally weighted 'ethos of equality' which, the Dassanetch hold, should be maintained by the age-peers of one clique.

Infants tend to mingle in a settlement without reference to their generation-set membership but, when they reach the ages of seven to ten, boys of the same set in an immediate neighbourhood coalesce into small groups based on mutual liking and interest. The formation of such 'close friend' cliques occurs simultaneously within each generation-set, as can be seen in Figure III.1.

During the second decade of their lives, which they spend as herders in livestock camps, age-peers are scattered throughout the pasture areas, but they often meet to share food, exchange information about grazing grounds and help each other out. Membership of an age-peer clique fluctuates at this stage as boys leave and join camps and as the stock they tend changes pastures. But membership of cliques is not haphazardly determined by pastoral movements; even young boys consider the relative social standing and resources of the families of their peers when they decide whether or not to join a particular clique. In its early years clique membership is loose, members join and leave, but the members of a clique undergo the 'hairdressing' (*me tagniya*) ceremony between the ages of seventeen and twenty. This marks their transition from boyhood to manhood. The ceremony takes place when and where the age-peers themselves decide, although they need permission from the senior elders of their generation set. Until they have undergone the 'hairdressing' ceremony boys are affiliated to a particular set, but are not formally and fully incorporated into the age-system. The hairdressing ceremony is an essential pre-requisite to social recognition of manhood, so all boys must become members of a clique. Participation in the ceremony marks the boundaries of a clique which should from then on form an intimate group of age-peers, and be a major social influence throughout a man's life. Ceremonial seniority may be accorded through membership of 'annuals' in such matters, for example, as the seating and meat distribution arrangements at certain generation-set ceremonies. But 'annuals' are not distinct or cohesive groups. They rarely, if ever, meet together. The Dassanetch say that 'a man grows up in his own generation-set (*hari*) and cannot live without a generation-set', by which they imply that a man's basic political rights and continuing social support derive from his membership of a generation-set and that a man is accompanied by his age-peers during all the major rites of his life. In summary, a man is a member of a generation-set which links its various members loosely and also of a clique of age-peers which maintains tight bonds between members who should consider themselves equal. This essay deals with cliques.

3

The second decade of a boy's life is critical in the development and consolidation of the ethos of equality of peers. The conditions under which youngsters associate and co-operate as equals are laid down in the stock camps where they all undergo similar experiences. Though they are under the supervision of elders, who may occasionally give them a hand, by and large they are left on their own. During adolescence, when the boys are separated from their natal households and near kin, the clique forms a substitute supportive group.[6] Age-peers depend on each other for practical help which causes high value to be placed on membership in an age-group. The relationship of a boy with his peers is not like that which often characterises his relationships with adults, who exploit his labour to strengthen their own social ties. His peers are his friends and allies who should help him in almost anything. Peers lend each other ornaments and tools needed for pastoral tasks, and look after each other's stock. All the social activities of the stock camps are carried out by peer cliques, who go to evening dances and go courting together. They pass time chatting and arranging each other's coiffures. They support each other in disputes with other herders, share milk and grain when it is brought from settlements and go together to 'lift' a sheep or goat. What will later become a formal group begins to crystallise. The desire and ability to co-operate, to share and to do anything for peers are the criteria for membership. A boy who does not conform to these standards will be left out of this circle of intimates, and usually leaves to join another clique where he is accepted and can get along. Membership brings the socially valuable reputation of belonging to a specific age-group of peers. This is the core of solidarity.

A young man chooses a name-ox for himself from the household herd, which should be different in colour and configuration from the name-oxen of his father. Henceforth he is identified with that particular colour configuration. Taking a name-ox is a mark of the youth's growing independence from his father's household and coincides with his increasing association with his age-peers. A young man keeps a small herd of similarly coloured name-oxen which form his 'cattle of the colour'. Although a man is identified with his name-ox, all his name-oxen are said 'to belong' to his age-peers to whom he is obliged to present one for a meat feast from time to time. The following example indicates how peers view their relationships.

Torko, a young man in his early twenties, exchanged a cow for an ox which was closer in colouring to his 'cattle of the colour'. Torko told me that it was his turn to give a name-ox to his peers, and as he did not possess an appropriate one he had suffered a disadvantageous exchange out of obligation to his peers. There is a host of proverbial sayings which men quote to explain why they have slaughtered beasts for their peers such as: 'How can a man refuse his *shele*, aren't he and they the same?', or 'We are one', or 'A man must give everything he has to his *shele*. For aren't they all one and the same?', or 'How can a man live without his *shele*? Who will support him? Who will care for him?'

The meat of a speared name-ox is shared among the age-peers in a ritual and communal meat feast. The owner is prohibited from eating its meat. As the Dassanetch put it, 'A man cannot kill his own name-ox because that would be like killing himself and he cannot eat its meat because that would be like eating himself, for aren't they one and the same?' Each peer in rotation metaphorically 'gives himself to his peers', who equally 'eat and share' him. The symbolism of transfer from the family to the set of equal age-peers is clear.[7] The ritual eating of name-oxen and other animals, indeed the general sharing of food, become occasions for the reinforcement of the values of equality and shared identity. Communal meals are consumed around the rim of a crescent of 'holy green leaves' (*miede*) which are laid on the ground in imitation of the way adults consume meat. This manner of eating demonstrates publicly that the youngsters form a specific and bounded peer clique.

Age-peers are expected to demonstrate solidarity and equality and they should not use *fargoginte* on each other. *Fargoginte*, which may be translated as 'coercion' or 'force', is a very broad concept and is used in many other social contexts. It is used when one person seeks immediate reward or benefit at the expense of another, by imposing his will or claiming superiority, in a situation where reciprocity should be the norm. To become known as a person who uses *fargoginte* in his relationships with others is a stigma. It is considered more reprehensible for young peers to overbear each other than it is for mature men, among whom competition and differentiation are recognised. I shall first illustrate some of the situations in which accusations may be made between young peers.

At the end of June 1969, a teenage shepherd, named Hakoliye, asked his elder brother's permission to slaughter a sheep for his age-peers. Permission was granted and Hakoliye invited some of his peers to come the following evening. One of the peers brought a friend who did not belong to Hakoliye's peer clique. During the meal no one said a word about it but afterwards they said to their peer who had brought his friend: 'He is different. What is he doing here? Is it a kind of *fargoginte*?' The accused defended himself by saying: 'He has been here before' (i.e. he is not a stranger and has stayed here on previous occasions). He was answered: 'You are just a tittle-tattle, we don't like it.'

Another accusation of using *fargoginte* took place when a group of peers was chatting informally in the shade of a tree. War, an extremely persuasive boy, was relating an incident in which two peers of the clique had been involved. War described how, while crossing the river with another peer (who was not present), their dugout had capsized. Since his companion did not know how to swim, War tried to help him. War dramaticaly imitated his companion's hand movements to illustrate his companion's fright. The peers laughed from time to time in response to War's dramatised tale but eventually a peer asked him: 'What are you telling us, is it not *fargoginte*?' To which War replied, 'No, leave it, the *kabana* (i.e. the peers) want to know.'

Another example concerns a quarrel between two teenage peers named Lomiede and Arkomo about who had first claim to a patch of grazing. When others discussed the incident phrases such as 'How could one do this to his *shele*?', 'You are both *shele*, why use *fargoginte*?' were tossed about.

Another incident which involved the use of sanctions by a peer clique was when Aigiet, a young man in his early twenties, found a lost sheep one evening. He slaughtered the animal with his knife and called two coeval affines to accompany him into the thick bush, where they roasted and ate the beast. The owner of the sheep later found out and made it publicly known. In consequence Aigiet was beaten by his peers, who each struck him once on his back and legs with their personal sticks. I witnessed the beating and one of the phrases which I heard was: 'We don't like *fargoginte*. Aren't we all *shele*? We are not thieves.'

These instances vary in their meanings. Pursuing one's own interests at the expense of the group and thus undermining the ethos of equality were features of the instances of Aigiet and the peer who brought his friend to the meat meal. War was accused of showing off and attempting to dominate his equals. Aigiet had attempted to show off to his affines and shamed his clique. In two instances (Aigiet and the uninvited guest) the accusations were intended to maintain the solidarity and reputation of the peer clique. Likewise, the quarrel between the peers about grazing rights was contrary to the obligation to co-operate and help each other. The *leitmotiv* throughout is reproof of selfishness, domineering or showing off at the expense of one's peers which undermines the solidarity of equals. A large part of the activities of peers concentrate on the maintenance of the 'solidarity of equals' which is highly institutionalised throughout the crucial period of youth. Each peer strives to prevent any other one from achieving a position of dominance. Consequently during their teens and twenties the behaviour of peers conforms to their shared image of equality. Such peer clique sanctions are usually much more effective among the young men than they are among senior age-groups. Youths fear the sanctions of their peers more than those of their elders.

4

Every man belongs to a generation-set and to one of the peer cliques of which 'annuals' are constructed. Each peer clique is originally based in friendship and affection which is later consolidated as the boys move into their teens. When they pass together from the grade of boyhood (*nigen*) to manhood (*kabana*), at the ceremony of 'hairdressing', the clique of age-peers is incorporated into the age-system. Thus lifelong membership is fixed in a social framework. The institutionalisation of the clique legitimises their activities as a group, which hitherto had been considered as no more than an aggregation of boys who liked each other. In their twenties at the stage of warriorhood young age-peers spend most of their time together. They chat, eat, drink and sleep together. Occasionally they raid other tribes and exchange the looted cattle, thereby both enhancing their *esprit de corps*, and strengthening ties between themselves. I have elaborated upon this in greater detail elsewhere.[8] This, however, is also the period during which differentiation commences in the roles each plays in the pastoral management of his natal household. The different status of each of the peers in his natal household determines, to a large extent, the amount of time he spends in the stock camps or in taking an active part in the pastoral and agricultural tasks of the household. The duties of a first-born son, who is obliged to stay with his father, differ both from those of a peer who has older bachelor brothers to take care of the household herd, and from those of a peer whose father is dead and who, therefore, has to take responsibility for his younger brothers and their stock.[9] All in all these very different social and economic demands are a result of the position each man occupies in his natal household. Differing household responsibilities cause each of the peers to participate in diffcrent activities and to enter into different relationships. Economic activities involve co-operation with many people and investment in future relationships which, in turn, contribute to the build-up of each peer's independent social and economic status. Variations in the positions occupied by peers in their natal households can, therefore, lead to increasing differentiation between peers which goes against the ethos of equality they all share. This conflict is further increased when some peers marry, have children, develop effective affinal relationships, establish more bonds and immerse themselves in economic and social activities which derive from their responsibilities as heads of independent households. Dassanetch men marry relatively late in life, usually at the end of their twenties or the beginning of their thirties. The discrepancy between social actuality and the ethos of social equality is well brought out at the circumcision ceremony. By one rule, only a man who has fathered a daughter may be circumcised, by another, all peers of a clique must go through the ceremony together. In practice, bachelors and daughterless husbands are circumcised along with their luckier peers.

The overriding of one rule by the other which permits unmarried or daughterless men to be circumcised, clearly expresses the contradiction between the ethos of equality and the reality of growing social differentiation. The framework of equality is maintained in the circumcision ceremony and the peers are seen as a single group of equals. However, the peers themselves are well aware that some of them have achieved a higher status by establishing their own households, by creating affinal ties but, above all, by having the potential to achieve a higher status in the near future due to the very fact of having fathered daughters and thereby being properly qualified to perform the important *dimi* ceremony.

The image of equality and the process of differentiation among peers do not correspond. The gap between them becomes more and more visible, not only in terms of the number of stock or wives and children each of them has, but also in their personal skills and ambitions and in the social prestige and credibility each has variously acquired. However, since peers remain formally affiliated to one set, which advances through the age-system as a unit, the solidarity of equals is strongly asserted at meetings and debates among equals (a subject to which I shall return). These debates aim to quell public doubts as to the reality of that solidarity. One of the elements in this assertion of the solidarity of equals is the avoidance of direct competition among peers. Nevertheless, a great deal of a man's activities involves the manipulation and the use of the norm of the 'solidarity of equals' as a means to achieve access to other people's resources. This could be best illustrated through a detailed case study, but shortage of space allows me to mention only some instances which show how the notion of equality is interwoven into competitive activities.

The peer clique which I discuss here consisted of eleven married men in their mid- to late-thirties. They were scattered in three settlements. The story is best followed through Figure III.2.

All, except H, were actively engaged in various daily work tasks and only two of them (B and H) had performed the *dimi* ceremony. I told me his views about the state of relationships among his peers and then said, 'We are one? [i.e. equals] No. It is only a way of speech. We are different. When I go to see H I see that he is a "big man". Everyone knows that he is a "big man". I go and eat meat. It is good. I am a little one.' The distinction I drew between his peers is obvious from Figure III.2. None of the peers had more than one wife and the differences between them (apart from B and H) in stock ownership were slight but there were, however, significant differences in relation

Equality among Dassanetch Age-Peers

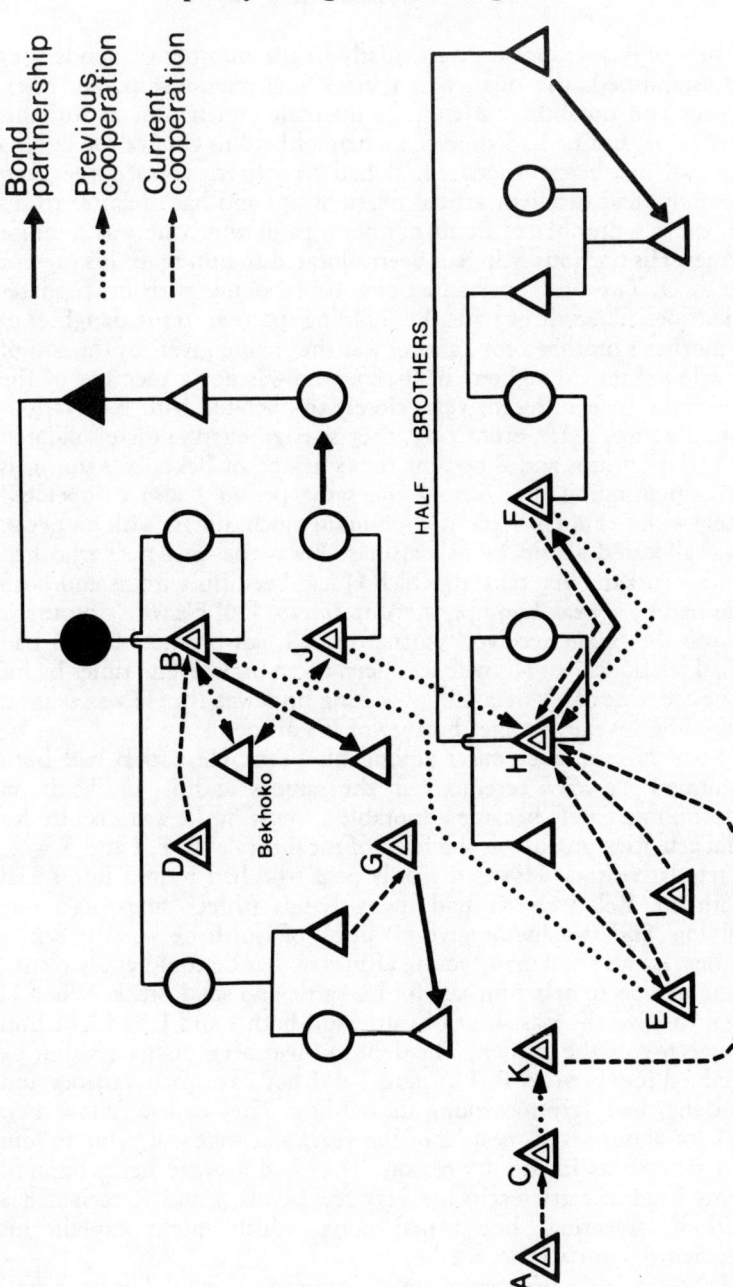

Figure III.2. Relationships within one peer clique (the eleven peers are marked with letters and a double triangle)

to their brokerage power, particularly in the number of bonds they had established, the quality of their affinal relationships and their prestige and notability. A did not maintain much contact with his other peers, but he had allocated a strip of land to C since the latter's strip had not been inundated. B had recently performed the *dimi* ceremony, had excellent affinal relationships and had, relative to his age, quite a number of bond partnerships in which he was a senior partner. His previous strip had been allocated to him by E, his present one by D. Two of his peers had established bonds with his cognates and affines. The wife of J was the 'holding' partner to the daughter of his mother's brother's son, and G was the 'name-giver' to the son of his wife's sister's daughter. Bekhoko, who was not a member of the peer clique, had in recent years closely co-operated with B in various pastoral camps until, eventually, they strengthened and consolidated their relationships and B became the 'smearer' of Bekhoko's son. It is worth mentioning that during the same period J also co-operated closely with Bekhoko. C did not maintain much contact with his peers. E was allocated a strip by H's affines. F was the only peer who had killed a Turkana in a raid, to which H had been his witness and both were tied by a weak bond partnership (*meto*).[10] F's wife's brother's son was the 'name-receiver' partner of H's half-brother. G had bad affinal relationships. His wife had been taken back several times by his affines because of his delays in allocating bridewealth. He was assisted in herding by the younger brother of B's affines.

H was *primus inter pares* among his peers. He and B had both performed the *dimi* ceremony in the same year but, unlike B, H almost immediately became a 'notable', whose home was a centre for social activities, mainly in the form of meat meals. E, F, I and K were his regular visitors. H was the only peer who had retired into social elderhood. Relatively he had many bonds (three 'smearing', one 'holding' and two 'name-giving') in all of which he was the senior partner. He also had many young affines so that he could easily recruit young herders to help him care for his cattle and small stock. When H 'went to *dimi*' he was short of cattle and both J and F had lent him animals to ease the burden. The debt to J had been discharged but he remained indebted to F. I, K and J did not have many affines and those they had were too young for herding. They had to follow their stock for about seven months of the year, and were only able to join their setlements in the dry season. They had average herds (around twenty head of cattle each) but very few bonds. J and K each had a bond of 'smearing' but I had none, which might explain his statement: 'I am a little one.'

Having roughly outlined the relationships between the peers, I shall refer to certain situations in which the incompatibility between the ethos of equality and the reality of differentiation becomes apparent.

One evening, a short time after the bond of 'name-giving' had been established between F's affine and H's agnate, H, F and some neighbours were drinking coffee in H's home. The recent difficulties which some herders had encountered with a Kenya patrol came up in conversation. The subject was dropped and then H made a remark which astonished me at the time. He referred to his debt to F and said, 'It is the dry season now, when the "big rains" fall, I will return the ox you lent me.' This astonished me not only because of its apparent lack of connection to the conversation, but also because H himself, who was in debt to F, had mentioned it without being asked. I will return to this in a moment, but shall first describe another conversation which took place between G and B. As noted, G's relationships with his affines were bad and he hardly co-operated with them. The bond G established with B's affines was a great relief to him, especially for the herding assistance which he was thereby rendered. One day G and B were chatting about whether to pasture near Mount Kuraz or near Erek and from time to time B made remarks such as: 'If the grass is good there [i.e. near Mount Kuraz] I'll let you know, you are my brother', or 'We used to eat from the same circumcision calabash'.

There are elements common to both instances. F was in debt to H, and G was dependent on B. However, neither was reminded of their debts by their peers, but each brought up the subject on their own initiative. By referring to his own debt to F, H indirectly diminished F's debts to him (visits, meals and a new bond-partnership of 'name-giving'). Similarly, when they were chatting about grazing plans, B was recalling his and G's clique membership and their common past experience as young herders who had shared all that they had. He thus obliquely brought out the difficulties which G had encountered in recruiting herdboys and his consequent dependence on B. I suggest that the common denominator in both instances is a desire to prevent inequality becoming obvious. When differences between peers become too apparent, it is very difficult, if not impossible, to maintain relationships on the basis of equal reciprocity. So, when inequalities are exposed men try to disguise any outstanding imbalance. So H, who was 'big', showed himself to be in debt to F, and B lessened G's dependence upon him by referring to the personal and intimate aspects of their relationship. The emphasis on reciprocity and equality mitigated the indebtedness. This is the very proper opposite of *fargoginte*. The above anecdotes indicate that a great deal of social tact is required to manage relationships between 'unequal equals'. No Dassanetch would specify exactly the obligations of one peer to another. They spoke in general terms such as: 'One should help one's peers', or 'One should give and share everything one has with one's peers, for aren't peers like one person?', etc. But what the 'solidarity of equals' definitely does imply is the free access of one peer to another. This ethos of equality is, of course, not restricted to Dassanetch age-peers. E.L. Peters has told me that great differences of wealth and status existed in the Maronite village he studied, but that, nevertheless, an ethos of equality was expressed in the free social access all villagers had to one another. Similarly, H. Lewis's comments that Galla tenants were considered socially equal to their landlords.[11]

The access Dassanetch peers have to one another is expressed not so much in visits, informal chats and coffee drinking (because anyone can visit and chat with any of his coevals), nor in direct access to each other's resources (i.e. meals, allocation of strips, lending of livestock, etc.), but more in the form of mediating access to other people's resources. The relationships between members of a clique have to be mediated. If we take the peer clique just described, for example, it can be seen from Figure III.2 that H mediates relationships to F, and B mediates relationships to G and to J. A man is also required to mediate between any member of his clique, if he is asked, and any outsider with whom he has a relationship. In the name of the 'solidarity of equals' he is under moral and social pressures to mediate relationships for, and to, his peers.[12] He does this because he must take into consideration the reactions of his peers and his long-term relationship with them. But, by the very mediation of relationships, he accumulates debts from among his peers and by opening up new ranges of social relationships for them, paradoxically, further increases the inequality.

Differences between peers are initially created by the number of strong bonds and the quality of affinal ties each possesses. Social possibilities are restricted by demographic constraints. The number of strong bond partnerships and affinal ties which can be forged are restricted by the number of births every year, the annual number of boys who reach physical maturity, the number of men who are circumcised and the availability of nubile girls. Each of these are in limited supply. In general, there is a marked absence of strong bonds between peers. It can be seen from Figure III.2 that no direct affinal ties and only weak bonds existed within the peer clique. However, there are not any rules or customs which either encourage or restrict the formation of bond partnerships with or between age-peers. During youth, when group solidarity is still strong, the most common strong bond established between peers is that of 'holding' at the circumcision ceremony which the age-peers undergo together as a group. Individual interests begin to develop after circumcision and peers become more and more differentiated as they become geographically and socially further apart (in terms of the allocation of land, co-operation in pastoral camps, dispersed affines, seasonal movements, etc.). As the number of boys with whom a strong bond may be established is limited, each individual must thoroughly weigh-up the pros and cons when establishing a bond partnership, in order to develop a strategy which will enlarge his field of relationships to the maximum possible extent. If a man's best interest lies with a peer he will establish a bond with him, but as a man matures age-peership simply becomes of less importance.

Peers compete for the same social ties.[13] The absence of strong bonds or affinal ties between peers could be explained by the fact that age-peership with its accent on equality is incompatible with 'bonding', in which the one partner is senior and the other junior. It is certainly difficult for two peers who are considered equals to enter into an unequal relationship, but a peer can mediate a bond partnership for a peer with a third person who is related to him. The essence of any bond partnership is the opportunity it gives for the creation of other relationships. Mediation between peers permits one partner to acquire more debtors than others and thus creates an unbalanced situation in which the mediating position of that particular peer becomes progressively stronger.

The equality of peers is emphasised when they are circumcised together, whereas the *dimi* ceremony brings out and legitimises the differences between peers. Performance of the *dimi* ceremony is a great step towards social elderhood and retirement from active pastoral management. Unlike the loose interpretation given to circumcision rules, the rule for *dimi* is absolutely inflexible: it depends on fathering a daughter. Hence, the differences between the times each peer 'goes to *dimi*' can be up to twenty years. The *dimi* ceremony publicly recognises an individual's potential ability to establish affinal ties through his daughter's marriage and makes a man a desired bond partner, since such partners will thereby acquire bridewealth rights. The post-*dimi* period, that is when most men are in their forties and fifties, is marked by increasing social differentiation between peers. Other factors such as a reputation for integrity, a man's social credit, the quality of his sets of affinal ties etc., come to the fore and individual differences become increasingly visible.

The recognition of inequality is marked symbolically in that, after 'going to *dimi*', a man gives up his name-oxen which had formally and symbolically represented the notions of the equality, unity and solidarity of the peer clique. It seems that as a man matures and becomes more individualised, the less his peer clique affiliation is relevant. The interests of peers become separated over the years so the role each plays in the networks of others becomes marginal. A man's membership of a peer clique and its position in a generation-set are not, however, forgotten and they indicate his formal rights to power. Furthermore, the overt value placed on the solidarity of equals and loyalty to the group remains high and maintains the stereotyped impression of a structure of peer cliques of equal coeval elders. This is clearly expressed in the Dassanetch language, in which a single term — *tigle* — embraces two concepts which can be translated as 'unity' and 'equality'. Thus, the expression *nien ni lule tigle* could be variously translated as 'we are all one' or 'we are united' or 'we are all equals' or 'we are the same'. The implication is that the two attributes are found together. During youth this is objectively so. However, as age-peers mature and approach elderhood an observer can see that unity and equality are by no means co-existent, as indicated in the words used by I which were quoted above: 'We are one? No. It is only a way of speech. We are different.' However, a peer clique is spoken of as if it were a united clique of equals within the age structure of the generation-set. *'Tigle'* expresses the view that ideally and formally the attributes of equality and unity are both applicable to the peer clique throughout its life and the lives of its members. Men constantly refer to the equality which should exist between peers throughout life. But a closer scrutiny shows that in daily life the stress is placed on collaboration and willingness to give mutual aid and, especially, on mediating new fields of social relationships, rather than on the minute balancing of individual inputs or comparing relative social standing. It is, in other words, a generalised reciprocity rather than a set of balanced transactions.

5

The clique of peers which I described above did not meet once as a group during my fieldwork. Some of the members who were living in one settlement spent their time together, but there was no special occasion when they all met. Members of mature peer cliques meet for meals and debates less and less. By the time a clique reaches elderhood some of its members will have died and there is a tendency for cliques that belong to the same 'annual' and generation-set to merge. Elders tend to see the hierarchical structure of the age system as a broadly based dichotomy between *lute* and *gasiet*, i.e. elders who are seniors and at the top, *vis-à-vis* youngsters who are juniors and at the bottom. On the other hand young men tended to specify the age structure according to its 'annuals' and even stressed the differences between adjacent 'annuals' and between cliques belonging to the same 'annual'. Elders perceive the age differences among them as small. They all belong to the 'yards' of their settlements where retired elders meet every evening and converse. Because the members are seldom co-residents, clique meetings are usually called at the home of one peer to coincide with an important local event. The aim of such meeting is seldom to reach any immediate conclusion. It is the gathering itself, and the long and open discussion in an atmosphere of equable equality, which is important. Peer clique debates are characterised by what Burns has called 'polite fiction', such as 'is used by married people and intimate friends in arguments, when each is concerned to maintain both the status of an intimate and the status of membership of a larger group whose prestige... weighs in the argument' (655). Elders only intimate any differences between themselves obliquely and

Plate III.2. Dassanetch age-peers debating after a meat feast

maintain the forms of politeness and fraternal equality, even though they are all well aware of the great differences of status which have crystallised among them over the years.[14]

A debate between peers is usually accompanied by a ritual meat eating at which the peers sit behind the sacred crescent of green leaves (*miede*). The debate starts after the meal, when each speaker in turn stands up, takes 'the spear of speeches' and commences. From time to time a speaker interpolates blessings and curses, to which the participants respond by repeating the last word of the blessing or curse. They are both addressed to God (*Waq*) and are usually for affluence, fertility for cattle and women, health for children, the destruction of wild beasts, and the punishment of neighbouring tribes. There is no specified time to bless or curse. One speaker may do so every few minutes, another only at the end of his speech, another may completely refrain. A speaker who cannot maintain a flow of speech, or who has little to say, will often resort to blessing and cursing. My impression was that whenever a speaker was unable to establish rapport with his peers, or when he touched on a controversial issue and felt that the clique might be displeased, he would bless or curse for a minute or two before continuing his speech, almost as a mechanical means of creating consensus. An observer cannot fail to notice the burden that such repetitions of blessings and curses imposes. Loyalty to the clique and the equality of peers is stressed throughout. An influential man rarely raises a subject which might be publicly opposed and, whenever he can, will tactfully conform to his peers' opinions. Tact is crucial. I do not recall hearing the reproving words *ma fargogo* (i.e. an over-bearing man) in a debate between retired peers. Since debates seldom end in a decision, lip service can be readily rendered to equality, and antagonism which might provide grounds for gossip suppressed. A powerful peer is more likely to appear to be fostering good-will than publicly demonstrating his power. The debates of peers afford an excellent opportunity to bring non-conforming peers into line, and to remind all of the necessity of not undermining the solidarity of equals. I recorded many occasions of debates between peers who had retired from active herding, during which prominent and powerful elders were tactfully reprimanded about their behaviour. In one debate an elder who had refused a loan of an ox to another was reprimanded in general terms as follows: 'We are one. Someone does not want to give cattle to his *shele*. This cannot be so. Aren't we all one? No one is more, no one is less.' It was not his difference in wealth, power, prestige, etc. which was questioned but rather his unfriendly refusal of aid, lack of consideration and arrogance.

Finally, the framework of the debates and their assertions of equality accentuate the inequality among peers by the very fact of assembling the differentiated persons together. The meetings of retired peers are a burden to most of them. 'Notables' are forced into situations in which their status and power are not given proper recognition.[15] This contrasts with the 'yard' debates at which it is difficult to separate the social and economic assets a man has from what he is saying.[16] On the other hand, the powerless, uninfluential and unskilled are made publicly visible; the less influential seat themselves in knots around the influential. The social gaps between peers are clearly manifested during the debates of peers. Ironically, inequality is emphasised in a debate which is supposed to be an expression of equality.

6

The stability and smooth continuity of the age-system is facilitated by the internalisation of the collective values of equality, group solidarity and loyalty. These values play a central part during the adolescence and the coming of age of every man; they underlie the limited range of images and of activities available to teenage boys and young men, but they do not suit the wider range of social and economic activities into which every man enters when he marries and establishes an independent household. From that time other factors, such as pastoral skills, ambition, the quantity and quality of bonds, useful affinal ties, personal credibility, etc. enter into a man's calculations which are likely to conflict with the ethos of equality and the solidarity of peers. However, in spite of this growing gap, the formal structure of the age-organisation of peer cliques does not change. Although age is the central defining principle of social organisation, there are two opposing structural principles which feature more prominently in different phases of the life-cycle of Dassanetch men. These two principles — the solidarity of equals, on the one hand, and competition and personal achievement, on the other — are both tied into different organisational contexts; the former is tied to a clique of peers and the latter to the development of affinal ties and bond partnerships.

The subject of this essay has not been so much to establish the inequality of peers, which is almost obvious once we shift our attention from common age to the actual structure of social relationships which each peer has, but rather the use of the solidarity of equals among peers who are unequal. The co-existence of the two conflicting principles both in the age-system itself and within the peer clique is expressed in ritual, in space and through time.

First, the transition from the cohesive peer group to an emphasis on networks has clear ritual markers. The circumcision and the *dimi* ceremonies, and the choice of a name-ox and its later relinquishment symbolically mediate the transition between these two principles. Second are the different organisational consequences which emanate from the different means needed on the one hand to join and to remain a member of a clique and, on the other to establish and maintain a social network. Clearly, to maintain a working balance between equality and competition in a small interacting group is more difficult than to maintain such within a 'group' the members of which only share nominal interests. In the second instance peers, although they are members of a clique, tend to meet as dyads or as triads, that is, as links in a network. This permits greater leeway to work out arrangements with one another based on mediation without threatening the concept of the solidarity of the peer clique. Thus, the peer clique must be at its most solidary when it meets as a group rather than when individual members of the group meet as dyads. Therefore, the transition from 'clique' to 'network' implies, first, that physical separation occurs, second that social separation (i.e. living in different camps and settlements in independent households) should take place and third that there be a minimal overlapping of the social characteristics that require peer clique expression with those characteristics that require economic self-interest. This is made easier because peers, once they have independent households, do not establish mutual obligations through strong bonds or affinal ties; this makes it easier for peers to maintain a semblance of equality when they meet. The progress through the life cycle of peers inevitably results in the formation of individual networks which are not 'dense' in terms of the strength of bonds that exist among peers. Thus, over time, the links between peers become weaker in comparison to the other links which each individual establishes. In consequence clique sanctions operate less effectively as attachment to a peer clique diminishes and as individual networks become stronger. The clique becomes reduced to a symbolic expression of solidarity on formal occasions such as the debates of peers. When a peer clique does function as a 'group', as in the debates, the transition that has occurred becomes clear. The debates demonstrate that equality can only be maintained for short periods and with difficulty. Moreover, the debates of peers, by demanding the expression of equality, in fact expose the differentiation and inequality which exist. That is, suppression of what is evident and known to all functions in much the same way as would over-representation. Demanding that no one should pay attention to a conspicuous feature almost guarantees that this feature will be at the forefront of awareness. Thus, the debates of peers show, symbolically and organisationally, that the solidarity of equals, except in a highly circumscribed and situational format, can only with difficulty co-exist with the separate individual network of the peers.

Finally, the image of equality is essentially an image of political power which, in the course of time, comes to represent the order by which power is transferred from generation-set to generation-set. It is expressed in the saying, 'A man and his peers grow up in their generation-set', which implies an orderly sequence of power transfer.[17] Paradoxically, the ethos of equality minimizes the rivalry for power between generations but opens up rivalry between these very persons who are considered to be, and who should remain, equals.[18] The ethos of equality is, in effect, one of 'pseudo-equality', based on age but unrelated to individual social credit, social ties, brokerage power or status. To put the argument slightly differently, to interact with another person one needs to have something in common with him. It is the notion of the equality of peers which is that 'something in common', and remains so, even though the originally homogenous peer clique becomes increasingly differentiated. It provides peers with a point of reference in the relationships between themselves and, in addition, affords access to new fields of social relationships and exchange with unrelated persons via the mediation of their peers. In their interaction, peers maintain the facade of equality and a peer will be careful to ensure that his behaviour corresponds to that image. The very use of one's peers, however, and the advantages some peers take of the social ties of other peers, in itself increases the inequality, since some peers accumulate more debts and power out of social brokerage than others. In other words, the ethos of equality among Dassanetch peer groups accentuates inequality, but the adherence to, and maintenance of, the ethos of equality supports the social processes involved in the sequence of power transfer and co-ordinates a weak kinship system with a centralised age-system.

NOTES

1 The fieldwork on which this essay is based was carried out during 1968-70. I thank the Hebrew University of Jerusalem and the Friends of the Hebrew University in England for their generous financial support. I am also grateful to the Victoria University of Manchester for the award of a Simon Research Fellowship during 1974-5 which enabled me to work on the subject of age-systems in Manchester. My thanks are due to P.T.W. Baxter and D. Handelman who read the first draft of this essay and made some valuable comments.
2 Social anthropologists who have studied neighbouring peoples, such as Dyson-Hudson (1966), Gulliver (1953, 1958, 1968) and Spencer (1965), have commented on the differences in status, power, wealth, respect and prestige between age-mates. They have also made it clear that men of the same age may be members of different ranked sets and, therefore, men of the same age may, through their membership of different sets, be ranked differentially.
3 The bond of 'holding' between women is an exception. In theory it is a strong bond, since it is established at the circumcision ceremony of a young girl, but the bond itself is considered weak and carries no rights to bridewealth: generally it is similar in nature to that of the bond of 'gift'.
4 For a more comprehensive exposition of Dassanetch bond partnerships, affinal ties and the build-up of social credit see Almagor (1978).
5 There are no rules which forbid a man to marry prior to being circumcised nor which restrict him from begetting children in elderhood. The elders, therefore, have no control over entry into new sets; sons normally follow automatically into the alternate set to their fathers. Sons born after their set has closed, i.e. after its fourth circumcision ceremony, follow into the set of what should by the rule be the set of their father's grandsons, i.e. their own sons. This raises a set of complex issues which I intend to pursue in a future publication.
6 This accords with Eisenstadt's hypothesis that there is a 'transitory' period in a man's life between 'kinship relations' and those regulated by pattern variables of achievement and specifity (50). Age bonds *per se* are formed in almost every society as bridges between the stage of early socialisation in the family and adult individualisation. I refer specifically to Eisenstadt's point that age groups are prominent in a society in which 'the family or kinship unit cannot ensure, or even impedes, the attainment of full social status by its members (54). This appears to suit the situation among the Dassanetch.
7 See Almagor (1972) and Evans-Pritchard (1956: Ch. XI).
8 See Almagor (1974).
9 See Almagor, *Pastoral Partners*, Chapter III.
10 See Almagor (1974).
11 See Lewis (1970:173) and Black (1972:617) for analogous situations of 'equality of opportunity'.
12 A somewhat analogous use of sanctions against the withdrawal of co-operation exists in Luristan. See Black (1972:626).
13 The co-operation of Bekhoko with two members of the same clique (B and J) described above is a case in point. It is worth noting that B and J,

who were competitors in one situation, i.e. to establish the bond with Bekhoko's son, were later tied through another mediated bond, i.e. the bond of 'holding' which B mediated to J.
14 Cf. Margolis (1975:374) who comments on a comparable situation in a Brazilian sugar plantation in which an ideology of equality was used to mask social distinctions.
15 A somewhat comparable situation exists in the debates among the neighbouring Mursi where 'men who are highly respected in everyday life, as the heads of large families and the owners of large herds, may never open their mouths in a public meeting.' See Turton (1975:176).
16 Generally speaking at the debate in the settlement 'yard' the social and economic assets as well as the prestige and credibility of the speaker are given expression. Cf. Comaroff, Turton and Bloch in M. Bloch (ed.), 1975.
17 Cf. Eisenstadt (1956:273).
18 I hope to show the incompatibility between formal concepts of the transfer of power, and the actual structure of power relations within and outside the age-systems in a future publication.

BIBLIOGRAPHY

Almagor, U. 1972. 'Name-Oxen and Ox-Names among the Dassanetch of Southwest Ethiopia', *Piadeuma* 18, 79-96.
———. 1978. *Pastoral Partners*, Manchester.
———. 1974. 'The War of the Ilemi Appendix'. Paper presented to Conference of the African Studies Association of the United Kingdom, Liverpool.
Bernardi, B. 1952. 'The Age-System of the Nilo-Hamitic Peoples'. *Africa*, 22, 316-32.
Black, J. 1972. 'Tyranny as a Strategy for Survival in an Egalitarian Society'. *Man*, 7, 614-34.
Bloch. M. 1975. 'Introduction' in M. Bloch (ed.) *Political Language and Oratory in Traditional Society*. London.
Burns, T. 1953. 'Friends, Enemies and the Polite Fiction', *American Sociological Review*, 18, 654-62.
Comaroff, J. 1975. 'Talking Politics: Oratory and Authority in a Tswana Chiefdom' in M. Bloch (ed.) op. cit.
Dyson-Hudson, N. 1966. *Karimojong Politics*. Oxford.
Eisenstadt, S.N. 1956. *From Generation to Generation*. Glencoe, Ill.
Evans-Pritchard, E.E. 1940. *The Nuer*. Oxford.
———. 1956. *Nuer Religion*, Oxford.
Gulliver, P.H. 1952. 'The Age-Set Organisation of the Jie Tribe', *Journal of the Royal Anthropological Institute*, 83, 147-8.
———. 1958. 'The Turkana Age Organisation' in *American Anthropologist*, 60, 900-22.
———. 1968. 'Age Differentiation' in *International Encyclopaedia of the Social Sciences*, 1, 157-62. New York.
Lewis, H.S. 1970. 'Wealth, Influence and Prestige among Shoa Galla' in A. Tuden and L. Plotnicov (eds.) *Social Stratification in Africa*, 163-86. New York.

Margolis, M. 1975. 'The Ideology of Equality on a Brazilian Sugar Plantation', *Ethnology*, 14, 373-83.
Notes and Queries on Anthropology (6th ed.). London (1951).
Spencer, P. 1965. *The Samburu*, London.
Turton, D. 1975. 'The Relationship Between Oratory and the Exercise of Influence among the Mursi' in M. Bloch (ed.) op. cit.

IV
Territorial Organisation and Age among the Mursi

DAVID TURTON

The purpose of this essay is to investigate the wider social significance of some of the data I have collected under the heading 'age organisation' during the course of fieldwork among the Mursi of southwestern Ethiopia.[1] I say 'wider' social significance because I am not concerned to establish connections between different parts of a self-contained age 'system'. I say 'some' of the data because which particular facts are relevant will depend upon which particular aspect (kinship, economic or political, for example) of the wider society is being considered. I am especially interested in Mursi politics and I have therefore chosen to concentrate on this aspect of their society here. Much of what has been written on 'age systems' in East Africa has, of course, been concerned with their so-called political functions, so this choice should allow the reader to judge whether my conclusions are any more satisfactory, and the assumptions upon which they are based any more sound, than those of other writers.

The Mursi, who live in the lower Omo valley, about 60 miles north of Lake Turkana, number 4-5,000 and are transhumant pastoralists and cultivators. Although they maintain the values and outlook of a predominantly pastoral people, they have only about one head of cattle per head of human population, and depend for about 75 per cent of their subsistence needs on the cultivation of sorghum. They are extremely isolated, in relation to the local administration of the Ethiopian Government, being hemmed in on two sides by the River Omo, and on a third by a mountain range[2] which forms the watershed between the Omo and its tributary the Mago (see Figure IV.1). Administration in the whole lower Omo region is minimal and is virtually non-existent among the Mursi. Their decentralised political organisation can be considered from at least two points of view: (*a*) the definition of and relations between more or less autonomous and self-sufficient territorial sections, and (*b*) the exercise of influence and the use of authority in public decision making.

Whichever of these two points of view is adopted, facts normally considered under the heading 'age organisation' are extremely relevant, but they are not the same facts in each case. Roughly stated, the first point of view involves an emphasis on groups of men of the same age but of different territorial sections, while the second involves an emphasis on men of different ages but of the same territorial section.

In other words, and according to the terminology which has become standard for writers on age organisation, the first involves an emphasis on age-sets, and the second an emphasis on age-grades. I originally intended to take both these points of view in turn, but gave up this plan for two reasons. Firstly, it would have resulted in a book rather than in an essay, and secondly, it was based upon the tacit but false assumption that the main purpose of an article on age organisation is to trace the connections between various parts of a putative 'age system', thereby showing how it 'works'. Once I had realised that the only connections worth looking for were between certain phenomena to do with age and certain other phenomena in the wider society, I also realised that there was no good reason why I should attempt to cover all the data I had collected, either on age or on politics, in one essay. I consider here then, only the territorial aspect of Mursi political organisation, and seek to show that certain facts to do with age are essential to a proper understanding of it. I begin by arguing, in the next section, that the present territorial organisation of the Mursi presupposes a continuing northward movement of Mursi-speaking people into territory already occupied, or claimed, by their northern neighbours the Bodi, and that this movement is achieved by the creation of new territorial sections, lying 'across the grain of natural resources' (Sahlins 1968:22). I consider first the external relations of the Mursi, and then show how these external relations are linked to their internal territorial organisation.[3]

1

Because they are hemmed in by very clear geographical boundaries, the Mursi are a conveniently self-contained and manageable unit from the point of view of the fieldworker. But this makes it easy to ignore the fact that they have very definite linguistic and cultural affinities with groups lying mainly to the west of them, towards and beyond the border between Ethiopia and the Sudan. With two of these groups, the Tirmaga and Chai, they share a common language and, especially with the Chai, intermarry. Their language is closely related to; but not mutually intelligible with, those of a number of groups lying further to the west, such as (in Ethiopia) the Suri and Bale[4] and (in the Sudan) the Didinga and Murle.

In this essay I am especially concerned with the relationship between the Mursi and their orthern neighbours, the Bodi, who number between three and four thousand and who belong to the same language group[5] as the Mursi and all the other groups mentioned so far. The Mursi and Bodi share an almost identical environment and economy, and although their languages are not mutually intelligible, many people on each side can speak the other side's language. They do not intermarry and their relations alternate between fairly long

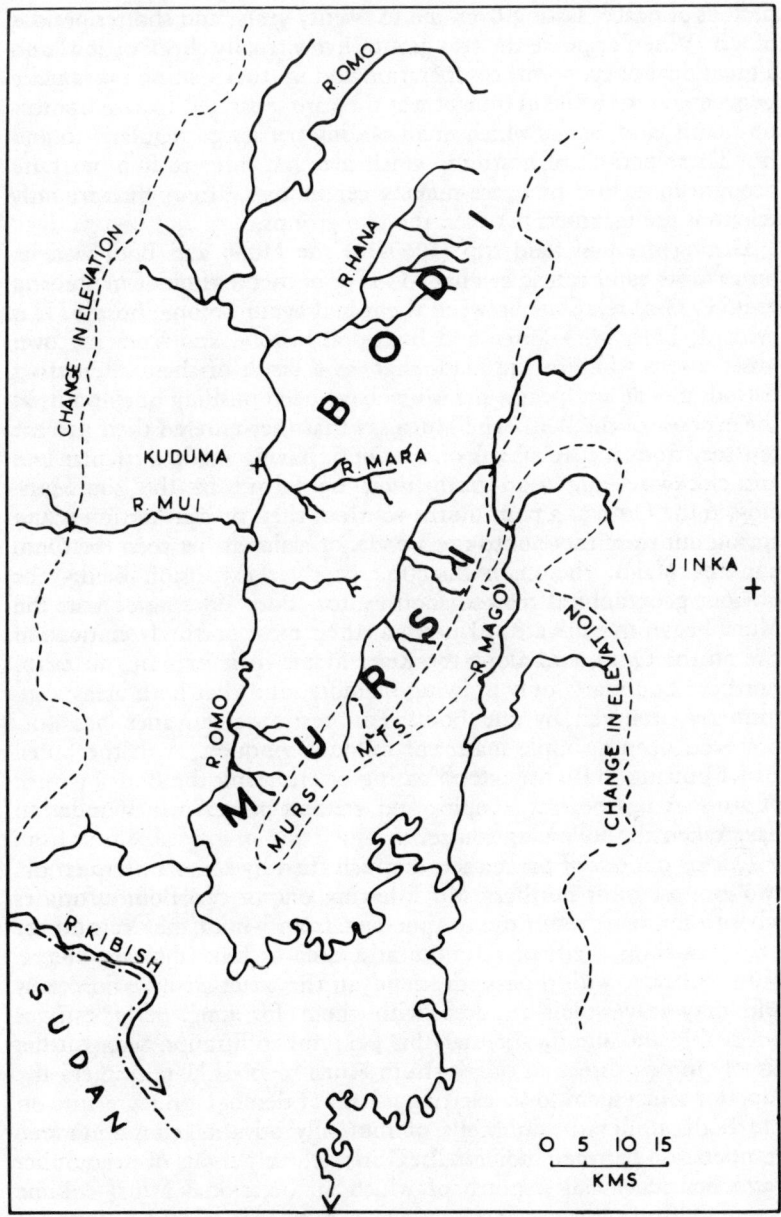

Figure IV.1. Map of Mursi and Bodi country

periods of peace, lasting from ten to twenty years, and shorter periods of war. When at peace the two groups live virtually cheek by jowl and a great deal of economic co-operation and mutual visiting takes place between them, while in time of war they are separated by a temporary no-man's land, across which small raiding parties go regularly to and fro. These periods of hostility, which may last three to four years are brought to an end by peace-making ceremonies, after which friendly relations are resumed between the two groups.

During my first field trip (1969-70) the Mursi and Bodi were at peace, and had been since about 1954, but by the time of my second visit (1973-4) relations between them had again become hostile. It is evident, both from Mursi and Bodi oral history, and from my own observations while in the field, that, as a result of these alternating periods of war and peace, the Mursi have been pushing northwards at the expense of the Bodi. The Mursi say that they entered their present territory from the west bank of the Omo, having made a circular and anti-clockwise migration from their homeland in the southeast, crossed the Omo at a point in the south of their present territory, and spread out from there onto the wooded grasslands between the Omo and the Mago; the main direction of their expansion being, for obvious geographical reasons, northwards. Both sides agree that the Mursi began to cultivate at Kuduma, their most northerly cultivation site on the Omo, and along the River Mara, their present, *de facto*, northern boundary, only in living memory, and that both areas were formerly occupied by the Bodi. This territorial advance has not, however, been a simple matter of military conquest, with the Mursi either putting to flight, exterminating or enslaving the Bodi by force of arms. It has been a complex and gradual process which seems to have taken the following course.

During periods of peace there is much friendly contact between the two groups, most northern Mursi having one or two Bodi associates whom they visit from time to time and from whom they can expect help — such as a gift of sorghum at a time of food shortage. Some Mursi cultivate with their Bodi friends in the latter's cultivation areas and may leave their children with them for long periods. It is noticeable and significant that this peaceful infiltration seems to be largely in one direction only — from Mursi to Bodi. The numerically superior Mursi seem to be exerting a kind of demographic pressure on the Bodi, under the umbrella of mutually advantageous economic co-operation between individuals. During these periods of peace, a *de facto* boundary exists, north of which an occasional Mursi will be found cultivating with a Bodi associate, but south of which there are no Bodi. Then comes a period of war, sparked off by a succession of apparently adventitious incidents, during which there is no friendly contact between individual Mursi and Bodi, and each side aims to get the better of, or at least to even the score with, the other by killing as many of their men as possible. But hostilities are prosecuted in such a way that simple numerical superiority is of no military advantage. Small parties, well armed with rifles and ammunition,[6] and having a perfect knowledge (from peace-time contact) of the other group's territory, will hide beside a bath, for example, and wait to kill a passer-by, or attack a settlement in the early hours, and be well on the way home by daybreak. This kind of 'tit for tat' is almost certain to be evenly balanced, and does not produce a definite result. What it does do, however, is gradually wear down each side, until, weary both with the loss of life and with the difficulties which the need to be constantly on a war footing put in the way of subsistence activities, they are ready to make peace.

Peace-making is accomplished by means of two successive ceremonines, one held by each group, at each of which a stock animal is killed in the presence of the other group's representatives. What really matters is not whether one side has lost more men than the other, but where these two ceremonies are held, since each side is supposed to hold its ceremony in its own territory. Thus, holding a peace-making ceremony at a certain spot is a way of making (and having acknowledged by the other side's representatives) a claim to *de jure* ownership of territory which formerly may have been owned only in a *de facto* sense. In which case, it may be said that the purpose of the fighting is to bring about a peace making ceremony, and that the purpose of this ceremony is to give legal ratification to a territorial encroachment which had already taken place, peacefully, before the fighting started. This can be illustrated from recent history. At the end of the last Mursi-Bodi war, in 1954, the Mursi killed their beast at a spot about twenty miles south of what had become, by 1970, their *de facto* northern boundary, the River Mara. When I was last in the field and spoke to both sides about the conditions under which they would be prepared to end hostilities, the Bodi, rather optimistically, insisted that the Mursi would have to withdraw from Mara and Kuduma, while the Mursi were adamant that any beast they killed by way of peace-making would be killed at Mara.[7] I now turn from the external relations of the Mursi to consider how this northward movement is linked to their internal territorial organisation.

The Mursi are divided into five named territorial sections or segments, which may be represented diagrammatically by means of a series of horizontal lines, at right angles to the Omo. It can be seen from Figure IV.2 that this east-west axis is dictated by the ecological 'grain' of the country, which is from north to south. Each section has to span the full range of natural resources in order to be, theoretically at least, self-contained and self-supporting. These natural resources consist of river bank land for flood cultivation at the Omo, bushland thicket[8] for rain cultivation several miles east of the Omo, and wooded grassland for cattle herding yet further to the east. Although

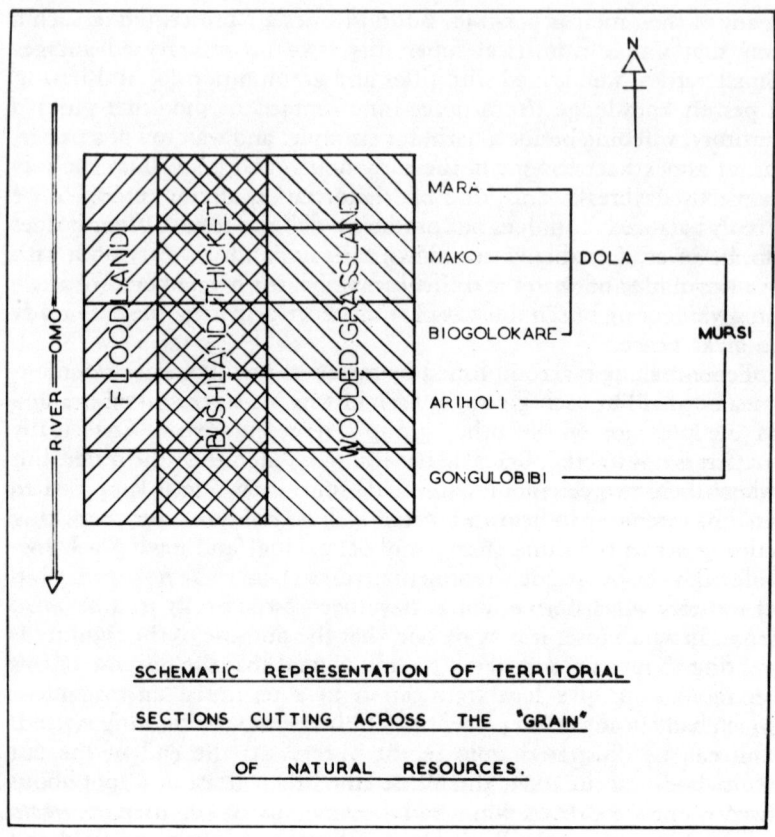

Figure IV.2

the transhumance movements by means of which the Mursi exploit these natural resources result in a high degree of individual mobility (there are no permanent settlements for example), this mobility takes place almost entirely along an east-west axis, at right angles, in other words, to the Omo, and parallel with the division into sections. For any one individual, then, the actual area covered during the annual cycle of subsistence activities is relatively limited, and indeed it is not unusual to come across people living, for example, in the north of the country, who have never visited the south, a mere fifty miles away.

Figure IV.2 also shows that three of the sections, Mara, Mako and Biogolokare, combine to form a unit of a higher order, called Dola, and that the other two sections do not form a similar unit, structurally equivalent to Dola. This grouping together of the three northern sections, each one of which, taken singly, is structurally equivalent to each of the two southern sections, seems, at first sight, anomalous. It does not correspond to any geographical or ecological division of the country, and the settlements of members of the three northern sections do not form a single, discrete grouping. Indeed, on this latter basis, Biogolokare would be more likely to form a single unit with the two sections to the south of it than with those to the north of it, since, as far as physical proximity and day to day contacts are concerned, its members are much closer to those of Ariholi and Gongulobibi than they are to those of Mara and probably also to those of Mako. Many members of Mara, on the other hand, have closer links with the Bodi (during period of peace) than they do with their fellow Dola-members from Biogolokare. Thus it seems that the unit called Dola must be seen as resulting, not from the convergence of three previously independent sections, but from the formation of new sections by means of a process which Dyson-Hudson has called 'replication' (1966:259).

This fits in well with the hypothesis of a long term and continuing northward movement of population, as a result of which new territorial sections, structurally equivalent to the existing ones, and cutting across the same three bands of natural resources, have been formed. It also fits in with the Mursi view of their recent history, except that they think of the three northern sections as having sprung from a single parent-section, called Dola. What is proposed here, on the other hand, is that there has been a general northward migration, the direction of which has been dictated by geographical features and by the availability of natural resources, and which has been exclusively fed, neither by the members of a single 'proto-section', nor even by the descendants of those Mursi who were the first to cross to the east bank of the Omo. Rather, one must envisage a continuing movement, not only from present day Mursi country, northwards, but also into it, from the west. Mursi/Chai intermarriage seems to play a vital part in this process, since one comes across many Chai in Mursi country who have married Mursi girls and who have come to live with their wives' people. Thus, just as one finds Mursi living among the Bodi, so one finds Chai living among the Mursi, but whereas intermarriage enables the Chai to infiltrate Mursi country peacefully, Mursi infiltration of Bodi country cannot, in the end, be peaceful. I have never visited the Chai, but I would expect that, just as there is virtually no southward movement of Bodi into Mursi country, so there is virtually no westward movement of Mursi into Chai country. The numerical superiority of the Mursi over the Bodi results, then, from the fact that the former have behind them a source of new immigrants, who speak the same language as themselves and with whom they intermarry, while the latter have before them the foothills of the Ethiopian Plateau, into which they can move only by displacing the sedentary agriculturists who already live there.

Each new Mursi section, then, has maintained with those immediately behind it ideologically closer links than it has with those further to the south, and the Mursi explain this by reference to the common parentage of the sections in question. In view of the above argument, however, it seems wiser to view this idea of common parentage as the main ideological justification of a link which has a more pragmatic and contemporary basis. This basis, I suggest, consists in the need to hold onto territorial gains and, if possible, to make further ones, in the face of rival claims by the Bodi. Since the territory into which the Mursi have been moving has been either occupied or contested, it has been necessary to bring maximum pressure to bear at the frontier.[9] It is evident, however, from the description given above of the tactics employed in Mursi/Bodi hostilities, that this pressure cannot be a matter of military strength. Rather, the maintenance of particularly close ideological links between the sections immediately behind the frontier facilitates the northward drift of population and therefore the gradual, peace-time, encroachment on Bodi territory, which has been shown to be the main mechanism of Mursi expansion. Thus it is no accident of demography that Mara, the youngest section, is also by far the largest in the size of its population.[10] A subtle, demographic pressure is brought to bear on the frontier by these arrangements, then, not a crude military one.

A second advantage of the special status of the three northern sections is, however, indirectly military, and has to do with the fact that the most highly valued material asset of the Mursi, the cow, is mobile. During periods of hostility cattle have to be kept as far back from the frontier as possible. The extent of Mursi and Bodi country together is no more than two thousand square miles and neither side can keep its cattle completely out of the reach of the other's raiding parties. But the further these raiders have to go into enemy territory, the greater the chances of their being overtaken on the way home, and of any cattle they may have stolen being retrieved. Thus, it is the cattle of the Mara section which, on the Mursi side, are most at risk during Mursi-Bodi wars, and at such times these cattle are sent thirty to forty miles south, to be looked after if not by, then at least in the territory of, members of the Biogolokare section. It is useful, therefore, for members of Mara and Biogolokare to think of themselves as having more in common with each other than either of them have with their fellow Mursi of the two southern sections, and therefore as having more binding obligations to each other. (It is interesting to note that the territorial organisations of the Bodi mirrors that of the Mursi. There are three Bodi territorial sections, named, from south to north, Gura, Hana and Chirim. Gura and Hana are linked, through the name Mela, in exactly the same way as the three northern Mursi sections are linked through the name Dola. Members of Mela think of themselves as a unit in opposition to Chirim.)[11]

What we seem to have in Dola, then, is an incipient 'society', the territorial span of which is related to the amount of opposition being experienced at the frontier, (other things, such as access to weapons, being equal, this opposition is probably mainly a matter of populaton size) and to the 'fall-back' distance necessary to protect cattle from raiders during periods of hostility. There will be no need for a greater span than is necessary to maintain ground already won, and to make further expansion possible — there is no value in unity for its own sake. As the front line advances, links with units now being left behind become more and more tenuous until they amount to no more than a vague memory of common origin. Indeed, it is not inconceivable that these units, when they have been left far enough behind, in time and space, should start expanding on their own account, in the same general direction as, and thus at the expense of, their former allies. At some time in the future, then, a 'society' which originated in the unit now known as Dola might find itself being encroached on from behind, rather as the Bodi are now being encroached on by the Mursi. Indeed, as will be seen, the members of Dola already protect themselves, symbolically, against such an encroachment from the south, using duelling poles rather than rifles. A useful image to represent all this would be a series of waves, seen in elevation, the crest of each wave representing a different 'society'. Although over a time span running into hundreds of years, these waves, or societies, are constantly on the move, merging into and out of each other, they appear stationary when observed over a single generation or so. The Bodi would thus represent a wave which is just about to break against the beaches of the Ethiopian Plateau, with another representing the Mursi (or rather Dola) coming in close behind it.

2

If one were setting out to describe the 'age-system', of the Mursi, one might be tempted to begin by observing that they 'have' age-sets, which are 'formed' in a certain way, which 'succeed' each other at certain intervals and which 'cut across' the territorial divisions of the population, thereby promoting 'integration'. For the Mursi do have a word, *teny*, which corresponds to what has usually been called an 'age-set'. The distinction between age-sets and age-grades has recently been succinctly stated by Paul Spencer: 'The term *age-set* is used here to refer to all those men who are initiated in youth during a definite span of time, and as a group share certain constraints and expectations for the remainder of their lives; and *age-grade* is used to refer to a status through which each person passes at some period of his life unless he dies first' (1976:153). An age-set, then, is a group, while an age-grade is a status. It is clear, however, from many accounts of East African age organisations (e.g. Dyson-Hudson 1966:174) that what is usually referred to, in these accounts, by the term age-set is not a group, but a category of men (and this, as will be explained below, is certainly true of the Mursi word *teny*). Gulliver has suggested that we use the word 'age-group' to mean a number of age-mates who 'engage in particular activities... and function as a group in relation to outsiders' (1968:159). Such an age-group is specifically not 'society-wide', while an age-set is; only another conceptual entity could be co-extensive with a society. From this point of view it would be pointless to describe 'society-wide' age-sets (or, for that matter, clans)[12] as helping to promote the integration of separate territorial sections, since the fact that the men of these sections acknowledge, for example, common age-set names is simply evidence of that integration. Such is the sort of conclusion, however, which is bound to follow if one sets out by treating conceptual entities (such as age-sets and clans) as though they belonged to the empirical rather than to the mental world. If, on the other hand, one acknowledges that they are conceptual entities but, nevertheless, makes a discussion of them the basis of one's analysis of actual behaviour, then one's method is at odds with one's theory. In this account, therefore, instead of beginning at the level of the 'tribal' institution and working down, to the particular, I begin at the level of the individual and his local group of age-mates and work up, to the general.

Most men, in any society, spend most of their lives as members of two kinds of family group, in one of which, their natal family, they are dependent, and in the other of which, their conjugal family, they are depended upon. The individual's transition from one kind of family to the other, however, is not necessarily instantaneous — there is liable to be an interval during which he is neither considered to be dependent on his natal family nor yet has dependants of his own. This interval will be relatively long in a society such as that of the Mursi, in which polygyny is the norm[13] and in which, consequently, there are, at any one time, more married women than married men. Given an equal sex-ratio, the easiest way for such a state of affairs to be brought about is for men to marry at a considerably later age than women (cf. Spencer 1965:96). While most women seem to marry between the ages of seventeen and twenty, most men do not appear to marry for the first time until their late twenties or early thirties. From the age of about fifteen (when he is old enough to look after cattle without being under the constant supervision of the parental generation) until the time of his marriage, a Mursi man is expected to live the year round in a cattle camp with his local age-mates, apart from the settlements of married men.

The Mursi word which I translate as 'territorial section' is *buran*, and this can also be applied to the local group formed by a single settlement of, say, half a dozen families. The five territorial sections I have described above are thus thought of in the image of separate residential groups. But the only residential groups which are co-extensive with sections are those formed by unmarried men, whose cattle camps consist, theoretically at least, of all the men of a certain age in a section. These camps are therefore identified with and represent the territorial exclusiveness of sections, this being particularly apparent in the practice, to be described below, of ceremonial duelling between unmarried men from different sections. The settlements of married men do not show the same exclusiveness, either where age or territory is concerned, because they do not consist of all the married men of a certain age in a section. Thus, it is during the approximately fifteen-year period of his life when he is more or less physically mature but unmarried that a man is most closely identified both with men of his own age group and with his own territorial section.

Fifteen years is a long time in a man's life, especially these particular fifteen years, between his mid-teens and early thirties. During this period he goes through a dramatic change, in terms of his physical maturity, the social expectations to which he is subject and the personal aspirations to which these expectations give rise. It is a period which covers the transition between the two basic age grades of jural minority, or boyhood, and jural majority or adulthood. I say 'basic' age grades because all males can be categorised by means of them. In Mursi, the two grades in question are those of *lusa* (boys) and *zuo* (adults), and each of these is further sub-divided into four grades of boys and three of adults. Here I am concerned only with the two which fall on either side of the basic boy/adult divide, since it is into them that the men found living together in cattle camps with their unmarried age-mates fall.

The junior of these two grades — the senior grade of boys — is that of *teru* and it corresponds to the period in a man's life falling roughly between his mid-teens and early twenties.[14] A *teri* (the singular form) is expected to be interested in his cattle, in dancing, in ceremonial duelling contests and in flirting and sexual escapades with unmarried girls (there is no ban on sexual intercourse before marriage). Although not formally prohibited from marrying, a *teri* is very unlikely to admit any short term interest in obtaining a wife. The most obvious public recognition of his jural minority is the fact that he is not allowed to speak at public meetings, unless specifically called upon to do so by an older man. Ideally he will live, more or less permanently, in a cattle camp together with all the other *teru* of his section, the cattle then under his care consisting of some that will form the nucleus of his own herd and others which he is looking after for his father, married brothers and/or uncles, and which are not needed at the family settlements. His ability to meet this ideal will depend, among other things, on the availability of a younger brother or cousin or take his place as a herd-boy in his natal family, and upon his family's cattle wealth.

The senior of the two grades under discussion — the junior grade of adults — is that of *rora*, or 'junior elders'. It corresponds to the period in a man's life between, roughly, his early twenties and late thirties. It is while occupying this grade, therefore, that a man is expected to marry for the first time. Until he does so, however, he continues to live, as before, in a cattle camp with his unmarried section age mates, attending dances and duelling contests and 'calling the girls'. But he is now openly intent on building up his herd in order to provide bridewealth for his prospective in-laws. As an adult he has a right to speak in public meetings, but as an unmarried one he is unlikely to do so, except perhaps to report on the state of the outlying pastures, or on a recent expedition to the border areas of the country, looking for the tracks of enemy scouts and raiding parties. Unmarried *rora*, being physically mature and yet not having the domestic and agricultural commitments of married men, are looked upon as a source of military manpower, providing the community with a sort of early warning system, or first line of defence, against attack from outside.

When he marries, a man ceases to live with his section age mates, and, indeed, his whole life style changes drastically. Firstly, he is no longer a member of a tightly knit group, exclusive both in terms of age and territorial affiliation. He forms links of co-residence and economic co-operation with men who may not only differ from him widely in age, but who may not even be members of his own territorial section. This latter situation is most likely to arise as a result of his marrying a girl from a different section. If such a girl continues to cultivate in her natal section, her husband may spend a large part of his time with her people. Conversely he may form economic and residential links with a sister's husband who has migrated from another section, to his own. Secondly, a newly married man is unlikely, after having provided his affines with bridewealth,[15] to have sufficient cattle to constitute a viable herd, and will therefore have to satisfy his subsistence needs, at least in the short run, primarily through cultivation. In marrying, therefore, he will have exchanged cattle, and a diet consisting predominantly of milk and blood, not only for the sexual services and procreative capacity of his wife, but also for her agricultural services, and for a diet consisting predominantly of sorghum porridge. Thirdly, he will no longer be a contestant in inter-section duelling contests (he may referee such contests) but he is now free to seek public acclaim in a physically less violent way, through his contribution to public meetings.

The physiological transition, to which the terms *teru* and *rora* give social recognition, is, of course, made gradually and imperceptibly by each individual. But the social transition is made suddenly, publicly and collectively by means of an initiation ceremony held, for all the *teru* of a section, on average, every fifteen years,[16] this being also, therefore, the average age span of the initiands. I describe the initiation ceremony and discuss its bearing on territorial organisation later. Here I wish to mention two implications which this fifteen year age span of initiands has for the facts I have been presenting above. Firstly, it is evident that for some individuals the transition from the *teru* to the *rora* grade, or, in other words, their initiation into jural adulthood, will accord more or less imperfectly with the particular stage of physical maturity they happen to have reached. In describing the fifteen years of a man's life between the ages of fifteen and thirty as falling, more or less equally, into two age-grades, therefore, I was ignoring discrepancies of this kind and considering only those individuals whose biographies typify the norm. It should be noted, then, that some individuals spend most, and others all, of this period of their lives either as *teru* or as *rora*.

Secondly, although the number of more or less physically mature but unmarried men in the society will remain constant from year to year (barring demographic fluctuations and/or a change in the normal age of marriage for men), the distribution of these men between the two grades of *teru* and *rora* will vary according to the time when the observation is made. Immediately after an initiation ceremony, most of them will be *rora* and most *rora* will be unmarried (the most senior may well have already married, as *teru*). Thus, one would expect to find, at such a time, a relatively large cattle camp of unmarried *rora* in each section. These camps will be large, but gradually decreasing in size, as more and more of their members marry. The cattle camps of the *teru*, on the other hand, will be small but increasing in size as every three or four years more boys are admitted to this grade. Immediately before the next initiation ceremony one would expect there to be no more unmarried *rora*, and each section to have a relatively large cattle camp of *teru*. (There may even be smaller cattle camps, made up of the senior occupants of the grade immediately junior to the *teru*.) In 1969/70, which was approximately nine years after the last initiation ceremony, Mara, the section with the largest population, boasted a cattle camp of *teru* and a cattle camp of unmarried *rora*, the latter having been ten and fifteen members. When I returned, about four years later, virtually all these unmarried *rora*, whom I had interviewed at their cattle camp in October 1969, were married and there was no cattle camp of unmarried *rora* in the Mara section.

Unlike any other type of residential group, therefore, the cattle camps of unmarried men, whether of the *teru* or *rora* grades, are co-extensive with territorial sections, of which they are thus a kind of ideal embodiment. But their members are in a state of what might be called social suspension, between childhood and adulthood. The whole essence of their life together as age-mates is that it must come to an end in order for them, individually, to become fully fledged members of society. The residential units they form are, therefore, essentially impermanent and this, in itself, demonstrates that various ideals which these units embody — including the territorial exclusiveness and autonomy of sections — are, for the society as a whole, nothing but illusions.

Since they cut across the full range of natural resources, each of the sections is, in theory, self-sufficient, both economically and politically. In fact, because of the vicissitudes of climate (especially the very localised rainfall and the variable Omo flood), a great deal of economic interdependence exists between the members of different sections, but individual ties of economic self interest cannot account for the territorial organisation of Mursi society. Members of Biogolokare, for example, cannot be described as having more to gain, economically, from co-operation with members of Mara and Mako than they have to gain from co-operation with members of Ariholi and Gongulobibi. And it is evident from the close links which members of the Mara section maintain with individual Bodi, despite periodic warfare and the gradual northward movement of the Mursi, that it is quite possible for economic co-operation to take place between fundamentally hostile and territorially exclusive neighbours. In the light of the argument in the first part of this essay, there is a far more telling reason why the autonomy and exclusiveness of territorial sections must be illusory. I refer to the need for especially close links to be maintained between those sections closest to the expanding frontier (and therefore most recently created), so that the migration of people towards this frontier can be facilitated in time of peace, and that the cattle of the 'front line' sections can be suitably protected in time of war. Mursi territorial sections are not autonomous units, in the sense of static permanent building blocks, at all.

There are two other ideals which the cattle camps of unmarried men, by embodying, show to be illusory. The first is that of the solidarity and self sufficiency of unmarried age-mates or, in other words, of men without women. To pursue this particular point further would take me too far away from my main theme. I merely wish to point out that the cattle camps I have described embody, to an extreme degree, the masculine ideals of Mursi society and yet are, in the long run, unviable social units, because women have no formal place in them. Secondly, unmarried men are the only members of the population who can hope to achieve, for any length of time, the ideal of a purely pastoral existence. The reality, for the population at large, is that, with only about as many cattle as there are people, around 75 per cent of their total subsistence needs must be provided by cultivation. These cattle camps, then, are built upon at least three illusions: the autonomy of territorial sections, the self-sufficiency of a purely male society and the viability of a purely pastoral economy. They seem to hold a message similar to that which Lévi-Strauss has attributed to some myths, and which may be roughly paraphrased as: 'These ideas are all very well in theory, but they will not work in practice. Try them out for yourself, and you will see.'

So far I have been concerned with the individual and his local group of section age-mates. I now want to discuss two kinds of ceremonial peformance which bring to the fore relations between age-mates of different sections and, in a structural sense, the relations between sections. The first of these performances I call 'ceremonial duelling'. It consists of a single combat game, or sport, in which the contestants, who are always unmarried, belong to the same age-grade but to different territorial sections. The second is the ceremony by means of which local groups of *teru* become *rora*, and which I call 'initiation'.

3

The duelling weapon is a pole about six feet long and weighing about 2 lb. In the attacking position it is gripped at its base with both hands, the left above the right. The aim is to land a blow with the shaft, and not with the point, on any part of the opponent's body, and with sufficient force to knock him over. Blows are parried by continuing to grip the base of the pole with the right hand, whilst sliding the left hand up the shaft. Each contestant wears a more or less identical duelling kit which is both protective and decorative. It includes a helmet and a hand guard for the right hand, both made of strong basket work, woven from the leaves of the doum palm, shin guards made of hide, rings of plaited sisal cord to protect the elbows and knees, a leopard skin over the front of the torso, a skirt made of hide cut into strips and a cattle bell tied round the waist. Bouts are fast, furious and short, (they usually last no more than thirty seconds) and are brought to an end, unless one of the contestants has been knocked over first, through the intervention of a referee, who attempts to come between the contestants. It is usually necessary for at least one of the contestants (nearly always the one who has been receiving most of the punishment) to be held back, by several spectators, before the referee is successful in ending a bout.

Contestants are always unmarried men, of either the *teru* or *rora* grades. Separate contests are held by the occupants of each grade, but contestants always come from different territorial sections. What significance should be placed upon the fact that they are chosen not only by age criteria (which may be said simply to ensure even matching) but also by territorial ones? Given that the contestants are unmarried men, and since such men live in residential groups which are co-extensive, in membership, with territorial sections, the answer to this question may seem clear: it is just a convenient, indeed an obvious, way of picking sides.

The trouble with this answer, however, is that there is no obvious reason why 'sides' need to be picked at all, since duelling, from almost every angle, is a highly individualistic sport. Firstly, the actual bout sets one individual in single combat, against another. Secondly, there

Plate IV.1. Mursi ceremonial duelling: a contestant ready for his bout

is no points system, or matching of local champions, which would enable one section to 'beat' another. Indeed, it is very unusual for unambiguous superiority to be demonstrated by one contestant during a single bout. Such superiority can only be demonstrated by knocking over one's opponent which, since bouts usually last less than thirty seconds, is a very rare occurrence. The duelling careers of some individuals are, of course, more illustrious than those of others and very considerable individual reputations may be made in this way. But they are specifically *individual* reputations, the men in question sometimes being remembered for many years after their deaths. Thirdly, the main conscious motive for taking part in duelling is sexual assertiveness: the young men say that they do it to impress the unmarried girls. But from this point of view it is undoubtedly more important to take part than to demonstrate superior skill. Indeed it is at least as honourable to sustain injuries as it is to inflict them. Contestants are proud of their injuries and will often leave the binding on an injured limb long after it has ceased to be strictly necessary.

Thus, if one considers the actual conduct of duelling contests and the conscious motivations of the participants, there would seem to be no reason why these participants should make up two local 'sides': no reason, in other words, why contests should not be staged by the unmarried men of a single territorial section. A second answer to the question posed above might be based upon the social context of duelling, and upon its 'latent' functions. Thus it might be argued that inter-section duelling contests provide a sort of 'safety-valve' for pent up antagonism between sections, this antagonism being the result of an underlying competition for natural resources between these ecologically identical units.

Such an argument, however, would ignore the following facts. Firstly, rights to property and resources are not vested in sections, while individuals can easily gain access, usually through affinal links, to even the most scarce natural resource — flood land at the Omo — in sections other than their own. Secondly, although duelling contests are preceded by a more or less intense build-up of tension and hostility between the young men of different sections, this is very largely manufactured for the occasion. It is not that contestants feel no solidarity with their section age-mates, or that they are not antagonistic towards their age-mates of other sections. It is simply that this solidarity and antagonism is at least as much a result as a cause of the duelling. So far from duelling being a safety valve for inter-section antagonism, it is likely that, without it, there would be less, not more, antagonism between sections. Thirdly, if duelling really were an outlet for antagonism resulting from competition for resources, it would be difficult to explain why only unmarried men take part in it. This latter fact does draw attention to a possible 'cathartic' effect of duelling, but any antagonism it thereby expresses and 'controls' is not so much

Plate IV.2. Mursi ceremonial duelling: a bout in progress

between territorial sections as between the young and the old. Duelling is certainly seen as an activity of immature youth which married men attempt firmly to control, both by acting as referees and, occasionally, by trying to prevent the contests from taking place at all.[17] This aspect of duelling, however, belongs in a discussion of authority relations, and not of territorial organisation.

A third answer to this question might be that it is simply in the interests of social harmony for hostility between individuals, which is presumably latent in duelling, to be directed outside the group of co-resident men. There is no doubt that duelling is an institution through which local loyalties are expressed and periodically intensified, but this answer fails when we consider the way in which the rule (that contestants should come from different sections) applies to the three constituent sections of Dola. It was noted above (p.101) that Mara, Mako and Biogolokare 'do not form a single, discrete grouping' and that members of Biogolokare are much closer, both geographically and in terms of day to day contacts, to members of the two southern sections, Ariholi and Gongulobibi, than they are, certainly to Mara, and, probably, to Mako. Yet, although members of the three Dola sections do oppose each other in duelling, they do so only when members of the two non-Dola sections are not represented in the contests. Thus, in October 1969, the unmarried *rora* of the Mara section took part in a day of duelling with the unmarried *rora* of the Mako section, at the latter's 'home ground', these being the only two sections represented. In June 1970, however, following a good harvest, there took place, at the Biogolokare 'home ground', eight successive days of duelling which attracted participants from all five Mursi sections. In these contests (which were immediately preceded by an outbreak of what could appropriately be called, in a phrase used by Spencer of the Samburu Moran, 'gang warfare') Dola members did not oppose each other, and neither did those of Ariholi and Gongulobibi. Thus, the division of contestants followed the structural division between Dola and the two southern sections, and was not a simple reflection of the intensity of social ties based on local contiguity. It should be emphasised here that Biogolokare, Ariholi and Gongulobibi settlements are likely, during the wet season, to be dotted about the headstreams of the same Omo tributaries and to be only a few hundred yards apart.

The distinctiveness of sections, then, is as much a result as a cause of the rule that contestants in duelling should come from different sections and this, I believe, should be seen as the rule's main significance. The Mursi themselves will define a section as a local division of the population, the members of which do not oppose each other in ceremonial duelling. The rules of duelling are therefore functionally similar to those of segmentary lineage organisation, in that they have a 'nesting' or 'massing' effect. This does not, of course explain the particular pattern of nesting which is revealed in the present territorial organisation, but this can, I believe, be accounted for on the assumption that there has been, and still is, a gradual northward migration of Mursi into territory formally claimed by the Bodi.

4

The second ceremonial performance which involves local groups of age-mates and which bears closely on the question of territorial organisation is that which I call 'initiation'. This seems to be the most appropriate term to use, because it is through this ceremony that the transition is made from the grade of *teru* to that of *rora*, and also, therefore, from the basic grade of *lusa* (boys) to that of *zuo* (adults). Of all the ceremonies which mark the individual's transition from one grade to another, this is by far the most elaborate, and thus of all the 'big moments' which he experiences in his progress through the grades, this is by far the biggest. (It will have become clear by now, of course, that while it confers new jural status on an individual, the transition to the *rora* grade makes virtually no immediate difference to his life-style and activities, a far more significant 'moment', in this sense, being his marriage, which may occur while he is still a *teri*.)

There are two reasons, however, why the term initiation could be misleading here, although I have no better alternative to offer. Firstly, for reasons outlined earlier, there is a very wide variation in the age at which men go through this ceremony. Some may be boys of fifteen, and others may be married men of thirty or thirty-five with children. Secondly, (and this is a point which will be continually emphasised in what follows) the initiands go through the ceremony very much as a group, and not as individuals. It is not just that a local group of *teru* is initiated together, but that no concessions are made, during the ceremony, to their separate individual identities. Nothing is done to them, as individuals (there is, for example, no circumcision) and nothing is done by them as individuals (there is, for example, no killing of a stock animal by each initiand). It will be seen later how the symbolism of the initiation ceremony emphasises both the solidarity of age-mates and their territorial — indeed residential — exclusiveness.

I consider first, however, the circumstances under which ceremonies are held (rather than what happens during them) for this focuses attention on the structural relations between sections. Since these relations are, in the long run and of their very nature, impermanent, and since initiation ceremonies take place at relatively infrequent intervals, it is necessary to emphasise that the following account is based upon information gained at one particular moment in Mursi history (i.e. 1969-74, the period spanning my two field trips). There is no suggestion, therefore, that the particular pattern of relations between sections upon which this account is based always has existed and always will exist — indeed quite the opposite is suggested. This qualification about time is not, as must be evident by now, inserted as a theoretical admission of something from which my analysis prescinds in practice. I am specifically not saying 'Yes, I know Mursi society must be changing, but since the only historical information I have is based upon oral accounts of the very recent past, I must — indeed ought to — ignore this in practice.' I am saying, on the contrary, that what I was able to observe only makes sense if a particular systematic change, which my gleanings from recent oral history sufficiently confirm, even if they do not fully document, is assumed to have been, and to be, taking place. It must be understood, then, that although I now outline the circumstances under which initiation ceremonies *are* held, this is based upon accounts I was given of the circumstances under which the most recent ceremonies *were* held, in 1961.

There are three points to mention here, one of which is evident from the last sentence: namely, that although different initiation ceremonies are held in different parts of the country for different local groups of *teru*, they are all held in the same year and during the same wet season, though not simultaneously. Secondly, the ceremonies are held in a particular order, beginning in the south of the country. The Mursi explain this priority of the south by observing that it was in the south of their present territory that they first crossed from the west to the east bank of the Omo. It is the Ariholi section which, on these grounds, is considered the most senior, for it is from the territory of this section that the Mursi see themselves as having expanded, after crossing from the west bank of the Omo. Ariholi thus stages its initiation ceremony first, and is followed by Gongulobibi. The constituent sections of Dola hold a third and final ceremony, after Gongulobibi. Thus (and this is the third point), although the unmarried *rora* of the Dola sections form cattle camps which are not co-extensive with Dola but rather with each of its constituent sections, they are moved into the *rora* grade at the same time, in the same place and as a single body.

The special conceptual unity of the sections which make up Dola is revealed then, by this rule, as it is by the rule that members of Dola sections do not oppose each other in duelling contests in which members of the other two sections take part. Although they express a conceptual unity — that of 'Dola-ness' — neither of these rules should be thought of as a survival from a time when Dola was a single section, since the idea that the present three-section Dola has grown from a single parent section simply helps the people represent to themselves a unity which is dictated by their northward migration into contested territory. If this migration continues, and a new Mursi section is formed, north of the Mara, there is no reason to believe that the constituent sections of the present Dola will continue to hold common initiation ceremonies, exclusive to themselves. On the contrary, there would appear, in this event, to be only two alternatives, neither of which would allow the exclusive conceptual unity of the present Dola to remain intact.

One is that the new section will be thought of as a fourth unit of Dola, so that four separate sections will then hold a common initiation ceremony. But there is already some logical tension between the symbolism of the initiation ceremony, which emphasises the solidarity and indeed the residential unity of initiands, and the separate cattle camps in which the unmarried men of each of the three Dola sections continue to live after they have been initiated. (This tension does not of course, arise where Ariholi and Gongulobibi are concerned, since each of these sections holds it own initiation ceremony.) This is another way of saying that there is a tension between the conceptual unity of 'Dola-ness' and the virtual self-sufficiency of the separate Dola sections in the management of day-to-day affairs — in the reaching of decisions, for example, about transhumance movements between the Omo and the eastern grazing areas. This applies particularly to the two Dola sections which are physically furthest apart, Mara and Biogolokare. There will presumably be a critical point beyond which geographical distance so reduces physical contact between sections that the job of organising a common ceremony with the particular symbolic content of that to be described soon, becomes not so much technically impossible as literally unthinkable. An observation already made in the first part of this essay should be stressed here. Namely, that although individual Mursi families are highly mobile over the course of a single year's transhumance their mobility is almost entirely along an east-west axis.

The second alternative, in the event of a new section being formed north of the Mara, is that the southernmost of the present Dola sections, Biogolokare, would break away from the conceptual unity which had hitherto bound it to Mara and Mako by holding its own initiation ceremony, as Ariholi and Gongulobibi do at the moment. As far as the rules of duelling are concerned one would expect Biogolokare to combine with the sections to the south of it, in opposition to those to the north of it — that the segmentary 'rift', in other words, which now separates Biogolokare and Ariholi would move up one to separate Biogolokare and Mako. Mako, Mara and the new section would then form a conceptual unit exactly analogous to the present Dola, holding initiation ceremonies in common and combining against the rest in ceremonial duelling. On no account, if the argument of this essay is correct, would a new section, north of Mara and thus in the front line of expansion against the Bodi, hold, like Ariholi and Gongulobibi, its own initiation ceremonies, thereby allowing the exclusive conceptual unity of the present three Dola sections to remain intact. If the northward movement of the Mursi continues, Dola, as it exists at the moment, is doomed. Indeed, if this movement were to continue indefinitely, so that the number of Mursi sections south of the 'segmentary rift' continued to increase, it might happen that those to the north of it, becoming proportionately fewer and having literally left behind such territorially anchored names as Mako and Mara, will be overtaken from behind like the present Bodi, and eventually be pushed into the foothills of the Ethiopian Plateau.

It now remains for me to show that there is a logical tension between the symbolic content of an initiation ceremony and the residence in separate cattle camps of those who have been through it together.

Since the most recent initiation ceremonies were held in 1961, eight years before I visited the Mursi, the following account of their form is based upon what I was told, and since I spent the greater part of my fieldwork in the north of the country, the most reliable information I have on this subject refers to the ceremony held by the three Dola sections in that year. I have no doubt, however, that the ceremonies held by the Ariholi and Gongulobibi sections were identical in all essentials — apart of course from their smaller catchment areas for initiands. Nor is it necessary, as it was when discussing the circumstances under which the ceremonies are held, to enter a proviso about the moment in Mursi history to which the information refers. As far as what happens in an initiation ceremony is concerned, the undoubted truth that even ritual activity changes over time can be ignored.

The ceremony lasts two days and I find it useful to divide the performance into four parts, of which I now give a rough outline.

1. *The beating of the initiands.* On the morning of the first day the *teru* (i.e. the initiands) construct around a shade tree an enclosure of branches, having two openings, one opposite the other. They then leave the scene. During the afternoon men of the *rora* and of the next most senior grade (*bara*, or 'senior elders', who are also referred to as the 'fathers of the *teru*') enter the enclosure, each man carrying a withy. Late in the afternoon the *teru* return. They kneel in a compact group outside the enclosure and are severely beaten by the older men, who circle the group, landing occasional but carefully aimed swipes with their withies.[18] The *teru* hold duelling poles with which they attempt to ward off these swipes but, since they are expected to remain kneeling in the same spot, they are easy targets. Meanwhile they have aimed at them not only withies but also words, since some of the more senior *bara* take it in turns to harangue them while the beating is going on, insisting that they are unworthy to become adults.

2. *The killing of the ox.* The next morning the *teru* return to the enclosure, three of them (in the Dola ceremony) driving an ox and a cow each, from their own herds. Two of these represent the junior and senior sub-clans of the Juhai clan and the third represents the Kagisi clan. (In the Ariholi ceremony there is a single pair of animals, belonging to a single representative of the Komorte clan, and in the Gongulobibi ceremony there is also a single pair of animals, belonging to a single representative of the Garakuli clan). The oxen are driven to one opening of the enclosure and killed by their owners, while the cows, their necks weighed down with bells, are allowed to wander off to graze. After this killing of the oxen, from which the whole ceremony takes its name (*nithai*) the *teru* enter the enclosure, within which the next part of the ritual is held.

3. *The naming of the initiands.* While the oxen lie where they were

killed, the initiands enter the enclosure, but stand one behind the other in a line which may thus stretch out through one of its openings. They hold on their shoulders (I am not sure whether the right or the left) sticks which are tied together, end to end, to form an unbroken line. One of the seniormost members of the *bara* grade present then walks down the line of initiands, banging with a stick the sticks they hold over their shoulders, and addressing them meanwhile with a name which they will keep for the rest of their lives. The oxen are then cut up and roasted for the older men by the new *rora*.

4. *The tying with kalochi*. Proceedings at the enclosure are now over. While the other men sleep off their meal, the new *rora* disperse into the bush and cut strips of bark from the *kalochi* tree (Grewia). Its bark is tough and flexible and is much used as a sort of general purpose string. The *rora* tie *kalochi* round their wrists, arms, knees, necks and waists, leaving long tassels which make a rustling noise when they walk. They then tour the local settlements, singing a song of which the following is one of the versions I collected:

> You girls, crawl into a hole;
> Make way for the *rora*;
> Make way for the lions.
> You boy, crawl into a hole;
> Leave the country for the *rora*;
> Leave the country for the lions.
> You woman, look at the *kalochi*;
> It says 'liang', 'liang'.
> You boy, crawl into a hole;
> etc.

Thus, during the three parts of this ceremony which takes place at the enclosure, the initiands are treated as a single body. They form a compact group during the beating and, although certain individuals are singled out for a specially severe haranguing, this is only so that the sins of the individual may be visited upon the group. The alleged misdemeanours of individual *teru* are dwelt on, not in order to correct particularly delinquent individuals, but in order to show that the whole group of *teru* does not deserve to receive, and therefore has no right to be given, adult status.[19] Secondly, the killing of the ox, which is clearly the central act of the ceremony, is not performed by each initiand for himself, but on behalf of them all by one or more representatives. Thirdly, during the name giving, the physical oneness of the initiands is emphasised by the fact they are made to hold an unbroken line of sticks.

The significance of the enclosure which is constructed for the ceremony also needs to be pointed out. It is called a *dir*, and this suggests that it represents a particular type of settlement, of which the cattle camps lived in by unmarried men are an example. The settlements of married men consist of a number of separate but contiguous brushwood compounds, grouped round a shade tree, with the compound openings facing inwards. The cattle camps of unmarried men, however, are constructed not only more roughly than those of married men, but also according to a different plan. The compounds face outwards from the central shade tree, and back onto an enclosure which is built round the base of this tree and which has two openings, one opposite the other. This enclosure is called the *dir* and, like the area round the central shade tree of a married men's settlement, it is predominantly a male domain. Women enter it only to bring food to the men, and in the case of the *dir*, they should be unmarried girls, at that. I was told that in the days before the Mursi had rifles, the *rora* would hang their shields from the branches of the shade tree in the *dir*, a practice which has been preserved in the imagery of public speaking, in which context one still hears the expression 'to take one's shield from the *dir*', meaning to prepare for military action.

It is only when the central rite of the ceremony, the killing of the ox (or, as in the Dola ceremony, the oxen) has been concluded that the initiands enter the *dir*, which until then had only been occupied by the initiated men. This seems to be a clear representation of their becoming not only adults but also members of a single residential unit. The word for the members of such a unit is *buran*, which can be used of any local group, and is used of that which I call a territorial section. The word for the physical structure lived in by the members of a single residential unit is *or*, and this is used also for the physical site or geographical extent, of a territorial section. Thus, the territory occupied by the southernmost of the three Dola sections, Biogolokare, is referred to by Dola members as 'the stomach' or centre of the 'settlement'. Mara, therefore, is thought of as being on the edge of the Dola 'settlement'. The *dir* which is constructed for an initiation ceremony symbolises therefore, both the residential unity of the initiands and also the physical extent of their territorial section. In the Dola ceremony these two are at odds, since Dola consists of three sections, the unmarried men of which live in physically separate camps with their unmarried section age-mates.

Finally, the giving of a name to the new group of initiates needs to be discussed. From one point of view, the ritual of name-giving emphasises the unity of a distinct local group of age-mates since, while receiving their name, they are made to stand in line and are joined to each other by an unbroken line of sticks. On the other hand, their new name links them to other local groups of age-mates, for the same name is used at each initiation ceremony held in the same year. In 1961 the name used was *benna*, stones, which had last been used about seventy years earlier. All men initiated in the same year, whatever their section, are said by the Mursi to form a *teny*, which word should be translated, according to current anthropological usage, as 'age-set'. One might say, therefore, that by going through an initiation ceremony an individual becomes not only an adult, but also a member of a named, society-wide age-set, of which he remains a member until he dies. The trouble is, however, that while this statement is logically true, it is very misleading in practice. It is particularly misleading if it is accepted as a basic proposition in attempting to understand the relationship between age phenomena and territorial aspects of political organisation, and this is why I did not want to begin my own account of this relationship with a discussion of age-sets. The essential point is that an age-set (*teny*) exists only as a sex and age specific category of the population. Membership (in the taxonomist's sense) of this category does not, in itself, affect an individual's behaviour. What does affect it, on the other hand, is membership of a local group of age-mates. This is well illustrated if one considers the rule that a man should not marry the daughter of an age-mate.

On the face of it this looks like a rule which governs the behaviour of men of the same age-set throughout the society, making the set a powerful force for integration, 'cutting across' local divisions. In fact, it does help to produce a degree of social integration, but in an entirely indirect way. For, in practice, the rule only applies to the daughters of a man's *local* age-mates. The term for such a girl is *ba*, but the Mursi say that the daughter of a man of one's own age but who lives a long way away is not one's *ba*. In other words there is a spatial element in the definition. The reason for this is clear, on the assumption that the purpose of the rule is to prevent one set of expectations about the free and easy behaviour which is appropriate between age-mates being brought into head-on collision with another set of expectations about the stiff and formal behaviour which is appropriate between son-in-law and father-in-law. If one rarely sees one's father-in-law the problem of such conflicting expectations will hardly arise, even if he is technically one's age-mate. So what looks, on the surface, like a rule about age sets turns out to be a rule about local age-groups. And if it promotes social integration it does so indirectly, through the contribution it makes to the practice of local group exogamy.

On one occasion during my first field trip I was puzzled to learn from a Dola man that he had become a *rori*, together with two or three others of his section, the year before, eight years after the last Dola initiation ceremony. When I enquired further I was told that 'the *buran* [local group] has not been cut.' On asking 'Which *buran*?' I was told 'The *buran* of the *rora*.' It is possible, therefore, for individual *teru* to join their local group of *rora* until a 'cutting' ceremony is held, and I was told that this 'normally' takes place two to three years after the main initiation ceremony. I discuss the apparent abnormality of recent history in the next section. Here I want only to point out that the Mursi speak of the 'cutting' not of the *teny* of the *rora*, but of their *buran* or local group, and that they therefore think of those individuals who become *rora* in the way just described as joining a local group of age-mates, rather than a society-wide category. As far as Mursi age-sets are concerned, then, we are left merely with the fact of a common name being applied to all men who were initiated at the same time. This does, of course, imply an idea of unity, but it is an idea which is co-extensive with that of being a Mursi. Age-set names have no more significance, for social integration, than any other cultural item which the Mursi think of as distinctively their own — such as the lip plates worn by their women, and the duelling poles carried by their men.

It would be easy to offer reasons why Mursi age-sets are politically redundant. Firstly, the Mursi are few in number, and they inhabit a well defined territory which is only about 1,000 square miles in extent. Secondly, because of the east-west axis of transhumance movements, there is relatively little need for individual families to travel from one section to another in the course of normal subsistence activities, and day-to-day co-operation in subsistence matters is therefore carried on almost entirely between people who are already well known to each other personally. Thirdly, because of the effects of clan and local group exogamy in such a small population, it is difficult to imagine any two Mursi being unable to relate to each other except on the basis of age-set membership.

The trouble with this kind of argument, however, is that it invites the question 'Why then do they have age-sets at all?', which in turn leads to conjectures about the functions which the 'age-set system' performed in the past, under conditions about which we have no knowledge, but which are presumed to have been different from those existing today. Writers on East African age-organisations seem particularly prone to this kind of conjecture, partly perhaps because the societies they have studied have fairly recently come under colonial administration. They are also prone to making theoretical statements of a similar kind, setting out, for example, the conditions under which age-sets will *not* have important political functions.[20] Such conclusions may be logical, but the fact that they are totally unenlightening suggests that they are based on false assumptions, the most important of which is, I suggest, that the phenomena in question form a system, which has a definite set of functions for a particular society. There must surely be something wrong with an approach which leads so frequently to conclusions about why certain kinds of behaviour are *not* socially significant.

5

In this section, by way of conclusion, I want to consider some of the apparently recent departures from 'normal' practice which are revealed by the investigation of age-organisation among the Mursi, no less than among other African societies. Explanations of such 'recent' departures from the norm fall into two broad categories, the *ad hoc* and the systematic. The first can be divided into two sub-categories, depending upon whether the explanations are offered by the participants or by the observer. An example of an *ad hoc* participant explanation is, 'We should have held ceremony x before now, but we have had a succession of poor harvests.' This type of explanation would be convincing (since bad harvests and other disasters, such as epidemics and war, are common enough occurrences in these societies) were it not so common. For it seems too much of a coincidence that so many peoples in East Africa should have had their age ceremonies delayed by adverse conditions just before they were visited by an anthropologist. Equally *ad hoc* is the kind of explanation, this time coming from the outside observer, which attributes recent 'abnormal' behaviour to colonial influences and to the subsequent loss by the 'age-system' of its former significance. The Mursi, at least, are one people who have never come under colonial administration, but who make just the same statements about recent departures from traditional practice as have been recorded for many other East African peoples. Into the same category of *ad hoc* observer explanations come those which attribute the irregularities and anomalies of a particular people's 'age-system' to the fact that they have recently adopted it from one of their neighbours, or that they are in the process of changing it to fit new ecological conditions. Both types of *ad hoc* explanation serve the purpose of protecting the belief, on the one hand of the participant and on the other hand of the observer, that there exists in a particular society an 'age system' which would, under 'normal' circumstances, 'work'. The trouble with both types of explanation is that, even if they are accepted as true (and they are, of course, extremely difficult to verify), they are relatively uninteresting if one is concerned with the wider social significance of the phenomena under study.

Systematic explanations attempt to preserve the idea of system by showing that what look to the participants like departures from tradition are in fact manifestations of an underlying, long term, regularity within the 'age system' itself. Subtle and ingeneous arguments have been advanced to this end by various scholars, but they do not overcome the major disadvantage of the *ad hoc* explanations just mentioned. Indeed the social significance of the so-called 'age-system' of a society seems to recede in proportion to the amount of effort which is expended in trying to show how it 'really works'. Another problem with this approach is that it makes us wonder why it should be necessary for the participants to fool themselves with *ad hoc* explanations when there is an underlying regularity within the system all the time. Why should they need to hide this regularity from themselves? If it is answered that they do not need to, but that they have not discovered it, one would have to ask what data the anthropologist has at his disposal that enable him to succeed where they have failed. As far as knowledge of the past is concerned he is rarely more knowledgeable than the people he is studying. It is more likely, surely, that *ad hoc* explanations are needed precisely because there is no deep seated regularity within the 'age-system' — or, in other words, because there is no such system. But why, then, should it be necessary for the people (and for the observer) to talk as though there were? The answer which is proposed here, for the Mursi, is that the beliefs and practices to do with age, which have been described above, help to sustain the illusion of a permanent and enduring 'Mursi society'. Understanding the true causes of what the Mursi see as recent departures from traditional practice in these matters means understanding that there is no such permanent and enduring entity at all. Thus, it is not the existence of a Mursi 'age-system' which is ultimately at issue, but the existence of Mursi society.[21] My final task, therefore, is to show how recent 'abnormalities' in Mursi age phenomena are related to the analysis made above of their territorial organisation.

The Mursi do not state a fixed interval which should elapse between successive initiation ceremonies, but the interval between the last two — between twenty and twenty-five years — was generally held to have been unusually long. It is extremely difficult to put even an approximate date to earlier initiation ceremonies, but the average interval between the last four seems to have been about fifteen years. The Mursi say that the holding of the last initiation ceremony, in 1961, was delayed by a succession of disasters, including a period of hostile relations with the Bodi, which came to an end in 1954, droughts and an outbreak of rinderpest. Similar reasons are given for the fact that the 'cutting' ceremony referred to at the end of the last section, which 'should' have been held two to three years after the last initiation ceremony, had not been held up to 1974. This ceremony, which took place according to schedule (around 1940) after the last initiation ceremony but one, should be held by the same territorial divisions and in the same order as the initiation ceremonies. That is, Dola holds a single cutting ceremony, which should, furthermore, take place in the 'stomach' of the 'settlement' — namely in the territory of the Biogolokare section from which Dola is seen as having originated. There is no such rule about the appropriate location for the Dola intiation ceremony, the last one having been held in the territory of the Mako section. It should be noted then that, while the special conceptual unity of Dola is expressed by both these ceremonies, the cutting ceremony gives this conceptual unity a territorial focus in its southernmost constituent section.

There is a third ceremony, of which I was not able to obtain an eye witness account since it was last held about seventy years ago. This is called 'the cutting of the cow's neck', from the fact that its central rite consists in completely severing a cow's head from its body. This is the only ceremonial performance, of any kind, for which the appropriate congregation is said to be society-wide. It also has a territorial focus: it should take place at that point on the Omo where it is believed the Mursi first crossed to the west bank. The stated purpose of this ceremony is to mark the transition to the *bara* grade of four successive sets of age-mates, or age-sets, such a series being linked by one of two alternating 'joint names', *gamal* and *kirin*. In practice this means that the ceremony should be held after every fifth initiation ceremony or, in other words, about every sixty years. When the next initiation ceremony is held and the present *rora* move into the *bara* grade, they will, *ipso facto* become the first set of a new *kirin* series. Thus, when they became *rora* in 1961, their immediate seniors, who then moved into the *bara* grade, became the last set of the previous *gamal* series. Immediately after the 1961 ceremony then, the new *bara* should have 'cut the cow's neck', but they have not yet done so, and there is no expectation that they will. Although some informants account for this by the familiar appeal to 'bad years', other give a slightly more subtle interpretation. They point out that, once a new series has been completed, a man whose set falls within it (i.e. men of the *bara* grade and above) should not marry a girl who was below marriageable age (about seventeen years) at the time the ceremony was held. This rule would affect quite seriously those who fell within the last set of a series — the youngest of whom might be about 40 years old — but it would hardly affect those who fell into the first set — many of whom would be dead by the time the series was completed. But, merely to point out that it has not been in the interests of the present *bara* to hold this third ceremony does not account satisfactorily for their success in putting it off. For if they could delay it just because it was against their interests to hold it, one must ask under what conditions such a ceremony would ever be held.

If the argument of this essay is correct it is not surprising that the interval between successive age ceremonies should vary, since these ceremonies must be seen as defining not only a cyclical series of temporal divisions of the population, based on the physiological aging of individuals, but also a linear series of spatial divisions, based on a continuous northward migration. Failure to hold a particular ceremony, therefore, when it is thought that the temporal limit has been reached, may result, partly, from uncertainty as to the appropriate spatial limit which should be set to its 'congregation'. In other words, these periodic age ceremonies play a part in the definition of the internal spatial divisions of the Mursi which is analogous to the part played by periodic Mursi-Bodi peace-making ceremonies in the definition of their external boundary. With this in mind and using what information can be gleaned from recent oral history, the particular 'abnormalities' just referred to might be explained as follows.

Since the last but one initiation ceremony (c.1938) the Mursi have consolidated their hold on the River Mara and on Kuduma. Indeed this consolidation has probably taken place mainly since 1954, when the last peace-making ceremony was held with the Bodi in the territory of the Mako section. It may be, therefore, that the last initiation ceremony was held up until 1961, by which time it seemed long overdue, because of the change this consolidation brought about in the alignment of the northern sections, Mara having now become by far the largest. Holding a common Dola ceremony at that time was, at the very least, a different matter from what it had been 20 or 25 years earlier, when, if the Mara section existed in any recognisable sense at all, it consisted of relatively few families who cultivated at Kuduma and along the Mara, but who thought of themselves, and who were thought of by others, as a northern outpost, rather as the Mursi who cultivate north of the Mara think of themselves and are thought of today.

But even if it is accepted that such considerations could delay the staging of a common Dola ceremony,[22] why was such a ceremony nevertheless held in 1961? The reason for this lies, I think, in the fact that the 'cutting' (of the *buran*) was last held around 1941, two to three years after the last but one initiation ceremony. As a result of this, firstly, no *teru* had been initiated since about 1941, so that by 1961 several were already married, with children, and secondly, virtually all the existing *rora* of the three northern sections who were alive in 1961 had been initiated together in a single ceremony. Pressure to hold a new initiation ceremony came to a head in 1961, presumably, because of anomalies connected with the first point — such as married men being technically unable to take part in public decision making — while the second may well account for the fact that the three northern sections held a single ceremony in that year. For virtually all the existing initiated men of these sections had been through such a single ceremony themselves, and it may not, therefore, have yet been 'thinkable' for one of these sections to act independently. Under what conditions, then, would such a break in the conceptual unity of Dola become 'thinkable', and how are these conditions linked to delays in the holding of age ceremonies?

This can be answered, I think, by considering again the 'cutting of the *buran*'. This ceremony, it has been noted, should be held according to the same territorial divisions and in the same order as the initiation ceremony. This follows from the fact that it is seen as closing recruitment to a particular local group of age-mates, who were initiated together, and not to a society-wide category, or age-set. It has also been noted that, unlike the Dola initiation ceremony, the precise location of which is not laid down, the 'cutting' of the Dola *buran* must take place in the territory of the Biogolokare section, which is seen as the 'stomach' of Dola. But this precedence of Biogolokare over the other two Dola sections, like the precedence of Ariholi over all the other Mursi sections, is historical, and does not reflect the present distribution of population. For, on the one hand, most Mursi are now members of Dola, and on the other, most Dola members now belong to the Mara section.[23] On the assumption that this had already become true by the early 1960s, it would have been even more anachronistic to hold a single ceremony at that time to 'cut' the Dola *buran*, a ceremony with its territorial focus in the Biogolokare section, than it was to hold a single Dola initiation ceremony, without such a territorial focus. The 'cutting' of the *buran* could, furthermore, be delayed indefinitely, without risk of creating the sort of anomalies which lead to an increasing pressure to initiate a new group of *rora*. It is true that newly initiated *rora* are still considered to be, in some sense, 'boys' until their local group of age-mates has been 'cut', but the sense in question is extremely technical.[24] In a similar technical sense a man is not considered to be a 'real' adult (*hiri hang*) until he has left the *rora* grade altogether and has become a *bari*, or senior elder. Becoming an adult is a gradual process, but becoming a *rori* is by far the most significant moment in that process.

These, I believe, are the likely reasons why the 'cutting' of the *buran* did not take place after the last initiation ceremony and why, indeed, it is unlikely to take place at all for the present *rora*.[25] Two implications of this failure to 'cut' the *buran* are relevant here. Firstly, it means that serious anomalies of the type mentioned earlier are unlikely to arise, since individuals can continue indefinitely to join their local group of *rora* in the years after it has been formed. Thus, if it is the build up of pressure from these anomalies which is instrumental in causing an initiation ceremony to be held at a particular time, there seems no reason to believe that the interval between the last initiation ceremony and the next will be any shorter than that between the last two, which was regarded as abnormally long. In other words, the reason why the last initiation ceremony was regarded as overdue was not simply because of the length of time (about twenty-three years) which had elapsed since the previous one (it has already been mentioned that there is no rule about how long this interval should be) but because, by 1961, many men who were heads of households were still jural minors. And this came about not because the twenty-three year interval just mentioned was abnormally long but because the 'cutting' of the *buran* took place two to three years after the last initiation ceremony but one. It would be mistaken, therefore, to attempt to assess what is an emically 'normal' or 'abnormal' interval between successive initiation ceremonies by means of the purely chronological measurement of time to which we in the West are accustomed.

The second implication of failure to 'cut' the *buran* is that, as the years go by, the proportion of Dola members who have been through a common initiation ceremony will steadily decline. For those Dola members who become *rora* in the years following the main initiation ceremony do so as members of a particular section, and not of Dola as a whole. Each section, in other words, acts independently when it comes to admitting individuals to its already constituted local group of *rora*. Thus, when the next initiation ceremony is held (which, because of the factors outlined in the previous paragraph is unlikely to be for some time) by no means all the existing *rora* of the Dola sections will themselves have been through the same initiation ceremony. The longer the delay before the next initiation ceremony, the greater the proportion of these *rora* who will have been initiated as members of a particular constituent section of Dola. Using the next initiation ceremony, therefore, to give public recognition to a new alignment of sections (by, for example, Biogolokare breaking away to hold its own ceremony) will seem less of a break with tradition than it would have seemed in 1961.

It may be objected that, in the above argument, I have concentrated on Dola and left out of account the two southern sections, Ariholi and Gongulobibi. What was to stop Ariholi, for example, holding its initiation and 'cutting' ceremonies 'on time', especially as it is expected to give the lead in these affairs to the other Mursi sections? The answer, I believe, and the reason why the Dola tail may be said to wag the Mursi dog, is that the precedence taken by Ariholi and Gongulobibi in the holding of age ceremonies, which makes it look as though they dictate the timing of these ceremonies to the northern sections, is purely historical and formal. It is just another means by which the Mursi preserve the idea of their own historical permanence. In practice, it is events in the north which, although they take place furthest from the historical 'stomach' of the country, nevertheless dictate the timing of age ceremonies in the south.

Failure to hold the third ceremony, 'the cutting of the cow's neck', is easily attributable to the same fact of northward movement and consequent territorial re-alignment. Not only is this ceremony said to be a 'national' one, requiring the presence of all men of the *bara* grade, from all sections, but it also has to take place at a particular place, associated with the first entry of the Mursi into their present territory. When it was last held, about seventy years ago, it seems likely that the Mursi were occupying only the immediate bank of the Omo (the present bushland thicket having been produced since by a combination of over-grazing and cultivation) and that they had not moved north of the area at present occupied by the Biogolokare section. The Mursi say that the same ceremony cannot be held again because there is no-one alive who can remember its details but, according to the argument being presented here, the real reason is that they are not the same Mursi.

Although they recognise that they have not always lived in their present territory, the Mursi believe that their society was created by God, at the beginning of time, and along with all the other peoples by whom they now find themselves surrounded. In this essay, however, I have argued that the people I have been calling 'Mursi' are merely a temporary coalescence, brought about largely by ecological and geographical features, in a huge migration of cattle-keeping people from the general direction of the southern Sudan into the Ethiopian highlands, where they are destined to become sedentary agriculturalists. I have tried to show that the definition of, and the structural relations between, Mursi territorial divisions are changing all the time, and that this change is being, so to speak, mediated by various activities and beliefs to do with age. On the assumption that every society has to seem more or less permanent (in the sense of having existed since the beginning of time) to its own members, the most general significance of the activities and beliefs I have been discussing is that they help to shield the Mursi from the realisation that their society is, by its very nature, ephemeral. This may also be the most general significance of segmentary lineage organisation among the Nuer. In which case, it is not so much an 'organisation of predatory expansion' as Sahlins has described it, but a means a camouflaging that expansion from the Nuer themselves. That is, it helps to preserve an illusion of permanence in a society which, like that of the Mursi, is not so much expanding but which, if one may so put it, is expansion.

NOTES

1. Fieldwork was carried out between 1969 and 1970 and between 1973 and 1974. I am grateful to the Social Science Research Council, the Central Research Fund Committee of the University of London, the Tweedie Exploration Fellowship Committee of the University of Edinburgh and the Royal Geographical Society, for their financial assistance. In writing this essay I have been helped by discussions with Dr H.J. Blackhurst and Dr P.T.W. Baxter. I also thank Mr Timothy Baxter for drawing Figure 2.
2. This range is called Ngalabong (from the Turkana name for the Mursi) on existing maps, but I prefer to call it the Mursi Mountains.
3. For a fuller treatment of the argument presented in the next section see Turton (in press).
4. These are the Zilmamu of earlier literature. For a brief account of existing sources for the Mursi and their neighbours, from a linguistic point of view, see Turton and Bender (1976).
5. This is called the 'Didinga-Murle isolated language group' by Tucker and Bryan (1956) and 'Surma' by Bender (1971).

6   The Mursi and Bodi obtain rifles (mostly the 8mm. Austrian Mannlicher, which was carried by the Italian troops who occupied Ethiopia from 1935-40) and ammunition from highland traders, in exchange for cattle, ivory and leopard skins.

7   Peace was eventually made in November 1975, after I had left the field, and the Mursi did indeed kill their animal at Mara, in the presence of Bodi representatives. For this information I am grateful to Dr Katsuyoshi Fukui, who carried out fieldwork among the Bodi in 1974-6.

8   That is 'an extreme form' of bushland 'where the woody plants form a closed stand through which man or the larger ungulates can pass only with extreme difficulty and in which the land has no value for grazing' (Pratt, Greenway and Gwynn 1966).

9   Sahlins (1961) has pointed the way here, with his argument about segmentary lineage organisation and 'predatory expansion' but, as will be seen, my emphasis is different from his.

10 The following table shows the section membership of all married male respondents in a complete census of cattle settlements carried out during July and August 1970.

Mara	Mako	Biogolokare	Gongulobibi	Ariholi	Total
127	82	72	56	28	365

11 Katsuyoshi Fukui (personal communication).

12 Mursi clans, like their age-sets, are conceptual entities which 'cut across' local divisions of the population.

13 Although most men have only one wife, taking all the married men in my census together, the incidence of polygyny works out at 1.66 wives per man.

14 The name *teru* probably derives from the word for the new green shoots of grass which appear with the first rain in grazing areas that were burnt off during the dry season.

15 Bridewealth amounts, ideally, to thirty-eight head of large stock, but in practice is unlikely to exceed twenty head. The essential point, however, is that, as a result of protracted negotiations, the groom's people are forced to give as much as they can afford.

16 This figure is based on a rough estimate of the dates of the last four initiation ceremonies. The timing of initiation and other ceremonies is discussed in Section 5.

17 The following sentences, which were written about the early history of sport in English public schools, suggests some similarities between it and duelling among the Mursi: 'Sport united the boys in a particular pattern of behaviour but from the point of view of the teachers and governors of the school it was dysfunctional. The boys were in frequent rebellion against their teachers and on at least two occasions the army had to be summoned to supress them. Sport which was organised entirely by the boys was the focus for the opposition of pupils to the established authority.' (McIntosh 1971:5-6).

18 This kneeling and haranguing is frequently seen in smaller, annual age ceremonies.

19 Cf. Spencer (1970:149): 'They [the Moran] are in a powerless position, and they simply cannot win in any circumstances. If a small group of them, or even just one individual, shows any irresponsibility through, say stealing stock, flirting with wives, or showing less than full respect for the elders, they are *all* held to be thieves, adulterers and psychopaths.'

20 Cf. Eisenstadt (1954:102): '... Age-set systems arise and function in those societies in which the basic allocation of roles is not overwhelmingly determined by membership in kinship groups, and where some important integrative functions remain to be fulfilled beyond these groups.' Also Gulliver (1953:166): 'It may be suggested that a deep seated age-organisation cannot exist where there are other important mechanisms of social integration.'

21 There is an analogy here with the *ad hoc* explanations offered by the Azande to account for inconsistencies in their beliefs about witch-craft. For the Azande to understand the true cause of failures of the poison oracle, for example, would mean their understanding not only that the poison works through its chemical properties alone, which is neither here nor there, but also that there is no moral order in the universe.

22 There is what appears to be an alternative explanation of the fact that the interval between the last two initiation ceremonies was relatively long — namely that the present *bara*, when they were occupying the *rora* grade, wanted to delay the 'cutting of the cow's neck', which was due to take place immediately after the next initiation ceremony, and which would have seriously curtailed their future marriage choices. From this latter point of view, therefore, it was against their interests to become *bara* and they would not, consequently, have exerted pressure to displace their immediate seniors. The difficulty with such an 'explanation', however, is that even after the 1961 ceremony had been held, the 'cutting of the cow's neck' still did not take place. Also just as it is insufficient to account for this last fact by appealing to the self interest of the present *bara*, so it is insufficient to use a similar explanation to account for the apparent delay in holding the last initiation ceremony. For even if it was in the interests of the present *bara* to delay this ceremony for as long as possible, this does not explain how the delay was actually brought about.

23 See note 8.

24 At meat-eatings, for example, the present *rora* may be taunted by their seniors, and told that they have no right to the portions of meat which are customarily reserved for 'adults' — but these are empty and jocular threats.

25 While my informants were always ready to speculate about the data of the next initiation ceremony, they had no interest in similar speculations about when the long overdue 'cutting' of the *buran* might take place.

BIBLIOGRAPHY

Bender, M.L. 1971. 'The Languages of Ethiopia: A New Lexicostatistic Classification and Some Problems of Diffusion' in *Anthropological Linguistics*, 13, 5.

Dyson-Hudson, N. 1966. *Karimojong Politics*. Oxford.

Eisenstadt, S.N. 1954. 'African Age Groups: A Comparative Study' in *Africa*, 24, 100-12.
Gulliver, P.H. 1953. 'The Age-Set Organisation of the Jie Tribe' in *Journal of the Royal Anthropological Institute*, 83, 147-68.
———. 1968. 'Age Differentiation' in *International Encyclopaedia of the Social Sciences*, Vol. 1. New York.
McIntosh, P.C. 1971. 'An Historical View of Sport and Social Control', in *International Review of Sport Sociology*, Vol. 6. Warsaw.
Pratt, D.T., Greenway, P.J., and Gwynne, M.D. 'A Classification of East African Rangeland, with an Appendix on Terminology' in *Journal of Applied Ecology*, V, 3, 369-81.
Sahlins, M.D. 1961. 'The Segmentary Lineage: An Organisation of Predatory Expansion' in *American Anthropologist*, 63, 322-45.
Sahlins, M.D. 1968. *Tribesmen*. Englewood Cliffs. N.J.
Spencer, P. 1965. *The Samburu: A Study of Gerontocracy in a Nomadic Tribe*. London.
———. 1970. 'The Function of Ritual in the Socialisation of the Samburu Moran' in P. Mayer (ed.), *Socialisation: The Approach from Anthropology*, A.S.A. Monograph. London.
———. 1976. 'Opposing Streams and the Gerontocratic Ladder: Two Models of Age Organisation in East Africa' in *Man* (N.S.), 11, 153-75.
Tucker, A.N. and Brayn, M.A. 1956. *The Non-Bantu Languages of North-Eastern Africa*, Part III of *The Handbook of African Languages*. London.
Turton, D.A. and Bender, M.L. 1976. 'Mursi' in M.L. Bender (ed.), *The Non-Semitic Languages of Ethiopia*. Lansing, Michigan.
Turton, D.A. 'A journey made them: territorial segmentation and ethnic identity among the Mursi' in L. Holy (ed.), *Segmentary Lineage Systems Reconsidered*. Queen's University, Belfast (in press).

V
The Jie Generation Paradox
PAUL SPENCER

The problem

The age span of descendants from a single ancestor increases within each successive generation, so that 'generation' becomes increasingly an inappropriate criterion for membership of a single age-set. The paradox of the Jie age organisation is that this is precisely the criterion they use, and they are said to adhere to it inflexibly. Referring to the age group based on a single generation as a 'generation-set', the four principles listed by Gulliver (1953:147-8) for the Jie are as follows:

Rule 1. *All* the members of one generation must have been initiated before *any* members of the next generation can be initiated. In other words, only one generation-set at a time can be open to recruitment.
Rule 2. A man *must* belong to a generation-set immediately following that of his father.
Rule 3. When a new generation-set is formed and its first initiations take place, at least some members of the grandfather's generation-set should still be alive.
Rule 4. Within each generation-set, there is a grouping of men of broadly the same age into named age-sets.

This exercise is primarily concerned with the anomalies that arise from the first two rules. As Gulliver points out: 'It will be appreciated that when a new generation begins to form sets there will be a large waiting list of men, some of whom will be middle-aged or more.' At the same time the youngest members of the previous generation will probably have to be initiated well before the usual age of about twenty years because of the pressures towards the formation of the next generation-set (Gulliver 1953a:152, 154; 1953b:44; 1958:920; cf. Lamphear 1976:38-40). Neither Gulliver as an anthropologist nor Lamphear as a historian consider at any length the extent to which this problem might increase with each generation if these rules are followed systematically.

The problem is aggravated by the practice of polygyny whereby some rather elderly men continue to take on junior wives, and by a form of widow inheritance whereby widows do not remarry, but continue to have children on behalf of their late husbands. Thus, even though a man's first marriage tends to be relatively late when he is perhaps thirty years or more, it is quite possible for there to be an age difference of fifty years between the first son of his first wife and the last son of his most junior widow.[1] In the next generation this gap between oldest and youngest could conceivably increase to 100 years, and to 150 years in the next and so on.

A possible solution to the problem of cumulative mismatch between age and generation is simply that the system is comparatively new and short-lived. It cannot persist, but must break down as the spread of ages increases with successive generations. It could be significant for instance that Gulliver studied the Jie in 1950 and confidently reported that there could be no violation of Rule 1: no new generation-set could be formed until all members of its predecessor had been initiated. Whereas Lamphear in 1971 noted that eight years after the formation of a new generation-set, there continued to be parallel recruitment by this new set *and* by its predecessor, and hence a measure of overlap despite Rule 1 (Lamphear 1976:45). This could be a symptom of the conflict between Rule 1 and Rule 2, in which case the period of overlap could be expected to increase with each future generation until there is continuous initiation of all living generations. This is in fact very close to the situation reported for the Turkana who have a myth of earlier descent from the Jie and give one a distinct impression of an earlier breakdown of the Jie system (Gulliver 1953b:53; 1958:920-1). Another neighbour of the Jie with a similar generation-set system are the Karimojong, and Dyson-Hudson (1966: 199) noted in 1956, before the formation of a new generation-set, that their system came close to breaking down, experiencing an 'aberration ... beyond the tolerance of the system.' However, with the change-over, one may note that the Karimojong system did not ultimately break down, but displayed a return to traditional order. Equally, from Lamphear's account the Jie system is clearly not new, nor is it said to be breaking down. The breakdown of the Turkana system is normally ascribed to their entering a different and more demanding environment that entailed a greater dispersal of population, whereas 'the Jie make conscious efforts to prevent a mixing of successive generations in order to prevent a breakdown of the formal structure' (Gulliver 1958: 920) and 'the Jie are adamant that the basic principle of their system can never be broken' (Lamphear 1976:35).

An alternative solution is that the system may have certain slip mechanisms which allow those men who are too young to drop a generation unobtrusively (or those who are too old to climb up). One of the major differences between the Karimojong and Jie systems is that the Karimojong admit to having such a mechanism for the most junior members of a generation whereas this is denied for the Jie. In this respect the Karimojong pose less of a dilemma and are more flexible. In another respect, however, the Karimojong have the more rigid system: no uninitiated man among the Karamojong may marry or raid or claim adult status, whereas these restrictions do not apply to the Jie. (Dyson-Hudson 1966:202-4; Gulliver 1953a:158; Lamphear 1976:36n).

Frank Stewart (1977) has recently proposed a solution to the paradox based principally on the notion of slip mechanisms. Among the Karimojong, he suggests, the flexibility which permits the youngest members of a generation to slip down to the next set takes care of the problem of underaging: those who are underaged for one generation become a suitable age for the next. This does not apply to the oldest sons who are overaged in relation to their generation-sets, and these have to wait. However, because of the restriction that prevents their marriage before initiation, they marry late and their oldest sons are born late. Hence these sons will not be more overaged than their fathers, and the problem is not a cumulative one.

This neat explanation cannot be applied to the Jie since they do not permit slipping by the underaged nor do they prevent normal marriage among the overaged; and hence the age span between senior and junior lines is likely to increase with each generation. To resolve this, Stewart (1977:220 ff.) suggests that the Jie slip without realising it. He evokes the notion of 'structural amnesia' which Gulliver discusses for the Jie (1955:113-7). As Gulliver presents it, this entails a process whereby the broad proliferating lineage of descendants from several brothers or cousins is tacitly narrowed down as less well remembered ancestors are forgotten and their descendants transfer their putative descent to better remembered men, former cousins become 'brothers', and distantly related lineages are drawn together. All Gulliver's illustrations refer to processes of this kind which do not violate the generation principle. Nowhere does Gulliver suggest that an ancestor may actually slip a generation. Stewart, however, suggests that this is precisely what does happen. In the process, he suggests, men who are grossly underaged identify their barely remembered ancestors with generations junior to the ones they might in reality have belonged to. In other words, Gulliver suggests a certain lateral amnesia in the context of discussing the dynamics of Jie descent groups, while Stewart shifts the context to the dynamics of the age organisation and proposes a certain vertical amnesia also.

Clearly Stewart has a point. Yet one notes again Gulliver's contention that 'the Jie make conscious efforts to prevent a mixing of successive generations in order to prevent a breakdown of the formal structure', while Stewart's evoking a notion of amnesia in this context implies that this is rather a shallow consciousness. The impression one has from Gulliver is of structural amnesia as a process which in constantly narrowing down the span of a lineage and coalescing ancestors serves to keep that lineage as a tight social unit in which generation is a more important principle for organisation than strict descent, whereas Stewart's extension of this notion implies a more fluid system altogether. If one accepts Stewart's explanation, then why should the Jie (and not the Karimojong also) deny it? Consistent with Gulliver's model, Lamphear's whole exercise is based on the strong corporate nature of Jie clans and of subgroups within a clan on the one hand, and of strict adherence to generational principles on the other (Lamphear 1976:23-4, 35).

Later in this exercise, a further possible solution to the problem of over- and under-aging based on Lamphear's historical material is considered. First, however, this search for hypothetical slip-mechanisms is surely skirting round the central issue. Without demographic data indicating the profile of age span with successive generations, one just does not know the extent of the problem. Societies with age organisations are ideally suited for providing an indication of true age in relation to demographic problems of this kind. Unfortunately, the Jie age system with its generational constraints is almost the worst conceivable, and to describe the sub-groups within each generation-set as 'age-sets' is up to a point a misnomer (cf. Gulliver 1953a:154). But in any case, none of the authors provide suitable census data and none found the apparent anomaly worth exploring. Each emphasises the importance of the basic rules, while the existence of slip mechanisms even among the Karimojong at a time of change-over and maximum strain is treated as a minor issue; the underaged are regarded by Dyson-Hudson (1966:204) strictly as borderline cases that can be dealt with as they occur without posing a major anomaly.

The problem in demographic terms is an issue that Stewart considers closely with reference to data collected in the United States. He is fully aware of the pitfalls of using such data from an advanced sector of Western civilisation and applying it to remote societies such as the Jie, and his discussion on this topic is therefore somewhat inconclusive.

Stewart (1977:55) does, however, make a tentative suggestion to which I must pay tribute, since the remainder of this chapter stems from this: 'We do not have all the demographic information necessary in order to form a clear idea of these generational processes among the Jie (though I imagine that one could combine what we do know about the Jie with data on more or less similar peoples and produce a hypothetical projection).' This is to suggest a mock-up, a simulation of the Jie system to explore it further. In fact, the right conditions do appear to exist among the Samburu for whom the relevant data are at least available. The Samburu are neighbours of the Turkana, and share many features in common with the Jie, including a similar pastoral basis to their economy, similar rules regarding the continued fertility of young widows on behalf of their late husbands, and first marriage for men normally after the age of thirty. This age of first marriage is generally a useful indicator of the range of polygyny which would therefore probably be similar among the Samburu and the Jie. Above all, with their non-generational type of age organisation, the Samburu lend themselves readily to age censuses, and this lends itself in turn to a simulation of the Jie system.[2]

The simulation

The basic assumption in this exercise is that demographically the Samburu are sufficiently similar to the Jie in terms of expectations of survival throughout life, age at first marriage, distribution of wives and fertility rates. Two points should be noted at once. The first is that among the Jie (unlike their Karimojong neighbours) the senior members of a generation do not have to delay their marriage until initiation; and for purposes of simulation this is a complication that need not concern us. Secondly Stewart cites the work of demographers who have based their calculations on *female* fertility and life expectation: it is the women who have babies and 'generation' is calculated along the female line. From a Jie point of view, however, it is the generations of men (alive or dead) and of sons born in their name that count. Thus somewhat perversely one is concerned with the 'fertility' of men, and calculations are based on the male line.

Table V.1 is derived from genealogical data for 646 males of a Samburu clan for whom data were available on their age-sets and those of their fathers. Age-sets were spaced apart by about fourteen and a half years, and this provided a base for estimating the range of age differences between fathers and sons.[3]

Table V.1. Age differences between Samburu fathers and sons

age-set	average span of time between age-set 'J' and subsequent age-sets.	recorded proportion of sons of 'J' in each age-set (age-set profile of second generation). %
'J' [age-set of members of first generation]		
'K'		
'L'	29.0 years	0.9
'M'	43.5 "	52.6
'N'	58.0 "	33.6
'O'	72.5 "	10.5
'P'	87.0 "	2.2
'Q'	101.5 "	0.2
Total		100.0

Source: Samburu clan census, Spencer 1965: 318-21. Sample base 646.

From this table one can extrapolate the spread of successive generations on the assumption that the third generation will bear a similar relation to the second as the second does to the first and so on.[4] In this way each generation is assumed to have the same 'fertility' rate as its predecessor and to differ only in its age profile. Figure V.1 indicates the spread of successive generations extrapolated from this table. It has been deliberately drawn on the assumption that there is no population growth, and hence the areas bounded by all curves are identical and the populations they represent for each generation are constant. The first curve is taken directly from the table, and subsequent curves are derived from it.

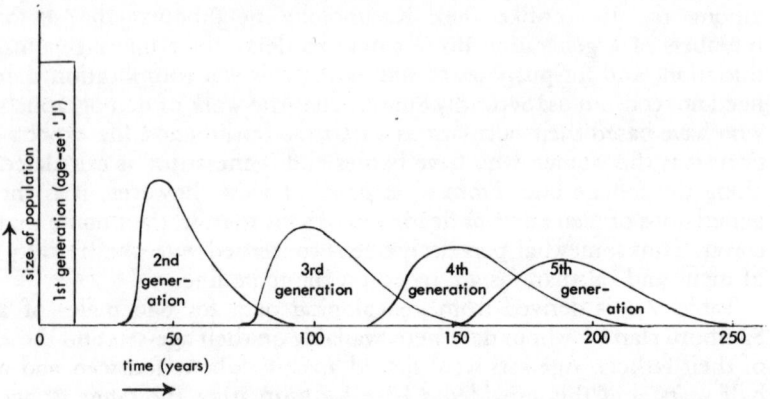

Figure V.1. Age spread of successive generations (Samburu clan census)

It may readily be seen in Figure V.1 that there is an increasing overlap between generations so that while there is a distinct gap between the first and second generations, there would in due course be a discernible overlap between the third and fifth. This is a clear indication of the extent to which the Jie system would get out of hand if the rules were applied systematically: the period of overlap (noted by Lamphear) would have to increase to a point where there is continuous overlap. One therefore has to look more closely at the problem in its early stages to discern how this runaway threat can be contained.

Gulliver estimates the interval between successive generation-sets at 20-25-30 years (1953a:148, 1953b:44), an interval which Lamphear (1976:45) and Stewart (1977:76) both question. However, Lamphear's own estimate of an interval of forty years is itself questionable; he himself suggests a mean age difference between a man and his eldest surviving son of perhaps thirty-five to forty years, and this would itself imply that the interval is geared to the senior line, while junior lines stemming from younger sons would progressively become underaged (Lamphear 1976:39n; cf. Stewart 1977:48). Table V.1 indicates that an interval of forty years would imply very serious underaging. On the other hand, again with reference to Table V.1, if there were an interval of eighty years between successive generation-sets, then there would be even more serious overaging.

The crudest and in some ways the safest assumption would be that the system is most likely to run with minimum difficulties if the span between successive generation-sets is identical to the average age differences between (Samburu) generations. Table V.1 suggests a span of about fifty-two years.

The next three graphs (also derived from Table V.1) approach the problem from a different direction.[5] Figure V.2 indicates the decrease in the proportion of younger sons who are too young for initiation during the period that their generation-set is open for recruitment as the span is varied from thirty years up to ninety years. Figure V.3 indicates the corresponding increase in the proportion of older sons who are too old, and have to wait as mature adults for their initiation into a new generation-set. These are the misfits of the system.

The upper curves marked 'A' show those who will be exactly twenty years old during the period that their generation-set is recruiting members. However, there appears to be a range of tolerance of about ten years on either side of this ideal age for initiation; even a man who has to wait until the age of thirty is unlikely to be married at that point, while some boys of ten years can if necessary be initiated (Gulliver 1953a:154; 1955:242; Lamphear 1976:33, 38, 40). The lower curves marked 'B' indicate the proportions of 'gross misfits': those who are beyond this range of tolerance and are grossly over- or under-aged. Thus the shaded areas between these curves represent the 'mild misfits' who lie within the range of tolerance.

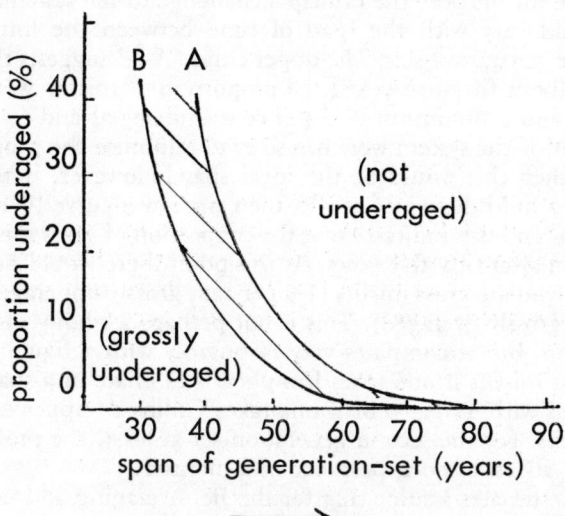

Figure V.2. Proportion of underaging at the tail-end of a closing generation-set

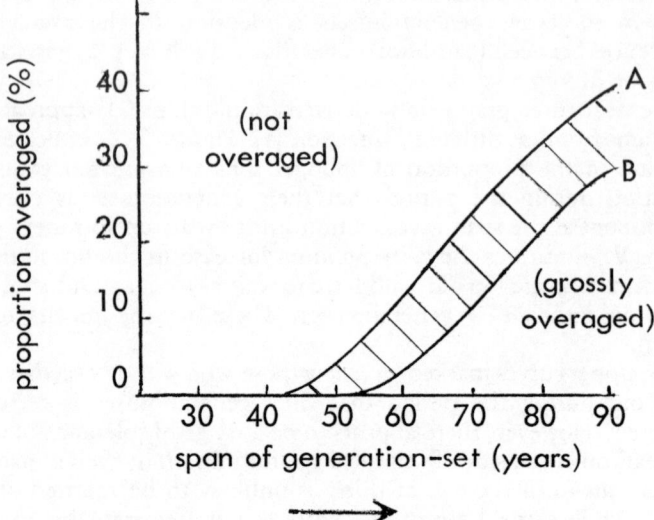

Figure V.3. Proportion of overaging in the vanguard of a new generation-set

Figure V.4 combines these two graphs and indicates the extent to which the misfits pose the principal challenge to the system, and how this would vary with the span of time between the formation of successive generation-sets. The upper curve 'A-A' suggests that with a span of about fifty-one years, the proportion of misfits would be 15 per cent and a minimum (8.5 per cent underaged and 6.5 per cent overaged). If the system were run so as to minimise the proportion of misfits, then this would be the ideal span. However, if the system tolerates a mild degree of misfit, then the lower curve 'B-B' is more pertinent, and this indicates that the proportion of gross misfits is at a minimum after fifty-five years. At this point there would only be 2.5 per cent who are gross misfits (1.9 per cent grossly underaged and 0.6 per cent grossly overaged). This is not perhaps a wholly insignificant proportion, but it compares very favourably with a figure of 12 per cent gross misfits if one takes Lamphear's estimate of a span of forty years, and with 41 per cent if one takes Gulliver's upper estimate of thirty years. For the second generation-set at least, the problem does not after all have the appearance of a monster.

These estimates assume that for the Jie, overaging and underaging are equally undesirable. On the other hand, the rule that prohibits an overlap of successive generation-sets while recruiting could be taken to imply that the system tolerates overaging and delay better than it

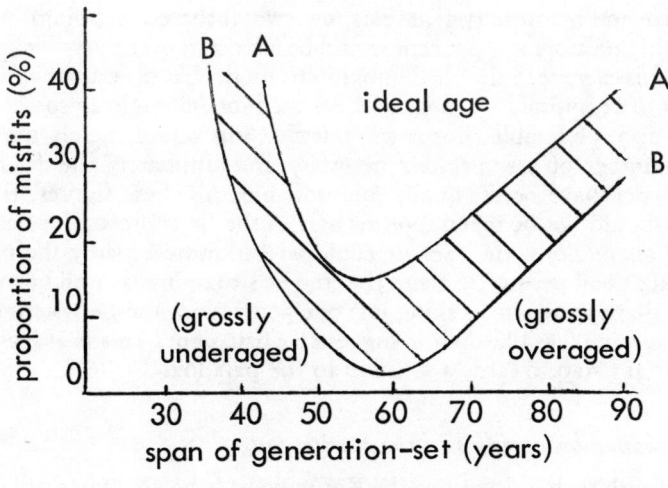

Figure V.4. Proportion of misfits (underaged and overaged) with varying span for generation-sets

tolerates underaging and an early change-over. If, for instance, at a time of change-over the Jie rate *two* grossly overaged men as no worse than *one* grossly underaged, then the optimum span would be fifty-six years; if *three* grossly overaged men are no worse than *one* grossly underaged then the optimum span would be fifty-seven years; and so on. In other words, the optimum is not especially sensitive to assumptions regarding the balance of undesirability.

Altogether, whatever the assumptions, one has a reasonably consistent estimate for an ideal generation-set span of about fifty-five years. At this span for the second generation, there would be 84.3 per cent who would reach the age of twenty years for initiation during the fifty-five year period of formal recruitment. There would be 10 per cent overaged before their set formally opened (9.4 per cent between 21-30 years and 0.6 per cent between 31-36 years), and at its close there would still be 5.7 per cent who are underaged (3.8 per cent between 10-19 years, 1.5 per cent between 0-9 years, and 0.4 per cent as yet unborn). Unless there is some slip mechanism to accommodate the gross misfits amounting to 2.5 per cent then this problem would be magnified in the third generation-set and progressively get out of hand.

It is possible at this point also to comment on Rule 3: that at the time of change-over the most senior generation-set who stopped recruiting some fifty-five years previously should still be alive but rapidly dwindling. Very roughly, the data on which this exercise is based suggest that at the third change-over since the inauguration of the system, only about 1¼ per cent of the second generation-set would still be alive and below sixty-five years (or fewer if there is slipping), while a further possible 2½ per cent would be alive and over sixty-five years.

In this exercise, a simple demographic model has been used without resort to a computer. A more sophisticated model might in some ways have been preferable, but it was felt that this would merely increase the number of assumptions necessary and ultimately the findings could well have been equally questionable. All these figures, therefore, should not be taken too precisely in the Jie context. Yet despite these reservations, the exercise could well indicate broadly the problem in a good perspective, and the true Jie situation may well be of the same shape and form. Taking just one generation, the Jie system does appear more feasible than it suggests at first sight. This is at least an important step towards a solution to the paradox.

The change-over crisis and the Karimojong

Faced with such a situation, the Karimojong, who are remarkably like the Jie in other ways, would have resolved the problem of cumulative misfit simply by allowing the (1.9 per cent) grossly underaged to slip a generation and by delaying the first marriage of the (0.6 per cent) grossly overaged by up to six years. Given the smallness of these anomalies, one appreciates the fact that Dyson-Hudson refers to these as borderline cases.

The value of Dyson-Hudson's study is that he undertook it at a critical point when a new generation-set was being formed by *fait accompli*. He provides some indication of how the system does in fact work, rather than how it could be made to work by some experimentally minded Samburu. Like Gulliver, Dyson-Hudson envisaged an ideal generation-set span of thirty years at most, and sought to explain the fact that the closing set had been recruiting for fifty-seven years partly because of recurrent drought and partly because the system itself under modern conditions was breaking down. Up to the time of change-over, there was increasing unrest as more and more uninitiated men took the law into their own hands, raiding when as 'boys' they had no right to raid, assuming personal ornaments to which they had no right, and even marrying prematurely. The fact that the situation was getting out of hand precipitated the change-over ceremony and the formation of a new generation-set; and this in turn led to a re-emergence of the traditional order as the older men succeeded in reasserting their authority. The deviants were now fully within the generation-set system and more directly under the control of the elders (Dyson-Hudson 1966:198-9).

A striking feature here is the proximity of the observed span of fifty-seven years to the simulated span of about fifty-five years. This prompts one to suggest that the symptoms of disorder, delay and innovation which Dyson-Hudson regarded as indications of eventual breakdown of the total system under modern pressures might in reality be indicative of the way in which the traditional system actually works (present tense). During the period leading up to a change-over, one infers, there is always an explosive situation with an increasing number of mature 'boys' who find the restrictions of the system increasingly irksome. As their numbers swell, the physical restraints that have governed them throughout their lives are no longer effective; and so long as they are kept outside the generation-set system they are not morally bound by the rules of respect for the more senior men within that organisation and are up to a point outlaws — and behave as such. Moral authority can only be exerted by permitting a change-over and bringing them into the system. The situation forces the elders' hand and a change-over ceremony is held.

Turning once again to the simulation, Figures V.2, 3, and 4 were presented previously in static terms to examine the implications of different generation-set spans on the problems of over- and underaging. If one now redefines the horizontal axis of these diagrams as 'years lapsed since the previous change-over' and the vertical axis as 'strain towards a change-over', then Figure 2 indicates a negative strain, with pressures for deferring a change-over until the underaged have come of age; and Figure 3 indicates the increasing positive strain towards change-over. The left-hand portion of Figure 4 indicates how during the first fifty-five years there is a decreasing pressure against change-over. Then after that point the pressures for a change-over increase very sharply. By the year sixty-one there would be an eight-fold increase in gross overaging over the previous six years (from 0.6 per cent to 4.7 per cent), while gross underaging would have decreased by two-thirds (from 1.9 per cent to 0.6 per cent). Thus while the problems of underaging at the tail-end of the retiring age-set slowly dwindle and continue to delay the change-over, the overaging of the unformed generation-set rapidly builds up and threatens the system. It is this build-up that sounds the warning to the elders and triggers off a new generation-set. In this way, the events observed by Dyson-Hudson appear to have their counterpart in the simulated model.

A similar process could occur among the Jie, except for Gulliver's insistence that the generation-set system and its associated ritual have little or no economic or political importance (Gulliver 1953a:164). Elsewhere I have questioned this and suggested that the system is more closely related to social control and the rules of respect for age than Gulliver concedes; from his own material, for instance, it does appear to play an important role in controlling the queue of bachelors for wives, and ultimately in celebrating the wedding itself (Spencer 1976:171). Lamphear independently confirms this impression noting the great respect that Jie should have for younger men of a senior generation-set, and the control that members of the senior generation-set have over the movement of cattle: 'To the Jie, seniority can be achieved only within the context of the generation-set system'; in the past, the authority and powers of the elders were of economic, judicial and political as well as of ritual relevance (Lamphear 1976:34-5, 36n, 153, 155, 157). Taking all this evidence together, one has a clear impression that the emphasis on generation-set ritual is a key feature in the moral order of Jie society and that any anomaly and challenge to the rules of precedence at a time of change-over would be an anomaly and challenge to the moral order itself.

The Jie and Karimojong may differ in their precise handling of the misfits, but essentially the dynamics of the generation-set systems are probably very similar, especially over a period of change-over. Certainly Gulliver does not offer any alternative model that could account for the persistence of the Jie system.

Jie and Karimojong: historical implications

All three authors stress the close links between the Jie and Karimojong despite their hostility towards one another: Gulliver (1952, 1953b: 28ff.) in environmental and ethnographic terms, Dyson-Hudson (1966:258ff) in terms of an evolutionary model, and Lamphear (1976) in terms of their oral histories. The contrasts between the accounts of Gulliver and Dyson-Hudson may partly reflect the fact that the latter undertook his study at a time of change-over when the strains accompanying the formation of a new generation-set were critical, while the former did not. Here I want to consider evidence that suggests that the Jie system is actually breaking down after all.

The authors agree that the Jie and Karimojong have a common origin. Lamphear (1976:107, 140, 200) estimates that an initial split into two separate groups by the early years of the eighteenth century led to the emergence of distinct Jie and Karimojong communities by about 1770 and 1840 respectively. Thus any significant differences between them today should have evolved since 1700. Lamphear does not focus on possible changes in the rules of the generation-set systems, but rather on the fact that prior to 1880 the Jie were a relatively small disorganised group whose warfare was based on the prowess of private companies of individualists underpinned by the generation-set organisation. Among their principal enemies were the Karimojong to the south and the Dodos to the north, each similarly organised to the Jie, but altogether superior in numbers. At this time, the Jie were clearly dominated by these more powerful neighbours (including also the Acholi to the west), and their survival as a group was threatened. The climax of his account is the emergence of a Jie leader between 1880 and 1910 who completely reversed their fortunes through his military and diplomatic skills. His initial step was to reorganise the principles on which the Jie army was based. He 'substituted an organisation based on . . . territorial divisions in place of the more unwieldy traditional organisation based on generation- and age-sets'. With this reorganisation, he led the Jie to take the offensive against their enemies and maintained their superiority until the advent of administration in the area. Lamphear does not suggest that in this process there was a clear change in the rules underlying the generation-set system, although it is clear that such changes as occurred were undertaken with full connivance of the senior elders and backed up by their ritual sanctions. Biological age rather than generation as such now played an important part in the newly organised army with clear roles for the older veterans, the younger warriors, and even [uninitiated] boys to gain their first battle experience. The inclusion of boys was consistent with the incorporation of other non-traditional elements to swell his small army. This reorganisation for survival appears to have been more profound than any other change that Lamphear reports and is specifically not matched by any corresponding reorganisation among the Karimojong or the Dodos (Lamphear 1976:230, 231, 233, 238, 239, 247).

For want of any alternative evidence, I would suggest that the Jie had a system similar to the Karimojong prior to 1880, and that the slip mechanisms to combat underaging and the constraints against serious overaging (as suggested by Frank Stewart, see above) would have applied to the Jie at that time. This is to infer that among the innovations of reorganisation which identified true age rather than generation as a key to effective warfare, uninitiated adults were incorporated into the Jie army along with men of a senior generation but similar age, and that this constraint which still persists among the Karimojong was first loosened among the Jie. It is a short step from this to suggest that once these men had been given the right to participate as full adults in this critical aspect of Jie survival, the prior restrictions to their marriage before initiation were also lifted:[6] generation as such had become an irrelevance and a significant step had been taken towards Gulliver's model of pure ritual somewhat separated (if not altogether divorced) from ultimate power.

However, removing the restriction on marriage among the uninitiated would also have removed a vital constraint on cumulative overaging: an overaged oldest son could now marry sooner, and his oldest son in due course could be even more overaged and marry even sooner. This would bring forward the pressures of overaging which could only be resolved by bringing forward also the formation of a new generation-set (in 1963). However this expedient would only serve to replace endemic overaging with a new situation of endemic underaging and increase the pressure to keep the retiring generation-set open to recruitment after the new generation-set has also been opened, thus modifying Rule 1. In fact one would have a situation very similar to that recorded by Lamphear in 1970.

Lamphear's chronology for the Jie is based on the assumption that the ideal span for successive generation-sets is of the order of forty years. However, if until recently they have had a system that is closer to the Karimojong then a more appropriate span would be of the order of fifty-five years. The following revised chronology which summarises the present argument is based on a presumed span of fifty-five years.

Table V.2. Revised Jie chronology
(following Lamphear 1976:36-7)

Generation-set	Suggested year of formation	Comments
Ngisir	1590	(ancestral group of Jie, Karimojong and Dodos)
Nigpalajam	1645	
Ngikok	1700	(Jie community emerges after this date, but no initial change to generation-set system)
Ngisiroi	1755	
Ngikokol	1810	
Ngikosowa	1865	(Jie generation-set rules modified after this date. First signs of overaging appear in about 1900, and these men are allowed to marry)
Ngimugeto	1920-3	(followed by Gulliver's study in 1950-1. He notes already considerable signs of overaging but reports strict adherence to Rule 1)
Ngitome	1963	(formed after an interval of only forty years because [it is suggested here] of the pressure from overaging due to the innovations of 1865 onwards. However Ngimugeto tail-end were still underaged, and they continued to recruit. When Lamphear left in 1971, this divergence from Rule 1 was still expected to continue.)

Thus ironically, while Gulliver and Lamphear give a clear impression that the Jie system persists intact and Dyson-Hudson suggests that the Karimojong system is breaking down, here I am suggesting that the two situations are reversed. Dyson-Hudson's evidence for breakdown appears quite normal in the situation of change-over and his span of fifty-seven years is not necessarily abnormal. The Jie evidence is more disturbing: it indicates serious overaging before the change-over of 1963 followed by serious underaging (possibly for the first time); the period since the previous change-over of only 40-43 years appears surprisingly short unless it is the consequence of cumulative pressures that will continue into future generation-sets. These could be symptoms of a breakdown of the Jie system rather as the Turkana system appears to have done in an earlier era.

Conclusions

In a number of ways this exercise is incomplete. The crudeness of the demographic model has already been noted. The simulation did not adequately consider the cumulative effect of misfitting after a succession of generations, but tacitly assumed that slip mechanisms would intervene at each change-over to prevent accumulation. The discussion on the Jie has not accounted for the apparent lack of slip mechanisms for the underaged, and again one is driven to assume that there must be, and always has been, some degree of slipping despite adamant claims to the contrary. Other nuances of the system and of the differences reported for Jie and Karimojong have been ignored.

The central feature of these generation-set systems as I understand them, however, is not their slip mechanisms or otherwise to accommodate misfits, nor the precise historical development of some of the associated rules. It is the problem of denying younger men a measure of power by maintaining a system that restricts privileges associated with wives, warfare and even (in their terms) personal ornaments. Not all age systems are necessarily gerontocracies, but this does appear true of the type considered here — or perhaps one might more accurately refer to it as a 'classificatory patriarchy'. It is a system which effectively pins down the youngest generation for a period and thereby interferes with a natural process of social development associated with age and maturation. In its immediate effect, it works in favour of the more senior generations who can monopolise the privileges, but ultimately it provokes a crisis as the younger generation become increasingly restless and capable of taking the law into their own hands, and the elders have to come to terms with this fact. The paradox of the system lies in the claim that there is an adamant adherence to the rules: no new generation-set can be formed until *all* the previous set have been initiated; nor until nearly all the set prior to that have died. If, however, this adamant insistence is interpreted as the rhetoric of elders determined to pin down the junior generation, then it does at least allow for a more pragmatic approach once the process has reached a critical stage. They are presumably rules intended to dominate and delay rather than rules that are strictly adhered to when the position becomes untenable.

The generation-set system is an imperfect formula which serves a central purpose. Alternative formulae with similar aims exist in East Africa and appear to display similar characteristics. Dyson-Hudson's account of the near chaos leading to the Karimojong change-over in 1956 and a subsequent return to traditional order is closely paralleled by an account of events leading up to and following the Arusha age-set change-over in 1959 (Gulliver 1962:447). Elsewhere in a separate exercise, I sought to relate the 13-14 year cycle of the Samburu age-set system to demographic factors associated with the privileges, especially marriage, that were monopolised by the older men in order to account for a certain oscillation in the system (Spencer 1965:167ff.). In effect the Samburu elders appear to have had similar aims to the Karimojong and (presumably) Jie, but were applying a different formula that entailed a more frequent but equally predictable cycle of events.

Thus the most important clue to a problem that appears at first sight to be one that accumulates with each successive generation lies in the notion of a developmental cycle with its characteristic build-up of pressures leading to a crisis point and the formation of a new generation-set. The notion of developmental cycles is more often associated with studies of the family where, by taking a sample of families at different stages of development, the anthropologist can place these along a continuum and identify the salient features. This is less easily done in the study of age organisations since with a sample of only one society and age-set system at one point in time, most anthropologists can only witness one phase in a more extended process. Nevertheless the age- or generation-set cycle is as much a process as a family and the realities of the system can perhaps only be understood in relation to the dynamics of this process.

It would be unfair to imply that the three ethnographers did not appreciate the developmental implications of the generation-set systems they studied or that they tended to gloss over them in their analyses. It is true to say, though, that the situations they witnessed typified different points of the total cycle, and it is only because of the rich ethnographic coverage they provide that a reconstruction of one rather critical feature of the system that they appear to have overlooked becomes possible.

NOTES

1 These figures are based on demographic data for the Samburu. It is later argued that the Samburu and Jie are comparable in this respect.
2 Gulliver 1953b:43; 1955:242; Lamphear 1977:33; cf. Spencer 1965:86, 96, 219. In one minor respect there is a generational constraint on the most senior Samburu sons of a generation who in theory should not be initiated into an age-set less than three below their father. A test on the Samburu data, however, indicated that any delay resulting from this does not lead to any discernible bunching into the first available sub-age-set: on average a Samburu has the same proportion of sons in the senior sub-set of the first available age-set (131/340) as he has in the senior sub-set of subsequent age-sets (120/300).
3 My earlier estimates of the period of the Samburu age-set cycle varied from thirteen years (1965:154) to fourteen years (1973:149). The present figure of thirteen and a half years is a deliberate compromise. Coupled with this is the lowering of the age of initiation by about one year per age-set over the period to which the data in Table V.1. refers. Thus for purposes of estimating the span between adjacent generations, age-sets were effectively spaced apart by an estimated fourteen and a half years.

4 This extrapolation for the third generation entails multiplying the final column by itself, so to speak. Thus 52.6 per cent of the second generation, who belong to age-set 'M' [= 'J' + 3], have 52.6 per cent of their sons in age-set 'P' [= 'M' + 3], and 33.6 per cent in age-set 'Q' and so on.
5 This again entailed extrapolation from Table V.1. Thus to estimate the spread of population with a span of fifty-eight years (equivalent to 4 × 14½ year age-set periods), it was assumed that the first generation were equally divided between age-sets 'J'. 'K', 'L', and 'M', and then the aggregate profile of age distribution of their sons was calculated accordingly. A graphical method was used to estimate the age spread of the first generation for periods not exactly divisible by fourteen and a half years.
6 Lamphear (1976:33) quotes the Jie as complaining: 'You people are growing up faster nowadays than in the past. Even children are marrying these days.' He interprets this as an allusion to the occasional marriage of men in their late twenties. Given the emphasis that the Jie also place on generation as well as age, however, it could quite conceivably be an allusion to the recent marriages and social recognition of mature uninitiated men who in Jie terms would also be 'children'.

BIBLIOGRAPHY

Dyson-Hudson, N. 1966. *Karimojong Politics*. Oxford.
Gulliver, P.H. 1952. 'The Karimojong cluster'. *Africa* 22, 1-21.
———. 1953a. 'The age organization of the Jie tribe'. *J.R.anthrop.Inst.* 83, 147-68.
———. 1953b. *The Central Nilo-Hamites* (Ethnographic Survey of Africa). London.
———. 1955. *The Family Herds*. London.
———. 1958. 'The Turkana age organization'. *American Anthropologist*, 60, 900-22.
———. 1962. 'The evolution of Arusha trade' in P. Bohannan and G. Dalton (eds), *Markets in Africa*. Evanston, Ill. Northwestern UP.
Lamphear, J. 1976. *The Traditional History of the Jie of Uganda*. Oxford.
Spencer, P. 1965. *The Samburu: a study of gerontocracy in a nomadic tribe*. London.
———. 1973. *Nomads in alliance: symbiosis and growth among the Rendille and Samburu of Kenya*. London.
———. 1976. 'Opposing streams and the gerontocratic ladder: two models of age organization in east Africa'. *Man* (N.S.), 11, 153-74.
Stewart, F.H. 1977. *Fundamentals of Age-group Systems*. London.

VI
Boran Age-sets and Generation-Sets: *Gada*, a Puzzle or a Maze?

P.T.W. BAXTER

1

The Oromo (Galla) speaking peoples were described by Seligman in 1930, summarising the knowledge of the time, as 'perhaps the most interesting people in Abyssinia.'[1] They are also by far the most numerous. They have especially captured the imaginations of travellers and ethnographers because of their ancient, enduring and complex system of age-grading, *gada*,* which, it has been consistently reported, has also served as the basis of a uniquely democratic political system.

The Boran have been assumed to be the ancestors of all the Oromo and the group above all which, relatively undisturbed by colonial rulers and economic and social changes, has maintained the ancient age-grading and political systems of *gada*. Other obviously distinctive features of Boran are that they are divided into exogamous moieties, that they have two hereditary ritual leaders (*Kaallu*) and are fairly straightforwardly monotheistic. The antiquity and complexities of the *gada* system are not in doubt, and I hope to establish the former and unravel some of the latter.

All accounts agree, in general terms, about certain central features of *gada* as a system of generation sets. These are: (*a*) A set of men assumes certain responsibilities on behalf of the nation for a fixed and standard time segment of eight years. For this period a set is usually described as 'ruling' or in 'power', or 'in office', and as 'retiring' when that period is completed. Set membership and set movement are both ascribed. (*b*) At a fixed and standard interval after a set has

---

*Because there is no single system for transcribing Oromo into English, confusion arises from the very form that the word *gada* takes. In transcribing Boran I have found the most satisfactory form to be *gaada*, and this form is kept in other related words such as *Aba gaada* and *gaadamoji*. The form *gada* has, however, been widely absorbed into the vocabulary of anthropology. In order not to confuse the reader more than can be helped, I shall use the form *gada* when referring to the system in the general sense, but when referring to that particular age-grade — and its members — which occurs in Boran society between *raaba* and *gaadamoji*, I shall retain the form *gaada* in order to preserve consistency within my system of transcription from Boran.

'retired', usually forty years, the set of its sons assumes 'office'. A set, therefore, consists of men who are all of the same genealogical generation. (*c*) A set of 'sons' cannot directly succeed the set of its 'fathers'. (*d*) There must always be a set in 'office' to ensure the welfare and continuity (the 'Peace') of the Boran nation. (*e*) Sets are sometimes called on to expend a great deal of stock and time on rituals.

It follows that if sons succeed fathers after a fixed interval then, *either* there must be other rules which control the span of time during which men may father sons, *or* there must be exceptions to the rules. Also, if there must always be a set in office and sons may not follow fathers then there must be other lines of fathers and sons to fill the time gap. If the gap is forty years, and each set has an eight year period in office, then there should be four other such lines.

The *gada* 'puzzle' or 'problem' (Legesse 1973: Ch. 4 and 1963:18) is that such a system, which defies demographic and political common sense, can work and have endured. I shall suggest that the complexities which *gada* has generated do not so much make a puzzle, which implies a solution, but are like a maze through which a way can be found. I shall also suggest that two of the difficulties reputed to the 'puzzle' do not exist, simply because sets do not 'rule' or have 'power' of a directly political kind, nor do they, as sets, administer affairs nor settle disputes. Firstly, a set of elders is not required to relinquish any power over persons or stock when they 'retire'; because they do not control anything when they are in office, they cannot be tempted to use office to build up 'power' which they then attempt to hold on to. 'Office' passes from set to set in an orderly way when it should do so, simply because it is an exhausting ritual burden that is being handed over and not an exploitable power over men and resources. Only ritual obligations reside in sets, and those involve giving away material resources in order to accumulate blessings; that is, the ritual desires of men stand, in part, opposed to their political and economic ambitions. So it follows, secondly, that men who are 'big' and powerful, but not qualified by ascribed set membership, are not only not required to be in the ruling set (indeed do not require even to hold office at all), but do not stand opposed to the set in office.

In brief, generation-sets are only very indirectly concerned with the disposal of economic resources and power. Sets as sets own no property, nor stock, nor water, nor grazing. I suggest that these negative features are common to many, maybe all, age-systems. Certainly the *gada*-systems of other Oromo, and of neighbouring peoples such as the Konso (Hallpike) and Sidamo (Stanley and Karsten, Hamer), also do not appear to control tangible power.

Nevertheless *gada* has been consistently described as having major political functions. The ethnographic survey on the Galla, which summarised the published data available up to 1955, accepted it as 'the basis of Galla social and political organisation', and the section entitled political structure dealt entirely with aspects of *gada*.[2] Legesse[3] writes that it is 'the foundation of the Borana socio-political system' and that 'kin groups, *gada*-classes and age-sets are the real bases of political and ritual behaviour' (1973:173 and 225). I shall suggest that Legesse's own analysis shows that, while *gada* provides a convenient political rhetoric and vocabulary, political power does not reside in sets and that *gada* only enters political affairs marginally.

Legesse is the most persuasive proponent of the view that *gada* has major political functions. He was fortunate to work in Ethiopia during the time a generation-set selects its six 'leaders' or 'councillors', and to be involved in the unusual competition which occurred between two candidates for selection to one of those offices. The population in Ethiopia is much greater and denser than in Kenya, and Legesse participated in assemblies of several hundred men (1973:208) and mentions five assemblies of 'several thousand' (1975:11). Legesse was able to see the political process in action in the populous homelands whereas I only saw it in the much more arid periphery. But, I do not think that our differences arise so much from the circumstances of our fieldwork but are more fundamental. We are in almost absolute and total agreement about the ethnography; indeed his is, in many areas, much fuller than mine and includes some data of which I was ignorant, so a nit-picking examination of points of difference would not be helpful. But we look at the data from different view-points and adopt different stances. These differences are in part a consequence of our different trainings and assumptions. I think that I see the Boran more from a comparative Africanist perspective and less from an Ethiopianist one; I do not think the intellectual achievement which *gada* represents, impressive as it is, to be as unique as he does. Subtle modes of symbolic thought are a feature of very many African cultures.

We both agree that *gada* is central to the way Boran talk about and perceive the world and their activities in it. Neither of us see *gada* as important in most practical daily activities such as herding; except in so far as it occasions heavy sacrifices and periodic assemblies of herds it hardly impinges on economic life. But Legesse does see the traditional system of government, even in Kenya, as based on the *gada* system (1976:10). I did not see generation-sets exercising power over persons or groups; nor did I see the 'officials' or 'leaders' of sets exerting any power by virtue of their offices. Office holders have high-sounding titles, such as Senior Chief, (*Haiyu gudda*), Owner of the Sceptre (*Abu Bokuu*), Chief of the War (*Haiyu A'Duulla*), but they do not control anyone. They stand for ideas rather than powers. In brief I suggest that the rules and rituals of *gada*, in all their apparent complexity, are communicating, by speech or symbol, a folk political theory or political philosophy, rather than either providing concepts which are those of sociological analysis or demonstrating a political process in action. Legesse and I differ in the weight we each give to the rhetoric of constitutions and statements of political value, both of which are in *gada*, and also in our views of what political institutions are.

In their manifesto for political anthropology Fortes and Evans-Pritchard(4) wrote:

We have not found the theories of political philosophers have helped us... for their conclusions are seldom formulated in terms of observed behaviour or capable of being tested by this criterion. Political philosophy has chiefly concerned itself with how men *ought* to live and with what form of government they *ought* to have, rather than with what *are* their political habits and institutions.... They have usually had recourse to hypotheses about earlier stages of human society... and have attempted to reconstruct the process by which the political institutions with which they were familiar ... might have arisen.

Boran elders enjoy chatting about political philosophy and theology, and *gada*, I suggest, is primarily a political theory or philosophy and the elders who are expert in *gada* are political philosophers and theorists. The exposition of *gada* propounded by Legesse is an exciting and subtle piece of political philosophy. *Gada* is a clever philosophical working model but it is still a folk model.

In an assembly an elder has influence by virtue of his established wisdom and power and never simply because he holds an office. Even the senior leader of a set (see below) is only attended to in so far as he speaks well that to which men want to listen. Set councillors become councillors because they are already qualified, trusted and prominent men; office confirms status but does not create it. In the case study which Legesse gives there was an unusually acrimonious struggle between two candidates and some elders lobbied hard when they had no 'legitimate' claims, according to *gada* rules, to do so (1973:206). But they did so, it seems clear, just because they feared that the controversial candidate sought the office for political purposes and because he was not a sound and reliable man to be trusted with the vital rituals for which an office holder is responsible.

Certainly the underlying concepts of *gada* dominate Boran ritual thought and behaviour, and *gada* offices are prestigious. They bring honour and confirm status and achievement and hence may be political assets also; just because *gada* is so pervasive aspects of it become involved in politics. But the logic of the *gada* system itself also militates against it having a central political role. Every man is obligatorily and ascriptively a member of a generation-set, so on every occasion that men meet set-members must be present. But, I can recollect no instance during my time in Kenya that members of a set met as a set (or even with a core of set-members or under the auspices of a set), for any other than ritual activities. Clearly men who, however heterogeneous in age and interest and influence they may be otherwise, live, and suffer, and sacrifice in a ritual village for several weeks, as some members of a set do, may well generate ties of interest which can be utilised politically — but so may any human activity which brings men together for a purpose. But almost every tie of kinship, affinity and stock friendship which a man has are likely to lead his political and economic interests away from *gada*. Indeed, some of the rules which control the selection to generation-set office are explicitly designed to prevent offices clustering into an asset which could assume political weight.

If a set, or a group of set members, had been involved in political activity I do not think that I could have missed it. I was looking for sets to have a political role because all I had read before I went to the field led me to anticipate one. There was ample opportunity for sets to reveal a political role if they had one; the Marsabit Boran were divided into factions over the appointment to the government chiefship, over the best way to try and block some unpopular new grazing regulations, and over their response to primary schooling. I sat in on many meetings and informal discussions on these and other divisive topics. Men split and grouped as their interests diverged by age, by the types of stock which they herded, by their grazing areas and by their intellectual convictions or prejudices; I never heard a whisper of *gada*-groupings or *gada*-officers having become involved in such practical issues.

Certainly set leaders are men of influence, because only men of influence are selected to be leaders. But, as Legesse demonstrates, even when a national assembly is held to make or amend laws 'regulating the distribution of resources' (94), sets do not form a bloc and any elder may speak. At the assembly Legesse attended set leaders led the blessings, but when decisions were required they were all 'removed from the role of leading the deliberations' (98), and became just single voices among a multitude.

My fieldwork did not coincide with the peak periods of *gada* activities, but I did witness a constant flow of ceremonies and rituals (Boran society sometimes appears to float on a river of prayers and blessings) which celebrated the values which are central to Boran culture and which are, therefore, central to the performances of *gada*. Themes such as the myths of the *Kaallu*, or symbols of complementary opposites such as virility : fertility, or marital vigour : gentleness, are repeated again and again (Baxter 1965). I listened to countless discussions about the relationships which should exist between man and man and between men and God which were couched in the idiom of *gada*. *Gada*, as I hope will become clear as I proceed, represents in an idealised form what social relationships should be through a four generational paradigm. In ascending order these are: a generation of non-responsible infants, one of irresponsible warriors, one of politically and economically responsible elders and one of economically non-responsible but ritually very responsible retired elders. *Gada* epitomises what social relationships should be, not what they are. In that sense *gada* is a political philosophy and a theology. As one informant succinctly put it: 'Generation-sets are our Book' (*luuba Kitaabu keen'a*), that is: 'They are to us at the Bible or Koran are to you.' *Gada* exists primarily, I urge, in the folk view as well as in mine, to ensure the well-being of the Boran and to regulate the ritual growth and development of individuals and to do so in such a way as to permit all men who survive life's full span to achieve responsible and joyful sanctity. It is this last, joyful aspect of *gada* as an institution which performs rituals that has struck intelligent non-professional observers, such as Plowman, Wingfield and Adamson, and not its political ones. What increasingly impressed me in the field was that, though in their speech and in their ritual activities (and I think in their thoughts and imaginations), *gada* was a dominant influence on Boran in Kenya, as an organisation it had little consequence for day to day social and economic life nor for political activities.

The account of the rules, organisation and rituals which follows is in accord with the other accounts we have, but differs from them in its interpretation of the political importance of *gada*. My argument is similar to that which Hinnant makes for the Guji in his essay.

2

With the caveat that it is not precisely in accord with Boran usage, I use *gada* as a convenient generic term to cover the genealogically based generation-set (*luuba*) organisation, the distinct but related age-set organisation, and the system of age- and generation-grading and its associated ceremonies and rituals. It is the mixing in action and in conception of these three distinct organisations and the changes in the parts over time which have generated incompatibilities and made the system appear so confusingly complex. Boran do not find *gada* puzzling because they do not seek to explain all of it together; as if it were something simple like cricket. They find their way through its maze of rules and of rituals, as they need to, without any trouble at all. It is only foreigners who use other, and more naïve, cognitive categories who need a guide or notice dissonance.

I had hoped to discuss *gada* without getting involved in the rules which regulate its mechanics, or at least to postpone consideration of them until the very end. But I should have realised that was bound to be a vain hope, because *gada* is a cognitive system rather than an instrumental organisation, and its rules provide categories for cognition in areas way outside the narrow boundaries of the sets themselves. Therefore I give the barebones of *gada* now which, though it involves some repetition, requires less than would any other expository sequence.

The mechanics can most readily be grasped through Figure VI.1.

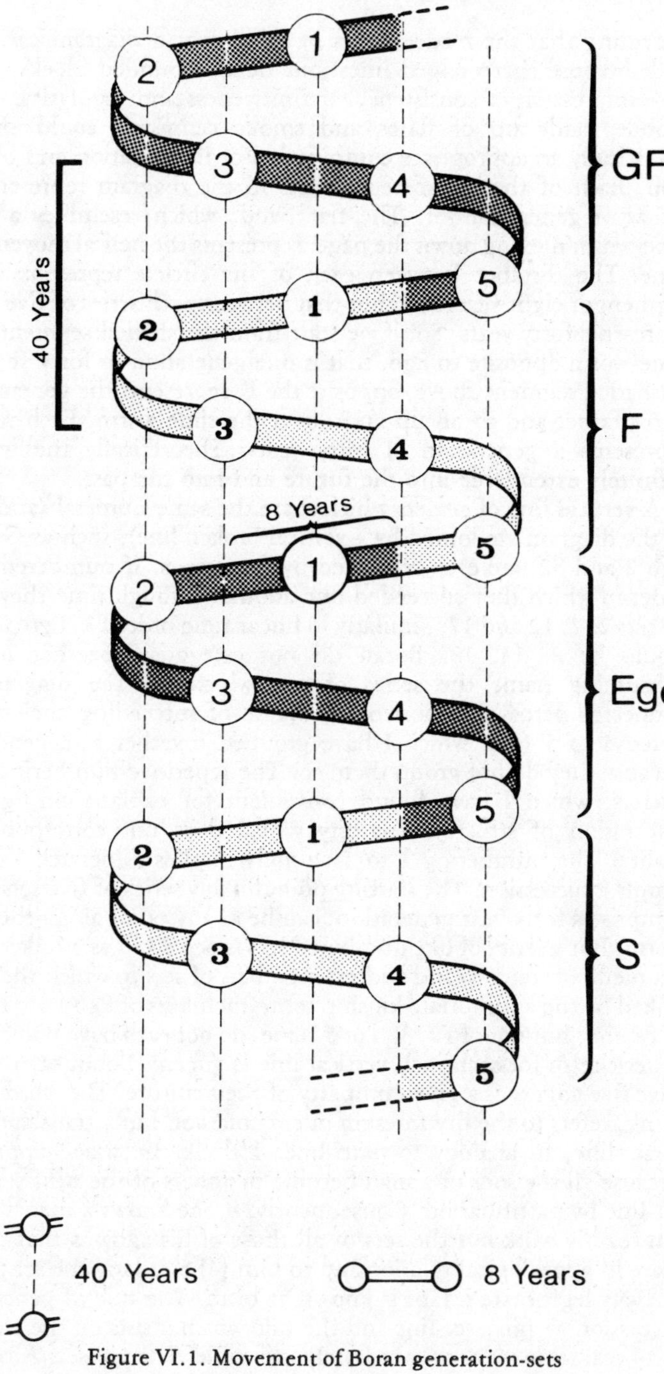

Boran Age-Sets and Generation-Sets

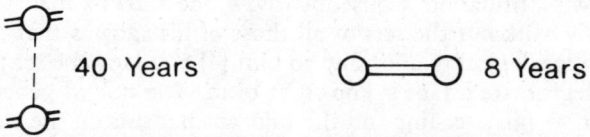

Figure VI.1. Movement of Boran generation-sets

providing that the reader keeps in mind that a diagram caricatures and, because sharp edged lines join clearly bounded blocks, gives a fake impression of consistency, definitiveness and regularity. Only a mobile made up of flares and smoke cannisters could simulate realistically an appropriate combination of illumination and obfuscation. Each of the numbered circlets in the diagram represents one *luuba* or generation-set. The flat band, which resembles a wiggly tape-worm moving down the page, represents the helical movement of time. The distance between each of the circlets represents a time segment of eight years and thus that between each series of five circlets represents forty years. So, if we start from the shaded segment of the time-worm opposite to Ego, that is one generation of forty years, the unshaded segment above, opposite the F, represents the generation of Ego's father and so on up and down the time-worm. Each segment represents a generation of forty years. Theoretically the worm is infinitely extendable into the future and into the past.

A vertical line of circlets which share the same numeral (and which in the diagram are joined by a vertical broken line), such as GF2, F2, Ego 2 and S2, are each separated by forty years. If numbered in the order in which they succeeded one another through time they would be sets 2, 7, 12 and 17. Similarly in linear time order F3, Ego 3 and S3 would be 8, 13, 18. Boran do not categorise together under a subsuming name the series of sets which, in the diagram, are connected across one horizontal wiggle of succeeding circlets numbered 1 to 5 (and which I have grouped together as a generation) because they do not group them so. The repetitive numbering of the circlets, which I have found convenient for explanation, gives an impression of structural rigidity which does not correspond with reality. The numbering 1 to 5 wrongly implies a hierarchy and not simply a succession. The starting point for any series of five sets, which comprise a forty year generation, can be at any point along the helical worm. But a series of like numbered sets is perceived as a linked series. Set members refer to and address members of sets to which they are so linked by the appropriate kinship term; members of Ego 1 are the sons of F1 etc., but not of F2, 3, 4 or 5. Lines do not each have names, but a generic term for each such vertical line is *gogesa*. Boran say that they have five *gogesa* as a given property of their culture. The word itself, I think, refers to the dry foreskin of circumcision but I translate it here as set-line, in analogy to patri-line. I think the usage appropriate because all the sons of a man become members of the next set in the set-line by patrifiliation. Consequently, if one knows a man's set one can readily work out the sets of all those of his agnates that one can place in genealogical relationship to him.[4] Similarly the set position of every legitimate infant is known at birth. The rule of generational succession within a set-line and the rule which insists on the eight and forty year time spans are absolutely inflexible. The age-sets *hariiya* (see below) and the age-grading aspects of *gada* (which endeavours to mesh human biological age with social responsibility) and modes of time reckoning also depend on the same eight year time segments. Clearly a system which continues to operate successfully, while flying in the face of biological probabilities, must require other subsidiary or secondary rules. I postpone consideration of some of these until later and others I ignore.

Each set-line then should encompass approximately one-fifth of the total population; as far as I could ascertain by simple field observations and reports no set-line appeared to have, or was believed to have, a greater population than any other. Set-lines are only relevant in the context of *gada* and, like their component sets, do not own any tangible assets of any sort. Boran hold that they have 'always' had their moieties and clans and *gada*, so that one would anticipate finding all members of one clan and sub-clan in one set-line and vice-versa. This does not occur and I was unable to discern a clustering of the two attributes, though an extensive survey might reveal them. Certainly when interrogating a stranger in order to place him, Boran ask for a man's set-name (not set-line, lines are not named), along with genealogical and clan information. They do not expect that one should relate to the other. The apparent anomaly does not cause concern at all. When questioned informants shrugged it off as irrelevant, as it is. Generally speaking, any elder could recite around five or six set names in his own set-line and about the same number, in correct order, back in direct linear time. Except for a few learned ritual specialists men are only concerned with their own set-line and the sets which are near to them, either preceding or succeeding, in the time-worm. Only a few very wealthy and influential stock holders maintain long ancestral pedigrees. But, from the genealogical checks which I was able to carry out, I found, on the one hand, that all the traceable agnatic descendants of any known ancestor belonged to the generation-set which was appropriate to their genealogical position, and on the other I recorded men of the same clan, but who had no traceable genealogical connection, who belonged to different set-lines. Simply the discrepancies are not evident in social situations only to an observer.

Every free-born Boran then is a member of a generation-set and there are five lines of such sets. Siblings, irrespective of age, belong to the same set. Members of a set, because they are of the same genealogical generation, may belong to very different social generations; in practice at any moment in time men long dead of old-age and unborn babies may belong to one set. The same sets are common throughout Boranaland and membership of a set is ascribed and a prerequisite of full citizenship. Sets do not appear to be associated with descent groups nor to cluster territorially.

Each set as a 'Father' (*Aba gaada*) and takes its name from his name; members refer to themselves as 'of the *luuba* of X'. To its members a generation-set consists of those men who are qualified by their descent to be members of that set, in that their fathers formed the preceding set in their set line, who came together to celebrate at the culmination ceremony of that set at the time of *gaadamoji*. There is a culmination ceremony every eight years and each set-line holds one in turn. The set organisation is said to be there to ensure that these ceremonies are held, because the wellbeing of all Boran depends on their being held. From another point of view the organisation generates a set of men every eight years who, for their own ritual needs, require the opportunity, as they enter the condition of *gaadamoji*, to undergo the culmination ceremony. Sets and ceremonies are as dependent on each other as chicken and egg. The succession of sets through two genealogical generations, i.e. along two loops of the time worm, provides the conceptual frame for an ideal form of age-grading, eighty years being a 'natural' span to run from naming during infancy to senility. The system also provides an orderly means of categorising past time and of relating it to the present and to linear and cyclical future and past times.

Before proceeding to further analysis of the generation-set organisatin and of the age-grading aspects of *gada*, I shall briefly describe those other features of Boran society and culture which are essential to the understanding of *gada*.

3

By preference Boran are cattle herders but they also keep sheep and goats and camels in the desert. Traditionally they look down on those who have insufficient livestock to follow a pastoral life and must cultivate the soil. Of recent years however the prejudice has been modified, at any rate in Kenya, as it has become more and more obvious that power now lies with the cultivating peoples. Pinched between the admonitions and rules of the authorities on one hand and of stock losses and encroachments on their grazing on the other, some have reluctantly settled to desultory farming. But there are few sites at which the nearby grazing and water are sufficient to permit even semi-permanent settlement with a herd although new modes of transhumance and family dispersal are developing to suit new conditions. Even in Kenya most Boran still rely very much on their livestock for a livelihood.

Boranaland straddles the borders of Ethiopia and Kenya. Over the last century or so Boran have in part drifted, and in part been edged by the Somali and the Guji, southwards and westwards. Boranaland in Ethiopia is goodish rangeland which is bounded in the north by the Ganale River and in the west by the Galana Sagan River. The area north of the Dawa River is known as Liban and that to the south as far as the Ethiopian scarp, which roughly coincides with the Kenya border, is known as Dirri. Dirri and Liban are the Boran homelands. The vast arid scrub and desert tract below the scarp is called Golbo[5] by Boran. As Hodson, the first British Consul for Southern Ethiopia, noted, Boran in Kenya 'have a much harder struggle than those in Abyssinia on account of the scarcity of water for their stock' (43). Almost all my fieldwork was carried out in Kenya and there I knew Boran of Marsabit best.[6] In Kenya access to grazing and to wells has been controlled by the government since the 1920s. Life has been less insecure than in Southern Ethiopia, but freedom of movement for individuals, families, camps and stock has been restricted, at times to the point of regimentation.

Boran in Kenya can, for simplicity, be considered as falling into three territorial groupings. First are those who water in the dry season at Turbi or Moyale or the wells between, most of whom graze back and forth across the border with the changing seasons, and maintain strong organisational and herding and ritual connections into Dirri and Liban. Second are those restricted to demarcated grazing areas on Marsabit Mountain and whose grazing cycles mostly consist of seasonal moves up and down the massif. I think all the Marsabit families maintain herding connections at the least into Dirri if not to Liban, and most have part of their family herds in Ethiopia. Most middle-aged men have spent some years in Dirri and homesteads move from Dirri to Marsabit, or vice versa, as its members decide that it is to their pastoral advantage to do so. Most are also likely to have herding connections in the Gabra grazing areas (see Torry's essay). Third are the Boran of Isiolo District who have been to some extent isolated from the north by the harsh desert which lies between them and either Marsabit or Moyale, by grazing and veterinary rules, and by the interpolation, between them and their relatives to the north, of wedges of grazing allocated to Rendille or Somali. Most Isiolo Boran accepted Islam in the 1920s and '30s and have been increasingly influenced by Somali culture. In the early 1950s they were more involved in the market economy and appeared much better off in stock and in consumable goods than Boran to the north (Baxter 1966 and Report HMSO 1962), but they suffered harshly during the confrontation between Kenya and the Somali Republic in the 1960s. I suspect that in Isiolo age-sets and generation-sets are more nostalgic items of folk memory than active organisations.

Boran have grazed and watered their stock over extensive areas of what is now Kenya since, at the very least, the middle of the last century and, with right and justice, regard the pastures and wells they use there as theirs. But Golbo is not vested with such intense sentiment as the traditional homelands[7] of Dirri and Liban to which, during archaic times, God is reputed to have sent down the two great *Kaallu* and revealed, in emblematic form, the basic values and institutions of Boran society, including the generation-sets. Each of the *Kaallu*, embodied in a direct lineal descendant, is ritual figurehead of one of the exogamous moieties; the *Kaallu* of the Gona moiety resides in Liban and of the Sabho moiety in Dirri. On no account should a *Kaallu* travel outside the homeland with which he is traditionally associated, which means that neither may visit Golbo. The relationship of the Boran nation through the *Kaallu* to God, the source of rain and of fertility, was established in, and continues to be centred in, the two homelands. Similarly the senior office holders of a generation-set, whose duty it is to maintain effective relationships between God and the Boran, are not permitted to descend into Golbo during their eight year spell in office. Informants spoke lyrically of the homelands where rain filled the wells to overflowing and the pastures were always lush. Even men who had only recently moved from Golbo, because the grazing and water were better there than from whence they came, spoke so. Such glowing asseverations are poetic statements containing mystical references to the attributes of God and to the ideal relationship which exists between him and the *Kaallu* and hence the Boran. God is said to distinguish the *Kaallu* by always providing bountiful rainfall around them, so that their villages may not need to follow the arduous transhumant or nomadic life which is imposed on most others. General statements about Dirri and Liban as homelands are different in kind to matter of fact statements about grazing conditions in specified places as they affect animal husbandry. For example, men might report that the grazing around Yavello, the administrative post near to the village of the Sabho Kaallu, was exhausted, but would not normally say that the grazing around the *Kaallu*'s village was exhausted, for to say the latter could imply that the relationship between the *Kaallu* and God was not as it should be. I was constantly urged to go to the homelands, and especially to stay in the village of a *Kaallu*, if I wished to comprehend Boran culture in its purity and fullness. (I was fortunate to spend a few days in the village of a *Kaallu* in 1966; the differences between daily life there and that which I had known in Kenya were not conspicuous.)

Kenya Boran often denigrated themselves to me as only being 'part-Boran' because of their separation from their ritual leaders and their remoteness from the oldest sacred sites at which generation-set rituals were performed and so by accumulation were full to overflowing with blessings. In 1951-2 elders in Marsabit cited the way in which custom, especially generation-set rituals, had been dropped by Moslems in Isiolo District and they forecast gloomily that the same would soon follow throughout Golbo. They said that only just enough participants had been found to carry out the last sequence of ceremonies, which had anyhow been attenuated. They persuaded me that it was likely that the rituals would never again be properly performed in Marsabit. But these gloomy prognostications were not fulfilled and, despite the prevailing drought and famine, the range of rituals was performed in the early 1970s; any curtailment of ceremony and sacrifice which occurred then was a consequence, I was assured, not of lack of concern but of dearth of stock. My brief revisit was after the conclusion of the ceremonies but it was clear, from the satisfied reports of participants and the accounts of the Revs. Houghton and Tablino (who witnessed parts of the sequence), that an extraordinary amount of organised effort and of stock were expended at a time when many of the Marsabit Boran were only surviving on famine relief. Such apparently lavish display was not improvident, because bearing stock were not slaughtered and every scrap of sacrificial meat was consumed; nor was it unfair, because no section of the community was over indulgent while others hungered. In Boran terms the sacrifices were an investment, and, anyhow, like the Nuer, they are almost 'always hungry and frequently starving' (Evans-Pritchard 1940:242).

Nevertheless, it is clear that involvement in *gada* activities are, and have been for as long as memory holds, weaker in Kenya than in the homelands. For example, the few men I knew who had held any office in *gada* had all been resident in Ethiopia at that time, or had had to move to Ethiopia for their period of active office. This different degree of involvement in set affairs reflects the differing histories and stock management practices of the Boran of the two countries. But the differences to which I have pointed are of degree rather than of kind and must not be exaggerated. Boran language and culture are extraordinarily homogenous; I could not detect any differences in dialect between any parts of Boranaland nor, with the exception of the changes in ritual practice and dress adopted by those who have joined Islam, any localised sub-culture traits. Boran who graze in Kenya are distant from the ritually active centres in the homelands, but all Boran, except those who have accepted Islam, share the same beliefs and participate in the same *gada* system. I do not consider that the Boran in Kenya and those in Ethiopia differ except, to some extent, in the degree of their attachment to details of custom. Legesse reports of families from Kenya who had made three trips to Ethiopia to join in ceremonies with the appropriate agnates (Legesse 1973:61). I know of men who similarly came from Ethiopia to Kenya.

Any Boran may, and very many do, travel freely anywhere in Boranaland. Almost all men also are likely to have stock rights and interests in herds managed by kin, affines or stock-associates who are scattered widely over Boranaland. A Boran likes to divide his stock, for management and maintenance, into separate herds of milch cows, dry cows, milch camels, dry camels and a flock of sheep and goats. Every family would like to own enough of each of the five categories of stock to make up a separate herd of each under the care of a member of the family. Obviously this is a paradigm of an ideal. Even at its peak point in the domestic cycle a family could rarely achieve such a wealthy and independent position from its own resources of stock and personnel. For our present purpose there is no need to examine the compromises which occur in daily life except to note that affines are most important (see Baxter 1970) and that adult siblings are likely to be distributed widely across the land. The heads of the homesteads of which any village is composed are likely to be men of approximately similar domestic and family status, each of whom is immediately responsible for a segment of the family herd which will be of the same type as that of his neighbours. As one would anticipate from this mode of stock management neither moieties, nor the clans and sub-clans into which they are divided, are localised, and the composition of villages and camps is not at all constant. A village commonly consists of from four to eight homesteads, with the stock which each homestead manages and from which it subsists. The homesteads that cluster together to form a village do so because, at that particular time, it suits them to do so; any homestead which perceives it advantageous to move off and join another village does so. The reasons for joining and staying in one village, rather than another, run from simple congeniality through useful mutual assistance to dependence verging on clientage. Formally defined relationships based on kinship, on descent or on age and generation groupings seldom constrain homestead heads to reside together, though men may, in answer to direct questioning, give such relationships as last resort explanations of why they continue to reside together. Each village takes its name from its 'father' (*aba*), who is likely to be a man of more than average wealth and with other attributes which enable him to maintain a semi-permanent core of a few households around him. Some such cores, made up of good friends whose labour forces supplement each other, may last for decades, because mutual trust is a vital resource to herdsmen. I have shown elsewhere (1972) that the cross-cutting net of territorially dispersed stock ties are the basis of Boran political and cultural homogeneity.

In brief, the groupings and social networks which men form for work or sociability are not directly affected by generation-set relationships either in daily practice or in folk theory. The fluctuating composition of the networks of relationships which men establish in order to pursue their livelihoods contrast with the rigidity of the groups and categories which order ritual life and restrict the choice of spouses. Workaday life gives an impression of casual opportunism in which men combine and separate according to criteria of mutual advantage, whereas ritual life appears to be a formally structured order in which men come together according to firm rules.

Ethnographic attention has focused, in particular, on the dual organisation of moieties and clans and the age and generation organisations. The formal, descriptive ethnography of conspicuous Boran social institutions is full, accessible and agreed,[8] so I only recapitulate the minimum necessary to make the workings of the age-organisation and of the generation organisation comprehensible. I deliberately exclude a number of subsidiary rules and exceptions which do not have any major influence. Also, in an almost desperate effort to see the wood for the trees, I only examine a few from the luxuriant Boran forest of symbols. I restrict myself so reluctantly because it is the intertwined meanings and ambiguities of the symbols which, above all else, demonstrate the associational and lateral logic which is the essence of *gada*.

4

Every male is a member of the exogamous moiety of his pater, that is the man to whom his mother was married, and is either a Sabho or a Gona. Each moiety consists of a number of named groupings which may be designated clans. Members of a clan presume descent from a common ancestor because they all share a common name, though the clan names are not those of those unknown and usually unregarded ancestors. Each clan is further divided into a number of sub-clans, many of which are further subdivided into 'branches'. The clans in the Gona moiety are bunched into two sub-moieties, Ful'leeli and Haroreesa, each of seven clans. These last two names, which are also the names of trees with ritual connotations, are not much used, even when probing an individual's social background, because in a context in which information is being exchanged they are irrelevant and redundant; the discriminations have no purpose in workaday relationships and, anyhow, every child knows which clans belong in each sub-moiety. The sub-moiety divisions are only relevant in the allocation of ritual offices and roles, and it was when discussing those, and the accompanying rules of *gada*, that I mostly heard the words. The Sabho moiety contains three clans and does not divide so neatly. One very large clan Karaiyu (also the name of a tree), which is divided into two clusters of sub-clans Diiyo and Basso, corresponds structurally, and in Boran conceptions, to one sub-moiety and the two other clans, Digalu and Mataari, to another. The Sabho sub-moieties do not have subsuming names which correspond to Ful'leeli and Haroreesa, and it is difficult to see what purpose such names could serve.[9]

Conceptions of unity in diversity, which are expressed through an ordered duality of the familiar left/right type, pervade Boran social structure and metaphysical conceptions: it is almost as if the Boran had a Gallic obsession to impose a seemingly logical set of constructs over the higgledy-piggledy of daily life. Boran representations of their social and ritual organisations and activities are intellectually tidy; protruberances are tucked in or covered over. For another example, Boran know full well that Golbo and Melba are territories which they have long grazed and which are crucial to their survival, yet they frequently speak of Boranaland as if it was restricted to the homelands and Golbo and Melba were extraneous appendages. As Boran express it, and as it appears if expressed diagrammatically, the moiety organisation seems like a fossilised segmentary lineage system, but it does not have a hint of genealogical referents at any level. Moreover, Boran hold that, with the exception of a very few branches which have diverged in the last century or so, the moiety, sub-moiety, clan or branch organisation has existed, in its present form, for longer than folk memory serves or cares. For our immediate purpose, which is merely to know only as much about the moiety organisation as is essential to understand that of *gada*, the important features of the moiety organisation are:

(*a*) Each moiety 'has' a *Kaallu*, which indicates that they are divinely approved, because it was from *Waaka* (God/Sky) whence the original *Borana Kaallu* came down to live among men. *Kaallu* are often called *Luubu Borana*, 'the life-spirit of the Boran'. Numerous secondary or supporting beliefs and practices, such as the rule that requires a *Kaallu* to breach the rule of exogamy and take his official wife from a prescribed branch of his own moiety, indicate the divine association between *Kaallu* and moiety.

(*b*) The rule of exogamy, which epitomises cognitive and structural duality, influences all choices of marriage partners (and to a lesser extent of lovers), and hence impinges on the compromises and equivocations of workaday life. Most importantly it follows that for any ego all other Boran are categorised as either agnates or affines, and that any other Boran can be categorised and addressed as one or the other according to age, sex and generation. Courtesy usage of the appropriate terms between otherwise quite unrelated persons is common.

(*c*) Moiety membership is linked to *Kaallu* and *gada* on almost every occasion at which prayers are spoken or a ritual performed. For example, daily prayers consist of two runs of paired phrases. The first run is ejaculated by an elder of one moiety and the second run by an elder of the opposite moiety. The lines of the prayers themselves each consist of phrases paired by their complementarity: prayers frequently run: Dirri Peace; Liban Peace; Gona Peace; Sabho Peace; GF1 Peace; F1 Peace; Ego Peace; S1 Peace and so on.

Boran ceremonies demonstrate consistent repetition of motif, theme and form[10] and a constant feature is that offices and tasks are apportioned according to moieites and sub-moieties. In particular generation-set offices, which are by far the most prestigious and demanding in Boran, are required to be allocated between the moieties. It is also argued, but not observed strictly in practice, that generation-set offices should not be concentrated in clans or become hereditary. (This conflicts with another Boran contention that the best guide to a man's suitability for any office or job is if his father or grandfather held it and performed well in it.) An explicit functional linkage is made between *gada* on one hand and moiety on the other through the rules which regulate the disposition of *gada* offices and during the discussions and lobbyings which precede any election to office.

But I think symbolic associations are more important than rule congruity. Items from the wide ritual gamut are combined and re-combined in differing orchestrations throughout the extensive repertoire of rituals. Symbolic associations and connotations interconnect throughout Boran culture, indeed throughout Oromo cultures,[11] so one would expect the dominant themes of the cycle of *gada* ceremonies to reverberate through other ceremonies as, indeed, they do. For example, a head of a homestead grasps a horse-whip (*liicho*), a primary indicator of active and responsible manliness, and dons a red, white and black check turban (*surri ruuf'fa*), a sign of Boran identity and exclusiveness, at domestic, at moiety and at *gada* ceremonies.[12] Connections through symbolic associations are myriad, but one particular object, the *kalaacha*,[13] links *gada* to the *Kaallu* and to the moieties. A *kalaacha* is a phallic metal horn worn at the *gada* culmination ceremonies and is associated in myth and in current usage to the *Kaallu* and to the verb — *kallu*, 'to sacrifice' or 'to slaughter'. Any enquiry about *gada* immediately evokes reference to, and an explanation of, the central importance of the *kalaacha*. Indeed men say that a primary purpose of *gada* is to enable properly qualified elders to 'put up' their *kalaacha* as replacements for their erect warriors hair tufts (*guutu*) which have been shaven off (see below). These associations are quite explicit and lie at the core of *gada*, and the moieties and the *Kaallu* are linked into *gada* both organisationally and conceptually.

Boran, who are keenly aware of distinctive features of their culture such as their moieties and their *Kaallu*, particularly remark that they have *luuba*, one of which is always responsible for the performance of ceremonies that are crucial to the welfare of all Boran. In this context a *luuba* is a generation-set; each of which is represented in the diagram by a circlet. One set succeeds another every eight years and each set in turn is responsible for maintaining the 'Peace of the Boran' for that eight years. The 'Peace of the Boran' consists not only of preventing internal strife and fostering active co-operation between men, but also maintaining proper relationships between men and God, so that the blessings of the latter, which are manifested particularly in rain and the fertility of stock and women, continue to flow. The Peace is based in *gada*.[14] A constant succession of sets is charged with the performance of ritual and sacrifices on which the welfare of the nation depends; each fifth of the nation (set-line) taking responsibility, through a named *luuba*, for an eight-year turn in the forty-year cycle. Within that set-line the one *luuba* of the appropriate generation takes its turn. The association of *luuba* to 'life-spirit' *luubu* (I have noted the frequent connection made with it and the *Kaallu*) is quite explicit in Borana usage.

5

The whole generation-set organisation, for which the word *luuba* is also by extension sometimes used, is of considerable antiquity; Boran hold that they 'have' generation-sets as they have *Kaallu* and moieties; that is they are one of the cultural characteristics which makes them Boran, so that therefore they must have had sets since they have been Boran. Some elders can recite the names of sets in their set-line which would run back into the eighteenth century. We also have supporting literary evidence, which was probably written by an ecclesiastic named Bahrey[15] from Gamo in about 1593. Which Oromo *gada* system Bahrey described is not clear but several of the features of *luuba* (and he used that word) recorded by him are still crucial features of Boran generation sets. I am not, of course, arguing that the organisation or purpose of sets has continued unaltered since the sixteenth century, but merely pointing out features of the contemporary Boran organisation which are reminiscent of the system delineated by Bahrey, and which are in accord with Boran statements about their antiquity and durability. I summarise the points from Bahrey because I have noticed, in discussions, a reluctance to recognise that the system could have retained such archaic elements in working order, as it were.

The sets described by Bahrey embraced all the nation into one system. A fresh set was installed every eight years, when five such sets had succeeded each other the sons of the first set followed in their turn and so on, so that each set of sons succeeded their fathers after forty years. These transfers followed 'at fixed times' (115) and the sets 'give themselves a collective name' (115). *Luuba* was stated to mean 'those who are circumcised at the same time' (115).[16] Bahrey also noted that newly formed sets had a military role and were likely to 'attack a country none of their predecessors have attacked'; and that those men who 'have killed men or large animals, they shave the whole head, leaving a little hair in the middle of the skull' (*gutu*) (122). Indeed Bahrey even noted the boast that the inhabitants of Shoa were not sufficiently doughty to count as men but rather were like 'oxen which speak and cannot fight' (127).[17] I heard the very same braggadocio some three and a half centuries later. It is implicit in his account that generation-sets grouped men and also had age-grading functions and that, in performance, these two features were conjoined. For example, he noted that circumcision and recognition of warriorhood were regulated by sets and, what is still an unusual and specific feature of generation-sets, that some men were obliged to abandon their children, because, although they were of an age to marry, they were not eligible to be paters. Bahrey attributed some political responsibilities to sets and stated that the people 'obey the *luuba* during a period of eight years' (115); but he also noted that the people 'have no rulers who can enforce his orders, and each man does what seems best to him' (114). This last suggests that sets in office were obeyed only so long as they gave orders which were not challenged.[18] That Bahrey did not comment much on the rituals of *luuba* is not surprising — he was after all a cleric, of a clearly pragmatic and enquiring mind, who was trying to explain pagan military successes.

6

Gada itself, it is apparent, contains internal contradictions; difficulties must arise from the rigidity of its rules and the multiplicity of functions ascribed to it and from its very enmeshment in so many aspects of Boran culture. It is used to group men for political and ritual tasks and also as the cognitive framework of the age-grading system on which each individual depends for an orderly transit through the stages of the life-cycle. On one hand the nation depends on there always being sets in appropriate conditions and levels of development to perform tasks on its behalf and, on the other, each individual depends on being able to pass with a set through the grade appropriate to his personal stage of development if his life is to be fulfilled. The reconciliation of these two needs, the societal and the individual, vexes many age-group systems, but is especially compounded by the rigidity of the forty-year generation cycle.

Boran distinguish several 'natural' stages of human development or 'ages of man', much as we do, each of which is marked by a name, such as suckling, crawler, child, youth, man, elder, dotard, etc., and at each of which certain behaviour is regarded as appropriate. There are more named stages during the early years of rapid development, but not ones which are marked socially by being classed or graded. The two most marked transitions occur: (i) when a man moves into full social adulthood by becoming 'father' of his own homestead (which combines being 'father' of a herd and of his own family of procreation); (ii) when he reaches the culmination of his life, at the *gaadamoji*, and withdraws from the activities and responsibilities of fatherhood. Many, of course, who survive to adulthood achieve the first but die before they are ready for the second; in one sense it is a distinction just to have lived for so long. These two stages are equivalent to the grades of *gaada* and *gaadamoji* (see below).

It is reasonable to presume, and convenient for the purpose of explanation, that *gada* has its origins in an age-organisation, but I do not intend to speculate on how or why it originated: we just cannot know. The stages of the male life-cycle can be fitted into two forty-year cycles so, for a start and for a couple of generations or so, age, generation and time can be kept in alignment but clearly (see Introduction), unless birth is controlled, the discrepancy between actual age and prescribed grade will increase from generation to generation.

Gada is a system of setting and grading in which every grade and every set is moving in relation to the others; the position of each part of the system is only explicable in relation to the position of other parts. Simply, because persons and sets are moving through time (or against time or with time) and because grades and persons and sets are sometimes in alignment and sometimes not, it is distorting to represent *gada* on a flat surface. Unfortunately age-systems still seek their Gerhard Mercator.

Let us assume that set GF1 on the diagram represents our imaginary and arbitrary starting point and that X, a first-born, is born into it while the set of his fathers are in the grade of *raaba guguurda* (see below) and just permitted to rear children. Let us also assume that each eight year time segment along the time-worm represents an age-grade, or an eight year component of a grade. Ideally then X should move through time in the grade appropriate to his set and age and, at one level of *gada* theory or theology, that is what should always happen. Those males, like X, who are born in step with *gada* (that is whose age is appropriate to their generation-set and their age-grade) are exemplars because in them theory and practice go together. They represent the paradigm of *gada*. They also stand for all their set and, during the rituals of *gaada* and of *gaadamoji*, for all Boran. The leader from which a set takes its name should be (probably must be) such a one.

Children in the condition of X are marked out for special care and attention and are known as *dabal'le*, the name of that grade. Any sons born to the father of X after the eight year time span represented by GF1, will be members of the set GF1, but will not be *dabal'le*. That is all brothers belong to one set but not one grade. The parents of *dabal'le*, particularly their mothers, are especially honoured for reasons that we shall see. Boys who are *dabal'le* wear their hair uncut and decorated with cowries, and are spoken of and addressed as if they were girls. Legesse notes acutely that *dabal'le* are 'among the principal mediators between men and God' and 'invested with powers and attributes similar to the *Kaallu* and other liminal persons' (1973:53). Their very remarkable rarity makes the *dabal'le* treasured representations of the ideal which wastage by death must reduce with time.

The next two grades are known as *gamme didiika* and *gamme gugud'da*. A *gamme* is the name given to the girls' tonsure; in childhood it is as round as a saucer but as girls approach marriage they allow the tonsure to diminish to the size of a shilling. *Didiika* means 'smaller' or 'junior' and *gugud'da* means 'bigger' or 'senior', which refers to the members and not to the size of the tonsure. Sets in the condition of *gamme* and *dabal'le* remain unnamed because they have not had leaders appointed.

The next grade is *c(h)uussa* and, though senior *gamme* may have started to act as warriors, by this grade all members are expected to be active warriors. The members of a set in this grade meet together as a set for the first time. They form village clusters at a number of regional sites and take their timing from the leader of the set of their fathers.

They sacrifice, or have sacrificed on their behalf, several head of stock. Their passage towards adulthood and responsibility for herding and fighting are signally marked by a series of acts, including the washing and shaving of their heads by their fathers, putting on trousers and receipt of gifts of stock and milking thongs.

Six councillors/leaders are selected for the set by the set of their fathers. The set then takes its name from the name of the senior councillor the *Aba gaada*. Ideally the leader should have a good pedigree and have established himself as a warrior and a man of good words. The set is expected to go on raids shortly afterwards, both as a public duty and to give each member a chance to put up his 'male tuft', *guutu diira*. This is the same tuft mentioned by Bahrey. *Diira* is simply 'male', the word *guutu* in different contexts means 'knob', 'handle', 'top', 'tuft', 'protrusion' etc., and 'full', 'complete', 'brimming', etc.; here it refers to a slender rat's tail of hair into which fibre is woven to make it stand erect. It is grown from the centre of the girl's tonsure and the surrounding locks are fluffed out into what looks like a fearsome caricature of a maiden's coiffure.

In order to erect his male tuft a man should have speared an enemy, a lion, an elephant or a rhinoceros. 'To spear' is a common synonym for 'to copulate', and the phallic symbolism of the male tuft is explicit. Men who have not earned their male tuft martially are allowed to erect one if they demonstrate their masculinity by fathering a child. (In practice exemptions are allowed by courtesy. I knew one man who was weak and impotent and married to a childless wife, but nevertheless he was permitted to erect his tuft; but people joked about it.) When the tuft is up and the hair around it sufficiently wild-looking and, ideally, gleaming with the butter of anointment, men say 'they have made their heads'. It is an envied condition and the high point of most men's lives.

The set is now an identifiable, named *luuba*. The six offices are distributed between the clans. Men in this grade 'beg for brides' and are reputed to be desired grooms, even though, as we shall see, they may not rear any children their wives may bear.

The next two grades, *raaba*, resemble the two *gamme* grades in that they extend for five years into the next eight year time segment (i.e.

into F I); *raaba* in that time segment are known as *raaba dore* or *guguurda*, 'senior' or 'larger' *raaba*, in order to distinguish them from those in the earlier condition of *raaba didiika*, 'junior' or 'smaller' *raaba*. Junior *raaba*, it is said, act wildly, aggressively and licentiously whereas senior *raaba* are said to settle down to domestic life and to learn public affairs. But, in practice, the behaviour of juniors slides into that of seniors and the transition is not abruptly marked. *Raaba* who have responsibilities thrust upon them, such as the headship of a family, must assume them.

A junior *raaba* may marry but he cannot retain his children. Any children his wife bears are said to be placed on the dungheap for the hyenas to take; i.e. they are gross anomalies which should not have occurred because their genitors were not yet recognised as potential paters. (In practice the children are taken and fostered by Waarta, the endogamous hunting and smithing caste, an ancestor of whom found the first *Kaallu*. By this subterfuge neither *gada* consistency nor natural feelings are too grossly violated). But a crucial consequence of this rule, which prevents men, such as X, bearing legitimate progeny until they are at least thirty-two years old, is that it prevents the birth of men who can have no legitimate progeny in their turn. This is a hard rule particularly as set-officials in that grade are expected to marry.

Whereas junior *raaba* must practise token 'infanticide', senior *raaba* rear up their sons. The ambiguous condition of junior *raaba* is marked by the rule which permits them, even encourages them, to marry but which forbids them to rear their children. The still uncertain condition of senior *raaba*, is marked in that their sons are brought up dressed as girls. The condition of junior *raaba* is especially signalled by their *guutu diira*, which they are all supposed to earn and to 'erect'. *Raaba* are reputed to go in bands from village to village, dancing and being made welcome and seducing the young wives of their elders. *Raaba* who have killed epitomise all the values of virility, 'bullishness', and martial ardour and strength which Boran expect their youngsters to embody and to maintain against their enemies and their own women. The foreign rulers of Boranaland have not always been able to distinguish the wild aspects of *raaba* from the gentle ones of *gaada* (see below) and have discouraged, even forbidden, any large gatherings of the celebrants.[19]

The period of *raaba* and its associated exploits and rituals grasp the imagination of Boran. I did not see the ceremonies but men revelled in telling me about them; descriptions of them based only on informants descriptions would more than double the length of this paper. Briefly, the rituals mark dramatically for those, such as X, the end of a childhood which, in *gada* theory, was extended to overlap delayed fatherhood. The juxtaposition of child: adult; junior: senior; wild: gentle, etc., is typical of Boran modes of thought, just as the

Plate VI.1. A Boran *raaba* with a *guutu* or 'male tuft'

equivocal ways of avoiding the logical consequences of that thought are typical of their behaviour in daily life.

The next grade is that of *gaada*. The set moving out of the condition of senior *raaba* takes over from the next set serially in line, that is from the set of the patri-line which preceded it in the cycle of patri-lines. This handing over extends over three years and the two *Aba gaada* should move their villages together for several spells of several weeks and, through the performance of a series of ceremonies and rituals, one set, and hence the representatives of one set-line and of one grade, hand over to the next.

Entry into *gaada* is marked by a most elaborate series of ceremonies which require the presentation by men who have completed this grade to men about to enter it of items required for the head-making ceremony which is the central part of the ritual. One of these items is aromatic gum *kumbi* (also used in many other rituals). Men about to enter the grade say they 'are going to look for *kumbi*'. They beg pinches of it from men who are either in the *gaada*-grade or who have passed through it. They mix bits they beg with lumps of freshly bought gum. In theory, as in the laying on of hands, there is an unbroken succession of transmitted gum. X should receive gum from GF 5 and hand some on to F2 and so on. Some of the gum is mixed in with the hair-style that is 'made' and some is pinched on to the eye-brows so that each looks as if he sports warts.

The ceremonials of *gaada* are lengthy and crammed with symbolic content. The wives and children of participants play important symbolic and practical roles as mothers and as milkers, because from entry to *gaada* a man is an elder and should live the leisured life of the milch cow villages. But most conspicuously a *gaada* 'makes his head', puts up his phallic symbol (ideally that of his father) and undergoes real or token circumcision.

Most conspicuously the *gaada* go on the great 'Pilgrimage of the Annointment' (*Muuda*), which is famous throughout all Oromoland and in which other Oromo join. It is almost a pan-Oromo gathering. At a site in Liban the *gaada* exchange gifts and blessings with the *Kaallu*. As part of the exchange the *Kaallu* have their snakes (puff-adders for Gona and others for Sabho) released from their bamboo containers into the long grass. The snakes are urged to go and graze. Snakes connote and connect many things but here, in particular, they stand for the *Kaallu* and, because of their ability to slough their skins and appear gleamingly new born, they stand for regeneration and continuity. They link the peaceful, domesticated village of men to the bush and wild animals. *Raaba* and *gamme* are often called wild animals (*binensa*); which is one of the reasons given in support of their unsuitability to be paters.

I understood that *Kaallu* only participate in the generation-system on this one occasion and are forbidden to intervene at all at other times. But they are ever present symbolically. The phallic symbol, for example, of each *gaada* quite deliberately recalls the great *Kalaacha* found with the first *Kaallu*, as does the turban (*suuri ruufa*) which each man wears, and a number of other symbolic objects. Each *gaada* also builds a special home for the festival, known as a *galma*, this is the name by which the home of the *Kaallu* is always spoken of because it is a permanent place of festival.

The set in the condition of *gaada* only accepts ritual responsibility for maintaining proper relations between the nation and God for the eight years it is in that grade; but the men who have entered the condition of *gaada* may remain active and effective elders until they become *gaadamoji*. This they do as the set of their son's, in its turn, enters *gaada*. For those who have 'completed their heads' life remains on a plateau. Formally the set that was *gaada* moves into the grade of *yuuba* for the remaining four time segments of the cycle, for X that is until the end of F5. *Gaada* and *yuuba* should busy themselves with public affairs and domestic cares. They should be active, wise and responsible, above all else, for the maintenance of the peace. Throughout the whole long generational span their wives should keep their *kalaacha* up-ended in a full milk pot. (In fact they usually store them away safely in a small dry pot.) The *yuuba* let their male tufts sag into a limp tag. Movement through each of the eight year time segments is only marked for them by the movements of the sets of their sons until the final grade of *gaadamoji* is reached. For X that is at Ego I. This is a grade few men live long enough to achieve. Those who do are greatly honoured and become in themselves a blessed sanctuary.

I have not witnessed the rituals of *gaadamoji* but to Boran it is the highest peak of life and they would tell of it constantly; Legesse reports observing a series of *gaadamoji* ceremonies (*jiila gaafa gaadamoji*) which 'was attended by twenty-two *gaadamoji* and several hundred celebrants' (1973:100).

The series of transitions from *raaba*, into *gaada* and into *gaadamoji* occur within the same set-line. Looked at horizontally, in segmented time, the participants are layers of generations. Looked at vertically, from the point of view of our imaginary X, the participants are his sons, grandsons and great grandsons, i.e. members of the same stock-holding family groups.

One of the practical consequences of *gaada* is that all participants need to have reliable affines and/or stock associates to whom they can trust the care of their herds while they are engaged in the lengthy ceremonies, because if one generation of close agnates are engaged in the *gaada* cycle it is probable that other generations of it will also be involved.

Also, because the ceremonies require a great number of sacrifices if they are to be efficacious, wealthy families who can donate stock dominate all the proceedings. The nature of the congregation, and also the extent of the sacrifice and the length of time spent on ceremonies, explains why a three year period is required for handing over from senior *raaba* to *gaada*. The logistics of assembly and movement of such numbers of people and stock in an arid habitat which is marked by erratic and extreme seasonal changes require that amount of flexibility.

I have called the ceremonies of *gaadamoji* 'culmination ceremonies' because participation in them culminates a man's life. A *gaadamoji* takes down his head', which includes his male tuft, and lowers his *kalaacha*, and enters into a condition of sanctity. Henceforth his very presence provides a sanctuary. He must always remain 'cool' and so should never show anger or lust. He should never raise his arm or his voice, and is thus prevented from herding and, effectively, from public activities. It is, of course, likely that even if our imaginary X had survived into his eighties and become a *gaadamoji* that his passions might anyhow be cooling in the course of nature. But as a *gaadamoji* declines from activity and rises into sanctity, his sons move into responsible activity and out of boisterous, lustful youth. The cycle turns and returns so that Boran perceive an order in events which, as Legesse expounds brilliantly (1973: Ch.7), combines with the recurrent refreshment of mankind.

Balandier writes that the enthronement of a king rejuvenates the kingship and 'gives the people... the feeling of a new beginning' (114). Similarly the holding of the culmination ceremonies, as does each naming ceremony for a first-born son, provides a fresh start at regular and predictable intervals along a known and trusted path. *Gada* insures and reassures.

The institutionalised 'infanticide' or abandonment of infants by *raaba* prevents children being reared up who could not, in a reasonably optimistic expectancy of life, hope to achieve *gaadamoji*. This simple mechanism prevents the generation of generations of anomalous men, who would prevent this cycle of regeneration in the ideal form in which it is constructed. In what I see as primarily a system of ideas about the human condition and situation, the primary purpose of this rule is the prevention of anomaly. Boran resent its harshness but, where the rule has been abandoned, anomalous children increase rapidly and produce more anomalous children in their turn. When the children of *raaba* are placed on the dung heap they are not proper children being abandoned; they should never have been born. They are thrown away as if they had never been, as impurities which pollute the social and ritual orders. Analogously an unmarried girl who conceives should be driven out to the bush and no bridewealth can be received for her; it would so cry out against the proper ordering of human affairs that it would pollute the herd. Girls should be virgins and virgins cannot conceive. A pregnant virgin is like the wife of a *raaba* in that neither should conceive — indeed, according to their social status as declared by their hair style, neither is capable of conception. The children of each are bastards who can have no proper age-grade nor set, and hence can have no proper place in society and its rituals. If X could produce legitimate children from, say, the age of eighteen and his grandsons and great grandsons carried on similarly, the gap between generation-sets and age would snowball out of alignment.

The rule which prevents *raaba* from rearing their children is felt to be an extremely harsh and onerous one. Mothers who have had to so abandon a baby — or worse, babies — are honoured and their private grief respected. It was the first *gada* rule to be avoided once the chance arose either by colonial protection or entering Islam. A semi-permanent village of the children of *raaba* had grown up near Moyale; its inhabitants were referred to pejoratively as Waarta and lived like Waarta. The proliferation of children who had no proper set, as has occurred among Moslems of Isiolo, is quoted by traditionalists as one good reason for not converting. A *raaba* who becomes a father controverts the cultural order imposed over unruly nature, he is, moreover, using children, God's greatest gift, to destroy God's order.

The problem of men born too late in time to go through with their set, *gultu*, is easily solved. The majority of living elders are *gultu*. A younger brother may be one whereas the elder was not. *Gultu* simply go through with a later set which, ideally, should be one in the same set-line, but that is not a rule. A *gultu* acts just as if he were a member except that he cannot take a set office. As we shall see, a *gultu* can effectively gain most of the satisfactions appropriate to junior grades of *gada* through the age-set organisation. He can obtain the blessings of a *gada* and sanctity of a *gaadamoji* as a 'passenger' and poses no threat to the *gada*-system. The only risk the system faces is that there will be insufficient men of the proper grade to fill the offices. But that, I think, is an unrealistic fear demographically and logically. If such an eventuality looked likely — some subsidiary rule would certainly be invented to circumvent the difficulty. I anticipate revolutionary social and political changes in Kenya and Ethiopia will swamp *gada* before it seizes up of itself.

Genealogical generation must give way eventually to chronological age when there is a confrontation. The organisation of age-sets and the alternative ways of marking stages in the life-cycle of *gultu* show that very clearly. I have described the latter elsewhere (1965) and shall not enlarge more here.

7

Even if generation and age and grade coincided in the sixteenth century they have not done so for a long time: I can see no overwhelming reason why they should have done so then. Generation-sets therefore cannot be an efficient means to mobilise troops and a quite distinct organisation based on closeness of age (*hariiya*) exists for that purpose. The *hariiya* or age-set organisation takes its timing from the generation-set organisation but is quite independent of it. The present organisation was devised about 1883 at a national assembly and replaced an earlier organisation which had proved unable to mass warriors effectively against Menilik and the Somali and the Guji when the nation had already been weakened by rinderpest, cholera and smallpox. *Hariiya* is used both of an age-mate and an age-set. Age-mates should share mutual love, loyalty and devotion, go on raids together and protect each other's wives from the sexual attentions of other sets, but permit sexual access to their own wives to members of their own set.

Age-sets take their timing from *gada* but have nothing to do with generation; very simply all the male babies born between one *gaadamoji* ceremony and the next are grouped into one set. A set is formed and given a 'father' and a name early in the short rains which follow after the *gaadamoji* ceremony. Members are not put into a named set until three eight year time-segments have elapsed. So X would know that his age-mates were all those boys born during GF 1, but he would not formally belong to a set until the *gaada* change of GF 3 and GF 4. At its naming members of a set can vary in age from sixteen to twenty-four. In practice older youngsters start to tag along as dry-stock herdsmen and as raiders before their set is formed.

Sets follow each other in linear order but Boran see them as forming two lines each of which shares a common name. So if the sets which consist of members born during GF3, GF 5 and F 2 are all named Damballa, then the sets of members born during sets GF2, GF4, and FI will all be named Waakor.

Fairly full information is available on age-sets elsewhere (Baxter 1954b and forthcoming). It is sufficient for now to note that members of recently named age-sets are expected to act like bush animals, and do act like them, just as *gamme* and *raaba* were said to act. I attended one local age-set ceremony in Marsabit in 1972 which was held over the weekend so that schoolboys and workers could attend. The participants acted just as twenty years earlier I had been told *raaba* should act. Age-mates go dancing and wenching together; and go game-hunting and raiding together in pursuit of their 'male tufts'. But as members move into middleage age-set membership fades into 'old boy' conviviality.

The age-set system meshes in its values, as well as in its timing, with the generation-set system. It forms a simple part of *gada* in that it cloaks one of the practical dilemmas created by *gada's* rigid timing. The age-set organisation still serves its traditional purposes. Young men still wander with the dryherds, and they still guard the water and pastures, and they still go off on retaliatory raids. They need trustworthy age-mates and they still enjoy the traditional rewards.

The generation-set organisation also continues to operate into modern times although it has neither practical utility nor political purposes. Neither the Kenya nor Ethiopian governments have utilised *gada* as a basis for indirect rule or for local government. Indeed it is doubtful if administrators have even been aware of its existence. I suggest that a major reason for the survival of *gada* has been its very lack of political visibility. It has not had either to buckle under or to oppose, but merely to continue.

For Boran it has served (*a*) as an organised way of ensuring that there is always a responsible segment of the nation responsible for maintaining proper relations with God, (*b*) as an organised way of ensuring that every man has the opportunity of a fulfilled ritual life while also fulfilling his obligations to the nation. It offers its own rewards.

The 'puzzles' in *gada* arise not from the way it fulfils its tasks, but from the obstacles created by its own categories. Men must follow the course around the obstacles not over or through them. The rule which requires 'infanticide' or, more properly, delayed paternity is such. It arises because the rules of *gada* as an age-grading system are incompatible with those of *gada* as a generation-set system. Given the premise, which has all the marks of a revealed truth, that generations must have a fixed time span then the rule becomes essential in order to maintain that assumption. *Raaba* and *gamme* should not have children, if they do that destroys the fixed time span assumption, therefore *raaba* and *gamme* must not rear up the children that their wives bear. Similarly if the rituals of *gada* are not performed God will withhold the rain and the world will spoil. But the rituals are always held. It is all as self-fulfilling and incontrovertible, so long as its premises are accepted, as any other closed system of belief; but perhaps just a little more intricate than most.

Gada is a dramatised philosophy or a way of acting out a folk faith rather than an instrumental organisation. When, therefore, men grumble about its onerous demands they are grumbling, as men do everywhere, about the demands laid on them by the religious obligations they delight in honouring.

NOTES

1 1930:120.
2 Huntingford, G.W.B., 1955:9 and 41-53.
3 Haberland (1963) emphasises ritual and rules rather than politics, but he attributes 'the highest political power' as well as 'the most important religious functions' (203) to the set in office. Legesse (1973: Ch. 8, 'Election 1963: the Analysis of Social Drama') shows, with insight and in detail, how *gada* values become permeated with other values at the election to *gada* office. Unfortunately, Legesse's subtle analysis has been crudely caricatured, for example by Stahl: 'The pastoral Oromo were organised in clans whose internal government was performed through a complex organization of age-groups and age-sets called the *gada* system' (33).
4 Common descent was so stressed by informants that in my first efforts to explain the generation-set system I translated *luuba* as descent-set.
5 The area between Lake Stephanie in the west, Dirri in the east and Golbo in the south-east in known as Malbe or Melbe. I know little about Malbe, but I think the relationship it has to the homelands is comparable to that of Golbo.
6 I am indebted to the CSSRC who financed my field research in Kenya in 1951-3 and to the Hayter Committee of Manchester University who enabled me to spend two weeks in Dirri in 1966. I was also able to revisit Marsabit for a few weeks in 1972 as consultant for the AUFS films *Kenya Boran*. The 'ethnographic present' in this chapter, unless the context clearly indicates otherwise, is 1951-3.
7 'Homelands' is not a direct translation from Borana, but Boran do speak of the 'lands of the *Kaallu*', and of 'lands of the Boran', and I think 'homelands' reflects Boran sentiment more accurately than heartlands.

8   See especially Baxter 1954a and b, Haberland 1963, Knutsson 1967, and Legesse 1973. The researches on which all these accounts are based were carried out independently. Haberland and I were in the field at approximately the same times, he in Ethiopia and I in Kenya. We managed one weekend meeting at Moyale. Legesse's fieldwork was later, but he writes (14, note 24) that he had 'not consulted Baxter's thesis', so that his work and mine could serve as 'totally independent bodies of data'. Pecci (1941) describes the formal mechanics of the generation-set system with enviable economy and lucidity; I confess that I missed his paper until some years after I had returned from the field. If I had read it before I went to the field it would have saved me months of puzzlement. Haberland and Legesse both contain comprehensive bibliographies on Boran. Stewart (1977) provides a comprehensive and critical assessment of the literature on *gada*.

Cerulli (1923) surveys the different meanings which have been given to words such as *gada* etc. by different authors. Legesse gives a particularly subtle and comprehensive résumé of different meanings and shades of meanings of *gada* as it is used by Boran; see especially 1973:81-105. The Oromo, like the Tuareg, have had a purgative effect on many European itinerants and moved them to write, so it is only too easy to heap up a mountainous bibliography. Unfortunately successive writers have often only reiterated and compounded the errors of their predecessors.

9   Legesse (1973), though he also stresses 'the principle of balanced opposition' (41) in Boran social organisation, suggests that Sabho is best seen as consisting of three sub-moieties rather than as three clans which cluster in two sub-moieties. The difference in our interpretation is not of immediate importance. (See also Haberland, 126-9).

10 See Baxter 1965.

11 See the essays in this volume by Hinnant, Blackhurst and Torry and also Cerulli 1922, Haberland 1963 and Knutsson 1967.

12 Both the whip and the turban, used as they are in so many contexts, are polysemous, but here I only want to refer to certain of their connotations. The turban, which represents a covering found with the first *Kaallu*, I often heard compared to a national flag.

13 Clear illustrations of *Kalaacha* can be seen in Plowman 1919. Wingfield 1948 (the painting by Joy Adamson), Baxter 1954a, Haberland 1963, Adamson 1967 and Brown 1971.

14 Boran have an overwhelming concern, which, as they know well, takes great efforts, with the maintenance of peace and order between all men of the nation — as in Queen Elizabeth I's striking words 'peace in all security' (quoted by Rowse 263) and the 'peace', *shalom*, of the old Testament. '*Shalom* — peace, harmony — between God and men is impossible where no *shalom* exists between man and his neighbour' (Phillips:22). Boran seek to construct and strengthen the Peace of the Boran with every daily greeting which they exchange, with every routine blessing which they ejaculate and with every daily prayer. Its maintenance is the primary public charge of every elder. 'Above all, the wise man was expected to be able to so manipulate words that order might either be maintained or restored' (Phillips:51).

Failure to maintain the peace, by the neglect of *gada* for the Boran, and other Oromo, would result in a confused and distempered universe as poetically described in the much quoted lament of Knuttson's informant: 'The bull refused to mount the cow... men no longer respected justice... and few children were born' (180). One is reminded of Hosea's lament for an Israel which neglected its God: 'There is no faithfulness or kindness, ... there is swearing, lying, killing, stealing... murder follows murder... the land mourns and all who dwell in it languish, and also the beasts of the field... even the fish of the seas are taken away' (4:1-3).

15 For a discussion of Bahrey's reliability and the probable provenance of the Oromo he describes see the Introduction to his History by Beckingham and Huntingford, and Legesse (1973:137-9).
16 *Luuba* is a difficult word. Bahrey associates it with circumcision and Tutschek gives it as 'the sexual parts of man', 'penis', though it is not a current colloquialism with that meaning. Foot, more recently, gives 'circumcised'. All authorities give something similar to Tutschek's 'life' or 'soul' for *luuba*, which is also common contemporary usage. The connotations of life and of penis, of course, are not incompatible. *Luuba*, like *kalaacha* and *gada*, has the structure of a 'complex word'.
17 See Andrzejewski 1962.
18 I have suggested that consensus politics suit arid zone pastoralism (1977).
19 I do not see how the custom of 'infanticide' 'facilitates warfare', as is suggested by Legesse (1973:73).

BIBLIOGRAPHY

Andrzejewski, B.W. 1962. 'Ideas about Warfare in Borana Galla. Stories and Fables'. *African Language Studies*, III, 116-36.
Adamson, Joy. 1967. *The Peoples of Kenya*. London (359-75).
Bahrey, 'History of the Galla' in *Some Records of Ethiopia, 1593-1646*, trans- and ed. by C.F. Beckingham and G.W.B. Huntingford. London. Hakluyt Society (1954).
Balandier, Georges. 1970. *Political Anthropology*. London.
Baxter, P.T.W. 1954a. 'The Social Organisation of the Galla of northern Kenya'. Unpublished D. Phil. thesis, University of Oxford.
———. 1954b. *Social Organisation of the Boran of northern Kenya*. London.
———. 1965. 'Repetition in Certain Boran Ceremonies', pp.64-78 in M. Fortes and G. Dieterlen *African Systems of Thought*. London.
———. 1970. 'Stock Management and the Diffusion of Property Rights among the Boran' in *Proceedings of the Third International Conference of Ethiopian Studies*, 1966, III, 116-27. Addis Ababa.
———. 1972. 'Absence makes the heart grow fonder', in Max Gluckman (ed.), in *The Allocation of Responsibility*. Manchester.
———. 1977. 'Film: The Rendille'. *RAIN*, 20; 7-10.
———. 'Boran age-sets and warfare' in D. Turton and K. Fukui (ed.), *Warfare among East African Herders*. Osaka (forthcoming).
Brown, Jean. 1971. 'Borana Kalaca: Cire Perdue Casting'. *Kenya Past and Present*, 1, 1.
Cerulli, Enrico. 1922. *Folk Literature of the Galla of Southern Ethiopia*. Cambridge: Mass.: Harvard African Studies. III, 8-228.

———. 1923. 'I riti della iniziazione della triba Galla'. *Rivista degli Studi Orientali*, IX, 480-95.
Evans-Pritchard, E.E. 1940. *The Nuer*. Oxford.
Foot, E.C. 1913. *A Galla-English: English-Galla Dictionary*. Cambridge.
Fortes, M. and Evans-Pritchard, E.E. 1940. Introduction to *African Political Systems*. London.
Haberland, Eike. 1963. *Galla Sud-Athiopiens*. Stuttgart.
Hallpike, C.R. 1972. *The Konso of Ethiopia: A Study of the Values of a Cushitic People*. Oxford.
Hamer, J. 1970. 'Sidamo Generational Class Cycles: A Political Gerontocracy' *Africa*, XI, 1:50-70.
Hodson, Arnold. 1927. *Seven Years in Southern Abyssinia*. London.
Huntingford, G.W.B. 1955. *The Galla of Ethiopia*. London.
Knutsson, Karl Eric. 1967. *Authority and Change: A Study of the Kallu Institution among the Macha Galla of Ethiopia*. Etnologiska Studier, 29. Gothenberg.
Legesse, Asmarom. 1963. 'Class Systems Based on Time'. *Journal of Ethiopian Studies*, 2.
———. 1973. *Gada: Three Approaches to the Study of African Society*. New York.
———. 1973. *Kenya Boran I: Flexibility and Change in a Pastoral Society*. Hanover, New Hampshire.
Pecci, D. 1941. 'Note sul sistema della gada e delle classi di eta presso le popolazioni Borana'. *Rassegna di Studi Etiopici I* Rome. 305-321.
Phillips, Anthony. 1977. *God: B.C.* London.
Plowman, Clifford H.F. 1919. 'Notes on the Gedamoch Ceremonies among the Boran'. *Journal of the African Society* XVIII, 114-21.
Report of the Northern Frontier District Commission. Cmnd. 1900. London (1962).
Rowse, A.L. 1955. *The Expansion of Elizabethan England*. London.
Seligman, C.G. 1930. *Races of Africa*. London.
Stahl, Michael. 1974. *Ethiopia: Political Contradictions in Agricultural Development*. Stockholm: Publications of the Political Science Association Uppsala No. 67.
Stanley, S. and Karsten, D. 1968. 'The Luwa System of the Garbicco Subtribe of the Sidama (Southern Ethiopia) as a Special Case of an Age Set System'. *Paiduma*, XIV: 93-102.
Stewart, Frank H. 1977. *Fundamentals of Age-Group Systems*. London.
Tutschek, Charles. 1844-5. *Dictionary of the Galla Language*. Munich.
Wingfield, Alys. 1948. 'Tribespeople of Kenya's Northern Frontier District'. *The Geographical Magazine*, 351-62.

VII
Gabra Age Organisation and Ecology[1]

W. TORRY

Gabra society is organised to allow human survival in an extremely adverse environment characterised by low annual rainfall and irregularly distributed surface water. Gabra respond to water scarcity by following seasonally fluctuating assemblage patterns which permit quick, opportunistic adjustments to continuously changing distributions of suitable pasturage and water, and by intense resource sharing between herding units which ease the impact of chronic economic reverses. I intend to portray the ways in which the Gabra age organisation allows persons to adjust to ecological stress by promoting largescale co-operation among population segments. I will also try to indicate how the *modus operandi* of the *gada* institution depends on some of the same ecological difficulties it endeavours to control. Gabra subsistence patterns are described first and then, secondly, the feedback between the organisation of the age grade system and economic organisation is considered.

Environment and subsistence

The Gabra are among the southernmost of the Galla (Oromo) speaking peoples and speak the same dialect as their neighbours, the Boran and Sakuyye. They number approximately 20,000 in a 52,000-square-mile territory which is bracketed by Lake Rudolph to the west and on the east by a vast plain which extends from the Marsabit foothills northeasterly to Moyale, on the Kenya-Ethiopia border. Herders move freely across the international border. Less than one quarter of the population normally lives near the Megado Escarpment, to the north in Ethiopia. The Gabra's only permanent allies, the Boran, surround them to the north and in small pockets to the south. Outlying Turkana groups appear to the southwest and Dassanetch camps occasionally intrude from the northwest. Neither the Gabra nor their neighbours, save for certain Dassanetch and Turkana sections, farm but subsist mainly on the products of their herds and flocks. This perforce brings the Gabra and most of their neighbours into stiff competition for access to some of the same scarce resources. Raids between Gabra and the Somali, Dassanetch and Samburu have been frequent and bloody.

The movement patterns of residential units follow a highlands-lowlands axis. The hot plains, which comprise three quarters of Gabra territory, are punctuated by low, rocky hills, vast barren salt pans, gravel patches and thick volcanic ridges. The annual rainfall is less than eight inches and falls in downpours during one or two week periods in the months of April-June and September-November. The growing period for most plants is brief so their nutritive value is correspondingly low, but the acacia, comminfera and assorted perennial grasses which dominate the landscape, with other xerophytic plants, do offer adequate forage to browsing stock.

The vegetation cover is one of alternating dense thickets and grass and low brush savannah. Highland zones are limited to Marsabit Mountain to the southeast, the Hurri Hills in the centre of the country and the Megado Escarpment to the north. Good spring-fed grasslands surround the lower flanks of some of these hill tracts but succeed into bushland and brush forest with increasing altitude. The hill clusters, most of which lie below 4000 feet, receive up to thirteen inches of rain per annum.

Shortage of surface water is perhaps the most critical environmental constraint. Except for Lake Turkana (Rudolph) permanent surface water lies only within a few widely spaced networks of wells and springs. The proximity of the Lake to hostile neighbours discourages herders from regularly visiting it. Gorai and Chalbi have the only large concentrations of water holes but they are separated by more than ninety miles of rough hill country, and the vast grasslands between them go virtually unutilised during the dry seasons because they lack water. Distances of twenty miles or more separate permanent water points. Gabra resources assume the form of a few islands of water surrounded by a sea of rock, sand and thornbrush.

Gabra do not cultivate from their own desire and lack of suitable natural conditions. Although their country abounds with several species of game animals they make little effort to hunt for food or to collect edible plants, but prefer to subsist from the products of their herds of camels, goats, sheep and cattle. Maize meal is purchased from local traders with proceeds from the sale of small stock and cattle, and is used to relieve desperate drought-induced hunger. During the dry seasons small stock become a vital source of meat, though their contribution to the milk supply is very small. Approximately 60 per cent of the milk during these oppressive periods comes from camels. The Gabra own too few cattle, less than 10,000 head, to be a major source of food.

Spatial organisation

Gabra occupy two types of residential unit, the main camp and the satellite or dry stock camp. Shortly after the rains, herdowners like to drive all of the access herds[2] back to the main camp, which typically consists of some fifteen to thirty tents occupied by a dozen or so family units. Herders prefer the grassy plains located some distance from foothills as wet season camp sites, and shortly after the rains these areas can accommodate all of a family's herds. A month or two after a series of good downpours the surface pools dry up, so that shifts of camp and the separation of the herds becomes imperative. Shortages of surface water accentuate the incompatible feeding requirements of the herds and impinge increasingly on herd management. Cattle are then sent to better-watered hill pastures. Gabra consider highland regions too cool, salt-deficient and tick-infested for camels and small stock, so cattle and their young male attendants move to these outposts, where they remain for several months until the next series of good downpours come to the plains.

As the dry season advances, main camps gravitate to the larger well complexes and washes of the hot plains. After a few waterless months the drinking requirements of small stock and camels diverge sufficiently to warrant further divisions. Sheep and goats must now drink at least once every five to six days. Travel through the hot plains become difficult and the animals rapidly lose condition. Enfeebled, they are usually relocated within four or five miles of water points. The flocks thrive in the low bush country which is laced with numerous washes in which shallow wells can be dug. Large tracts of this sort abound in the southeast and north central parts of the territory, and it is to these regions that the bulk of the flock are sent, in the care of both young men and women.

Small stock country has too few water holes large enough or bush sufficiently dense to support large camel herds continuously during the dry months, and by the third rainless month the camels need more water than forage plants can provide. Herders begin to send these beasts to water at wells at Chalbi and Gorai, and they come here from every part of Gabra country. Each herd visits the wells once in every ten to fifteen days. Each of the well complexes contains over twenty wells and on any day thousands of camels may come to them.

Camel milk is the dietary mainstay for the bulk of the population, so that most of the people remain at the main camps with the camels throughout the year. The concentrations of camels that visit the well complexes graze down the surrounding forage, hence main camps settle some distance from them. Herders tend, on the average, to live some twenty miles from camel wells during the advanced stages of the dry seasons. Strong youths take the pregnant and bull camels to lusher frontier ranges in order to relieve local grazing pressure during these oppressive periods.

The prevailing pattern of seasonal displacements then is one between wet season hill-flanks and dry season interior plains. The orbits of any given camp can, and frequently do, change from year to year. The compass of main camp displacements only very occasionally exceeds one hundred miles. Main camps shift to fresh sites about once every four to five weeks but satellite units move more frequently. These displacements occasion two basic types of aggregation — the camp and the neighbourhood. A family and its dependent herds are spread widely between the dry stock camp and the main camp during the dry seasons. However, the range of tracts containing good camel pastures within easy reach of suitable water is limited, and restricts camp sites to certain regions only. Herders prefer to be near neighbours during periods of intense privation so that they can borrow such essentials as labour, water containers, milch stock and pack camels. Hence, maximal clustering among camps occurs during the dry months, despite the dispersal of their occupants.

Satellite camps consist of little more than a network of make-shift kraals and adjoining brush windscreens. Camp residents dwell in small, spherical tents of goat or sheep hide and sisal fibre. Women are charged with the onerous task of dismantling tents, loading all the family possessions on to pack camels and then reassembling the camp when a new site is reached.

Subsistence patterns cannot be examined in depth here, but the salient socio-economic problems must be outlined because they affect the everyday operations of the grade system. These subsistence exigencies can be described briefly as a series of shortages, involving labour, food and key resources.

(a) *Labour shortages.* The economy is extraordinarily labour-intensive and many essential tasks are arduous. During the long dry seasons the domestic labour force is parcelled among a number of different herding units, each separated in space. Stock are taken long distances to wells, and women travel with pack camels far from the main camps to fetch water. Almost every able bodied person, including children from the age of seven, is pressed into service. My data indicate that the average individual is employed six hours a day seven days a week in activities solely related to the acquisition and preparation of food.

(b) *Food shortages.* The amount of time and energy which is expended in production activities is inversely related to the quantity of food produced. Dry season conditions force people to work longer and harder but so undermine the productivity of the herds that starvation diets prevail. At this time, according to my calculations, only about one quart of milk and a few ounces of meat are available daily to the typical individual, well below the 2200 calories of food a day which is conventionally suggested as the minimum needed for human subsistence.

(c) *Shortages of operating equipment.* Pack camels transport family possessions between campsites and carry the heavy water containers between the camp and distant wells. Most active pack camels are stationed at the main camp but some are sent to sheep/goat camps where they fetch water. Pack camels are used frequently during droughts and, overworked and undernourished, they do not perform at full capacity. There are never enough healthy beasts of burden to meet the demands of every herdowner, nor are there sufficient water containers to go around to all who need them.

(*d*) *Shortages of water points.* Ordering the activities of large aggregations of persons and stock around the few dry season wells and springs is a major organisational problem.

Because of the conditions I have just outlined, it is difficult for the family or camp unit to achieve economic self-sufficiency. Within the span of a year or two many occasions arise which prompt men to borrow stock, helpers and equipment from neighbours. The unpredictable nature of climatic conditions and the fortuitous incidence of stock diseases and enemy raids can bring instant ruin to herding units. Each man thus requires access to a large network of persons from whom he can claim support. The *gada* system links the herdowner to a wide range of persons who are obliged to render such assistance, and it also embodies a politico-judicial apparatus for enforcing claims for assistance. It also facilitates the sharing of scarce dry season tracts and heavily used water points. A politico-ritual system which can influence the organisation of social activities beyond the level of family or camp is necessary to effect the large-scale co-operation that permits the Gabra herding enterprise to endure.

Social organisation

Both the grade system and the camp community are built on a foundation of phratries and their internal divisions, hence I shall describe these units first.

The largest segments are politically autonomous units, which I shall call phratries. There are five phratries named Gara, Galbo, Algana, Odola and Sharbana. The larger ones probably number around five to six thousand persons. Although the egalitarian character of Gabra policies provides that no one group can claim exclusive access to any one piece of territory, phratries nonetheless tend to be associated with customary ranges.[3] A variety of important social activities, among which is the arrangement of marriages, are regulated through the phratry. My census of over four hundred marriages revealed that more than 60 per cent of all Gabra marriages are contracted within the phratry and in some the rate reached 85 per cent. Each phratry embraces an independently operating system of generation-sets and grades, the activities of which are co-ordinated by a committee of political and ritual functionaries.

The phratry asserts its identity through numerous rituals, nuances of dress, stock brands and myths. In addition to these diacritics, ethnic roots are drawn upon to emphasise group distinctiveness. For instance, most Odola trace their ancestry to Somali and Rendille forbears and none claims descent from the Boran, who are the traditional enemies of those tribes. On the other hand, many Algana proudly boast of having a Boran pedigree and few claim to be of Somali or Rendille stock. Algana and Odola indeed belittle one another for having adopted the distasteful habits which each attributed to the neighbouring tribe it dislikes. This contempt, real or feigned, is expressed by jestful insults.

Although phratries tend to be quasi-endogamous, and despite the great pride a Gabra manifests in his phratry membership, there is no evidence to suggest that such identification in any way strains intra-tribal harmony. Indeed the ecological exigencies of stock management already described inhibit this possibility. Men from all phratries mix at the wells and at satellite camp grazing tracts, join together to attack or to repel a common foe, establish complex trade partnerships and occasionally co-reside and intermarry.

Each phratry has a dual division, Yiblo and Lossa, but these only play a major role in the organisation of ceremonies. More important in the structuring of social activities are the exogamous, named patriclans. A man's clan affiliation determines the range of clans from which he can acquire a spouse. In times of need a man turns first to his clansmen for help. A major economic operation undertaken by a clan is the redistribution of stock from the affluent to the impoverished. Clansmen can also adjudicate disputes among themselves and levy fines on each other. Clan meetings are usually presided over by *Jallaba*, who are men selected from each clan to political offices associated with the phratry council.

Clans are not territorial units. Indeed, herding requirements, a rule of one year uxorilocal postmarital residence, and a tendency for persons to reside with various affines long after marriage, combine to disperse clansmen widely. However, as I hope to make apparent later, the operation of the grade system assures a considerable degree of clan cohesion. Each clan owns esoteric rituals and paraphernalia, stock brands and wells. Clans embrace lineages.

My census of the composition of more than fifty main camps indicates that the majority of co-residents in any camp are also phratrymates, many of whom are also affinally related. A typical camp consists of a core of one or two elders, some of their male and female married children and married siblings of the spouses of those children. In the larger camps, several criss-crossing strands of such brother-sister linkages exist, (Torry 1976) thus giving such camps a bilateral appearance which is reminiscent of bushmen or Algonkian bands (cf. Lee 1972; Helms 1965). If classificatory affinity is taken into consideration these inter-household bonds appear even more intricate.

Each clan exhibits traditional preferences for marriage into a limited range of other clans, which may belong to its own or to other phratries. Fathers take special pains to see that their eldest sons get wives from one of the preferred clans and particularly from the clan of their mother; similar, but less strenuous, attempts are made for younger sons. Members of these marriage-linked clans are addressed by affinal terms and treated with more than ordinary respect. A man is expected to exhibit similar behaviour towards the affines of all his agnates. Members of such marriage linked clans are addressed by reciprocal affinal terms and are under special obligation to render mutual assistance. This system of classificatory affinity multiplies the possibilities of neighbours entering into established patterns of association.

Every camp has a founder or headman. The composition of camps may change from one season to the next but some men retain a headmanship for many years, and the son of an influential headman often takes over from a deceased father.[4] But some camps form for a season or two and then disband. Whatever its lifespan a camp always takes the name of its headman.

The position of headman lies at the juncture of three connected spheres of political integration — the camp, the neighbourhood and the phratry. Normally a moderate degree of intelligence and stock wealth are sufficient credentials for the attainment of headmanship. Irrespective of the personal attributes of its holder, this position is endowed with certain well-defined prerogatives and duties, one of the most important of which is the supervision of local ceremonies. Most seasonal thanksgiving rituals are performed on an intra-camp basis. Ideally, both animals and coffee beans are sacrificed in strict order of precedence of the sacrificers, according both to the phratry and clan affiliations of the stock owners and the degree of ritual importance associated with the category of beast being offered. Headmen arrange and oversee these activities. Minor quarrels between neighbours are also brought to the attention of the headman, who should convene a meeting of available elders to press the disputants to a quick settlement. More energetic leaders occasionally represent their camps in neighbourhood assemblies which meet to work out neighbourhood watering schedules, to map out migration strategies and to plan for inter-camp rituals.

The population of the larger camps exceeds two hundred persons distributed among some forty to fifty tents. Headmen of big camps often retain their positions for several years and their influence derives as much from high positions they hold in the phratry as from personal qualities. Indeed the majority of founders of the larger camps surveyed were either *Jallaba* or high ranking members of the priestly clans known as *Xallu* clans. In many such instances the headman is a phratry leader as well as a leader of a local community.

Gabra camps are seldom isolated and it is unusual to find a camp located more than a mile or two from its nearest neighbours. The most common pattern is the *rera*, a cluster of two to five camps each within a few hundred yards of each other. These groupings, which I shall refer to as neighbourhoods, share a nearby shady meeting spot and often move together throughout the year, though only exceptionally do they remain together beyond the time of one annual cycle. Neighbourhoods which are located within a radius of around five miles are considered part of the same district (*arda*). The men of a district also make a shade-covered clearing, at which they hold occasional district meetings. At these meetings such important matters are discussed as the organisation of stock raids, defensive manoeuvres, the dispatch of scouts to reconnoitre the pasturage, the adjudication of difficult disputes, the arrangements for phratry rituals and assistance for men who have been the victims of stock epidemics or raiders. District-wide watering schedules may be formulated there. Neighbourhood elders appeal to the custodians of wells for watering rights on behalf of men they represent. The schedules specify the time and the exact well at which each herder in the district may water. Stiff fines may be imposed on men who consistently attempt to water out of turn. At times more than twenty-five camps may participate in such district meetings which are usually presided over by senior phratry officials who collectively press the assembly to maintain decorum and to arrive at consensual decisions.

After a series of good downpours the central phratry assembly, or *Ya'a*, may call meetings which will be attended by men from several districts. The organisation that makes these huge aggregations possible will be discussed presently.

Grade organisation

Every Gabra male automatically enters at birth a generation-set or *luba*, which consists of all the males of his phratry who are the sons of his father's *luba* mates. Until they are installed into the grade from which the highest official (the *Hayyu Aadula*) of the father's *luba* is appointed, men are collectively known as 'the sons of' that official. Two *luba* are interposed between those of a father and his sons. In Gabra theory each clan, and hence each phratry, embraces a full range of extant *luba*. Each set (*luba*) moves sequentially through a series of grades. The ceremonies (*Jilla*) through which *luba* are installed into given grades ideally occur once every eighth year, from which it follows that a son's *luba* succeeds its father's into a given grade after twenty-four years.

There are two principal grades, the *Xomicha*, or political elders, and the *Dabella*, or ritual elders, two pre-grades, the young men *luba* and children *Idjole*, and one post-grade, the retired elders, *Jarsa*. Retired elderhood is a residual grade which lies at the end of the grade-line and may contain more than one set. Regardless of the grade their *luba* occupies, men are not considered to be adult until they marry. Most men marry in their early to mid-thirties, prior to which they must have been circumcised, usually in their late teens or early twenties. The circumcision ceremony is performed on an individual rather than on a communal basis.

Bachelors spend most of their time herding stock and have virtually no role to play in community-wide policy making activities. Indeed it is regarded as improper for bachelors to make a habit of attending assembly meetings of any sort. Uncircumcised lads are allowed even fewer privileges and are barred from the battlefield, forbidden to marry or participate in mortuary ceremonies. Bachelors are denied the right to sacrifice stock which is one of the most cherished prerogatives enjoyed by Gabra males.

The grade system bears significantly on an individual's social persona after he marries and enters the political elder grade. Most political officers of a phratry belong to that grade. Political elders are collectively known as 'bulls' and sacrifice certain categories of bull stock at large public ceremonies on behalf of the entire phratry. Symbolically they embody the strength and generative powers of the phratry and tribe. Political elders lead assemblies at all levels.

The transition from political to ritual elderhood involves a dramatic status change, in that henceforth men should retire from the political domain and rarely, if ever, go on raiding and hunting expeditions. At the transition ceremony they vow to avoid all acts of violence except for defending villages from enemy attacks. Office-holders retain their offices until their deaths but their authority diminishes progressively and they perform their duties in what is essentially an emeritus capacity.

Through their initiation ceremonies, ritual elders acquire *garoma*, a quality of heightened virtue or piety which enables its holder to give potent blessings. Much of this mystical power is believed to emanate from ritually treated *materia sacra* that are enclosed within the folds of a band-like headpiece which is the most conspicuous emblem of this grade. Ritual elders play a major role in blessing persons at communal ceremonies and *rites de passage*. Sterile women who seek fertility and owners of stray stock who pray for their safe return also approach ritual elders to ask for help. The establishment of peace and fertility through prayer are among their chief duties. In contrast to the masculine, or bull-like, qualities associated with political elders, ritual elders are regarded in a euphemistic sense as women. For instance they are referred to by feminine forms of pronouns and verbs and are prohibited from lighting brush fires, from holding their genitals when urinating, from wearing trousers and from travelling at night. They abstain from stock watering and do not walk behind their male

Plate VII.1. A Gabra political elder

travelling companions. They only sacrifice sheep and gelded stock, for these animals are equated with the female sphere of life and with public peace. Indeed, many of the ceremonies which ritual elders perform *ex officio* involve the safety and welfare of women. Moreover, ritual elders, like women, are excluded from the execution of rites which emphasise masculine activity. These lie in the province of political elders. I am not suggesting, however, that ritual elders are expected to behave effeminately.

When men leave this grade they discard their ritually doctored headpieces and replace them with a thin strip of coarse cloth which is the insignia of retired elders. Henceforth they only have minor public responsibilities that are confined to assisting ritual elders in the execution of public ceremonies and substituting for them if none is present in an area in which a ceremony is being planned.

An individual's grade has a bearing on many of his social prerogatives, including seating positions at public gatherings, the division of war booty, position in stock watering rotas, aspects of costume, the order in which invocations are recited at ceremonies, the type of stock sacrificed at feasts and the species of ritual in which men are obliged to participate actively. Members of one *luba* pass through the grades together, and only one *luba* at a time occupies a grade. *Luba* mates share a special joking relationship and address one another as *jal'*, or peer. But they only meet, as a formal group, during the *luba* installation ceremonies, *Jilla*.

The timing of *Jilla* is determined calendrically. The most important component of the system of time-reckoning is a cycle of seven twelve month years. The seven years of a cycle and the seven days of a week share the same nomenclature. Each named day and year has propitious or unpropitious associations and all ceremonial activities are programmed around these associations. With the exception of the Gara, all phratries hold their *Jilla* during the highly propitious year of *Gumata* (Friday). The Gara, because they are the most senior phratry, carry out their festivities one year before the others. Traditionally, the other phratries follow the Gara lead and should first apply to the Gara council for blessings and engage in ritualised exchanges of incense and sheep with them before moving to their own ceremonial grounds to perform the *Jilla*. Each phratry performs its own ceremonies independently but all follow the same time sequence.

The *Jilla* consists of a long pilgrimage which initiands of both grades make to the clan shrines of the mythical founders and heroes of their phratries. Initiands travel over most of the circuit of ceremonial sites together and, at one special ceremony, authority is formally handed over from the leaders of the *luba* retiring from the grade to those about to enter it. The *luba* making the journey perform numerous sacrificial rites at specific sites, and these are arranged and sometimes conducted by clansmen of the ancient heroes being commemorated at the site. These ceremonies require substantial co-operation between persons of different *luba* and different clans.

During the trip initiands of each grade undergo long periods of instruction. They are accompanied by their families and the bulk of their milch stock, along with a number of sacrificial animals. Ritual elders-apparent tutor the political elder-initiands in the conduct and responsibilities expected of them in their new roles, while a few particularly knowledgeable men, who are about to move into the retired elder grade, travel with the prospective ritual elders in order to instruct them in their turn. The *Jilla* grounds of all but the Odola phratry are situated in southern Ethiopia. The Odola site is near Sololo in Kenya, not far from the Ethiopian border. These pilgrimages may involve treks of 200 to 300 miles during the course of one year.

Each clan is entitled to appoint from it ranks a number of political functionaries, or *Jallaba*, from each *luba* entering the political elder grade. The number of *Jallaba* who are elected ranges from two to twelve and is dependent both on the size of the clan and of the *luba*.[5] Fathers tend to be succeeded by sons but there is no fixed rule of hereditary transmission. *Jallaba* are ranked according to the seniority of their clans and lineages but such distinctions are of little consequence outside the organisation of ceremonies. The influence a *Jallaba* exerts on an assembly *vis-à-vis* other *Jallaba* is determined more by wisdom and personality than by pedigree.

Political elder-initiands assemble to nominate *Jallaba* at a series of meetings which precede the pilgrimage to the *Jilla* grounds. Once their *luba* has been installed, these men hold phratry offices for life, but their authority wanes as they move into other grades. Like all officeholders *Jallaba* are ceremonially confirmed by the senior *Xallu* of the phratry and serve both their clan and their phratry. They preside over all important meetings of clansmen and neighbours. All *Jallaba* should collaborate to adjudicate a case regardless of the clans of the parties involved. The Gabra seem more concerned with the wisdom and prestige of a particular *Jallaba* than with his clan, so that disputants rarely go out of their way to seek *Jallaba* of their own clans to mediate for them. *Jallaba* in no way form discrete councils and the office carries with it no specific ceremonial functions. If *Jallaba* of more than one grade attend a council meeting, those of the political elder grade take precedence.

The most prestigious political positions are those of *Hayyu*. These offices are in theory hereditary and confined to the highest ranking lineages within specific clans. Each set entering the political elder grade confirms two *Hayyu*. One is from the senior of the dual divisions (Yiblo), and the *Hayyu Aadula*, and the other is from the junior division (Lossa) and is known simply as *Hayyu*. The *luba* of the Hayyu *Aadula*, is eventually named after him once it is installed into the political elder grade.

Hayyu are installed in office together with the *Jallaba* of their *luba* by the senior *Xallu* of their phratry and by the two *Hayyu* moving out of the political elder grade. *Xallu* are said to be the 'makers' of *Hayyu* and *Jallaba*. Phratry-wide rituals, under the supervision of the *Ya'a*, or central assembly, cannot be performed without the participation of *Hayyu*. The *Hayyu* represent the embodiment of procreative powers of which the political elder grade is a manifestation, and the blood of the bull stock these men sacrifice at important ceremonies is smeared on the *Hayyu* so that men and stock will proliferate.

The duties of *Hayyu* are essentially politico-jural and concern members of their own phratries. Generally, very complicated breaches of law or cases involving important elders, including *Jallaba*, that cannot be effectively handled in lower level assemblies are brought to the attention of *Hayyu*. The assemblies that *Hayyu* preside over are the highest courts of appeal in Gabra. During good wet seasons these officials convene huge meetings which draw non-phratry and phratrymen alike from all corners of Gabra country. Cases which have accumulated over the long dry season are heard at this time. *Hayyu* are also instrumental in determining whether the phratry should conduct its *Jilla* during the year for which it is scheduled. If they insist influential *Hayyu* can stall the ceremony for at least another seven years. *Hayyu* of each phratry can carry out most of their duties independently of one another, although some phratries require that the *Hayyu* of the political elder grade be present if the central assembly is to perform its phratry-wide rituals. If both *Hayyu* live in the same district, as they commonly do, they collaborate to resolve important disputes. *Hayyu* are enjoined not to live outside their phratry rangelands, as are all members of the *Ya'a* assembly.

Each phratry has its own assembly, the *Ya'a*, a term which signifies both the camp these elders occupy and the assembly they form. Under no circumstances do the *Ya'a* of more than one phratry reside within the same district. Ideally, the core of the *Ya'a* assembly is comprised of four High *Xallu*, at least one *Hayyu* of the Yiblo division, numerous ritual elders, and the custodians of the sacred drum, horn and firesticks. *Jallaba* act somewhat as deputies to the *Ya'a* but, unless they are ritual elders they tend to remain in their own camps. The *Ya'a* camp is constructed around a large, oblong bush fence, or *nabo*. Sacrificial ceremonies are conducted periodically within this enclosure on behalf of all Gabra, but especially members of the phratry. The High *Xallu* from the ritual elder grade of the Yiblo division is the leader or 'father' of the *Ya'a*; hence he is the spiritual leader of the entire phratry.

The sacred drum custodian (*Aban Dibbe*) comes from the ritual elder grade of the Yiblo division, and the drum is owned by the *Xallu* clan. The sacred horn custodian (*Aban Magalata*) hails from the Lossa division and must be a political elder. The sacred horn belongs to one clan but like the drum, its stewardship is temporarily given to other clans if the *luba* of the clan which owns it lacks an elder who is competent to use and protect it. The sacred firestick custodian (*Aban Uchuma*) comes from the ritual elder grade of the Lossa division. These firesticks are owned by one clan and they are kept exclusively within that clan even if custodianship is conferred upon an individual from the political elder grade. The distribution of officers and grades is represented in Figure VII.1.

The *Ya'a* constitute a mobile administrative and spiritual hub of phratry affairs, and all major religious ceremonies of the phratry are conducted by these elders. The assembly is constantly visited by men, who sometimes travel great distances, to beg for favours, to make offerings, and to seek information concerning technical, legal and ritual matters. I outline below only some of the more important and interesting duties of the assembly:

1. The most severe or complex violations of tribal law eventually reach the *Ya'a*. For example, if a maiden is seen having sexual intercourse or

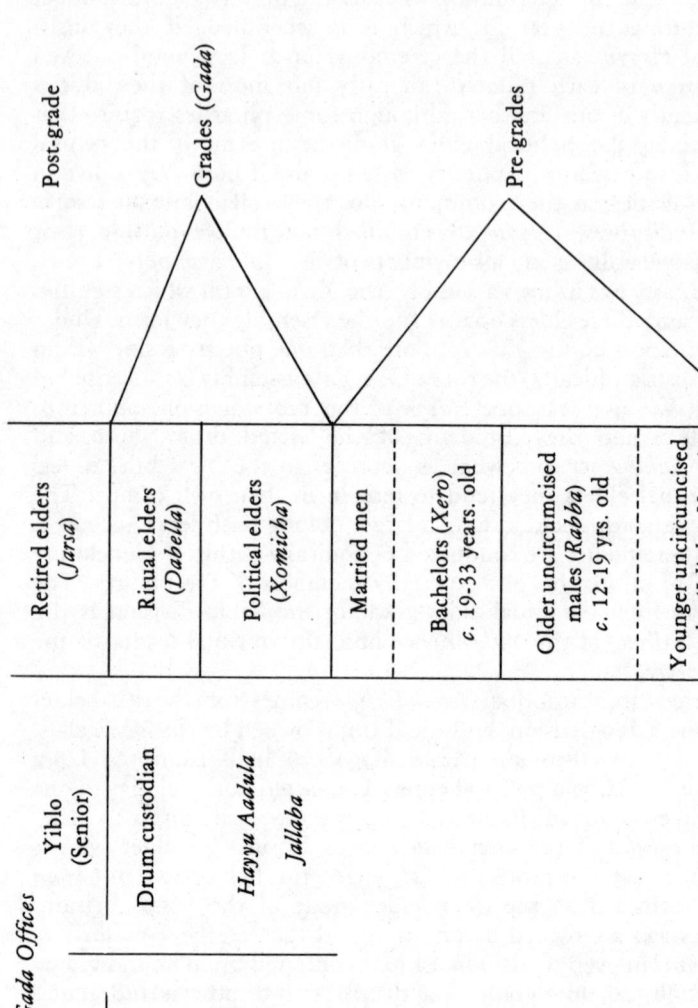

Figure VII.1. Distribution of grades and gada officers

becomes pregnant, she and her consort are sent before the Phratry Council and the couple are forced to undergo a series of rites of defilement which symbolise their disaffiliation from the tribe. A murderer is treated in much the same way. Men gravely abused by their agnates communicate their plaints to the *Ya'a* who then adjudicate them.

2. All plans for opening and closing the grades and for organising all major *Jilla* ceremonies are the responsibility of the *Ya'a* acting under the direction of the *Hayyu* and High *Xallu*.

3. Foreigners who wish to become Gabra apply for membership in the clan and phratry of their choice (generally those of a friend or affine) through the *Ya'a* of that phratry. Upon approval the *Ya'a* administer purificatory rites which 'naturalise' the applicant. They may also present him with a small herd with which to begin his life among them. On the other hand, a man who has been so offended by his agnates that he wishes to join another clan of his phratry applies to the *Ya'a* to expedite this transfer for him. These arrangements are quite rare, I was told, and cannot be executed without the permission of the *Ya'a*.

4. The *Ya'a* are empowered to fine miscreants and to enforce penalties if needs be. In exceptional instances they can send a deputation of strong young men to the camp of a culprit and forcibly take stock from him.

5. The *Ya'a* can requisition stock for a public ceremony from anyone of their phratry except *Xallu* and *Hayyu*. Occasionally drum custodians require contributions of sheep to provide fat to rub into the leather bindings of the sacred drums, and horn custodians require the blood of goats to 'feed' the sacred horn. When the *Ya'a* plan a phratry-wide sacrifice during a propitious month, they can select a camel from the herd of a wealthy stock owner if they are unable to provide a sacrificial beast from among their own herds.

6. The *Ya'a* camp is the administrative capital of the phratry although throughout the year many leaders live scattered over the extensive grazing territory of their phratry. It is impossible for all officials of the phratry to assemble for many of the important meetings and sacrifices that the *Ya'a* request. However, the Gabra have devised strategies to compensate for the dispersion of their members so that political and ritual isolation is minimised. *Kora deeda*, or meetings in the bush of elders from a number of districts are one such device through which the integrity of the phratry structure is maintained. If weather permits these ceremonies are held at least once each year. A central feature is the sacrifice of a goat by a political elder as representative of a particular clan. The *Hayyu Aadula* is then

annointed with the blood of this beast by every political elder attending. All of the men of this grade who are present rub their foreheads and spear shafts with the blood and the sacred horn is also annointed. War songs and dances follow and goat-skin bracelets, cut from the hide of the sacrificial animal, are distributed to the participating political elders. All *Hayyu, Jallaba* and High *Xallu* of the phratry must receive these tokens. As relatively few of these persons attend the sacrifice, they are transmitted to them some days or weeks later through a chain of couriers whom the *Ya'a* instruct to deliver them. The Gabra consider it essential that their phratry officials possess tangible evidence of having received or partaken in the blessings attendant on their sacrifices. I have seen bracelets which have been transmitted over 200 or 300 miles before reaching their destination. Similar occasions also arise when *Ya'a* call officials to their camp for consultations.

The *Ya'a* play no specific role in the organisation of inter-tribal fighting, but where relations between Borana or Rendille and the Gabra are concerned, the *Ya'a* of particular phratries are requested to negotiate a peaceful settlement.[6] Gabra contend that the *Ya'a* have peace-making rather than war-making functions.

The duties of the occupants of the above offices which pertain to the establishment and maintenance of social order can be summarised as follows:

1. Most disputes which involve the use of wells, the transfer of stock, feuds over women or property, refusal to pay fines or a multitude of types of petty squabbles are brought to the attention of neighbouring elders. If they cannot effectively resolve the disagreement, and there are no *Jallaba* on hand, they may call one.

2. Many *Jallaba* are influential, especially within their own clans, so that relatively few issues pass beyond their level of jurisdiction. *Jallaba* preside over discussions about who will donate stock to an impoverished agnate and they possess the authority to put pressure on agnates to contribute stock to those phratry rituals which demand the sacrifice of animals from their clan. *Jallaba* can levy fines on all but the highest phratry officials. They have special responsibilities for organising raids against enemy tribes.

3. *Hayyu* usually handle only very serious and involved cases which *Jallaba* have failed to settle. *Hayyu* are appealed to for their services; they do not volunteer them. The summit of jural authority exists at this level, but in exceptional cases such as murder, *Xallu* and the triumvirate of ritual custodians are also enlisted to pass judgement. Men who flaunt all established authority risk the curse of the High *Xallu*, which is tantamount to outlawing. *Hayyu* and other *Ya'a* often act together, especially in cases where the declared offence involves ritual matters.

Irregularities in the system

Gabra believe that the grade system should operate according to the scheme I have outlined. The system, however, does not and cannot work precisely in this manner. The age at which men and women marry, the marital status of men on the eve of the *Jilla* and a host of ecological factors conspire to create a discrepancy between the ideal and real operation of the grade system. I will go on to indicate why the very failure of the system to conform to Gabra norms allows it to persist and how this paradox is rooted in herding ecology.

The individual must satisfy the following prerequisites in order to be eligible to enter a grade: (*a*) his *luba* must be up for initiation; (*b*) he must be married. Men who marry after their *luba* is installed become active grade members for as long as their set remains in the grade. But initiation is a precondition for placement into office.

While men commonly marry for the first time in their mid-thirties, most Gabra girls are brides by the age of sixteen. This marriage arrangement produces a wide age differential between fathers and sons and between siblings. A two to three year post-partum restriction on sexual intercourse also maintains wide age intervals between male siblings. The way these factors jointly affect the movement of *luba* through grades can best be illustrated by a simple hypothetical example (see Figure VII.2).

Pete, aged thirty-four, marries a girl of fifteen. Two years later the couple have their first son, Bill, and ten years later Alex, their second boy, is born. In the year 1900 Pete is forty-three and his *luba*, Xa, enters the political elder grade. By this time Bill is seven years old. Let us assume that *Jilla* are held every eighth year. In 1924 Bill's *luba*, Xb, is installed as political elders. Will Bill and Alex both be initiated with their other *luba* mates? Bill, at thirty-one, may or may not be ready to marry at this time. Even if he is not he is certainly bound to do so some time during the next seven years and, when he does, his political elderhood becomes automatic. Alex at twenty-three will probably be too young to enter this grade but in all probability will marry during the period his set is in the ritual elder grade, so that both he and Bill will definitely reach this category of elderhood. An analysis of the prospects of Bill and Alex's children becoming initiates reveals some of the implications of these events.

Suppose that Bill and Alex, like their father before them, marry at the age of thirty-four, have their first sons at thirty-six and their second at forty-four. As the *Jilla* commence every eight years, Xc, the *luba* that Pete's grandsons belong to enters the political elder grade in 1948, in which year the ages of Ken and Karl, Bill's sons, and Allen and Adam, Alex's sons, will be 19, 11, 11, and 1, respectively. Their bachelorhood disqualifies them from becoming active political elders throughout the period their *luba* occupies this grade. Nor will they

Figure VII.2. The movement of *luba* through the grades

		F1 Luba Xa 1900 Pete	F2 Luba Xb 1924 Bill	F2 Luba Xb 1924 Alex	F3 Luba Xc 1948 Ken	F3 Luba Xc 1948 Karl	F3 Luba Xc 1948 Allen	F3 Luba Xc 1948 Adam
1900	Xa	43 yrs. old						
1908		51	7 yrs. old					
1916		59	15					
1924	Xb	67	23	7 yrs. old				
1932			31	15				
1940			39	23				
1948	Xc		47	31	3 yrs. old	3 yrs. old	3 yrs. old	1 yr. old
1956			55	39	11	11	11	9
1964			63	47	19	19	19	17
1972	Xd			55	27	27	27	25
1980				63	35	35	35	33
1988					43	43	43	41
1996	XE				51	51	51	49
2004					59	59	59	57
2012					67	67	67	65
2020	XE							
2028								
2036								
2044	XG							

In this diagram, first sons are born when their fathers are thirty-six years old and second sons are born eight years later, when their fathers are forty-four years old.

marry in time for initiation into the next grade. They will never have a chance to enjoy the full prerogatives associated with these grades, including incumbency of office. The progeny of these men will also be excluded from the grades. However, such men, known as *hafto*,[7] bear no stigma because of this exclusion.

If *Jilla* were delayed through say, one, two or three cycles, would the disjunction between physical age of individuals and the social age or status bestowed on them by virtue of the movement of their *luba* through the grades be reduced at all? To answer this question, let the set-progression during the period under consideration be held back for one cycle so that *Luba* Xa decides to postpone its *Jilla* from 1900 to 1908. The *Jilla* of succeeding *luba* are perforce then delayed eight years. Xb, the *luba* of Bill and Alex, is then installed into the political elder grade in 1932 rather than in 1924, by which time there is a good chance that these men will be married and subsequently make the grade. But none of their children will ever be able to join their *luba* through the grades. A postponement of *Jilla* for sixteen years increases even more the percentage of men eligible for grade membership. Certainly then Bill and Alex could go through initiation with other Xb's and Karl could join the Xc's when they go through the grades. But Pete would certainly have died before his *luba* was initiated. With a three cycle delay (twenty four years), Pete's sons and those of his grandsons considered here would be able to enter both grades although Pete would not.

Clearly, the delays which the Gabra construe as idiosyncratic allow the grade system to persist. A delay-free system would produce a progressive drain on grade membership and a corresponding expansion in the ranks of the retired, unless, of course, a corrective of some sort were introduced. The judicial and policy making machinery, and the ritual regulatory apparatus needed to activate it would crumble without a regular influx of personnel to fill key offices and to keep the ritual elder grade 'alive'.

If the age at marriage of Gabra males and the *Jilla* intervals were both reduced, might not such transition problems be resolved? Probably so if it were not for the problems ingrained within the Gabra mode of subsistence. Under this regime such modifications might at the least be ineffective and at the most be patently disastrous. The prolongation of sub-adulthood among men by delaying marriage until they are in their thirties guarantees for herd owners, a large reserve of subordinate males to enlist in herding chores at distant satellite camps or in laborious watering ventures near home.

Once a man founds a family and assumes more supervision over the herds, his incentive and ability to spend long periods working stock away from camp is considered diminished.[8] Moreover, main camps are nerve centres within social networks. They become arenas for major ceremonies, virtually all assembly meetings and major economic transactions. The dispersal of elders beyond immediate contact with large communities of peers would certainly impair many vital politico-economic operations which herding units perform, particularly those pertaining to the organisation of well-watering schedules.

The seven year spacing between *Jilla* may seem long, but the severe logistical problems that are involved in planning and conducting these ceremonies discourage the Gabra from adopting intervals shorter than this. *Jilla* generate a multitude of highly structured activities. First, several months of planning are required. Clan representatives meet to consider who among them will offer sacrificial stock once the phratry pilgrimage reaches the clan shrines. The nomination of clansmen to *Jallaba*-ship is also considered. Decisions on the clan level are co-ordinated through frequent communications among *Jallaba* of various clans and the *Ya'a* assembly. Once the cavalcade of pilgrims begins its one year journey, men must set aside an enormous amount of time to carry out rituals and, eventually, to settle outstanding cases.[9] For some these festivities are little more than a highly inconvenient interruption of stock production activity.

Jilla participants must also plan for the deployment of their herds while they are away. Herders cannot — and have little desire, to — take all of their stock with them. To do so would produce an intolerable burden of men and animals on local resources and deprive both small stock and cattle access to the rangelands that meet their specific feeding requirements. If herders had to supervise the grazing activities of many different kinds of animals, much of their energy would be diverted from ceremonial activities; so they take most of their camel herds with them along with a small flock of milch goats and some sheep and oxen for sacrifice. Travellers enlist kith and kin remaining behind to look after their stock for them while they are away. Men who are unable to get this assistance may excuse themselves from the *Jilla* with the consent of the *Ya'a* assembly and clan elders, although persons acceding to high office receive such aid through the *Ya'a*. On the whole the Gabra have mixed feelings about *Jilla*. They welcome the chance to move into new grades and to join others of their clan and phratry in these festivities. But they are less than enthusiastic about parting from their herds and driving their camels to remote rangelands.

Jilla make additional economic demands on herding units. They require of some individuals a large capital outlay. New clothing, tea, sugar, coffee beans and cornmeal are needed for ceremonies and rations. These supplies are purchased from the sale of livestock and a family must part with additional animals for sacrifice in numerous rites. Through the *Jilla*, then, a herder accumulates a short term economic deficit in exchange for the possibility of social and ritual advancement.

But the facts that constrain Gabra from holding *Jilla* more frequently do not explain why these ceremonies are sometimes delayed for very long periods. The chief reasons offered, and indeed the only major ones that I have been able to determine bear directly on ecological processes — climate and warfare. To begin with, the continuous aggregation of hundreds of persons and their herds would hardly be possible under conditions of drought. The Gabra hold their transition ceremonies shortly after a series of good rains, when forage growth is luxuriant, surface water is abundant and milk plentiful. Camel milk is a major ingredient in most feasts. Pack camels are then in good enough condition to enable family units to make frequent shifts of camp, and small stock get sufficient browse to fortify them on their long journey. Moreover, long dry spells worry men to the point of distraction about the welfare of non-resident herds, and they so diminish the health of livestock that the market price of sheep, goats and cattle plummets to the level where it is hard for men with small holdings to get the cash to buy *Jilla* provisions. A number of *Jilla* have been postponed because of droughts. *Jilla* are also postponed when parts of the country have been under attack by strong enemy forces. Turkana raids in the early part of this century, Dassanetch expansion in the 1920s (following the prohibition by the Kenya Government of the ownership of firearms), harassment from the Ethiopian army in the 1930s and late 1940s, the English-Italian war (as Gabra see it) of 1940-1 and the Somali raids of the 1960s have forced all the phratries to postpone their *Jilla* time and again. It is difficult for the Gabra to mobilise large fighting forces during *Jilla* years because youths are widely dispersed herding while the elders are preoccupied with rituals. Gabra insist that the *Jilla* grounds be absolutely safe before the ceremonies are held.

The prolongation of *Jilla* over extended periods, system-maintaining as it may seem, still raises a basic question regarding system performance. Office holders die off as the years pass. Many are already in their forties and fifties when they enter the grades, and when there are successive *Jilla* delays, most die before their grade time. Shortly before the last *Jilla* of 1972-3, the Algana had one surviving *Hayyu* and only a handful of *Jallaba* and ritual elders. Decades had passed since the last Sharbana functionaries had died. Among the other sections the grades were also depleted but not as heavily. The question that arises then is, given frequent *Jilla* postponements, what is to keep the politico-ritual machinery of the phratry from becoming undermanned to the point that its operation is impaired. Or, to put another way, how much is sacrificed for the future by postponement?

The Gabra combat this problem of manpower attrition by what I term anticipatory succession. Although men who have not been initiated into an office cannot legitimately hold it,[10] they substitute for others on a *pro tem* basis. For example, after a *Jilla* lapse of thirty two years, the Algana phratry was left with only one *Hayyu* and no more than a half dozen *Jallaba*, so Algana treated married men currently under consideration for these positions as *de facto Jallaba* and *Hayyu*, and elders of the *luba* next in line for installation into the ritual elder grade who were held in high regard were called upon to perform the duties.

The custodianship of ritual objects automatically shifted to those persons temperamentally and morally suited to hold these positions provided that they were from the proper clans and the *luba* next to be installed. The drum was held, for instance, by an individual in the political elder grade and the horn by someone who would become a political elder during the next *Jilla*. The *Ya'a* was presided over by the senior *Xallu* of the phratry, an office which is transmitted by primogeniture. The phratry assembly was very small but it still conducted major ceremonies. Local ceremonies and dispute settlement on all levels were handled by *pro tem* officials. The Gara and Galbo phratries had conducted there ceremonies more recently and had more properly installed officials.

Conclusions

At first glance the complexity of the Gabra system seems inconsistent with the simplicity of their technology and the low level of consumable energy they acquire from their habitat. Their physical environment is so harsh, and the competition among neighbouring tribes for scarce resources is so intense, that it is impossible for herdsmen to accumulate surpluses. Hunger is more the rule than the exception. If they did not own multi-species herds Gabra would have to seek another place to live. The low productivity and diverse, and sometimes conflicting, feeding requirements of the herds when coupled with the highly irregular distribution of key forage points are factors which conspire to place enormous demands on the Gabra social system. Foremost among the organisational problems are achieving an extensive flow of goods and services from the prosperous to the needy and insuring that great aggregations of men and stock can jointly use scarce dry season tracts and well complexes. The grade-system acts as a regulatory apparatus effective beyond the household and camp, as a device for articulating and ordering the activities of a spatially dispersed but economically interdependent population. It cross-cuts clans and generates a system of political and ritual leadership roles built around a central council which unifies the interests and directs the destinies of many persons. The many ways that phratry officials promote a broad scale of co-operation among herdowners is a prerequisite of economic survival. Phratrywide, neighbourhood and camp rituals, the arrangement of watering schedules, stock redistribution and the settlement of disputes are among the major activities falling within the command of *Jallaba*, ritual elders and the *Ya'a*.

NOTES

1. Paul Baxter has read drafts of this manuscript and made numerous helpful suggestions. I wish to express my gratitude both for his assistance and for the encouragement and invaluable advice he and his family offered me during early stages of my fieldwork. Information in this paper was collected through extensive interviews with all categories of age grade officials, in conjunction with the observation of a wide spectrum of ceremonies and legal cases requiring the participation of these functionaries. Many of these activities occur during grade initiation ceremonies (*Jilla*), which I did not have the opportunity to observe, but general field experience provided the insight necessary to formulate questions and critically evaluate answers about events which occur during *Jilla*. Fieldwork among the Gabra was carried out between November 1969 and May 1971 and during June and July 1973. Research was funded through an NIMH predoctoral training grant, Columbia University ISRP funds and aid from the Range Management Division of the Kenya Ministry of Agriculture.
2. Each herdowner is typically the warden of several animals belonging to others, while some of his stock in turn are on loan to associates. By 'access herd' I refer to livestock that a man is actually keeping at his residence at a given time — that is those at his immediate disposal — whether or not he owns all of them.
3. Wells are the property of individual clans although Gabra from all phratries are normally free to use them. During this century repeated Dassanetch harassment has driven the Sharbana phratry from its homeland near Lake Rudolph and Sharbana are now scattered over the Kenya portion of the tribal territory. Odola never had a discrete area and have traditionally resided within or near Galbo camps.
4. The camp of a deceased headman who has older surviving sons is known by the name *ola ilman ebelus*, the camp of the sons of so-and-so. The eldest son acts on behalf of family in camp-related matters; if he is unmarried he collaborates with the more senior of his neighbours to run the camp.
5. Clans, especially small ones, are occasionally unable to place a large number of men into the political elder grade at one time, for reasons considered a bit further on. When no men qualified for high office are among the initiands, the clan simply foregoes its privilege to appoint *Jallaba* until the next *Jilla*. Most clans select from two to six *Jallaba* per *luba*. The number must be even.
6. Algana tend to have the most contact with Boran, and Galbo and Odola with the Rendille.
7. This noun is derived from the verb *hin hafa*, meaning 'to remain behind'.
8. Stock is not alienated from fathers to sons until after the herdowner's death.
9. At the end of the *Jilla* year the new *Ya'a* assembly convenes to settle cases which have arisen during the course of the *Jilla*.
10. Exceptions to this convention are the High *Xallu* and custodians of the sacred paraphernalia of the phratry. *Xallu*-ship passes from father to senior son and is confined to one lineage. The ritual objects must always

have a custodian who is married. If he dies or loses his wife, an elder from his clan or another clan authorised by custom to provide custodians is appointed. If men of the appropriate grades are no longer available from these clans, persons in the *luba* class next to be installed are sought.

BIBLIOGRAPHY

Dyson-Hudson, N. 1966. *Karimojong Politics*. New York.
Helm, J. 1965. 'Bilaterality in the Socio-Territorial Organisation of the Arctic Drainage Dene', *Ethnology*, 4:361-85.
Lee, R.B. 1972. 'The Kung Bushmen of Botswana' in M.G. Bicchieri (ed.), *Hunters and Gatherers Today*. New York, 327-70.
Torry, W.I. 1976. 'Gabra Residence Rules: Some Ecological Considerations', *Ethnology*, 15:269-85.

VIII
The Guji: *Gada* as a Ritual System [1]

JOHN HINNANT

Introduction

The Guji are a Galla or Oromo speaking people of Ethiopia located in Sidamo Governorate-General on the northern border of the Boran. [2] The Boran and Guji *gada* systems probably had a common origin and share many similarities of organisation, in terminology and in the values they celebrate, but each has also developed differences. Both have an apparent age or generation grade organisation which provides role-models for males which are predicated on the assumption that every male passes through a similar ideal life-cycle, each stage of which is marked by a rite of transition. For the Guji, these role-models are irrelevant in most everyday life. The Guji generation grade organisation which I will refer to as *gada*, [3] has leaders named *abba gada*, who have councillors, but the authority of these leaders is almost entirely limited to the ritual of *gada* itself. The political authority and most of the legal responsibility they once had is gone.

When I began my fieldwork in the summer of 1968, it appeared to me that *gada* was a basic preoccupation of the Guji. The rites of passage between *gada* grades (most of which on the local level are performed household by household) were in progress, and over the next few months I attended many and observed people acting in terms of the role-models appropriate to their grades. By January 1969, when the dry season was reaching its peak, all *gada* rituals ceased. People reverted to interacting as neighbours, kinsfolk, and friends. Nowhere on the local level could I find evidence of social action or social status based specifically on *gada*. Since my research design centered on the study of *gada* as a social system, this was extremely disconcerting. As my study progressed, it became clear that *gada* persists primarily as an enormous outpouring of ritual which requires the preparation of vast quantities of food and the slaughter of many cattle.

The basic anthropological problem of the Guji system is, then, to explain why the ritual is so important that it is maintained even though other aspects of *gada* are defunct. In order to do this it is necessary to describe certain aspects of social organisation, the central tenets of Guji religion, the structural rules of *gada*, and the nature of the office of *abba gada*.

Social and territorial organisation

Gujiland is extremely variable in its topography and Guji live at widely varying altitudes. The western part, in the Rift Valley, consists primarily of hot lowlands. Northeast of the Rift, a mountainous ridge rises dramatically from the valley to slightly under 3000 metres elevation. To the southeast, the central part of Gujiland consists of vast highland pastures occasionally broken by hills and stands of trees. Farther south the land descends in gradual stages, large forests become increasingly common which drop away to hot grasslands.

The Guji see themselves as a confederation of several independent but closely related peoples. Each of these peoples, called a *gosa*, which I shall translate here as 'tribe', has its own territory which takes its name from the *gosa* and a leader named *abba gada* (father, or leader, of *gada*).[4] This paper is concerned with three tribes, the Uraga, Mati, and Hoku. I join Haberland (1963:348) in calling them, collectively, the Southern Guji.

Each tribal territory is considered to be the homeland of seven patrilineal, exogamous, non-totemic clans[5] (*balbala* — doorway, or *firra* — friend). Each clan is divided into a variable number (3, 4 or 5) of named primary segments or 'houses' (*mana*), which are in turn divided into a great number of patrilineages (*sanya*). A few individuals can trace their lineal ancestry as far as fifteen generations but none can trace back to the founder of the 'house', much less that of the clan. All Guji also belong to one of two moieties, the *Akaku* and the *Dalata*. Membership of a moiety is governed by house affiliation, so while all the lineages of one house belong to the same moiety, the houses of any one clan do not; each clan of all three tribes contains both *Akaku* and *Dalata* houses. (The clan of the great *Kallu*, the *Obitu*, is an exception and is discussed below). The *Akaku* moiety is considered senior and embraces the lineages which have rights to hereditary offices while the *Dalata* are considered 'later born' or junior.

The office of the great *Kallu* stands above all the Guji tribes and serves to unite them through *gada*. Historically the *Kallu*, who always lives in his own territory outside Southern Guji, mediated between the *abba gada* of the various tribes when disputes arose concerning territorial boundaries. He remains the person who legitimises the *abba gada* when they take office, and thus in him also rests the ultimate responsibility for maintaining the *gada* system.

The Guji see themselves as devoted herdsmen, even though they depend for subsistence upon a variety of agricultural crops. Residence patterns reflect their preoccupation with the needs of cattle. People live in round straw houses which cluster into neighbourhoods (*ola*) separated by expanses of pasture and crop lands. A neighbourhood consists of lineage mates, fellow clansmen and friends. The families of a neighbourhood share food and labour, settle their disputes together, and attend one another's ceremonies. Each individual is also involved in an extensive network of kinsfolk and affines, who can be called upon to assist with rituals, agricultural labour, and for the exchange of cattle.[6]

Guji society has undergone great changes during the seventy-five years since it was conquered and incorporated into Ethiopia by the armies of Emperor Menelik II, and several garrison posts were established. The military was gradually replaced by civil administrators, courts, and tax collectors, and the usurpation of Guji territory by northern Ethiopian landlords began. A type of indirect rule was instituted. A few men, who had not held office in the traditional system, were appointed to government headmanships (*koro* and *balabat*) and each made responsible for the maintenance of peace and collection of taxes in a specified geographical area. Any breach of Ethiopian law which they discovered was, and is, reported to the Ethiopian courts. The independent political and legal authority of the *abba gada* was abruptly ended and the *Kallu* was incorporated into the Ethiopian system as a headman.

Today the garrison posts have evolved into towns, most of which are interconnected by the two north-south roads which pass through Gujiland. These towns are primarily enclaves of Ethiopian culture, few Guji live in them and townsmen seldom travel through the countryside. Guji come to town to attend markets and courts and perhaps to spend some time in the drinking houses. When they leave the towns, they return to a world which is still very much of their own making.[7]

Guji religion

The Guji conceptualisation of *gada* is rooted in religion and the symbolic dichotomies which are related to it, so I shall summarise some of its basic elements before I discuss *gada*.

The high god, *Waka*, is central to Guji religion. Guji assume that he, along with the earth, sun, moon and stars, has always been present. The coming of the peoples and animals of the earth, on the other hand, are explained in myth as the direct and indirect creations of *Waka*. A few elderly informants remembered myths of creation which describe how the first men fell from *Waka* (the word means both god and heaven) and found women already on the earth. The myth now most widely known is a modified Adam and Eve story in which the first man Adan and the first woman Harda Awan fell from *Waka* to a paradise on earth (*darartu* — the flowering). After the temptation of the woman by a snake and the expulsion from paradise, the woman gave birth to both the animals and to children who became the forebears of all peoples. Other myths explain the founding of the clans, the transmittal of the rules of *gada* from God to man through the agency of the great *Kallu*, and the wresting by man of the control of society from the hands of woman in the person of a wicked queen.

Once the earth was populated and the rules of society were established, God withdrew from the earth. However, he did not end his concern with humans and his effect on the lives of men is all pervasive. Guji see his pleasure or displeasure with them in terms of abundance and deprivation. The paths to each are clearly marked and are conceptualised in terms of law (*sara*).

At the time of creation God gave a body of laws which must be obeyed to ensure continuous well-being. These laws are of two broad types: jural rules and regulations concerning obeisance to God. The latter are products of the *gada* system and will be discussed below. The former have the concept of *nagea*, peace, as their ultimate concern. Congruent with this principle is the emphasis on restoring peaceful interaction between disputing parties.

To be in a state of peace through reconciliation (*arrarsa*) is essential for participation in any religious ceremony, particularly for the recipient of the benefits desired from it. It is believed that if a person participates in a ceremony when not in a state of ritual purity through reconciliation he will gain no supernatural benefit and may indeed anger God. As a result, when it is known that there are arguments involving participants, adjudication and reconciliation must precede the main ritual action.

An individual who experiences misfortune, such as chronic illness in the family, cattle disease, poor crops, or involvement in frequent disputes, believes that it is because he is not in God's good grace. The afflicted must take action which usually begins with a consultation with an adept. One of the questions the adept asks is whether the afflicted has an unresolved dispute. If so, the afflicted person should first seek reconciliation with the one he has offended then seek reconciliation with God through a ceremony of propitiation. Reconciliation with both man and God is a prerequisite for well-being.

There is one concept, *kayyo* (which may be loosely translated as destiny, or perhaps providence) which subsumes the entire philosophy of interaction between man and God. *Kayyo* has several interrelated aspects. First, and most generally, it represents the degree to which individuals have achieved the ideal state of peace and the rewards which flow therefrom. When a man has many cattle and children and an abundance of food his *kayyo* is good. It is also good when his relations with others are peaceful and he has achieved respect and high office. Such a man is frequently asked to play the role of ritual assistant at ceremonies in the belief that his *kayyo* will spread to the other participants. If such indications of good *kayyo* are lacking a person is presumed to have bad *kayyo* and must take social and ritual action to correct this dangerous situation. Bad *kayyo* (which is evidenced by a lack of plentitude) is also believed to be contagious so people avoid those who are thought to have chronically bad *kayyo*. In sum, chronic misfortune breeds further trouble through exclusion from other people who fear its spread.

Kayyo is controllable through reconciliation ceremonies with man and with God. It is also controllable through the *gada* system. As a man rises through the various ranks his ability to hold ceremonies for propitiation and to be increasingly 'listened to' by God increases. Those in the upper ranks have the greatest ability to control *kayyo* for themselves and others because they have achieved a state of purity (*kolulu*).

There are many types of divination which attempt to predict future *kayyo*. When a hazardous undertaking is begun, a careful search of preceding events is made to detect clues of the *kayyo* (here, success) of the venture. For instance, before a marriage is contracted a careful search is made for clues which might indicate the *kayyo* (future success in marriage and fertility) of the couple.

Kayyo, then, is a type of balance between man, nature, and divinity which people may affect by their actions. It serves as a sanction for following both custom and law. Most important, it serves as the central conceptual tool which Guji use to explain events and to try to control their personal fortunes. It is expressed and manipulated through a number of symbolic distinctions in ritual and in everyday life. Many of these distinctions are simple dichotomies between things which cause or reflect good *kayyo* and those which are less auspicious. During many ceremonies deliberate attempts are made either to heap negative *kayyo* on a sacrificial animal which is to be discarded, or to combine positive symbols when a sacrifice is made (and the animal eaten) in order to ensure positive results.

Of all the distinctions which are basic to Guji values that between men and women is the most important. Women are often equated with negative symbols and men with positive ones. Women are associated with the left side and men with the right, with odd numbers as opposed to even, down as opposed to up, and junior as opposed to senior. Men are seen as straightforward, honest, and fit to dominate, and women as deceitful and foolish. These contrasts are expressed repeatedly and are amplified in a number of stories. The creation myth is interpreted as showing that women lead men astray. The myth of the wicked queen who created chaos and discord with every act until she was overthrown and killed by men, is another. Men claim that a woman is only worth half a man, citing as evidence the difference in the ransom paid for male and female war captives. When people walk down a path, all men precede all women. Women may not speak on any formal occasion without permission. The only humans consistently referred to with the male pronoun are adult Guji males. Children of both sexes and men from all other societies are often referred to in the feminine. Within the *gada* system, men of junior rank are said to be like women. The ultimate level of the *gada* rank system, *jarsa kolulu* (the pure old man), is given both masculine and feminine attributes; it is the rank which represents senility.

Men in their prime see themselves as a class apart from the rest of humanity. They combine seniority and great relative worth with the strength and virility of mature physical prowess. The men also see themselves as the only ones capable of maintaining the social order. Boys and old men do not really belong to this class, nor do 'lesser' males from other societies.

The contexts of male/female discussed above all reflect value-laden contrasts, but in the important context of fertility, male/female symbolism is complementary. When a baby is born, the midwife touches its head to the earth and says 'mother is the earth' (*harda lafa*). Then the head is held high while she says 'father is the sky or god' (*abba waka*). The association between woman and earth and man and sky is pervasive. For instance, when an animal is sacrificed for good *kayyo* the blood spurting upward is for God and man, that spilling downward is for fertility of the earth and woman. In these blessings with blood, there is a directly physiological association with human reproduction. Men take blood in their right hands and rub it on the middle of their foreheads (*kallacha*), the centre of strength and virility. The phallic association here is made explicit by an *abba gada* who, when conducting blessing ceremonies, wears a metal phallus on this part of the forehead. In the blessing they rub blood on the phallus and on the concave side of a shield which is placed on the earth, and represents the vagina. When women are present at blessings men rub blood on them while they sit as passive recipients. Blood is placed on the side of the neck where a pulse can be felt (*lubu*, life or pulse), on the breasts, and on the thighs. Men stand while blessing themselves; women sit on the earth while being blessed by men.

It seems evident that the active role of man in sexual intercourse and of God in providing sun and rain are perceived to be similar. Women are viewed as passive bearers of children, the earth as the passive grower of grass and crops. Men and God maintain social order; women and earth through their unpredictability challenge that order.

Two other concepts are interrelated closely with Guji religion, *gada*, and the perceived relationships between the sexes. The concept of *kallacha*, or virility, is the key symbol of the *gada* system and its leadership. The *abba gada* are called people of the *kallacha*, as are the clan segments which provide the *abba gada* in each tribe. The use of *kallacha* to symbolise the system is consistent with the conception of *gada* as a male institution, both in its emphasis on the active male role in quickening fertility (as will be shown below) and in the dominant role attributed to men in the idealised social order which *gada* attempts to create.

The concept, *woyyu*, which permeates several contexts, is directly associated with two types of poisonous snakes (called *boffa* and *butta*) and through them the earth. The great *Kallu*, who stands above all, is considered the ultimate *woyyu*. Poisonous snakes are kept in his house and are used in a ritual described below. The curse of the *Kallu*, the most potent in Guji, is described as being like the bite of a poisonous snake. Affines, between whom strained, even venomous, relations are likely to be common, are said to be *woyyu* to each other.[8]

Members of a number of *woyyu* clan segments have the power to curse, just as do all members of the clan *Kallu*. Elders with hereditary *woyyu* are considered to be the most effective judges because of the power of their curse. *Woyyu* people must never marry into the clan segments which provide the *abba gada* because the marriage might be infertile or the parents and children might die prematurely. The heritable powers of the dangerous *woyyu* and of the fertility controlling *kallacha* must not be mingled; they are inimical principles. But there are occasions when these powers are brought together. The *abba gada* and the *Kallu* synthesise their distinctive powers in opposite ways. The *Kallu*, who is born *woyyu*, puts on a *kallacha* during ceremonies so that he can bless people and increase their good *kayyo*. The *abba gada*, who is born of the *warra kallacha*, shortly after taking office kills a poisonous snake and burns it to ashes, which he then rubs on his *kallacha* in order to acquire the power to curse. No other *woyyu* may wear the *kallacha* (or even enter the house of the *abba gada*); no other member of the *warra kallacha* may have anything to do with snakes. It will be seen that the oppositions and combinations of these two powers are of central importance in the conceptualisation of *gada*.

The structure of Gada

Before *gada* can be discussed as a religious system, the organisation rules governing recruitment to and transitions through the various ranks must be explored along with the role models which the system creates.

The rules are complex and it is impossible to explain them without the use of many vernacular words. The next two sections will be easier to follow if frequent reference is made to Tables VIII.1 and 2.

To anyone familiar with age-grade organisation, the institution of the Guji at first seems familiar. *Gada* divides the stages of life, from childhood to old age, into a series of formal steps, each marked by a transition ceremony at which activities and social roles are formally defined in terms of both what is permitted and what is forbidden. The aspect of *gada* which throws the concept of age grading into confusion is that of recruitment. A strict age-grade system assumes that an individual's social passage through life is in tune with his biological development. An individual enters the system at a specific age and

Table VIII.1. Duration of ranks

Rank	Duration	Enters rank in junior or senior cycle
soluda	1 *balli*	Junior
daballa	1 *balli*	Junior
karra	2½ *balli*	Junior
kussa	½ *balli*	Senior
raba mido	1 *balli*	Junior
dori	½ *balli*	Junior
gada	1 *balli*	Senior
batu (yuba)	1 *balli*	Senior
yuba	1 *balli*	Senior
yuba guda	1 *balli*	Senior
jarsa gudurru	1 *balli*	Senior
jarsa kolulu	1 *balli*	Senior
jarsa raka	until death	Senior

passes through transition rites at intervals appropriate to the passage from childhood through full adulthood to senility. However, recruitment into the *gada* system is not based upon biological age, but upon the requirement that an individual remain exactly five stages below his father's level. Recruitment is thus based on the maintenance of one socially defined generation between father and son.

The Guji word for the *gada* system as a whole and for each rank is *balli* (see note 3). The ideal length of one *balli* is eight years. If a father and his son are separated by five *balli* (ideally forty years) they are thereby prevented from occupying either political or priestly ranks at the same time. The forty-year interval thus effectively prevents adjacent generations from competing for status. The Guji consider this separation to be necessary because adjacent generations are considered to be antagonistic and dangerous to each other, while alternate generations are considered equivalent and harmonious.

All of a man's sons occupy the same *balli*, regardless of age, which creates a great potential difficulty. A polygynous man may begin sireing children by his first wife while in his early twenties and continue sireing children by junior wives until his late sixties (including children sired by his wives' lovers); his children may vary in age by more than forty years. If all of these offspring are put in the same *balli* and are required to follow the role model expected of that *balli*, the elder children will be unduly restricted, and the younger will be forced

The Guji: Gada as a Ritual System 215

Table VIII.2. The contemporary *gada* sequence by classes

gada grades (*balli*)	I Before *abba gada* takes office (and after lower rank change) 1971	II Immediately after new *abba gada* takes office (and before he sends messengers ordering lower rank change)	III Before next new *abba gada* takes office (and after lower rank change)	Duration in *balli*
none (waiting)	dalana	dalana	harmufa	
soluda	halchisa	halchisa	dalana	1
daballa (gudurru)	mudana	mudana	halchisa	1
karra I	robala	robala	mudana	1
karra II	harmufa	harmufa	robala	1
karra III	dalana		harmufa	½ or ½
kussa		dalana		
raba mido	halchisa†	halchisa	dalana	1
dori	mudana		halchisa	½
gada	robala*	mudana	mudana	1
batu (yuba I)	harmufa	robala	robala	1
yuba (II)	dalana	harmufa	harmufa	1
yuba guda (III)	halchisa	dalana	dalana	1
jarsa gudurru	mudana	halchisa	halchisa	1
jarsa kolulu	robala	mudana	mudana	1
jarsa raka	harmufa	robala	robala	1+

to occupy senior positions which are equally inappropriate. In the next generation the children of the younger sons may not achieve full adulthood within the *balli* until they are old men. After a period of several generations few members of any given *balli* will be of the appropriate age to carry out the activities of that rank. In the past, the Guji attempted to solve this problem by restricting the number of years during which a man could sire legitimate children. The rules governing restrictions on procreativity, which have been abandoned for at least seventy years, will be discussed after the basic outline of the contemporary system has been presented.

The ideal gada life cycle

Before examining the structural rules governing the contemporary *gada* system, it is useful to examine the ideal role models which it generates. It must be remembered that the ideal life cycle contained in these role models does not coincide with the actual sequence to be observed today.

While it is no longer possible to observe people playing roles based on *gada* other than during ceremonies, I was able to elicit from informants the ideal role-model appropriate to each rank. In the vernacular the same word is used for both the ranks and for members of those ranks; I follow Guji usage. The first two ranks (see Table VIII.1), *soluda* and *daballa*, are those of childhood and early adolescence. The *soluda* herd small animals, but are too junior to have any social responsibility or ritual power. Both are under the control of their fathers. The death of a 'child' of either rank should not be mourned; in a sense the deceased is a non-person without a proper name, and is 'buried in the dung of horses'.

Next the boy passes through the name giving ceremony (*makabasa*) and becomes *karra* for two and a half *balli*. The ceremony is held separately by each family whose sons have reached the appropriate rank.

It is the first ceremony held exclusively for the junior initiates, and is the only formal recognition of the transition. 'Name-giving' recognises socially both the individual's new adult personality and his position in the *gada* system and releases him from absolute subservience to the father. *Karra* may speak in public debate and address the *abba gada* and begin to participate in ceremonies. After his 'namegiving' a man is properly mourned when he dies.

A *karra* has important economic responsibilities. He herds the fullgrown cattle and takes them to the mineral springs in the wild lowlands for long periods. He can hunt large game animals and raid the herds of neighbouring peoples either alone or in a party.[9]

Following *karra*, at the time a new *abba gada* takes office, the rank *kussa* begins, which marks a break with the orderly development of

The Guji: Gada as a Ritual System

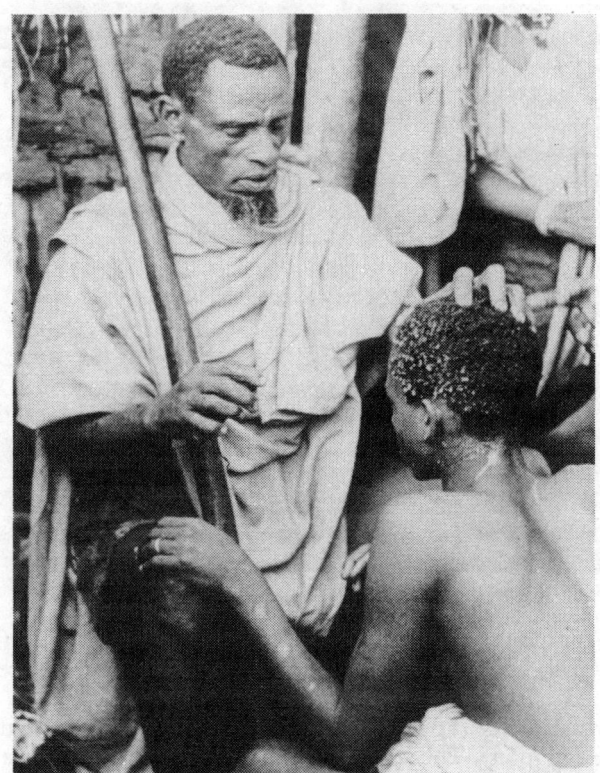

Plate VIII.1. Guji: a father cutting his son's hair during *makabasa*

socialisation. In the ranks before *kussa* a person gradually becomes involved in social and economic life. After *kussa* those who wish to be respected in later life must begin to display the characteristics of calm, dignified, intelligent, settled behaviour. However, during *kussa*, men may become like wild animals, strip naked and go into the forests (where they can be heard calling like hyenas) and if they find a woman there, may have group sexual intercourse with her without fear of punishment. The *kussa* paint their bodies with a mixture of red earth and butter (*sorsa*) and wear their hair long and unkempt.

The *kussa* rank, with all of its 'wild' attributes, is a period of status reversal (Turner 1969:177-8) but it does not involve a substitution of childhood for maturity, or humility for hierarchy. Rather, the reversal is between society, with its orderly rules, and the disorderly aspects of nature. It is a period of licence which occurs immediately before entry to the ranks of greatest constraint. I was told that *Kussa* formerly participated in organised war parties led by a 'father of battle' of *gada* rank. It was such fighting units of Galla which, during the sixteenth

Plate VIII.2. Guji: cutting the *wudessa* pole

century, conquered large parts of the old Ethiopian Empire (Bahrey 1954: *passim*) and more recently driven the Boran from present-day Southern Guji territory.

Individuals enter the next rank, *raba mido*, after passing through the *banti* ceremony. The ceremony itself is the first in which a role is assigned to the wife, who receives an elaborate head ornament (*mido*). As a *raba mido* for the first time a man is permitted a following (*yaa*); that is, he is in a position to be listened to and obeyed by others, particularly those of *karra* rank. *Raba mido* marks a slight increase in ritual authority. During the transition ceremonies, the *raba mido* organise lower ranked people for music and dance. The role of a *raba* is almost a parody of officiousness as he bustles around, beating with a stick all who fall asleep or are sluggish. During *raba* a man receives his first ritual implement, a forked stick (*ororo*), which he uses to pass along the backs of sacrificial animals while supplicating for health and abundance.

The final rank before *gada* itself is *dori*, which lasts only one-half of a *balli* (ideally, four years). Each *dori* cuts a long fluted pole (*wudessa*) which becomes his main ritual implement for the remainder of his active life in *gada*. He cuts one such pole for each of his wives who has borne him a son. There are few differences between the social roles appropriate to *raba mido* and *dori*. In the ritual sphere, however, *dori* marks the end of the novice period and the beginning of full participation as a senior man. The fluted poles are taken to all *gada* promotion ceremonies and to sacrifices for good *kayyo*. Those who possess poles are considered to have become more effective supplicants for *kayyo* both for their families and for 'the country' than they were before. When the *dori* become members of the rank of *gada* they should be at the height of their political and economic power. Able men of *gada* rank are respected in debate and adjudication, and provide the leaders of each tribal territory in the persons of the *abba gada* and his following.

The three ranks after *gada* are all named *yuba*. Guji say that a *yuba* is like an Ethiopian Orthodox monk. He withdraws from economic activity, gives control of his cattle to his eldest son and retains only five for himself. He gives up debate but may still be consulted as an expert on law and custom. In effect he leaves the affairs of daily life to the junior generations and ceases to compete with them.

Yuba dominate religious activities, at least one must be a principal actor at promotion ceremonies, and they are consulted on all matters concerning the proper performance of *gada* ritual. *Yuba* are the most effective supplicants for good *kayyo*, and the funerals of those who have passed beyond 'name-giving' require several of them in attendance. But this recognition does not simply depend on attainment of the rank; a *yuba* who has not shown evidence of good *kayyo* during his lifetime, that is, has not had many children or owned many cattle, is considered out of favour with God. He will not be invited to ceremonies because his blessing would have no positive value and might even work against those he blessed.

The first stage of *yuba*, named *batu*, is a period of transition into full priesthood. A *batu* has the obligation to pass on his knowledge of the duties and rituals of the crucial *gada* rank to those who have just entered it. The second and third stages are increasingly free from secular concerns and increasingly pure (*kolulu*).

The final three ranks, *jarsa*, acknowledge a paradox. A *jarsa* should be the wisest and most revered of all men. He has passed through the entire life cycle and achieved purity, but at the same time he has lived so long as to become biologically senile. In acknowledgement of this conflict of social and biological identities, the *jarsa* ranks combine great respect with freedom from social or ritual tasks. When a *jarsa* dies he is buried with honour on the path leading to the cattle kraal.[10]

The first *jarsa gudurru*, wears the same braided hair style as children of *daballa* rank. Members of both are referred to in the feminine gender, have no daily responsibilities and are cared for by kinsfolk. At the second, that of *jarsa kolulu* (the pure old man), an individual shaves off his previous hair style (*gudurru*), and enters more fully into the period of structural senility. He may go from house to house begging for food and is always fed. He may even kill a cow on the path and eat it, so long as he uses a woman's knife (*ala*) and does not attempt to slaughter in a hidden place, such as a forest. When a *jarsa kolulu* dies he is buried in the cattle kraal, the most honoured place of all. The third *jarsa* rank, *raka*, marks the final retirement from *gada* and lasts until death.

One informant divided the *gada* sequence into four grand stages: youth, which consists of *soluda, daballa* and *karra*; adulthood, which incorporates *raba mido, dori*, and *gada*; priesthood, which includes the three *yuba* grades; and retirement, which encompasses the three *jarsa* grades. (The informant omitted *kussa*, probably because it is a break with the ordered sequence of life.) To some degree stages one and two are mirror images of three and four. The ranks of *raba mido* through *gada* involve a gradual increase in the individual's authority in secular affairs, and the three *yuba* provide a gradual withdrawal. The ranks of growth progress from birth through irresponsibility to social accountability, while the *jarsa* ranks decline from the venerated *yuba* rank through progressive social relinquishment of responsibility to death. Significantly, individuals in both the first and fourth stages are not considered to be true men and are referred to in the feminine. Also the *gudurru* hair style of the *daballa* and *jarsa gudurru* ranks stresses the parallel nature of life's beginning and end. Indeed that the *jarsa gudurru* stage of a grandfather partially overlaps in time with the *gudurru* stage of his grandson (see Table VIII.2) is another way of indicating the equivalence of alternate generations.

Gada is very much a male-oriented institution and I have only needed to mention in passing the wives of *raba mido* and *dori*. Women are referred to as the wives of their husband's rank and only play minor roles. For instance, during 'name-giving' a mother will not let her son's hair be cut until he has been promised a calf by his father. During *raba mido* the woman receives the *mido* ornament from her husband which is removed when he becomes *dori*. The *mido* is then divided into three pieces; two are given to her senior brothers and one to her husband. In exchange for these she receives a cow from each man. After *dori*, the woman plays no active part in *gada* ritual, other than singing and preparing food.

The operation of the contemporary gada *system*

The full system of ranks and the complexities which arise from the variations in the time periods of ranks, which in folk theory should be constant, were not fully comprehended by most of my informants, but they were by the leaders and by those seniors who had been active. My model of the system is based on interviews with these informants and data from surveys.

The complexity of the contemporary system makes it appropriate to describe it one dimension at a time. The first dimension to be discussed is the duration of each rank; the second is the operation of the *gada* classes.

The Guji: Gada as a Ritual System

Reference to Table VIII.1 (Duration of Ranks) shows that the various ranks last from one-half to two-and-one-half *balli* each. The concept of a *balli* (or *luba*) and factors in determining its length are central to understanding the system. A *balli* refers to the duration of the central *gada* rank which, ideally, is eight years. Among the men who enter the *gada* rank during each time period, one is chosen as the leader for each tribal territory. His title is *abba gada* (father, or leader of *gada*). At this point it is sufficient to say that the *abba gada* of Uraga controls the timing of the entire *gada* cycle and that the others follow him. The day he passes through the investiture ceremony and becomes the new *abba gada*, the new *balli* begins. When he takes office all the other people of *dori* rank become *gada*. The *gada* whom they displace, become *batu* and so on throughout all the senior ranks. Any survivors of the most senior rank, the *jarsa kolulu*, become *jarsa raka* and retire forever. None of the lower ranks has a promotion ceremony at this time, with the exception that those in the final phase of *karra*, become *kussa* which leaves no one in senior *karra*.

After the *abba gada* has been in office for at least four years, he sends out messengers to order members of the lower ranks to hold promotion ceremonies. All occupants of each rank move up one step, including *kussa*, who become *raba mido*, leaving no one in *kussa* rank.

The second dimension of *gada* is the division into classes. Each patrilineage belongs to one of five *gada* classes (*missensa*). (See Table VIII.2). These classes are: *dalana, halchisa, mudana* (*birmaji*), *robala* and *harmufa*. Recruitment to the classes is by patrilineage, rather than by clan or clan segment. For example, if a man of the *handoa* clan is *halchisa*, so are his father, grandfather, and so on, but the other hundreds of patrilineages of *handoa* are distributed among all five classes in an unpredictable manner.

Since there are only five classes and a large number of *gada* grades, the generations of a given class occupy different grades. For example, in 1971, the 'middle' generation of the living *robala* class was in *gada* grade. The sons of *robala* were *karra* and had just passed through the name giving ceremony. Any living fathers of the occupants of *gada* rank would be *jarsa kolulu* (see Table VIII.2 for complete list). When the senior cycles moves up one rank, all members of the *robala gada* group will become *batu*. Any of their fathers still alive would become *jarsa raka*. When the next promotion of the junior cycle occurs the sons of the *robala gada* (cum *batu*) category will move to the next stage of *karra*. When informants speak of the progression through the various *gada* grades, they refer to the movement of classes rather than of individuals. They avoid confusion by saying that *robala* is *gada*; the sons of *robala* are *karra*; and the fathers of *robala* are *jarsa kolulu*. In other words, informants focus on the middle, or active, ranks and relate the other living generations to them. When the Guji view the progression through *gada* grades, they see each class in the senior or junior cycle moving upward with the next junior class taking its place.

When the *abba gada* finally divests himself of rank (after anywhere from the ideal eight to sixteen years) and becomes *batu*, the *balli* period ends. A new group of *dori* become *gada*, with one of their members becoming *abba gada*, and a new *balli* begins.

For the senior ranks, then, one *balli* is the period between the time an *abba gada* takes office and the time he leaves it. For the junior ranks, one *balli* is the period between the time one leader sends messengers to order the promotion ceremonies and the time the next one does so.

There is thus a dual cycle, with all but two of the lower grades holding promotion ceremonies four (or more) years later than their fathers. One exception is the final stage of *karra* whose members become *kussa* when the leader takes office and who leave this half *balli* to become *raba mido* when the other lower ranks are promoted. Another exception is the half *balli*, *dori*, whose members become *gada* and thereby enter the other (senior) cycle.

While fathers and sons are prevented from competing for high status positions due to the rule which separates them by five ranks, there is a great deal of rivalry and aggressive joking between adjacent classes. Classes whose members are in a junior position in terms of the active political grades jokingly urge the senior classes to leave their grade. The more senior class members tell men of the adjacent junior class that they are *tuta*, like women. Indeed, the 'female' anatomy of the junior men is described in minute detail during *gada* ceremonies and at other times. Thus the obligatory hostility frequently found between adjacent grades in age grade societies is engaged in by the classes rather than by the *gada* grades (*balli*) which are occupied by fathers and sons, who can never directly succeed one another.

The effects of adding the above information concerning the gada classes to the model can be seen from Table VIII.2. In this chart the grades are held constant, while the classes pass through them in three time periods. Column I represents the time when on the orders of the old *abba gada* the lower ranks have held their promotion ceremonies, and is in fact the actual position of the classes in March 1971, when I conducted a survey in the territories of all three tribes. Column II predicts the position of the classes just after the next *abba gada* takes office. At this time all of the classes in the senior grades move up a grade, beginning with *dori* (*mudana*), who becomes *gada* (leaving no one in *dori* grade). At this point the senior *robala* have been promoted out of the system. The classes in the junior grades remain as they were, except those in the final stages of *karra* who become *kussa*.

Column III shows the progression four or more years later after the lower classes have again moved up. *Dalana* has been added at the top (*soluda*), and the other junior classes have all moved ahead a step, including the *kussa*, who have become *raba mido*, leaving no one in *kussa*.

The Guji: Gada as a Ritual System   223

The dual promotion system continues making junior and senior progressions each time period until five *abba gada* have come to power and *robala* is once more the *abba gada*, in this manner travelling full circle.

Implications of the system

This system has certain implications. To begin with, from the perspective of the patrilineage, it can be seen from Table VIII.2 that three living generations are contained within the system with two exceptions. These are the top and bottom entries in the '*gada* grades' column and consist of the senior generation of classes which are retiring into the *jarsa raka* grade (*harmufa* in column I, *robala* in columns II and III) and the junior generation of classes which are 'waiting' to become *soluda* (*dalana* in columns I and II and *harmufa* in column III).

Second, since all members of a patrilineage belong to the same class whatever their generation, a man who is *robala* in column I finds not only all of his own brothers in the *gada* rank, but also all his patrilateral cousins of the same generation. If he has followed the preferential marriage rules of *gada* and has married into his own class (as discussed below), all of his wife's brothers and cousins of her generation are also *gada*. If his father married into the proper class, all of the male relatives of his mother of his generation also share the same rank.

Since *gada* is considered to be the grade of greatest secular activity, it is useful to examine the structural position of the fathers and sons of the *gada* to determine whether either one can compete along any dimension. The fathers of *robala* who are *gada* in column I of Table VIII.2 (marked with *) are *jarsa kolulu*. They have not only retired from power, but also become structurally senile, and thus effectively removed from the affairs of men. The sons of a *gada*, for the first four years he holds the rank, are still *daballa*. They are in one sense children and in another non-persons who have yet to have an officially recognised 'name'. They, too are not in a position to compete with the *gada* father. During the second half of his tenure as *gada*, a man holds the name-giving ceremony for his sons which ushers them into manhood and the *karra* rank. Even as *karra*, the sons are restricted to a range of activities, which cannot offer competition to the father.

The descent system is articulated with *gada* through the classes. In this respect *gada* differs from a true age-grade organisation in which age-grades cross-cut the descent system and the family. *Gada*, on the other hand, incorporates the lineage and cross-cuts the clan. That is, lineages of a given clan are spread through all five classes, and conversely some lineages of all twenty-one clans of southern Guji belong to the same class. If the classes cross-cut the clans, they obviously cross-cut the three tribes. This is one means of countering the tendency for the tribes, which have separate territories and leaders, to become socially and ritually separate.

Third, it is clear from the cyclical nature of the classes that they prevent the *abba gada* and his assistants (*yaa*) from becoming a set of hereditary leaders. An *abba gada* may not pass his office directly to his sons because the other four classes must first come to power before his class again has its turn. The same applies to his following. In each class though the leader is chosen from among a limited number of patrilines a rotating system distributes office among five distinct groups.

Finally, *gada* creates a preferential marriage rule through the classes. The *kayyo* of each class is believed to be different, so that it is better for a man to marry a girl of the same class and of the same generation within the class. In this way their *kayyo* will be the same. Thus, if a man is *halchisa* and in the *raba mido* grade (marked with a † on Table VIII.2, column I), his father will be in *yuba guda* grade. If this marriage class rule were prescriptive, men of each class would be restricted to choosing a wife from among only 20 per cent of the marriageable women, but it is only preferential. Its sole sanction is that of the possibility of acquiring bad *kayyo* from marrying into other classes.

There are further preferential restrictions related to this rule. If a man marries outside his class, it is particularly bad *kayyo* to marry into the immediately junior class ('she is like a daughter') or the immediately senior class ('she is like a mother'). This illustrates the paradoxical view that although genealogical generations are kept five grades apart, adjacent classes (or grades) are considered to be like genealogical generations.

Changes in the rules

From Table VIII.2 it would appear that there is a problem in the contemporary *gada* system over life span. Even if an individual entered the first (*soluda*) rank at birth, he would have to live much longer than a normal life span before reaching the rank of final retirement. The present system incorporates adjustments which have been made to reconcile these difficulties, despite the seemingly rigid structure. Once during each *gada* period, when the old *abba gada* is about to leave office, there is a great assembly of the men of *gada* grade. At this time the rules of *gada* are discussed and agreed changes are incorporated. No historical record of the sequence of changes resulting from these deliberations exists but it is possible to piece together a general picture of one previous system from the accounts of informants.

Probably the most important change which created the seemingly unworkable structure of the contemporary system was the abandonment of the rules restricting procreativity. In the past only men of certain ranks could sire legitimate children. Children born when their fathers were in inappropriate ranks were either abandoned or adopted by men in the appropriate ranks. This practice has been defunct since well before the beginning of the twentieth century.[11] Prior to then, apparently, a man could marry only when he had reached *raba mido* (see Table VIII.2). At the time of the *banti* ceremony, which is the transition rite into that grade a man's wife appears in a promotion ceremony for the first time and dons an elaborate head ornament, the *mido*. Her husband receives a haircut, the *banti*, which involves shaving a circle of hair from the crown of his head. This haircut is identical to the hair design of marriageable virgins. Women are given this haircut for the last time on their marriage day. It is possible that, in the past, the initiation ceremony into *raba mido* was also the marriage ceremony, with husband and wife symbolising their 'virginity' with the cutting of *banti*.

According to Haberland's information (390), the next rank, *dori*, was the first in which a man could legitimately sire children. I was not able to confirm this. In the contemporary system a *dori* is expected to have already fathered children. I heard a lengthy debate during one *dori* promotion ceremony about whether or not a man could cut the fluted *wudessa* pole because he had not yet sired a son. He was finally permitted to cut the pole, but it was apparent that the decision was not wholeheartedly accepted.

If there was a lower limit to marriage and the sireing of legitimate children, was there also an upper limit? One of my oldest and most knowledgeable informants stated that when a man had passed from *gada* rank through *batu* to *yuba*, he should neither acquire additional wives nor father children. This statement is in keeping with the nature of a *yuba*, who must retire from active participation in the affairs of daily life and devote himself to ritual.

An hypothesis can be suggested. The lower limits to marriage and procreation in the past were set by forbidding marriage until *raba mido* and possibly compelling the abandonment of children until the next rank (*dori*) was achieved. The upper limits to acquiring new wives and procreation may well have been set by the social and economic position of the *yuba*, if not by actual law. A *yuba* is unable to acquire additional wives because he may only possess five head of cattle. This restriction on procreation tended to limit the age range of children entering each rank and thus partially prevented men being born into inappropriate grades.

Today children are not abandoned and only two rules exist to cope with the problem of inappropriate age. First, if the father is still in the childhood grades (below *karra*) when he sires sons, the offspring have no rank at all. Their exclusion from the system can be countered through adoption by a man of higher rank. Some of the instances I encountered were handled in this manner,[12] while other parents simply accepted the removal of their sons from the system. Second, at the other extreme, the presently stated upper limit on recruitment of children into the system is set by the rule that sons born to men of *jarsa* rank have no rank.

What cannot be built on earth or in the sky?
Who does not have rank, except [or only] the sons of *jarsa*?

Today the problem of the sons of *jarsa* could hardly occur, since there are virtually no people of *jarsa* rank, but should sons be born to such men they can be adopted by someone of the next lower generation.

Through cross generational adoption they would thus become their fathers' 'grandsons' and would be placed in the *daballa* or *karra* grade which is appropriate for their chronological age.

This rule has some bearing on the maintenance of *gada*, since the current shift in the Guji system is toward very few people in the upper ranks and a large number being born while their fathers are in the very junior ranks. There are at least two reasons for this shift. During this century the rank changes have not occurred at the proper time and each set of transition ceremonies has been delayed several years for reasons too complicated to discuss here. Second, as the system of ranks is presently constituted, a man who enters the system as a small child of *soluda* rank cannot possibly become *jarsa* until he is well into his eighties, even if the rank changes occur on schedule every eight years.

The increasing accumulation of people in the lower ranks has apparently led to the addition of junior ranks to the antecedent system. Guji claim that *soluda* and *daballa* are recent additions which were innovated by the Hoku tribe and gradually spread. It is likely that these childhood ranks were added to absorb rankless people into the system, which in the past began with *karra*. Evidence from ritual tends to confirm this. A son now becomes *soluda* during the hair-cutting ceremony in which his father becomes *raba mido*. He becomes *daballa* when his father cuts the *wudessa* pole and becomes *dori*. In both cases the son's transition ceremony constitutes a very minor part of the ritual and could have easily been tacked on in recent times.

A prototypical gada *system*

There are enough clues available to posit a prototypical *gada* system. The Guji system presumably began as a true age grade system as Legesse (1973:137) has suggested the Boran system did also. For reasons unknown the rule of recruitment by generation rather than by age was added later.[13] Just after the generation rule was applied, the system probably had the following characteristics (see Table VIII.3).

Table VIII.3. A prototypical *gada* system

EGO's rank	EGO's age when he changes rank	Father's rank
		raba mido marries; children abandoned
born		*dori* children legitimate
makabasa ceremony	8	
karra		*gada*
		batu
	28	*yuba* gives up wealth; new children unwanted
kussa	32	
raba mido marries; children abandoned	40	*yuba guda*
dori children legitimate	44	*jarsa gudurru*
gada	52	*jarsa kolulu*
batu	60	*jarsa raka*
yuba gives up wealth; new children unwanted	68	
yuba guda	76	
jarsa gudurru	84	
jarsa kolulu	92	
jarsa raka	until death	

Let us assume that EGO's father married as a *raba mido* and sired EGO as his first legitimate son when he was a *dori*. EGO would have his naming ceremony and become *karra* when he was eight years old and remain *karra* until he was twenty-eight. When EGO became twenty his father would have left *batu* and become a full *yuba*. Assuming that EGO's father ceased sireing children at this point, EGO's youngest full brother would be twenty years his junior. There would then be a maximum twenty years span in the ages of both as they passed through the system together.

EGO would become *kussa* and a warrior at age twenty-eight, marry at thirty-two and begin sireing legitimate sons at forty. At forty-four he would become *gada*, and begin his priesthood during *batu*. At sixty he would cease to sire children and become a full *yuba* and finally retire from the system as *raka* at age ninety-two.

Throughout the sequence EGO would be slightly old for the roles expected of each grade, whereas some of his younger brothers would be of the appropriate age and the very youngest would be too young to participate in at least the first ranks. The youngest would retire when he was seventy-two, twenty years younger than the firstborn.

The youngest would be in an unusual situation as regards marriage. He could legitimately marry when he reached *raba mido* at age twelve, but it is extremely unlikely that he would until he was at least into his late teens. His period of legitimate procreativity would thus have been slightly shorter than that of his brother, assuming that *yuba* sets an upper limit on procreation.

There are several difficulties implicit in this model. First, the evidence that there has been an upper limit to procreation is tenuous. If there were an upper limit the ages of people in each rank would be kept within workable limits. If there were no upper limit fathers would continuing sireing children to the biological limits of their wives, and children would be born into increasingly higher ranks. Finally, the Boran (Legesse 1973:159-160) situation would occur, in which men are retired from the senior grade while quite young. The only counter to this would be that the sons born to *jarsa* would have no rank, but could be adopted.

Second, no information is available to explain why the marriage rule was abandoned,[14] but it is possible that the rule was creating a severe age deviation and that this was perceived and the rule modified.

The third problem is the long duration of *karra* rank. If the system has been modified by adding to the junior end it is possible that *karra* in the past had a duration of only eight years instead of the present twenty-year span.

Attempts to reconstruct a prototypical *gada* system are obviously speculative. However, certain aspects of the historical development of the system are clear. First, as a structural system *gada* has been unstable since the rule of recruitment by generation (rather than age) was instituted. Assuming that the social roles generated by the *gada* grades were in the past the basis for the division of labour, individuals must often have found that they were of the wrong age to fill the age specific roles. This was especially so after the restrictions on marriage and procreation were abandoned. Individuals must have found increasingly that they were either promoted out of the system while still young or, more likely, that they were in the non-man's-land below the most junior rank. In view of the chronic problems which the structural system generated the possibility of adjusting the rules during the council was essential for the continued functioning of the system.

Second, the roles of *gada* do not appear to have been amenable to change. The system of roles reflects the developmental cycle of men in a warlike herding society. Incorporation into Ethiopia made institutionalised warfare impossible; just as journeys by young men to the lowland with their cattle also generally ceased when that land became the property of landlords who charged rent, and as hunting virtually ended after the introduction of guns resulted in the annihilation of game. Population increases and land pressure have increasingly driven the Guji to more land-efficient agriculture and increased sedentarisation.

The first and second points are probably connected, as the instability of the system may of itself have led to an increasing detachment of the role structure from actual life, but if restrictions on procreativity were already terminated when the period of rapid change began, the age problem may already have led to the abandonment of the roles as unworkable. The roles, in this case, would no longer be moulded by social reality. The roles are however still played in the temporally limited confines of ritual. In this context, the acting out of activities from the past serves as a 'cultural memory' which stresses the assumed uniqueness and power of the Guji past. Also the components of role-play in *gada* ritual, which are based on interaction and hierarchy within the family, still contain the timeless values of the society, and thus still provide relevant information for the contemporary society.

Finally, it should be clear, from an examination of the structural system that the explanation for the persistence of *gada* lies outside it, since the structure of *gada* is itself something to be tolerated but not maintained for its own value. Informants attempted to tell me this throughout my fieldwork. Many were aware of the general flaws in the system, but stressed that they did not participate in *gada* just because of its structure. The rest of this paper will discuss the aspects which informants did stress, the meaning behind the system as expressed in ritual and through the activities of the *gada* leaders.

Leadership of the gada *system*

Part of the meaning of *gada* is embedded in the local level rites of passage from rank to rank, which I have not the space to describe.[15] Perhaps of greater significance is the leadership of the system and the cycle of rituals which it maintains. The following condensed description of the handing over of office and the duties of the *abba gada* is intended to demonstrate that it is these leaders who maintain both the religion as an active ritual system and provide the primary sense of common identity and destiny in Guji.

Authority of the abba gada

One of the vital roles of the system in the past was to provide and legitimise political, legal, and religious leadership. The largest territorial and political units in Southern Guji are the three tribes each of which contains the homeland of seven clans. Over each tribe there is an *abba gada* who has a number of advisers and assistants. The formal influence of each *abba gada* is limited to his own people and territory. The tribes and their *abba gada* are ranked in terms of their fictive birth order. Only the great *Kallu* stands above these nearly equivalent leaders.

An *abba gada* does not, and apparently also in the past did not, have a broad range of political control over his people. Usually he only leaves his own settlement to carry out his ritual tasks. Very few of his people come to him. He does not, as a routine of his office, collect food and other types of goods and then redistribute them in return for loyalty and the carrying out of assigned tasks. He does not appoint political or legal officials other than his own assistants whose primary duty is to serve him. In fact, he has very little influence over the daily lives of his people.

While I could find no evidence that the *abba gada* had greater power in the past it is evident that he did have some responsibility for aggressive warfare and for the defence of his territory against invasion, but he could not himself fight because one of the requirements of his office is that he never spill human blood. Apparently he did, however, appoint the leaders of battle, the *abba dula*.

The one occasion when he emerges as the political leader of his people is the time of the periodic rituals, especially those concerned with handing over rank. The *abba gada* of Uraga sends word to the other *abba gada* that the first phase of the rank change is due to occur four years after he takes office, and the others in turn tell their own people. This process is repeated when the *abba gada* hand over their duties and the upper ranks change. The *abba gada* has the right to command the collection of the vast quantities of food and the many cattle required for the ceremonies and to lead the people on the long pilgrimage to the sacred places. Today, three-quarters of a century after the conquest of the Guji, it is only the powers associated with the *gada* ritual which remain.

Soon after a new *abba gada* takes office he proclaims the laws which will apply during his time in office, including the laws governing *gada*. My impression is, however, that his ability to create and enforce secular law has been seriously eroded.

He and his advisers remain the highest court of appeal in the traditional legal system, and any difficult matter which cannot be solved on the local level may be brought to them. In matters of the proper form for *gada* ritual he remains, even today, the proclaimer of, and final authority on, the entire ritual sequence.

Each *abba gada* is assisted by a number of men of his own grade, called collectively a *yaa*. The division of labour within the group reflects the responsibilities of its leader. The largest subgroup, the *cedabba*, may number in the hundreds. It is its duty to carry out the orders of the *abba gada*, deliver messages, bring miscreants to justice and punish them, and maintain the houses of the *abba gada*. The second group, the *hiyyu*, is responsible for knowing Guji law and for acting as a judicial body to hear cases. The third group, the *faga*, are the repository of ritual knowledge. The *yaa*, with the exception of the two *faga*, are far too numerous to be in constant attendance and assemble only at the time the *abba gada* takes and gives rank. For the remainder of his eight years in office they only attend in small groups. The frequent movement of *yaa* members between their homes throughout the tribal land and the *abba gada*'s settlement is the basic means of communication between the *abba gada* and his people, since he himself only leaves his home on specific ritual occasions. *Yaa* members are also seen as authorities on *gada* in the countryside where they represent their leader.

The giving and taking of office

The handing over of leadership is a complex ritual sequence which lasts one full year, ideally from one September to the next.[16] It comes as the culmination of a long sequence of events (all of which canot be described here), including the lower rank promotion ceremonies. One event which must be mentioned is the selection of the new *abba gada*, which occurs at least four years before the handing over. The selection is secret and it was only possible to obtain a general picture of the procedure. Even the identity of the new leader is kept secret until he takes office.

Within each tribe there are three clans (the *warra kallacha*) which contain a small number of patrilineages whose members are eligible to become *abba gada*. All five classes are represented among these patrilineages. As the classes succeed each other through time, the appropriate patrilineages of each class are examined for the most likely candidate by the last (retired) *abba gada* and his *yaa* from that class.

The office of *abba gada* is considered to be so important that a preselection process occurs. When members of a class are in *kussa* rank one very young man of the appropriate lineage is made the candidate of that class for each tribe and is given a following of other men of *kussa* rank. When he reaches *raba* he is designated the *abba raba*, a position with very few duties. When he performs ceremonies or appears in public his conduct is carefully watched and should he behave inappropriately, or become ill, he is replaced. When he reaches *dori* rank he becomes *abba dori* and continues to be closely watched. Only if his behaviour is exemplary is he finally selected. Informants indicated that throughout this entire time candidates may be, and in fact are, replaced if they are considered unworthy.

No informant would acknowledge that secular political competition is ever involved in choosing among available candidates and indeed I was assured that candidates are extremely reluctant to take office.

The ideal candidate is he who best meets the ideal of absolute physical perfection, handsomeness, dignity, and membership of the proper lineage. The descent criterion is crucial because only certain lineages have the power to transfer God's *kayyo* to earth, and *kayyo* is what the system is all about.

The handing over

The actual handing over period is, quite literally, a year out of time. The old *abba gada* first orders procreativity to cease and then visits the sacred shrines in his territory and removes his *kayyo* from them. Finally, he visits the great *Kallu*, terminates the law of Guji for his *balli*, and hands over his powers to his successor, who then spends a year infusing his *kayyo* and that of his class into the territory.

The procedure begins when the *abba gada* of Uraga sends a message to the other *abba gada* telling them to notify their people of the rank-change. All three then send their messengers throughout the countryside alerting their people. People are told to close their affairs for this *balli* period. Women should not become pregnant and those who are should 'quickly give birth' before the *balli* period ends; marriage is also forbidden. 'All of the grass of Guji' must be burned from the land in September.[17]

The order to suspend childbirth and marriage refers back to the concept of *kayyo*. The *kayyo* of each of the five classes is different and should be kept separate. The year of transition between one class and the next creates a temporal no-man's-land which should not be crossed. At this time the annual firing of the grass throughout Guji is endowed with symbolic content. The burning of the grass is to the land as the shaving of the head is to a man.[18] To be shorn of hair is to lose an identity, and to burn the grass is to end a tenure in office and a period of time; both anticipate rebirth.

Everyone is very much aware of events during the handing over. The people not only contribute to the ceremonies but also attend those which occur in their local area and keep track of the various stages of the cycle. During this time Guji comes alive as a society sharing a common set of beliefs.

The sequence begins when the *abba gada* and their councillors begin to move to the meeting point, the *maa bokku* tree (the most sacred tree in Guji), making sacrifices at several shrines along the way.[19] They wait there through the rains of October into November.

In November the time of milk and plenty *gutu* (fullness) begins. The three *abba gada*, together with the *abba raba*, *abba dori*, and their councillors all assemble at the tree and begin to travel crosscountry to the house of the great *Kallu*. Each *abba gada* takes cattle which must be given to the *Kallu*.[20]

The work of the *Kallu* was summarised by one informant as follows:

The *Kallu* gives *kumbi* [incense] and blesses the people. To receive *kumbi* the *abba gada* each give one hundred cattle. There is also one male goat which leads them [all], and which is decorated with beads. The beads must be tied over the neck to between the horns. They must go over the four legs and reach to the ground. Each of the tribes selects three very big bulls. These nine are put aside. A message is then sent to the *Kallu*. He refuses them [the messengers]. Again they are sent. Then twice more. He refuses. When finally the fifth message goes to the *Kallu*, he accepts. The cattle are driven in. When they come to his house there are people appointed by the *Kallu* to keep the cattle out of the house with sticks. The people from the *abba gada* must drive some cattle into the house. When this is done the *Kallu* accepts them.

Next people, including the *abba gada*, tell their problems to the *Kallu*. The *Kallu* orders his servants to kill a certain number of bulls and prepare a certain amount of mead. They stay there for two nights eating and drinking. He then tells them the solutions to their problems. He also tells what will happen to the people in return for their gifts and prayers.

As the procession approaches the house of the *Kallu*, I was told, he puts out his snakes painted with red earth and butter, to 'poison the enemies of the *Kallu*'. When the *abba gada* enter the house of the *Kallu*, they must crouch down and more or less 'duck walk' to their seats, which are set in order of tribal seniority.

The *Kallu* then begins his deliberations with the leaders. He first discusses any business remaining from the *gada* period which is ending.[21] He then asks about the qualifications of the new leaders and about the events leading to the *gutu* as well as plans for the rest of the handing over. When he has confirmed that all is correct he gives out the incense and blesses the leaders. After the *gutu* is concluded the *gada* leaders return to the sacred tree for the next stage of the handing over, the *gumi*.

There are several levels of interpretation of the *gutu*. The first relates to the myth of the coming of the first *Kallu*. When he came to earth from God he brought with him the rules of the social order, including *gada*. It is therefore appropriate that the living *Kallu* should legitimise the leaders. The *abba-gada* show their subservience to the *Kallu* by stooping before him, indicating thereby that they, like all others, are lesser beings. They symbolise the *Kallu*'s legitimisation of the *gada* system.[22]

Incense from the *Kallu*[23] is believed to make *gada* leaders and their councillors honest and truthful if they hold it in their mouths for several hours. Incense is kept by the religious advisers of the councillors who feed it to the leaders. The potential candidates for leadership (from the *warra kallacha*) are also given *kumbi* as small children and again when, as *kussa* they return from the forest. The *Kallu* gives the incense separately to the *abba gada, abba dori,* and *abba raba,* who, it will be recalled, are members of three different classes. Members of one class never give incense to members of any other class, so that the incense given to each is kept within that class. The incense which they hold in their mouths cleanses the members of the *warra kallacha* from any actions which might have rendered them incapable of holding office. These future leaders, who will be responsible for maintaining the law, are impressed with the need to adhere rigidly to law and custom. Individuals who violate social rules are passed over for leadership, since the *kayyo* of miscreants is inevitably bad. By giving incense the *Kallu* acknowledges the legitimacy of the leadership and, by giving it separately to the representatives of each class, he asserts his position above them all and recognises that they are separate but equal. In addition, the members of each class in power bear witness to the legitimacy of the others through the receipt of incense.

In summary, the *Kallu* endows the council with part of the special attributes his ancestor brought from God, which allows them to become conduits in turn for God's reward of *kayyo*. The *Kallu* does not participate directly in the transfer of authority, which comes later; rather, he supports the legitimate basis of the whole system. The positioning of the *Kallu* above the organisation, but not within it, is emphasised both by his physical exclusion from the three tribal territories and by the fact that he has no *gada* rank whatever. The patriline of the *Kallu* is thus the only one which may not participate in the organisation. His impartiality in the role of ultimate validator of *gada* is thus structurally guaranteed. The *Kallu* holds office for life and the office is inherited (ideally) in the direct line of first sons. The *Kallu* provides continuity of authority in a system in which the other members are replaced at regular intervals.

After the *gutu* the various groups return to the sacred tree for the great assembly at which the outgoing *abba gada* settle any legal or ritual problems which remain from their time in office. The *abba dori* and *abba raba* do not attend but use this time to feed incense to their councillors.

The Guji: Gada as a Ritual System

Any man who has passed through the name-giving ceremony may speak at the assembly and may also speak for those of lesser rank who must remain silent. Cases within each tribe are said to be brought to the appropriate *abba gada* for settlement. (However, I could find little evidence that this still occurs.) The ritual and rules of the system are scrutinised and changes may be suggested.[24] Finally, the old *abba gada* end their law and prepare to travel to the actual handing-over after having sat at the sacred tree from December until early August.

On another level the *gutu* is a confrontation from which a synthesis of the powers of *kallacha* and *woyyu* is produced. The *Kallu* puts up a great show of resistance to contact with the *gada* councils when they first arrive. He rejects their messengers and, later, their cattle. Significantly, he sets out snakes to poison his 'enemies' when they arrive. Clearly these acts have symbolic content, since it is the *Kallu* who has arranged the appointment; a statement is being made concerning the need to keep these very different powers separate. Finally the powers of procreativity, the specifically male-associated *kallacha* with the power of *kayyo* from God, are able to penetrate the resistance of the ultimate *woyyu*, who has sent out as the specific symbol of his power the earth-dwelling snake. When the leaders finally succeed in driving their cattle into the *Kallu*'s house they are rewarded with incense, without which they would have no powers at all. Without the earth-and-woman-associated *woyyu* there can be no male-associated procreativity of the *kallacha*.

The actual handing over takes place in the lowlands near the Ganale Gudda River. The men of *dori* rank gather in three separate areas by tribe and await the leaders, who arrive in late August. There are two preliminary ceremonies. The *abba gada* and *abba dori* hold separate stripping ceremonies (*huluku*). The *abba dori* passes under the *huluku* to remove any negative thing from his past that would interfere with his impending performance as *abba gada*. The old *abba gada* walks under the *huluku* to remove any inauspicious things which have accrued during his time in office.[25]

There is also a blessing ceremony (*muda*) performed by the *abba dori* at the time of the handing over. At the many other blessing ceremonies I have seen, a sacred tree and the heads of people attending the ceremony were anointed with butter to ask for abundance in the coming year. During the local level ceremonies the male head of each family present puts butter on the tree and requests benefits for his family. (See Knutsson:147 and 150; and Haberland: 396, for discussions of *muda*).

The actual handing over of rank proceeds as follows. The *abba gada* orders the construction of a large settlement for his councillors and takes up residence. The *abba gada*-elect comes with seven councillors, one from each clan of his tribe, to the house of the *abba gada*. Three times he calls out *'ya warra kanna'* (this people). He receives no answer. The fourth time the *abba gada* acknowledges with *'yo'* and the *abba dori* enters and is given a stool. After a brief discussion about the period that has just ended the *abba dori* takes a feather from the hair of the retiring *abba gada*, and puts it in his own hair and the men exchange seats. Next the new *abba gada* goes outside and mounts a white bell-bedecked horse. The assembled members of his class (who have just left *dori* and become *gada* with him) shout *'gada, gada, gada, gada'*. Finally there is a great feast for the newly promoted and their leader.

One element of hidden symbolism should be mentioned here. When the *Kallu* is approached by the *abba gada* during the *gutu* he refuses them admission four times and then lets them enter on the fifth try. When the *abba dori* calls out for admission to the house of the *abba gada* the latter remains silent three times and then acknowledges his successor on the fourth attempt. Women are associated with odd numbers and men with even. The seemingly ambivalent nature of the *Kallu* appears to be expressed here in contrast with that of the *abba gada* who is surrounded by male symbolism.

After the rank change the new *abba gada* is visited by his predecessor and his councillors, who advise him about his responsibilities and any problems or changes within the institution itself. The new leader then proclaims his law and begins a year-long trek around the sacred shrines of his tribe, bestowing his *kayyo* in each area. A new period of time has begun.

The first stop during this trek is particularly significant. The new *abba gada*, accompanied by his councillors and many men of *gada* rank, comes to the sacred area at Adola.[26] One informant commented on the special meaning of this area:

The *woyyu* of the land is a spirit below *waka*. It is also called *woyyu* of Adola. *Woyyu* of Adola can do many things — kill people, no water, no food, prevent a person from leaving Adola. The Amhara especially believe this. However, it goes back in Guji to Harda Hawan. She created it. If it becomes angry, people should slaughter and let the blood fall on the ground. *Woyyu* lives in the ground. *Woyyu lafa* becomes angry if people fight or if they kill wild animals. All of this applies to the one area only.[27]

As I understand it, it is at Adola[28] that the *abba gada* burns a snake and rubs the ashes on his phallic head ornament. One informant provided the following statement:

The snakes have poison and the *kallacha* is painted with this poison so that if the *abba kallacha* curse someone the curse will be poison. It is to frighten people to show that the *abba kallacha* are poison in terms of curses. The Kallu and the *abba gada* are the same as *Waka*. The *Kallu* himself is a snake. He keeps snakes in his house.

Kallala is a cloth put on the heads of *abba gada*. At this time after he takes the rank, he sings a song.

Buti bola buta — snake dropped into the hole
naden name futa — woman married a man
bola boffa boni guta — the holes of the snakes are dry
bola dura dayan guta — penis filled the vagina of a girl

The *abba gada* then throws the *kallala* from his head at his sister.

I cannot provide a full exegesis of this song and action here but it is clear that a parallel is being drawn between the snake and the earth, the penis and the vagina. The penis, symbolised directly by the *kallacha*, is, by itself, only the agent of procreativity. The snake is only capable of poisoning or refraining from poisoning. Certainly 'the holes of the snakes are dry' would not be associated with fertility. Indeed *boni*, which I have translated here as dry, is the word for the dry season, the period of greatest suffering. It would thus appear that both an equivalence and an opposition are being drawn, just at the time the *woyyu* is added to the *kallacha* for the final synthesis of powers.[29]

The remainder of the pilgrimage to the sacred shrines is apparently less remarkable. Each *abba gada* and his entourage visit each shrine in their tribal land in order to infuse, through their leader, the *kayyo* of their class into the earth. This symbolic intercourse with the earth is considered vital to the survival of Guji. I was told that if these ceremonies were not performed there would be 'No rain, no grass, no cattle, no crops. All would die.'

After the year of sacrifices, the *abba gada* returns to his home[30] where, a year later, he is circumcised as, ideally,[31] are all men of *gada* rank. After his circumcision he holds an important ceremony, *jara*, which involves the sacrifice of a bull and a blessing.

During his time in office the *abba gada* has many constraints placed on his behaviour. He must always be calm, be settled in his ways and show wisdom. He is under particular constraints concerning women and the earth. A virgin bride is selected for him by his councillors from an appropriate clan[32] as the wife of his *gada* period. If she is his first wife her hymen is penetrated by one of the councillors on the marriage night so that the *abba gada* 'will not perspire'. If she is not his first wife, the *abba gada* penetrates the hymen himself. (A nuptial night is often a contest and the woman occasionally emerges still a virgin.) It seems likely that the hymen is penetrated by a councillor so that an inexperienced *abba gada* will not fail. For the living embodiment of virility to fail on his marriage night would hardly be appropriate or encourage faith in his *kayyo*. He must also not keep a mistress which, considering that such relationships are generally institutionalised, makes him almost unique. The wives of the *abba gada*, on the other hand, may have lovers, but they must never use their husband's bed. The *abba gada*, *abba dori*, and *abba raba* are all forbidden from digging in the earth for any purpose, and no one else may dig within their settlements.

Sexual intercourse by the *gada* leaders, both literal and symbolic, is very carefully regulated. Their virility is vital to the survival of Guji and must therefore be carefully controlled for the general good. Female contacts are only dangerous if they are random. Just before my arrival in the field the *abba gada* of Mati had been deposed and replaced by another man of his lineage. I heard many explanations for this, including 'digging in the earth', having mistresses, and that he had no dignity, but I was later assured that the real problem had been 'mistresses'.[33]

The *abba gada* devotes himself to ritual throughout his term. He holds an increase ceremony for his tribe twice yearly. After four years he orders the lower rank changes and holds the naming ceremony for his sons. Finally, as his time in office nears its end, he prepares for promotion to *batu*.

Conclusions

Present-day Guji society is an example of a type for which a ritual/feast cycle contained within a generation system provides the basis for what Geertz (34) calls the 'logico/meaningful' integration of society. *Gada* accomplishes what the elaborate, and more static, cosmologies of many other societies do; it makes sense of, and humanises, the universe.

Gada is a perpetually unfolding process. At no one point in the eight-year cycle is the total system revealed. For the Guji time may be seen as a circle segmented into five equal, but carefully isolated, pieces each consisting of the tenure in office of one of the five *gada* classes. Members of the society travel around the circle and learn through ritual the position of the individual within traditional society and the nature of universe, and the position of society in the overall scheme. This knowledge is not passive. The individual is presented as constantly changing and progressing; the society as continually using powerful ritual tools to recreate and direct its destiny. *Gada* ritual in fact consists almost entirely of individual and societal rites of passage.

During the part of the cycle when men throughout Guji pass through promotion ceremonies, household by household, the ideal position of the individual within a total system of roles is brought out. A child entering the system at *soluda* rank finds that his own ceremony is a tiny addition to that of his father's. The ritual actions performed on him use both of his parents as the major actors. Men of senior ranks are involved, but at a distance. It is only with the name-giving rite, which marks the transition to adulthood, that the 'youth' first has a complex ritual devoted exclusively to him and his brothers.

Men of *gada* rank in many ways stand for society itself. When an individual passes from *dori* to *gada*, he does not do so in his own home. When a new *abba gada* takes office, all men of his rank attend the ritual and are all promoted with their leader. Their interests and legitimacy have passed beyond the local setting and they follow the new *abba gada* for his year of pilgrimages to the sacred shrines.

For *yuba* there is no rite of passage as such; their withdrawal from secular concerns and the assumption of the state of purity is the nearest mortal approximation to divinity itself. Informants indicated that little attention is paid to the *jarsa* rank promotions.

The local ceremonies, then, do several things. They make statements about the position of the individual in the family and the neighbourhood.[34] They provide, step by step, the path to a closer relationship with divinity and, through this, the increasing ability to supplicate for *kayyo*. In the past the role models of *gada* created the division of labour among men by socially-defined age. This third function is attenuated to the extent that a fieldworker, arriving during the inactive part of the cycle, would not be able to discover the existence of *gada* through the observation of social interaction on the local level. Only during ritual is it possible to observe role play in the rituals themselves. Nevertheless its probable that *gada* was once a key dimension of social organisation.

On the societal level *gada* creates a legal and political leader who is a high priest with attributes of divinity. That is, the *abba gada* is not only a ritual expert, but also the embodiment of the well-being of the tribe through his *kayyo*. The *gada* system provides a solution to a serious problem created by such a leader. The Dinka spear-master (Lienhardt 1961:298-319), for example, elects to be buried alive when he becomes enfeebled so that the countryside will not become like his body. The *gada* leaders should take office while still in their prime and are removed routinely at the end of their *balli*, thus avoiding the problem of the transfer of their physical decay to the land. This is crucial since the system is, in one sense, a 'fertility cult' in which the *abba gada* acts as the conduit through which the blessings of the supernatural flow to man and the sacrificial signs of obeisance of man flow to God. The concept of *kayyo* is thus the key idea, in both *gada* and Guji religion, which is developed through an enormous outpouring of ritual observances on both the local and societal levels.

Through *kayyo* and the related concepts of *kallacha* and *woyyu* the system becomes more than just a fertility cult. They, and the associated subsidiary symbols, develop the tensions between the active (and forthright) male principle and the passive (and ambivalent) female principle. Symbols are dichotomised into male associated (right, even numbers, senior, and so on) and female associated (left, odd numbers, junior, and so on) ritual objects and actions. *Woyyu* expresses a particular type of ambivalence. The concept develops around the earth-dwelling snake, but the people who have ritually active *woyyu* are males from certain hereditary lines. The danger in *woyyu* serves society by making potent pronouncements of those who would judge and rule. *Woyyu* is never associated with fertility in the way that *kallacha* is, but the reconciliation reestablished by *woyyu* people is essential for good *kayyo*.

These concepts achieve their most powerful expression during the handing over of leadership. It is not coincidental that this is also the time when, in people's minds, the parochial ties of the neighbourhood and region are transcended by those of the tribe and, ultimately, the Guji people. The *abba gada*, old and new, traverse the entire territory holding ceremonies. Household heads of the appropriate ranks leave home and join the assemblages. Most homes contribute something to the enormous quantities of food needed to maintain the vast throngs over the two-year period. Wherever people gather they discuss the content, performance and meaning of the great rituals which are addressed to the people as a whole and to the beliefs they hold in common.

In a very real sense all but three years of a *balli* period contain events that turn people's minds to *gada* and anticipate the handing-over. Each local ceremony is seen as a complete event but also as a small piece of a vastly larger cycle; not only does the symbolism in part refer to the total system, but also conversations inevitably turn to the *abba gada* and the grand scale rituals.

During the year when the *abba gada* is terminating every one is bound by the prohibitions he lays down at the beginning of the year. Historically the assembly was the final summation of a dying segment of time. Today the making of adjustments in *gada* itself is the only business over which the *abba gada* retain jurisdiction.

That time and destiny periodically die and are reborn is basic to Guji. As each class takes its turn in office it is as if the world itself were born anew. The new segment of time is not unpredictable, however, for the circle of time is repetitive. The cumulative history of each class is remembered from the past. There was a sense of grim resignation when a drought developed during the tenure of the *robala* class in the late 1960s; informants recalled that when *robala* was last in office there had been a major drought and an outbreak of cattle disease, followed by human death from starvation. It was also during *robala* that Menelik's forces conquered the Guji. The present disaster was seen, even by the *robala abba gada* of Mati, as the inevitable result of the general *kayyo* of the *robala*. It was widely believed that the problem could be ended by the removal of *robala*, which had already lingered beyond its eight years.

Each traditional Galla society lacked any basis for overall unity other than the *gada* system which, in the past, was basic to both social organisation and, very likely, to religion. It also provided the organisation for recruiting men for periodic warfare. For the Guji it still provides the basis for unity through its ritual. It is not simply having *gada* that makes Guji unique, since almost every society impinging on its boundaries has traditionally possessed a similar system, but rather the meanings contained within their own particular system which, for Guji, makes them a people with a unique destiny and a unique strength.

To the anthropologist *gada* is an institution which has served to integrate Guji society both structurally and cognitively. For the people themselves it is the primary means of controlling *kayyo* and it is *kayyo* which humanises the universe and makes it predictable.

NOTES

1. The research upon which this paper is based was conducted between August 1968 and May 1971. Funding was provided by grants from the National Science Foundation, the Committee on African Studies, and the Department of Anthropology at the University of Chicago. Travel funds to attend the symposium at the University of Manchester were provided by the Center for International Programs and the African Studies Center, Michigan State University. I wish to express my gratitude to Paul Baxter, David Turton, and Hector Blackhurst for their hospitality.
2. See Paul Baxter's discussion of the Boran, Chapter VI.
3. The Guji refer to their generation system as *balli*, reserving the word *gada* for one grade within the system. I use the word *gada* for the entire system in order to be consistent with the literature.
4. These leaders will be discussed later. Tribe has become a vexed word but I have used it here because it is conventional to do so in the Ethiopian literature. In a Guji myth of origin Mati, Hoku and Uraga were three brothers each of whom had seven sons who became the founders of the seven clans of each *gosa*. Each *gosa* had first claim to a particular territory. A more accurate translation of *gosa* might therefore be phratry. (cf. M. Meggitt 1965:5-8).
5. Members of a given clan can be found throughout the tribal territory.
6. A man maximises the survival potential of his herds by distributing them widely among the many altitude ranges where his kinsmen and in-laws live. He, in turn, receives cattle from them.
7. A full discussion of local level organisation will be contained in a forthcoming monograph.
8. If a poisonous snake enters one's house, it is said that an in-law has come to visit. A cloth is spread on the floor for the snake and butter is put near it, just as in-laws are given butter when they visit.
9. I am not clear at what point in *karra* these youthful exploits begin.
10. All adult males who have passed through 'name-giving' but who have not reached *jarsa* rank, are buried outside their houses on the right side of the door (their wives being buried on the left). Those below *makabasa* are dumped into the ground away from the house without ceremony.
11. Haberland (1963:390) writes that one of his informants indicated that the practice had ended before his birth in 1885.
12. For example, the father of one of my assistants was of childhood rank when my assistant was born. My assistant had been adopted by his grandfather and thus become his own father's 'brother' both genealogically and through *gada*. Despite the humour father and son found in this

paradox, the son treated his father appropriately in other contexts and retained his inheritance rights.

13 Using a computer-simulated regression, Legesse (2974:154) found that the Boran system added this rule more than 340 years ago. In fact, as Legesse points out, the generation rule must have been in effect more than 450 years ago for its military organisation to have been operative during the Galla invasion of highland Ethiopia.

14 The Guji, who tend to blame all social problems on their incorporation into Ethiopia, laid the abandonment of marriage rules to this, even though they had very likely been abandoned previously.

15 These ceremonies, many of which I attended, will be described in a forthcoming monograph on *gada* and social structure.

16 The information concerning the handing over, which I did not have the opportunity to observe, was collected from: the *abba gada* of Uraga, Mati, and Hoku and their Councillors; the great *Kallu*; the *abba dori* (future *abba gada*) or Uraga; the historian (who is responsible for a wide range of traditional knowledge) of Mati; and a number of senior men who had observed some part of the sequence.

17 Guji have a calendar of seasons and months, the commencement of *adolasa* roughly coincides with September. The grass is normally fired each September, before the heavy rains of October. In this instance it expresses the idea of termination.

18 During the *makabasa* 'name-giving' transition rite from childhood to manhood all of the hair is shaved off the heads of the initiates 'to remove all the bad things of childhood'.

19 During this sacrifice they performed the *huluku*, a number of which I have seen. This consists of passing under a vine suspended between two trees. It is a form of 'stripping', aimed at ridding the participants of bad *kayyo*. It is often performed after misfortune or when people are moving to a new area following a death in the family or ill-fortune with cattle or crops.

20 The number of cattle is said to be one hundred; a number which is frequently used to indicate 'many', just as one thousand indicates the largest possible number. The *Kallu* set the number of sixty, but I have heard others give estimates as low as twenty. Whatever the number, the herds of the three leaders are kept separate.

21 For example, the *Kallu* told me that two things must be settled at the next rank-change. At the last *gutu* the previous *abba gada* of the Uraga did not have enough cattle and passed on his debt to his successor. Also, there is the case of the *abba gada* of the Mati who was forced out of office during the current *balli* period and replaced by another man to whom the *Kallu* had not given incense. The *Kallu* does not recognise him and is angry with this replacement, who does not have his blessing.

22 Informants generally referred to the *gutu* as 'going to the *Kallu* to get *kumbi*'.

23 *Kumbi* is used in household and spirit possession ritual by other Ethiopian peoples. It is readily available in the local market. The *kumbi* mentioned here must come from the *Kallu*.

24 Legesse (98) reports that the *abba gada* are subject to criticism during the Boran assembly of the multitudes. Guji deny that their *abba gada* is criticised to his face.

25 There is an additional ceremony for the *gada* class which is being promoted to *batu*. One man of *gada* rank has his hands tied behind his back and then others say, 'Let the bad things of this *gada* go with him.' He is then driven from the house of the ceremony.
26 The area surrounding the town of Kebre Mengist, which was formerly named Adola.
27 The text is yet another indication of the association between *woyyu* and woman and the earth. Also consistent with *woyyu* is the punishment of people who fight. It is especially interesting that this *woyyu* is associated with domesticated animals, particularly cattle.
28 I am not certain whether all three *abba gada* have the snake ceremony at this place or in their separate territories.
29 When the *abba gada* leaves office and becomes *batu*, he loses his *woyyu* powers. This is in contrast with the people of *woyyu* who have their power for life.
30 Men of *gada* rank, in addition to participating in their leader's ceremonies, each slaughter a bull at their own homes.
31 Nowadays boys are often circumcised when they are young.
32 The *warra kallacha* of each tribe may only marry into certain clans of that tribe. For the Uraga, *galalcha* is the best, 'pure' clan. It is also the clan from which the *Kallu* chooses his first wife. This restriction is particularly important for the first wife, the *harda bola* (mother of the hole), who assists at ceremonies and who ideally bears the first son and heir.
33 For other young men, who are expected to have as many mistresses as possible, this would not cause social censure. My initial suspicion of political intrigue in this case was groundless. The man who replaced the deposed leader had neither the knowledge of nor the desire for the office, and the councillors for both men remained the same.
34 Again, it should be noted that limitations of space do not permit analysis of social organisation.

BIBLIOGRAPHY

Bahrey. 'History of the Galla' in C.F. Beckingham and G.W.B. Huntingford (eds.) *Some Records of Ethiopia, 1593-1646.* London (1954).
Geertz, Clifford. 1957. 'Ritual and Social Change: A Javanese Example'. *American Anthropologist.* 32-54.
Haberland, Eike. 1963. *Galla Süd-Äthiopiens.* Stuttgart.
Knutsson, Karl, E. 1967. *Authority and Change.* Gothenburg.
Legesse, Asmarom. 1973. *Gada: Three Approaches to the Study of African Society.* New York.
Lienhardt, Godfrey. 1961. *Divinity and Experience: the Religion of the Dinka.* London.
Meggitt, M.B. 1965. *The Lineage System of the Mae-Enga of New Guinea.* Edinburgh.
Turner, Victor W. 1969. *The Ritual Process: Structure and Anti-Structure.* Chicago.

IX
Continuity and Change in the Shoa Galla *Gada* System[1]

HECTOR BLACKHURST

Introduction

Among the Northern Galla, the formal organisation and practice of *gada* have either been abandoned or continue in a form which, when compared to that of the Southern Galla, is both simple in structure and sparse in ceremonial elaboration. In his book *Authority and Change* Knutsson reported on the decline of *gada* among the Macha Galla. This essay is concerned with a neighbouring group of Galla, the Tulama or Shoa Galla. Like Knutsson, I propose to discuss changes in *gada* that have taken place during the last century and my analysis of these changes owes much to Knutsson's work. However, while Knutsson was dealing with a situation where *gada* had disappeared and had been, he argues, replaced by another institution, my problem concerns an attenuated system which is still operating.[2] In addition to discussing the changes in Tulama *gada* therefore, I shall also examine the reasons why *gada* has taken the form it now has.

Gada was both a political and a religious institution with a tribal and inter-tribal organisation and the most notable change in the system has been its reduction to a series of almost wholly domestic rituals. This reduction in the span of *gada* is the result of the emergence in Tulama society of new forms of political relationships prompted, in part, by the incorporation of the Tulama into the Amhara Kingdom of Shoa, and, in part, by pressures within the *gada* organisation itself. The reasons for the persistence of *gada*, despite these changes, are to be found in the religious significance of the system which is largely independent of the changing political environment.

Social organisation

The Tulama or Shoa Galla inhabit the central areas of modern Shoa Province, Ethiopia. These are their homelands, that is, the area in which they claim to have settled after the Galla migrations of the sixteenth century. However, not all Shoa Galla live in Shoa Province and for people themselves the geographical criterion is less relevant than a genealogical one in determining tribal status: a Shoa Galla is a member by agnatic descent of one of the Galla tribes which form the loose grouping called by others the Shoa Galla, but which is given various other designations by its members. No precise definition can be given to this grouping. Lists of component tribes given by ethnographers vary and the people themselves have no definite roster of tribes, rather an indefinite list of attributes possessed by people whom they consider to be like them. The Shoa Galla I studied did not live in Shoa, but were a group of immigrants living round the small town of Adaba in north-western Bale Province some 140 miles south of Addis Ababa. They had moved there some thirty years ago either directly from Shoa, or after settling briefly in Arussi Province to the north of Bale.

The Shoa Galla in Bale, and those in the Shoan homeland, live, for the most part, in the middle ranges of the Ethiopian plateau (5-8,000 feet). They are peasant farmers and grow a range of cereals and pulses, chiefly *teff*, wheat, barley, peas and beans. They also keep sheep, goats, horses and cattle, and, in a casual way, chickens. Agricultural production is the responsibility of the domestic group. The necessary labour is, as far as possible, drawn from this group and all agricultural equipment and land is owned jointly by the head and his wife. Ideally, the composition of this domestic group is that of the family, a man, his wife, and their sons and daughters. The various agricultural and domestic tasks are allotted on the basis of a division of labour by age and sex and the tendency is to limit as far as possible long-term dependency on others outside the household for labour or equipment.

A married man should be an independent household head. On marriage, sons cease to labour for their fathers and set up a new independent, enterprise with their wives, correspondingly, daughters leave their natal homes on marriage to go to live with their husbands. The marriage contract which requires the families of both bride and groom to make equal gifts of property to the couple is designed to ensure that they have at least the nucleus of an independent household. In most instances, the property acquired at marriage is only a nucleus. Few men are so well endowed that they have immediately all the land and equipment they require. Even if they have, it is clear that, in the early years of a marriage, the demands for labour cannot always be met from within the household. The ideal of independence must, to some degree, be compromised, and outside assistance sought. Labour and equipment can be hired and, at peak times during harvest, advantage can be taken of a number of types of collective working party based on neighbourhood or membership of voluntary associations. Some or all of these solutions can be used by a man faced with a shortage of labour or equipment, but for the younger married man a more usual solution is to remain closely associated with his father. After marriage a son may continue to farm some of his father's land and to borrow his equipment. However, despite this continuing dependence, marriage does alter the relationship between father and son to the extent that the son is now working with his father rather than for him. He may be dependent on his father, but, strictly speaking, he is not a dependant.

This dual character of the relationship between a father and his married son is reflected in patterns of residence. At marriage, or shortly thereafter, a son builds his own house, an indication that a fledgeling independent domestic unit has been brought into being. However, it is rare for a son to build away from his father's homestead. The new house is usually within or close to the father's compound, an indication that the two households, though nominally independent, are still closely interconnected.

This pattern of the father-son relationship after marriage develops, with variations, between a man and all his sons. For a time at least most young men remain with their fathers after marriage. Younger sons may be dependent not so much on their father as on an elder brother, but the cumulative effect of these ties is to produce a pattern of residence familiar from many patrilineal African societies. The residential unit consists of a man and his wife, their unmarried children and their married sons, their wives and children. Most Shoa Galla in the area I studied live in such agnatically based hamlets. There are, of course, variations in the precise composition of these groups; not all groups of brothers reside together and occasionally a son-in-law stays with his wife's father. However, the pattern is sufficiently prevalent for it to be treated as typical.

I have described the development of this type of residential unit by reference to ties of economic dependence, sons on fathers, younger brothers on elder brothers. These ties of dependence never entirely obliterate the independence of each constituent household of the hamlet. As each son's household grows this independence becomes more marked and, in practice, the hamlet can persist as a residential unit long after it has ceased to have any coherent economic unity. However, the absence of day to day co-operation in production in a hamlet may conceal other types of long-term interdependence between its members. Economically, the hamlet may be bound together by the interests shared by a group of brothers in their father's estate. All a man's children are entitled to an equal part of his estate and a son's expectation of inheritance can induce him to remain close to his future landholding despite short-term difficulties. Even in the absence of such material inducements, membership of a hamlet has definite and persisting advantages which derive from what Bloch (1973) has called the long term nature of kinship obligations.

The relationship between brothers is central to hamlet organisation. The ideal of brotherhood held by the Shoa Galla is not unusual. Brothers should love one another and support one another in difficulty. A group of brothers should present a united front to outsiders such that a harm done to one is done to all. Brothers should treat each other as equals, though this equality is tempered by a mild ranking according to birth order so that the first born (*angaffa*) is treated as being to some degree the father's deputy and benefits slightly from preferential inheritance. These sentiments are familiar from many societies and the Shoa Galla are probably no more successful than others at putting them into practice. Nevertheless, a brother, other things being equal, is the person most likely to help one in a difficult and perilous situation. The relationship of brotherhood is expected to sustain demands greater than those made on any other relationship and, because of that, probably does.

This feature of brotherhood is integral to the relationship and does not need to be maintained by a continual series of reciprocal gifts and services. The relationship does not preclude such reciprocity, but it does not require it to persist. Many day to day short-term requirements can be met by arrangements with outsiders without jeopardising relations between brothers. However, these outside relations are based largely on mutual convenience and advantage and are formed to meet a defined and limited need. Situations of crisis are not easily dealt with by means of such relationships. By its nature a crisis is unplanned and unpredictable and may require extraordinary measures to be solved. Short term relations of convenience are not designed to meet such situations, but brotherhood, with its strong moral obligations, is. To live in a hamlet with one's brothers, therefore, offers long-term security even though day to day co-operation may be slight.

This somewhat protracted discussion of the household and the hamlet has been necessary because the hamlet and the relationships upon which it is built play an important part in the present day practice of *gada*. In the following section I describe the present day organisation of *gada* and an associated ceremony of transition.

Gada *organisation and the transition ceremony*

The contemporary Shoa Galla *gada* system has five grades: *itimako, daballe, folle, doroma* and *luba*. For convenience, I shall number these grades from *itimako* (I) to *luba* (V). A man remains in each grade for a period of eight years and a full career in the grades lasts forty years. Men who have passed through grade V are called *huba* or *yuba*. This term does not denote the existence of a sixth grade, but refers to a category of people only. This category is not internally differentiated into separate *yuba* grades and men do not pass out of *yuba* into a higher grade.

Recruitment to the grades is based on the position reached by a man's father in the system. A son should always be forty years behind his father, consequently a man enters grade I as his father leaves grade V. This rule applies equally to all a man's sons. All sons enter *gada* at the same time and pass through the grades together. Sons born after their siblings have entered *gada* join their brothers in the appropriate grade whether or not this is the first in the series.

These are the basic rules of the contemporary Shoa Galla system. Its affinity with other, more complex systems is apparent but its sparseness of structural elaboration contrasts markedly with these systems. This contrast is heightened when the actual operation of the system is considered. Formally, there are five grades as I have described but in practice only two of these grades, *luba* (V) and *folle* (III), have any significant role to perform. These grades do not correspond exactly to grades in the formal structure but are formed by amalgamations of the formal grades.

During the month of June at the end of an eight year *gada* period many ceremonies are held to mark the transition of men from grade IV to grade V. Strictly speaking, the people who are the principal actors in these ceremonies are *doroma* (IV) who are about to become *luba* (V), but, during the ceremony, they are referred to as *luba* and the fact that they are or have been *doroma* is ignored. Outside the context of the ceremony of transition, neither *doroma* nor *luba* have any significant role in connection with their *gada* status. During the ceremony the *doroma* are called *luba*, so, in practice, the *doroma* is merged into the *luba* grade.

Unlike the *luba* (V), the *folle* (III) are active throughout an eight year *gada* period in addition to playing a significant role in the ceremony of transition. However, the groups referred to collectively as *folle* are, in practice, made up of people from the three grades of *folle* (III), *daballe* (II) and *itimako* (I). The first two grades have no independent activities but are seen as apprentices who are learning *gada* from the real *folle*. They are rarely referred to by their appropriate grade name and are distinguished from the real *folle* only by the negative criterion that they cannot perform certain ritual roles which are reserved for the real *folle*.

The real *folle* and their associates can be seen on many occasions throughout a *gada* period, indeed, they are frequently difficult to ignore. Their traditional dress is distinctive consisting of a monkey skin head-dress (*chate*) and clothes made from the skins of wild animals, principally monkeys, lions and leopards. They are armed with circular hide shields and carry long staves (*fororsa*). The animal-like and aggressive appearance this dress gives to the *folle* is matched by their behaviour. They rarely move without running in a curious loping fashion and accompany their movements with shouts, roars and grunts. Throughout the eight year period, the *folle* attend many religious and secular festivals. Here they career through the crowds in small groups, shouting and rattling their long staves on their shields. Eventually, they form a circle and begin to sing and dance. Their songs are characteristically obscene and use phrases which would not normally be heard in public. This obscenity is both expected and licensed

Plate IX.1. Shoa *folle* dancing at a *gada* ceremony

and forms an integral part of the way in which the *folle* are meant to behave.

However, while a large part of the *folle's* behaviour resembles that of wild animals, they do have an important moral duty: to seek out and to punish a man believed to be living with a widow without having married her (*sigaba*). The punishment given by the *folle* consists of beating the man and tearing his clothes. Theoretically, their victim has no redress against the *folle*, a fact which is celebrated, in appropriate style, in the short ditty:

arangaban bala inkabu
sigaba danya inkabu,
nansala.

the arangaban tree has no leaves
the *sigaba* has no judge,
I will swive him.

I have never witnessed the shaming of a *sigaba*, but *folle* claim that they still search them out.

The *folle's* behaviour contrasts sharply with that of the *luba* at the transition ceremony. Traditionally, the *luba* (V) were the grade from which the tribal leaders of the Shoa Galla were chosen. In keeping with this, the *luba* act throughout the ceremony with dignity and deliberation. They dress in white robes and a white turban with a chaplet of the creeper called *kalala* (Stephania Abyssinica). During the ceremony their ears are pierced and decorated with a pair of ear-rings called *loti* which, I was told, were worn traditionally by a man who had killed a lion, an elephant or a man. The *luba* always move slowly in the ceremony and their song is a slow, haunting chant; they act like elders and leaders while the *folle* act like wild animals or adolescents.

The two operational grades of *folle* (III) and *luba* (V), the associated structure of grades and the rules of recruitment together constitute the greater part of *gada* as now practised by the Shoa Galla. Apart from the activities of the *folle*, *gada* plays little part in the everyday social organisation of the Shoa Galla and differing *gada* status does not affect interaction between people outside the ceremonial context. However, during the transition period, *gada* springs to life and a great deal of time, effort and resources are spent to mount the series of transition ceremonies.

Each ceremony is held to mark the transition of a man, or group of men, into the *luba* (V) grade. All the ceremonies I attended were held for a group of *luba*. In all instances the group was composed of full brothers who were residing in one hamlet. The largest of these ceremonies took place in the hamlet of a group of six brothers, the sons of Leka, who had died some four years previously. In general outline this ceremony was similar to the others and to informants' accounts of how the ceremony should be performed. I therefore propose to use it as the prototype of the transition ceremony, but I shall also indicate some of the variations between the actual performance and the texts given to me by informants.

The six brothers who are the principal actors in the ceremony I call, Alemu, Badada, Chala, Dida, Elicho and Fayissa. Seniority by birth is of some importance in the ceremony and I have accordingly named the brothers in such a way that the alphabetical order of their names corresponds to the order of their birth, Alemu is thus the firstborn and Fayissa the last born.

The brothers range in age from approximately sixty to thirty. The land on which their hamlet was built was bought jointly by the brothers before their father's death. The purchase was made largely at the instigation of Chala and he now owns the largest share of the land. Some of this is used for his own house site, cattle byre and eucalyptus grove and his mother's house and a small area is farmed by him. His brothers all own just enough land for a house site, cattle byre and eucalyptus grove. None of the six men owns other land and all are dependent on renting or sharecropping arrangements for access to sufficient agricultural land.

Although formally equal, all six brothers can be differentiated from one another by reference to their economic and social standing. Chala is undoubtedly the most prominent and forceful as his leading role in the land purchase shows. He still provides what overall leadership there is in the hamlet and he is helped in this by the fact that his two elder brothers, Alemu and Badada, are not successful men. Alemu is rather feckless and happy-go-lucky and Badada has, for many years, suffered from a severe and untreated case of gonorrhoea. Among the younger brothers, Dida and Elicho are ambitious and increasingly successful while Fayissa is still too young to have become a significant force in the hamlet.

Relations between the brothers were, on the whole, amicable, but not intense. Mutual co-operation between them was slight, but the inequalities I have described gave rise to a pattern of dependence between the richer and poorer households. Thus Chala's mother lived on land owned by her son and Alemu received, in an informal way, a flow of goods and services from Chala. Chala, Dida and Elicho all gave assistance to Badada and Dida and Elicho kept a brotherly eye on Fayissa. Between the three successful households, however, co-operation was minimal.

The effects of these inequalities are apparent in the transition ceremony both in the logistical arrangements made to mount the ceremony and in deviations from the ideal in its performance. Nonetheless, the fact that the ceremony was held jointly by all the brothers indicates that, whatever their internal divisions, there was an overall unity between the constituent households of the hamlet.

The ceremony proper began near midday with the arrival of a group of about ten *folle* at the hamlet. They ran through the hamlet singing raucously and briefly visited the house of each brother. Finally, they came to Chala's house, formed a circle outside and began to dance and sing in earnest. After a while, Alemu and Chala came out of the house and presented the *folle* with a pot of beer, a number of round loaves coated with a mixture of butter and chilli powder and small containers of roasted grain mixed with butter or honey. Chala urged the *folle* to eat. They accepted the invitation and, seated in a circle outside the house, helped themselves to the food and drink while Chala and Alemu went inside.

When they had finished, the *folle* began to sing again, this time including in their songs laudatory references to Chala. He and Alemu then came out of the house and stood on the threshold while the *folle* gave a series of blessings, using such phrases as:

Gather the water together and let it rain for us.
Let the rain fill the streams.
Let the country be filled with peace.
Let *gada* return to us with peace.
Don't let drought come back to us.

Let the barren give birth.
Let those who have given birth give birth again.
Let God protect *gada*.

After the blessings, the *folle* moved off singing towards Dida's house. Dida had combined with Fayissa for this part of the ceremony as Alemu had with Chala. The two brothers fed the *folle* with the same foods as Chala and the same type of blessings were given by the *folle*. Finally, the *folle* went to Elicho's house where both Elicho and Badada were the hosts and the feeding and blessing were repeated for the second time.

When the *folle* had been fed in this way by all the brothers, they returned to Chala's house. Chala had, by now, attired himself fully in the dress of a *luba* and was wearing a white turban and white robes. His ears had been pierced and a small twist of black and red cotton threaded through the lobes, a substitute for the more decorative, and more expensive, *loti*, or ceremonial ear-rings. Chala was accompanied by his wife who was now also dressed in white and was carrying an axe on her shoulder and holding a milk churn. The couple were greeted by the leader of the *folle* and a man who had previously passed through the *luba* (V) grade, and, accompanied by them, they moved at a stately pace towards the house of Alemu.[3] Chala was singing a slow, mournful chant which was in marked contrast to the wild antics and noisy singing of the *folle* who followed.

Alemu and his wife came out of their house as the party approached. The two brothers kissed and Alemu joined Chala in the chant as the party moved off towards Dida's house. On the way the two brothers crouched on the ground three times. After Dida, Elicho and his wife joined the party, then Fayissa and his wife and finally, Badada. Each brother joined the group by kissing his siblings and all joined in the chant which had been started by Chala. However, both Badada and Fayissa received special treatment. Before he joined his brothers Fayissa had his head covered with a bundle of fresh green grass by the *folle*. This was done because he was the youngest (*kutisu*) of the brothers. Badada was in a difficult position because, at the time of the ceremony, his wife had left him. He had not found a substitute and had to beg the forgiveness of the *folle* for this irregularity. They granted it.

All the brothers were now gathered in a group. They continued to chant almost in competition with the *folle* whose shaggy clothing and riotous singing and dancing contrasted with the dignified mien and white robes of the *luba*. Slowly, the brothers began to leave the hamlet and, as they did, the shrill ululations of the women in the congregation added a new sound to the cacophony of singing, shouting and stamping.

The procession of *luba*, and their wives, the *folle* and those who had come to watch the ceremony now walked to a nearby ford some five hundred yards from the hamlet. At the ford, three *folle* waded through the water to the far bank, the *luba* with their wives stood in the water by the near bank with the rest of the *folle* and the onlookers linked up on the near bank, having first plucked small bundles of fresh green grass.[4] A few moments of confusion followed with a number of people talking at once, but one man eventually made himself heard. He was standing on the near bank. He took off his cloak, addressed the *luba* and told how he had quarrelled with one of the *folle*'s wives who had insulted him. The woman, who was also there, put her side. One of the *luba* then referred the matter to the *folle* on the far bank. They replied that it was bad that *folle* should quarrel and the two should make it up. Everyone said. 'Amen'.

A second man then spoke up and said that he too wanted to give a party for the *folle*. His friend had done it and he was angry because he was so poor that he was unable to. Would the *folle* forgive him? The matter was referred to the *folle* on the far bank and after some discussion between them and their colleagues by the near bank, the man was blessed and forgiven.

A third man then walked into the stream and spoke. He said that he had sown, reaped and threshed a field of barley, but, before he could store the grain, he had had to go to Addis Ababa. While he was away a thief had stolen some and his landlord had also helped himself to more than his share. He had taxed his landlord with this but the man had refused to do anything. He asked the *folle* to curse the landlord and the thief which they, and the whole congregation did, using the phrase *Rabi habalesu*, 'May God destroy them'. The aggrieved man then bowed and returned to the near bank.

There was a short pause. Then one of the men who had passed through *gada* accompanying the *luba* asked if there was a member of the Galan tribe present. A number of men in the congregation gave their tribes until finally a Galan stepped into the middle of the stream. On this occasion, the Galan was a brother-in-law of the six *luba*, but his affinal status is irrelevant in this context. What is important is his tribal status. Galan are held to be the firstborn (*angaffa*) of all the Tulama tribes and their blessings are required on many ritual occasions. Even if the only Galan present is a juvenile he will be asked to call the blessings.[5] The *luba*'s brother-in-law was an adult, but he was a little drunk, and called a somewhat slurred string of blessings.

After the Galan, each of the six *luba*, in descending order of seniority, also called a string of blessings to which the whole congregation gave the response. Then the wife of each of the *luba* stepped forward and placed her axe in the stream at her husband's feet. On top of the axe she placed a bundle of fresh green grass and poured milk from the churn over the axe, the grass and her husband's feet. The whole congregation then took their bundles of grass, dipped them in the stream and splashed water on their feet and forehead. The grass was left on the bank and the congregation began to move away, but some of the *folle* stayed in the stream and began to splash each other and anyone else who stayed to watch.

Meanwhile, the *luba* had retired to a small hillock near the stream where they were addressed by one of the men who had passed through *gada*. He exhorted them to kiss each other and to avoid quarrelling in the future. The procession then reformed and the *folle* escorted the *luba* back to the hamlet and accompanied each one to his house in ascending order of seniority. With that, the principal part of the ceremony was completed, but the celebrations went on into the night and continued for two or three days.

The sequence of events in the ceremony matched fairly closely descriptions of the ceremony given by informants. There was, however, one major deviation. Informants stressed that the feeding of the *folle* and the collecting of the *luba* should be done in descending order of seniority. In this instance this was not done. A full examination of the significance of this deviation is beyond the scope of this paper, but it seems clear that the deviation was a tacit recognition of the fact that the ranking of the brothers by seniority and their ranking by other criteria did not correspond. In practice, Chala was treated as if he were the first born and his two senior, though less prestigious, brothers were relegated.

Many such ceremonies are held at the end of an eight year *gada* period, each one marking the transition of a man, or a group of men, to the *luba* (V) grade. So far as I could determine, no special ceremonies are held to mark the passage of men through the lower grades. At the end of June the complete transfer is deemed to have taken place.

Changes in the organisation of Gada

Traditionally, the members of the *luba* (V) grade were those from whom the tribal leaders of the Shoa Galla were chosen. The eight year *gada* period limited the term of office of these leaders, but the grades themselves provided a basis only on which an elaborate hierarchy of councils and offices was built. Knutsson (1967:177) has reconstructed this political hierarchy as it existed among the Shoa Galla (see Figure IX.1).

This diagram refers principally to the situation as it is believed to have existed in the period between 1600 and 1700, that is to say after the Galla had moved from their southern homelands up into the central parts of Ethiopia. In this period, the various, small, tribal groups who now form the Shoa Galla were settling in Shoa Province. According to traditions I collected, the Galla who moved into Shoa

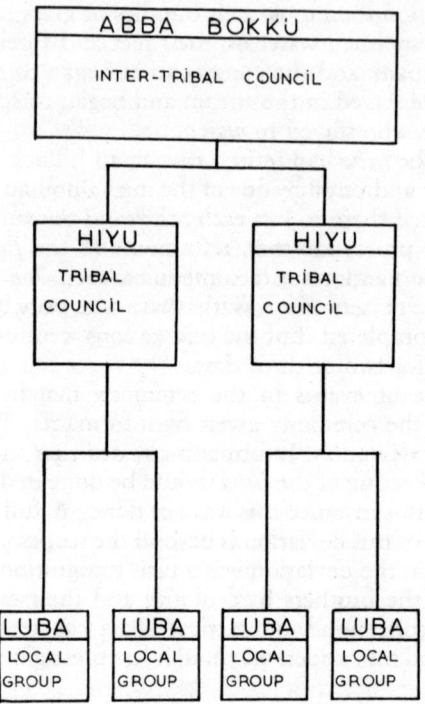

Figure IX.1. Tulama *gada* hierarchy

already had a tribal organisation at the time of the immigration. The present tribal distribution is the result of that organisation being followed in the pattern of settlement, rather than a subsequent identification of groups of people with particular areas giving rise to tribal divisions.

Although these Galla immigrants were divided into tribes, they retained a supra-tribal political organisation. In the diagram, three levels of the political hierarchy are shown: the local group, the tribal council and the intertribal council. The passage of men through the various grades of the *gada* system was supervised at the levels of the local group and the tribe. Local *luba* sent delegates to the tribal council which was led by an official called *hiyu*, hereafter tribal leader, who was himself elected from among the *luba*. The tribal council in turn sent a number of delegates to the intertribal council. From among the members of this council were chosen the supreme leaders of all the Shoa Galla, and a number of lesser officials.

The supreme leaders were a triumvirate comprising the *abba bokku* (father of the sceptre), hereafter intertribal leader, and two others, known collectively as 'the three spears'. Below them in the hierarchy were the *abba chaffe* (father of the council) who served as a chairman of the council, the *abba dubbi* (father of speech) who acted as the link between the permanent officials and the whole council, and the *abba sera*, (father of the law), an expert on law and custom whose duty it was to memorise the results of the assembly's deliberations. Other, lesser officials were also chosen.

The hierarchy had both political and judicial functions. Councils at any level could debate issues, formulate policy and act to settle disputes, but supreme political and judicial authority were vested in the intertribal council under the intertribal leader. The authority of this leader was dramatically represented in the ceremonies held to mark the periodic changes in the personnel of the council. When an intertribal leader left office at the end of an eight year period the 'law' was symbolically suspended by the retiring leader only to be restored by his successor. At this time, major changes in tribal custom seem to have been discussed and, if accepted, were binding on all for the next eight years.

Although the hierarchy was both a political and judicial structure it should not be regarded in its most elaborate form as permanent. The most senior officials seem to have been resident at the intertribal council headquarters, a place called Oda Nabbi, close to the Awash River. But the full council and the tribal councils were probably more periodic, coming together largely for the great ceremonial gatherings which marked significant points in the cycle of *gada* grades.

The loose confederation of tribes that made up the hierarchy is clearly vulnerable to centrifugal forces. Such forces, Knutsson argues, led eventually to the break up of the intertribal confederation. Following settlement in Shoa, tribal expansion continued, people moved away increasingly from the central areas to find more land and local interests began to predominate over those of the confederation. Competition over land between confederation members further exacerbated the growing divisions between the tribes until the confederation itself was abandoned. The highest level of the hierarchy was lopped off and each of the Shoa Galla tribes became an independent political unit.

The disintegration of the confederation was probably a gradual process, and political separation does not seem to have caused the abandonment of all the symbols of the union. Both Harris and Isenberg and Krapf who were in Shoa during the 1840s report internecine fighting between the Galla there, an indication that politically the federation was by then defunct. However, both authors also report that Oda Nabbi was a central Galla shrine, whither, to quote Harris 'the tribes flocked from far and wide to make vows and propitiatory offerings' (1844-49, vol. III). The site of the intertribal council appears from this account to have retained importance as a religious centre after its political significance had waned.

By the middle of the nineteenth century *gada* as a political system had become a tribal, as distinct from intertribal system. This change in the span of *gada* was due to changes that took place within the confederation of tribes. However, from the mid-nineteenth century onwards the Tulama were increasingly brought into contact with the aggressively expanding Amhara Kingdom of Shoa. Contact between the two peoples, both peaceful and war-like, certainly existed before this period, but only now were the Tulama subjected to a co-ordinated campaign of expansion which, under Menelik, would incorporate into the Empire many of its present-day southern Provinces.[6] Individual Shoa Galla tribes were either conquered by the Amhara armies or capitulated peacefully. Alliances were formed between the Amhara and some of the Galla to subdue other Galla.[7] Eventually the greater part of the Galla on the Shoan plateau were incorporated into the Amhara Kingdom. Incorporation into a centralised kingdom, either peacefully or by arms, necessarily affected the political organisation of the conquered tribes. However, the structure of leadership among the Galla was not immediately altered. The Amhara did not simply abolish *gada* officials and the *gada* system and replace them with their own political and administrative officers. There was, rather, an element of indirect rule in the administration of the incorporated areas. Nonetheless, the incorporation did juxtapose two contrasting political systems and this juxtaposition affected *gada* in two ways: first, it exaggerated tendencies already within the system towards a further weakening of its political functions, and second, it created a situation where two political systems were in competition with each other for the allegiance of the people.

I have, so far, treated *gada* as if its structure accounted for all political relations among the Shoa Galla. Such a view implies that the sole authority recognised by the Galla was that vested in *gada* officials, either local *luba*, or the tribal leaders. It also suggests that authority within the system derived from the reverence in which the system and its associated offices were held and that *gada* was to a great extent insulated from the competition for control over material resources and men which is normally associated with political activity. At one time this may have been true, but certainly by the end of the nineteenth century there are reports that indicate that *gada* was becoming increasingly enmeshed in just this kind of competition.

De Salviac (183 ff.) is particularly informative on this feature of *gada* organisation. Writing of the northern Galla, he describes a situation where each tribe has its own *gada* hierarchy with a tribal leader, now referred to as *abba bokku*. Even at this late stage he reports a nominal allegiance to an '*abba bokku* superieur', but stresses that this allegiance is more often broken than observed. The tribal leader and his immediate colleagues were settled permanently at the site of the tribal council where could be seen 'the numerous herds of cattle brought in tribute, taking advantage of the rich pasture' (de Salviac :184). The rendering of tribute by the people to their *gada* leaders adds an economic dimension to the political hierarchy of *gada* and suggests that the *gada* officers were part of a redistributive economic system. Tribute flowed up the hierarchy to the *gada* leaders and was distributed by them, possibly as gifts to individuals, but certainly through the slaughter of cattle for the many rituals associated with the *gada* cycle. In this way, the leaders were able to fulfil the expectation that they would be generous and openhanded, an expectation that continues today. Thus the term *luba* was glossed for me as 'a giver, a generous man', the proof of his generosity being the feeding of the *folle*.

However, as de Salviac makes clear, the expectation of generosity was balanced by the realisation that individuals would use the system for their own benefit. Indeed, he argues that a degree of exploitation was institutionalised in the system. At this time, the *luba* (V) grade was divided into two sub-grades of four years each. The term *luba* was used to describe the whole eight year period and the second four year period while the term *dori* was used for the first four year period. The transition between sub-grades was marked by a mid-term ceremony. At this ceremony the *dori* call together the tribe and confess the faults which their inexperience and greed for wealth have led them to commit. They then promise that for the next four years they will behave with moderation. During the first four years, the constitution, as de Salviac (186) somewhat floridly expresses it:

holds that the *dori* are novices or apprentices and closes its eyes to their pranks caused by the first intoxication of power. Endowed with a maternal tenderness which spoils its terrible children it allows them to oppress their subjects to hasten the acquisition of a fortune from their ephemeral royalty ... the axiom is formulated thus: four years for the *dori*, four for the law [my translation].

Whether or not this period of licence was followed by four years of good government is difficult to determine. De Salviac reports that an impartial tribal leader may retire poor and some have been known to sell their sceptres, but he gives the impression that this was a rare event.

Even allowing for possible exaggerations on the part of de Salviac, it is clear that the hierarchy of *gada* offices offered opportunities for the accumulation of individual wealth. This tendency towards accumulation and economic differentiation within the *gada* system was matched by similar developments in the wider society. De Salviac (195) reports the existence among the Galla of a number of wealthy and respected men who did not owe their position to holding *gada* office. Such men were known as *abba laffa* (landowner) or *abba biya* (owner of the country). These men, according to de Salviac (195), formed 'another social order based on property and fortune, constituting a veritable landed nobility'. Apparently outside the normal, tribal pattern of land tenure, they owned in some instances thousands of hectares of land. This ownership was legitimated by tracing descent from warriors famous at the time of the Galla invasions, but men with large holdings of cattle could also acquire land by purchase.

These landowners became landlords. They settled rent-paying tenants on their land over whom they exercised paternal authority. They also raised armies from among their clients which were used in the whole tribal army, or, under private command, could be called on to defend the landlord's holdings. The growth of a landed nobility and the accumulation of individual wealth by *gada* officials threatened the integrity of *gada* because both developments tended to produce centres of power outside the political hierarchy. Thus, *gada* officials who exploited their authority for their own benefit were able to exercise power derived from their control of material resources. Such power was not lost at the end of an eight year *gada* period with the result that retired *gada* leaders were in competition with their successors. Indeed, it is possible that retired *gada* leaders converted some of their wealth in cattle into land and themselves became members of the landed nobility. The landowners, whatever their origin, were also in competition with the *gada* leaders. A significant indication of this is their ability to raise an army. The marshalling of troops and the conduct of warfare were technically the sole responsibility of one *gada* official called the father of war (*abba dula*). The fact that landowners also were able to mobilise armies inevitably weakened the power of the father of war. Equally, the authority and respect accorded to the landowners weakened the authority of the tribal leader, for now, instead of being the sole authority he became one of a number of authorities. The control that he and his associates had was consequently no longer direct, but was mediated, and hence constrained, by the control of the landowners. Where once there had been one embracing hierarchical structure, there was now a parcelling out of power among a number of authorities, none of them supreme and each in competition with the other. A process of balkanisation was beginning.

This process was accelerated by the Amhara conquests and the subsequent incorporation of the Galla tribes into the Shoan state. Like many colonising powers the Amhara looked for indigenous authorities among the conquered peoples through whom they could administer their new territories. Markarkis (107) reports that the Amhara governors of the period regarded the eight year rotation of the political office associated with the *gada* system as an alien practice. They recognised the current *gada* leaders as the tribal authorities and encouraged their retention of office beyond the prescribed period. In addition, they gave administrative authority to some of the heads of the large landholding families and in some instances appointed people who had succeeded in ingratiating themselves with the conquerors.

The Amhara, therefore, ratified the proliferation of positions of power outside the *gada* system by granting administrative authority to the large landowners. At the same time they froze the senior offices of the *gada* system itself making their incumbents government-sponsored representatives. They also, by their mere presence, created further opportunities for the establishment of new positions of influence outside either the landed families or the *gada* officials. Undoubtedly, after the conquest a number of enterprising Galla began to act as brokers between the conquering power and their own people. Such men need not have been given official recognition by the Amhara, but by establishing informal links between the Galla and the Amhara they would have been able to make themselves important and influential figures among their own people in some ways more able effectively to represent the interests of these people than the official, recognised, leaders. As a result of the conquest, therefore, the exclusive political authority that was once vested in the *gada* system was further dispersed. In addition, all the various positions of authority within Galla society were downgraded, for now final authority lay neither with the *gada* officials, nor with the landed nobility, but with the Shoan kingdom. The recognition given by the Amhara to the indigenous authorities lessened the power of those authorities because recognition showed that they were now subordinate. Final authority had passed out of the hands of the Galla and politically speaking they were no longer whole societies, but parts of a larger whole. In these circumstances the political hierarchy of *gada* became superfluous. The political arena had changed so much that the type of political relations found in the *gada* system were no longer relevant. The *gada* hierarchy was not abolished, it was bypassed, ignored, and finally, forgotten.

The decline of *gada* as a political institution was not a prelude to the complete breakdown of the whole *gada* system among the Tulama. *Gada* has persisted. To understand why it has done so it is necessary to appreciate that *gada* is not simply a system of government, it is also a religious system.

To many of the nineteenth century travellers in Shoa, *gada* appeared first and foremost to be a religious institution. Thus de Salviac (193) reports that even when the political power of the *gada* leaders had declined the Galla continued to offer them gifts regarding them still as the true representatives of God. Harris (1844:49, Vol. II) says of the council site at Oda Nabbi: 'Paying adoration only to stocks and stones and bending the knee to none but idols and serpents they here lavish votive oblations of butter and honey to secure the favour of the Deity.' Similarly, Krapf (1860:76) reports 'The Galla have priests called Lubas as distinguished from the Kalijas who are their magicians, exorcists and medicine men.'

The religious element in *gada* is made explicit in the following legend which describes its origin:

> A long time ago the rain stopped for six years. Some people were wandering about and they came across a place where a prophet (*nabbi*) lived, a prophet like an angel of God. They went to him and said that the rain had stopped and the cattle were dying, the crops were dying and men were dying. The prophet told them to go to the river with *kalacha*,[8] *bokku, folle, luba, daballe* and *itimako* and to asperge (*fachassu*, lit. to sow) the water. If they did that, he said, it would rain. When they had done this they went home and pierced their ears, circumcised themselves and let the wound bleed. When they had done this, it rained. They did those things then and believed in them and, look it is the same today, it is the law.

Here, *gada* is shown to be divinely inspired, handed down from God through his prophet. Furthermore, its performance is shown to secure the well-being of the people, ensuring the rain necessary for their livelihood. There is also an implicit contrast in the story between the circumstances of the people before and after they were given *gada*. The aimless wandering of the first part suggests a purposeless and discoordinated life. In contrast, after their meeting with the prophet, the people are organised into distinct groups with particular tasks to perform. The fruits of this organisation are peace and prosperity.

Correspondingly, other texts show that the penalties for failure to perform *gada* are disease, death and want. Haberland (1963:530) reports that in the 1870s King Menelik called to his court the leaders of the Gulalle tribe of Shoa Galla and forbade them to practise *gada*. They obeyed but in 1876 there was a serious epidemic of rinderpest which the Gulalle ascribed to their failure to observe *gada*. They petitioned the King who revoked his previous prohibition. My own informants told me that if a man neglects *gada* his cows would give birth to calves that are deformed. If he is a trader, or so poor that he has no cows, his children will be afflicted with blindness, withered arms and club feet. The most expressive text describing the consequences of forgetting *gada* has been collected by Knutsson (1967:180) for the Macha:

> When *gada* was destroyed they left *gada*. The bull refused to mount the cow, men no longer respected justice.... There were no longer any real elders and few children were born. The cows gave birth to deformed calves. Pregnant women gave birth to their children at the wrong time. They bore children without hands, and calves were born which had no tails. When the *gada* system was destroyed everything else was also destroyed. When *gada* no longer existed, there was no justice.

From these texts there emerges a view of *gada* which shows that the significance of the system transcends the purely political. It contains a view of the world which links the natural order with the social order; disturbance in one threatens the other. Only by observing the rules of *gada* can social order be maintained and the natural order relied upon to provide fertility and prosperity.

Fertility and prosperity, the well-being of cattle and children, are fundamental concerns of any peasant society. Despite all the major social and political changes of the last century, the Tulama have remained small-scale, peasant farmers, intimately dependent on their cattle, the land and the weather. The contemporary Tulama have, so far as their livelihood is concerned, the same interests as their forebears. *Gada*, in its religious aspect, is directly tied to these concerns and not to a particular social or political order. It has persisted because it expresses these concerns and purports to ensure that livelihood and prosperity will be maintained.

To say that *gada* has persisted despite political and social changes suggests that the system is unaffected by the social and political environment in which it operates. Certainly, this is the view of the Shoa Galla themselves who maintain that the *gada* they now practise is exactly the same as that of their ancestors. In a formal sense this is true; the five grade structure and the eight year *gada* period are features common to both the contemporary and the past system. However, while the structure has remained the same, the form in which *gada* is celebrated ceremonially has altered in response to the events of the last century.

During the period that the political hierarchy of *gada* existed, the *gada* system united each tribe into a coherent whole. Thus, local members of the *luba* (V) grade were not only local dignatories but also national leaders who, through their place on the tribal council, linked their local area to the centre. Similarly, the *folle* (III) and some of the *doroma* (IV) had tribal roles to perform as warriors or the executive arm of the council. *Gada* rank was, at this time, a significant tribal status. The celebration of key points in the *gada* cycle reflected this tribal importance. Major *gada* rituals were not just local celebrations but were held at the site of the tribal council in the presence of the whole tribe and the changes in *gada* status were ratified by tribal, and not just local, consent.

The political changes of the last century removed the basis of this tribal cohesion. Power, which had been contained within the *gada* hierarchy was parcelled out among local dignitaries and supreme power was vested in the Shoan State. Consequently, political allegiance was no longer commanded by one central authority within the tribe but was dispersed; the local magnate with his supporters displaced the *gada* leader. In these circumstances, the celebration of *gada* on a tribal basis becomes both difficult and meaningless. The organisation of *gada* ritual on a tribal level requires a central, co-ordinating authority. In the absence of such an authority, the mobilisation of the whole tribe becomes a daunting logistical exercise. It is not, of course, impossible and it is conceivable that local leaders could jointly have organised their local populations in a co-ordinated ritual enterprise. However, to do so would, in effect, be to undermine their own status. Their power was derived from the control of local areas; any claim or suggestion that there was a tribal authority superior to the local leader would threaten their power. Far from organising a central *gada* ritual it would be in their interests to prevent any such ritual being held. By retaining power at the local level, they had reduced the importance of *gada* status by removing from it much of its political significance; to have then staged a ritual which, amongst other things, celebrated the tribal importance of *gada* would have been contradictory.

However, the antipathy between the local leadership and *gada* is based on more than a conflict between centralised and dispersed authority. The symbolic representation and legitimisation of power are also at issue here. The local leaders could have used the symbolism and ideas of *gada* to legitimise their authority. Such ideas and symbols were traditionally associated with leadership and would have been recognised and accepted by the people. Furthermore, the *gada* organisation could have formed the basis for the mobilisation of local populations, even without a tribal organisation. However, the type of authority symbolised by *gada* is inconsistent with the authority of local leaders in that the latter is not subject to an eight year limitation and is not circumscribed by the obligations and expectations of traditional office. To exercise and legitimise their power the local leaders needed a new set of symbols and they found these in the Amhara system of stratification not in their own culture. *Gada* was, therefore, not integrated into the changed political situation at either the tribal or the local level.[9]

Were *gada* merely a political institution the result of this lack of integration would, most probably, have been the disappearance of the system. However, as I have argued, *gada* was sustained because it is a religious system. The failure to integrate *gada* into the local level of leadership deprived it of an institutional setting in which it could operate, but it did not reduce its meaning as a religious system.

The expression of the ideas and values in *gada* requires some form of social organisation, and in the absence of any tribal or local arena for *gada* the largest and most enduring structured sets of social relations on which to base *gada* are the hamlet and its constituent households. The domestication of *gada* ritual can, therefore, be seen as the direct corollary of the decline of the political importance of *gada*. Successively higher levels of Tulama social organisation have been removed, the intertribal confederation gave way to tribal divisions and the tribes themselves were broken down into smaller political units. The organisation of *gada* has reflected this process and its major institutional setting has changed from that of the intertribal council site to the hamlet composed of a group of brothers and their dependents.

Described in this way, *gada* may appear to have become a largely domestic ritual simply for the lack of any other institutional setting.

However, an examination of the rules of recruitment to *gada* and of the symbolism of the ceremony of transition shows that, regardless of its political functions, *gada* is closely tied to household and hamlet organisation. The rules of recruitment ensure that fathers and sons are separated by *gada* so that neither is in competition with the other for the status that *gada* rank confers. At the same time, since a father must always be ahead of his sons in the *gada* cycle his domestic authority is supported by his status in the *gada* system. *Gada* rank also unites brothers. All brothers belong to the same *gada* grade and have the same status throughout their career in the system. *Gada* thus ignores even the slightest ranking by order of birth which differentiates a solidary group of brothers. Finally, although fathers and sons are, so to speak, divided by *gada* and placed in two, separate cycles, they are united by the very fact that they are in the system. Membership of the *gada* system is a right which can be lost, those who have retained this right owe their status to their father. Their father, in turn, owes his status to his father, and so on. The right to practise *gada* therefore, links both fathers and sons to their agnatic ancestors; the living and the dead together constitute a corporate '*gada*-owning' group.

The purpose of *gada* for its practitioners is to ensure the health and fertility of men and animals. This aim is explicit in the myth describing the origin of *gada* and is also apparent in the nature of the sanctions thought to be applied to those who neglect *gada*, that is the death or deformity of their cattle and children. Similarly, in the ceremony of transition, the series of symbolic acts which take place at the ford are expressive of the central ideas of *gada*. The three elements, water, grass and milk are related in that water, or rain, promotes the growth of grass, the grass is eaten by the cattle who produce the milk. At the ford, this cycle seems to be reversed: milk is returned over grass to the water, after this, the congregation uses grass to agitate the water, in effect making their own rain. Whatever precise interpretation is given to these actions, their reference is clear: fertility, growth and prosperity.

The benefits which are expected to flow from the performance of *gada* are directed towards the whole community. However, the successful exploitation of these benefits is not a communal responsibility but is the task of individual households which are the property owning and property exploiting units of Tulama society. It is, therefore, understandable that the symbolic acts at the ford should be performed by a husband and wife, for, in the conjugal relationship, human procreativity and fertility are combined with the fertility of land and cattle.

The rules of recruitment to *gada* and the emphasis on fertility have this in common: both are closely tied to relations within the hamlet, but, at the same time, can refer to wider sets of relations. Thus the rules of recruitment not only reflect an ideal pattern of relations between fathers and sons and between brothers, they also provide a model for relations between and within generations in the society and derive a system of authority from the model of domestic authority. Similarly, the notion of fertility, at its most general, can refer to society but it also has a specific reference in the household group of husband and wife. The political hierarchy of *gada*, as it were, drew out and elaborated the domestic elements in *gada* and applied them more widely. The disappearance of the political hierarchy eliminated the framework on which this elaboration was constructed, but the domestic elements remained and were easily integrated into the institutional setting of the household and the hamlet.

Conclusion

In its present form the *gada* system of the Tulama, is principally a small-scale, local institution. This essay has been restricted to an analysis of the causes of this reduction in the span of *gada* but this is not to deny that, even now, *gada* transcends the purely domestic and becomes involved in wider sets of relations between hamlets or between the Shoa Galla and other groups. Certainly, an analysis of *gada* in its domestic aspect does not account for the full, contemporary significance of the system. However, the contrast remains. The past involvement of *gada* in a tribal political system gave it a specific form and significance. The disappearance of this political system has directly affected *gada* firstly by narrowing the ceremonial arena of *gada* celebrations and secondly by highlighting the religious, as distinct from the political, features of the system.

NOTES

1. The fieldwork on which this paper is based was carried out between 1969 and 1971 with a grant from the Social Science Research Council.
2. Knutsson argues that the structure of positions of authority at one time provided by the Macha *gada* system was replaced by an ecstatic religious cult under the authority of cult leaders called *kallu*.
3. In the ceremony the man who has passed through the grades and is accompanying the new *luba* is called *irko*. The *irko* is in fact repaying a debt to the *luba* for the *luba* should be the man who acted as leader of the *folle* when the *irko* himself held his own *gada* ceremony.
4. The *folle* who cross to the far bank are real *folle* and not *itimako* or *daballe*.
5. There is an association here between the word *galan(a)*, the ceremony and a myth which accounts for the senior status of the Galan tribe. *Galana* means a river or stream and the *gada* ceremony takes place on the banks of a stream. In addition, Shoa Galla account for the seniority of the Galan in a myth which states that originally the Gombichu tribe were the first

born but that they lost this status when the tribal founder, Gombichu, who could not swim, asked Galan to cross a river ahead of him when the two men were out walking (Haberland 1963:527).

6   The history of the relations between the Shoan Kingdom and the neighbouring Galla is more complex than this brief summary would suggest. Details of the gradual expansion of Amhara control can be found in R.H. Kofi Darkwah (1975:1-34).

7   See Greenfield (1965:97).

8   *Kalacha* is an item of ritual paraphernalia which, I was told, is a piece metal shaped roughly like a man. The first *kalacha* fell from heaven but duplicates can be made by blacksmiths, cf. Knutsson (1967:89). I showed informants pictures of the Guji and Borana phallas-shaped *kalacha* but they maintained that those were not *kalacha*. Haberland (1963:540) reports however that the Shoa Galla *kalacha* is phallus-shaped.

9   This situation can be contrasted with that of the Macha *kallu* who combine many of the traditional *gada* symbols with their non-traditional cult. (Knutsson 1967:206).

BIBLIOGRAPHY

Bloch, M. 1973. 'The Long Term and the Short Term: the Economic and Political Significance of the Morality of Kinship' in Goody, J. (ed.), *The Character of Kinship*. Cambridge.

Darkwah, R.H. Kofi. 1975. *Shewa, Menilek and the Ethiopian Empire*. London.

Greenfield, R. 1965. *Ethiopia: A New Political History*. London.

Haberland, E. 1963. *Galla Sud-Athiopiens*. Stuttgart.

Harris, W. Cornwallis. 1844. *The Highlands of Aethiopia* (reprinted Farnborough, 1968).

Isenberg, C.W., and Krapf, J.L. 1843. *Journals* (reprinted London, 1968).

Krapf, J.L. 1860. *Travels, Researches and Missionary Labours During an Eighteen Years' Residence in Eastern Africa*. (reprinted London, 1968).

Knutsson, K.E. 1967. *Authority and Change*. Gothenburg.

Markakis, J. 1974. *Ethiopia. Anatomy of a Traditional Polity*. London.

Salviac, P. Martial de. 1901. *Un Peuple Antique au Pays de Menelik*. Paris.

Index

Abrahams, R., 1, 15, 25, 45, 57
Acholi, 38, 50, 64, 144
Adaba, 246, 254
Adamson, Joy, 156, 180 n13
Addis Ababa, 246
Adola, 236
age-regiments, 2, 10, 17
age-systems: as cognitive categories, 5, 245; and women, 11; antiquity of, 20-1; discrepancies in, 8; durability of, 20-5; rules of, 2, 4
Algonkian bands, 188
Almagor, U., 1, 10, 25
Anywar, R.S., 38, 50
Arssi, 11, 21, 24
Arusha, 14, 15, 31 n9, 32 n14, 54, 147
Arussi Province, 246
Awash River, 257
Azande, 130 n21

Bahrey, 28, 168-9, 171, 181 n15, 218
Balandier, G., 176
Bale, people, 96; province, 246
Barber, J.P., 64
Baxter, P.T.W., 1, 6, 11, 18, 21, 91 n1, 128 n1, 164, 180 n10, 207 nn1 and 2
Beckingham, C.F., 181 n15
Beidelman, T.O., 65-6 n3
Bender, M.L., 128 n4
Bernardi, B., 69
Bischofberger, O., 38
Black, J., 91 nn.11 and 12
Blackhurst, H.J., 1, 6, 28, 29, 128 n1, 180 n11
blessings, 16, 22, 28, 46, 54, 155, 162, 167, 177, 180 n14
Bloch, M., 92 n16, 247
Bodi, 26, 96, 98-9, 101-2, 109, 113, 116, 125
Bohannan, P., 31 n8
Bohannan, L., 31 n8
Bonte, P., 31 n11

Boran: 3, 8, 10, 13, 15, 16, 18, 21, 24, 31 n9, 151-182, 183, 198, 205 n6, 207, 226, 228; *Aba Bokuu*, *Aba gaada*, see Boran generation-sets, officers of; assemblies, 153-5; *gaadamoji*, 151, 160, 169, 174-7; *gada*, 151-181, (as a cognitive system) 156, 160, (as a political system) 156, (as a system of sets) 151, 170-8, (political functions of) 152-3; *gada* grades, (*chuusa*) 170-1, (*dabal'le*) 170-1, (*gaada*) 151, 169-75, (*game*) 170-1, 178-9, (*raaba*) 151, 171-3, 175-6, 178-9, (*yuuba*) 175-6; generation-sets, officers of, 151, 153, 159-60, 171; Gona, see Boran moieties; *gultu*, 177; *guutu*, 167, 171-2; *hariiya*, 10, 21, 159, 177-8; Islam, 161-3, 176; *Jilla*, 160, 175; *Kaallu* 151, 155, 161-2, 166-8, 174, 179 n7; *kalaacha*, 167, 174, 175, 180 n13; *kumbi* 173-4; *luuba*, 156-60, 167-9, 171, 181 n16, *luubu* 166, 168; moieties, 162, 165-7; *Muuda*, 174; 'Peace of the Boran', 167, 180 n14; Sabho, see Boran moieties; set councillors, qualifications for, 154; set-line (*gogesa*), 158-9, 168, 175; snakes, 174; stock management paradigm, 163-4; *Waaka*, 166
Boranaland, extent of, 160-61.
Brazilian Sugar Plantation, 92 n14
Brown, Jean, 180 n13
Bryan, M.A., 128 n5
Burns, T., 86
Burton, J.W., 66 n3
Buxton, Jean, 14

Cerulli, E., 180 n8
Chai, 96, 101
Chalbi, 184-5

Chirim (Bodi territorial section), 102
Comaroff, J., 92 n16
curses, *see* blessings

Darkwah, R.H. Kofi, 267 n6
Dassanetch: 9-12, 25-6, 69-94, 183, 205 n3; affinal relationships, 71, 78-80, 82, 84, 88; absence among peers, 85; age-groups, 70, 72; age-mates, 69; age-peers, *see* Dassanetch peer cliques; age-set, 69; age-system, 69, 72, 73, 74, 79, 80, 85, 88; annuals (*chad*) 72, 73, 75, 79, 86; blessings, 87; bond partnerships, 71, 82, 83, 84, (and inequality) 79, 84, 88, (demographic concentration) 84, (and bridewealth rights) 85, (and competition) 89; bridewealth, 71, 82; brokerage, 82, 90; boys hairstyle (*nigen*), 73, 79, (and circumcision) 72, 82, 84, (and equality) 80, 85; clans, 70; curses, *see* Dassenetch blessings; *dimi* ceremony, 71, 72, 82, (and inequality) 80, 85, 89; elderhood 82, (and cliques) 86; equality (ethos of), 73, 75, 76, 78, 79, 80, 82, 88, 89, 90; *fargoginte*, 77, 78, 83, 88; generation-set (*hari*), 72, 73, 74, 75, 76, 79, 85, 86, 90; gift, bond of (*shisho*), 71; God (*Wag*), 87; hair-dressing ceremony, 72, 78, (and clique formation) 75; holding, bond of, (*herno*), 71, 82, (between peers) 84; kinship system, 90; land, allocation of, 70, 82, 84; lips, bond of (*afo*), 71; marriage, 79; meat feast, 76, 77, 82, 87; men's hairstyle, (*kabana*), 73, 78, 79; *miele*, 77, 87; name-giving, bond of (*neto*), 71, 82; name-ox, 76, 89, (symbolism of) 77, (after dimi) 85; peer cliques (*shele*), 73, 64, 76, 77, (recruitment to) 75, (and *fargoginte*) 78, (and equality) 78, 86, 87, 88, 89, (differentiation within) 79, 83, 84, 85, (avoidance of competition within) 80, (and

Dassanetch, *cont*.,
debt) 83, (accessibility of members) 84, (debates) 86ff, 90, (as opposed to network) 89-90; spearing, bond of, (*uru*), 71, 82; social credit, 71, 85, 90; stock camps, 75, (and cliques) 76; stock loans, 82, 83, 84, 88; *tigle*, 85-6; tribal sections, 70; warriorhood, 79; yards (of settlement), 86; (debates in) 88
Didinga, 38, 50, 96
Dinka spearmaster, 239
Dirri, 160-62, 179 n5
Dodos, 144-6
Dodoth, 38, 50
Driberg, J.H., 38, 50, 54
Durkheim, E., 24
Dyson-Hudson, N., 6, 16, 18, 20, 32 n13, 38, 45-6, 54, 57, 58, 62, 65 n2, 91 n2, 101, 103, 134, 136, 142-7

Ehret, C., 20
Eisenstadt, S., 31 n10, 37, 91 n6, 92 n17, 130 n20
Erek, 83
equality, ethos of, 25, 69-93
Evans-Pritchard, E.E., 4, 18, 19, 47, 69, 154, 163

family and sets, 12-14, 22
Firth, R., 66
Fortes, M., 154
Fukui, Katsuyoshi, 129 nn7 and 11

Gabra: 21-2, 28, 161, 183-206; assemblies, 191, 194-6, 202, 205 n9; camels, importance of, 184-6; ceremonies of sets, (*Jilla*) 190, 193-8, 202-4, 205 n10; custodian of drums, 195; custodian of firesticks, 195; *Dabella,* ritual elder, *see* Gabra grade organisation; *garomo*, 191-2; *gada* 183-204; grade organisation, 190-8; grade-system, (irregularities in) 199, 201-2; (hypothetical example) 199-201; *Hayyu, see* Gabra officials of sets; headmen, position

Gabra, *cont.*,
of, 189; herd management, 184-5; *Idjole, Jarsa, see* Gabra grade organisation; *jallaba*, 188-9, 193-8, 202-4, 205 n5; *Jilla, see* Gabra ceremonies; *luba*, generation set, 190, 193-8, 201-4, 205 n5, 206 n10; marriage, 187-9, 201; marriage-linked clans, 189; *nabo*, 195; neighbourhoods, 190; officials of sets, 188-9, 193-8, (duties of) 198-204; phratries, 187, 190; shortages (of equipment) 186-7, (of food) 186, (of labour) 186, (of water points) 187; social organisation, 187-90; spatial organisation, 184-5; subsistence, 183-4; *Xallu*, ritual leaders, 194-8, 204; *Xallu* clans, 189; *Xomicha, see* grade organisation
Gada: as a puzzle, 6, 152; provisions of, 27-8; as a grade, 170-1; Boran, 28, 151-82; Gabra, 28-9; Guji, 29; Shoa, 29
Galan (Shoa Galla tribe), 254, 266 n5
Galla, *see* Oromo
gangs, 3, 4, 13; gangs and age-grading, 4; gang rape, 17
genealogical generation 6-8, 159-60, 177
Geertz, C., 238
generation-setting, 2
Gennep van, A., 7-8
gerontocracy, 14, 19, 147
Gluckman, M., 17, 27, 32 n18
Golbo, 161, 162, 165-6, 179 n5
Goldschmitt, W., 19-20
Gombichu (Shoa Galla tribe), 266-7 n5
Gorai, 184-5
Greenfield, R., 267 n7
Greenway, P.J., 129 n8
Guji: 8, 21, 156, 160, 207-43; *Abba Dori*, 232, 233, 235, 237, (and *Kallu*) 234; *abba gada*, 207, 208, 212, 213, 222, 223, 224, 230, 231, 232, 233, 236, 237, 238, 239, (authority ended by Ethiopian state) 209, 240, (and timing of

Guji, *cont.*,
gada system) 221, (responsibility for warfare) 230, (as court of appeal) 231, 235, (selection of) 231ff, (relation to *Kallu*) 234, (and symbolism) 236, (circumcised) 237, (and marriage) 237; *Abba Raba*, 232, 233, 237, (and *Kallu*) 234; 'adjacent' generations, 214; 'alternate' generations, 214, (relations between) 214; *Banti* ceremony, 225; *birnaji*, (gada class), 221; blessing ceremony (*muda*), 235; calendar, 242 n17; *Cedabba*, 231; children (abandonment of) 225, (adoption of) 225, 226, 228; clans, *balbala*, 208; *daballa* (*gada* rank), 216, 220, 223, 226, (compared to *jarsa gudurru*) 220, (recent addition to cycle) 226; *dalana* (*gada* class), 221, 222, 223; *dori* (*gada* rank), 218, 222-5, 228, 232, 235, 238; landlords, 209; *faga*, 231; father/son relationship in *gada*, 223; *gada* classes (*messensa*) 221, (recruitment to) 221, (relation to grades) 221-2, (between adjacent grades) 222, (relation to patrilineage) 223, (relation to history) 240; *gada* system: (recruitment) 214, (ideal cycle) 216ff, (role dominated) 220, (contemporary operation) 220ff, (relation to descent system) 220ff, (compared to age grade system) 223, (changes in rules) 224ff, (distribution between grades) 226, (prototypical system) 226ff, (unstability of) 228-9, (disjunction between age and grade status) 229, (leadership) 230, (cognitive function of) 238, (basis of unity) 240, (rank in system) 219-24, 228, 238; *gada* rank (*balli*) 207, 214, 222, 240, (duration of) 214, 221, 239; God (*Waka*) 209-12, 219, 239; Gujiland, 208ff; *gumi*, 233; *Halchisa*, *gada* class, 221, 224; *harmufa*, *gada* class, 221-3; *harra*, *gada*

Guji, *cont.*,
rank, 216, 220-6, 228; head ornament (*mido*), 218, 220, 225; *hiyyu*, 231; *hoku*, 208, (innovators of new grade) 226; horses (*mara*), 208; incense (*kumbi*), 233-4; *jari* ceremony, 237; *jarsa gudurra* (*gada* rank), 212-20, 226, 239; *jarsa holuku* (*gada* rank), 212, 219-21, 223, 226, 239; *jarsa raka* (*gada* rank), 220-21, 223, 226, 228, 239; *Kallu*, 208, 232, (relation to *abba gada*) 208, 230, 234, 235, (made headmen) 209, (agent of God), 210, (role in handover ceremonies) 233, (association with snakes) 233, 235, (myth of origin) 234, (and symbolism) 236; *kayyo*, 210, 212, 218, 219, 232, 234, 235, 237, 239, 240, 241, (controllable through *gada* system) 211, (divination of) 211, (related to *gada* class) 224, (and *abba gada*) 236, (associated with *Kallacha* and *Woyyu*) 239; *kussa* (*gada* rank), 216, 221, 222, 228, 232, 234, (and status reversal) 217; leader of battle, *abba dula*, 230; *maa bokhu*, 233; male/female distinction, 211, 239, (in relation to fertility) 212; marriage, (preferential rule of in *gada*) 224, (relation to *gada* cycle) 225; Mati, 208, (*abba gada* of deposed) 233, 238; moieties, 208; *muduna* (*gada* class), 221-2; name giving ceremony (*makabasa*), 216; neighbourhoods (*ola*), 208; patrilineages, 208; peace, 210; pilgrimages, 231; procreativity, (restrictions on) 216, (abandonment of restrictions) 225, (upper limit) 228; *raba mido* (*gada* rank), 220-2, 224-5, 226, 228, 232; *robala* (*gada* class), 221-3, (and *Kayyo*) 240; sedentarisation, 229; *soluda* (*gada* rank), 216, 220, 222-6, 238, (recent addition to the cycle) 226; stripping ceremonies (*huluku*), 235, 242 n19; tribe (*gosa*); 208; *Uraga*, 208, (*abba gada* of) 230;

Guji, *cont.*,
virility (*kallacha*), 235, 237, 239, 240, (symbol of *gada* system) 212, (associated with *wayyu* and *kayyo*) 239; *warra kallacha*, 231, 234, 243 n32; *woyyu*, 212, 235, 236, 240, (associated with order) 213, (associated with the *Kallu*) 213, (associated with affines) 213; *wudessa* (ritual staff), 218, 226; *yaa* (assistants to *abba gada*), 224, 231-2, *yuba batu* (*gada* rank), 219-22, 225, 228, 238; *yuba ii* (*gada* rank), 219-20, 225, 228, 239; *yuba guda* (*gada* rank), 219-20, 224-5, 239

Gulalle (Shoa Galla tribe), 262
Gulliver, P.H., 1, 5, 14, 18, 30 n1, 31 n9, 38-9, 54-9, 62-5, 91 n2, 104, 130 n20, 133-6, 138-9, 142-6, 148 n2
Gura (Bodi territorial section), 102
Gwynn, M.D., 129 n8

Haberland, E., 179 n3, 180 n8, 208, 225, 235, 267 nn5 and 8
Hallpike, C., 32 n15
Hamer, J., 152
Hana (Bodi territorial section), 102
Handelman, D., 91 n1
Harris, W. Cornwallis, 257, 261
Helm, J., 188
Hinnant, J., 1, 7, 28, 156, 180 n11
Houghton, Rev. S., 163
Huntingford, G., 8, 17, 38, 179 n2, 181 n15
Hurri Hills, 184

Ibo, 30 n3
infanticide, 7, 169, 172, 176, 179, 181
Isenberg, C., 257
Isiolo, 161, 176
Islam, 161-3, 176

Jakobson, R., 47
Jensen, A.E., 5
Jie: 17, 25-6, 38-40, 45, 48-50, 54-9, 62-3, 133-49; fertility rate, 137-8; mismatch of age and generation, 134; overlap of generations, 138-9;

Index

Jie, *cont.*,
  simulation, 137-142; slip mechanisms, 134-6, 141-2; underaging and overaging, 135-6, 139-41, 143, 145-7
Jones, G.I., 30 n3

Kalenjin, 50
Karamoja District, 38, 50
Karimojong, 3, 16, 18, 20, 25, 38, 45-6, 50, 57-8, 63, 134-7, 142, 144-6; cluster, 49, 54, 59
Karsten, D., 152
Katabok area, 43, 63, 67
Kebre Mengist, *see* Adola
Keiser, R.L., 3
Kikuyu, 21, 23, 32 n17, 38
kinship systems, relationship to age and generation systems of, 38
Kipsigis, 16, 38
Kitgum, 64
Konso, 32 n15, 151
Kotol, P., 65
Korya, 83
Knutsson, K., 180 n8, 181 n14, 235, 245, 255, 257, 262, 267 n9
Krapf, J.C., 257, 261
Kuraz, Mount, 83
Kuria, 38
Kuper, Hila, 2, 5

Labwor: 15, 25, 27-67; age-groups, 40, (importance of seniority in) 41, (initiation into) 41-2, (closure of) 43, (authority of) 43, (promotion between) 44, (number of) 48, (relation between provincial groups) 51, (relation between alternate groups) 52; age-mates, 51; age-principle, 37, (conflict with generation) 37, (compared with generation) 61; age-system (relation to military organisation) 55, (relation to kinship system) 55, (relation to Jie and Turkana) 58, (as incipient *civitas*) 60; *ameto*, 43, 44, 49, 52, 54, 55, 59, (distribution of) 50, (punitive functions) 50-1, (normative role) 60; Bongo

Labwor, *cont.*,
  age group, 43, 44, 51, 53; buffaloes (*Ekothowa*), 39, 29, (as distinguished from *Ekoria*) 39-40; circumcision and sacrifice, 47; *Edewa* age-group, 49; *Enyang' among* age-group, 49, 62-5; *Eribanya* age-group, 43, 44, 53, 62-5, (fight with *Erukojwi*), 52; *Erukojwi* age-group, 51, 53, 62-5, (close of) 43-44, (fight with *Eribanya*) 52; generation groups, 39, 54, (recruitment to) 39, (system of dual social classification) 40, (relation to age groups) 49; generation principle, 37, 61ff, (conflict with age) 37, (elementary quality) 61; God (*Rubanga*), 46; Honey badgers (*Ekoria*) 39, 49, 62-5, (as distinguished from buffaloes) 40; initiation (*kwogo*), 41, (rituals of) 44-6; iron working, 38; Jie age-system, 38, 55-6, (influence on Labwor) 39, (relation to kinship system) 56-7, (and Labwor on Turkana) 58-9; *Madanga'a* age-group, 49, 62-5; population increase, 48; sacrifice, 46, 54, (and initiation) 47; Turkana age system, 38, 55-56, (relation to kinship system) 56-7, (and Jie and Labwor) 58-9, (alternations) 55
Labwor Hills, 38
Lake Rudolph, *see* Lake Turkana
Lake Turkana, 70, 95, 183, 205 n3
Lamb, G., 32 n17
Lambert, H.E., 32 n17
Lamphear, J., 6, 55, 57-8, 62-5, 66 n5, 133-6, 138-9, 143, 148 n2, 149 n6
Langi, 38, 50, 54
Lango, 50
Lawrance, J.C.D., 20, 38
Lee, R., 188
Leeke, R.H., 64
Legesse, A., 4, 152, 153-5, 163, 173, 175, 176, 179 n3, 180 n8, 226, 228, 242 n24

Lévi-Strauss, C., 5, 47, 61, 66 n6, 108
Lewis, H.S., 84
Liban, 160-2
Lienhardt, G., 239
Lower Omo Valley, 70
Lowie, R., 30 n1
Luckham, B., 30 n2
Luling, V., 27, 29
Luo, 50, 67

McIntosh, P.C., 129 n17
Maasai, 3, 13, 17, 20, 23, 38, 47, 54, 61, 65 n3
Macha Galla 245, 262, 267 n9
Mago, River, 95, 98
Mair, Lucy, 19, 30 n1, 32 n14, 60
Mandari, 14
Maquet, J., 10
Mara, River, 98-9, 125
Margolis, M., 92 n14
Markakis, J., 260
Maronite village, 84
marriage and sets, 9, 15
Marsabit, 155, 161, 162, 178, 183-4
Masai, *see* Maasai
Mayer, P., 31 n8
Mauss, M., 24
means of production and sets, *see* property and sets
Megado Escarpment, 184
Meggitt, M., 5, 241 n4
Mela (Bodi territorial section), 102
Melbe, 161, 162, 165-6, 179 n5
Menelik, 209, 258, 262
Middleton, J., 19
Moroto, 64
Morulem district, 48
Moslems, *see* Islam
Moyale, 161, 176, 180 n8, 183
Murle, 50, 96
Mursi: 26, 92 n15, 95-131; age-grade, 96, 103, 105-7; age-group, 104; age-set, 96, 103, 119-121; Ariholi territorial section, 100-103, 108, 113, 115-6, 127, 129 n10; beating of initiands, 117; Biogolokare territorial section, 100-103, 108, 113, 116, 119, 123, 125-7, 129 n10; bridewealth, 106, 129

Mursi, *cont*.,
n15; cattle camps, 104-5, 107-8, 119; Dola territorial section, 100-3, 113, 115-6, 119, 123, 125-7; duelling, 103, 105, 106, 109-113, Garakuli clan, 117; Gongulobibi territorial section, 101-103, 108, 113, 115-6, 127, 129 n10, initiation ceremony, 113-120, 123-5; Kagisi clan, 117; Komarbe clan, 117; Kuduma, 98-9, 125; lip plates, 121; Mako territorial section, 101-3, 108, 113, 116, 123, 129 n10; Mara territorial section, 100-103, 107-8, 113, 115-6, 119, 125, 129 n10; marriage, 106; peacemaking, 98, 124-5; polygyny, incidence of, 129; population (total), 95; sorghum, 95, 98, 107; territorial-section, 99-103, 108-113; Tuhai clan, 117
Mursi Mountains, 128 n2

Nalder, L.F., 38
Nandi, 8, 16, 38, 47, 66 n6
Needham, R., 1
Ngalabong (Mursi Mountains), 128 n2
Nilo-Hamites, 50
Notes and Queries on Anthropology, 69
Nuer, 18, 19, 26, 47, 66 n3, 69, 128, 163
Nyakusa, 12, 20, 30 n7
Nyakwai, 45, 50

Obonyo-Jabwor, C., 65
Omo River, 75, 95, 98-101, 111
Orma (Warra Dai) of Tana River, 21, 24
Oromo, 6, 7, 12, 19, 21, 25-7, 38, 84, 151-2, 167-8, 174, 179 n3, 180 n8, 181 n15, 183
Oromo Liberation Front, 27n
over-aging, *see* under-aging

Paulme, D., 11, 30 n1
Peristiany, J., 12, 38, 50
Peters, E.L., 12, 83
Phillips, A., 180 n14

Plowman, C.H.F., 156, 180 n13
Pokot, 38, 50
polygyny and set-problems (Jie), 133
Poro, 30 n5
Pratt, D.T., 129 n8
prayers, 166, 180 n14
Primitive Government, 19
Prins, A.H.J., 30 n1, 38
property, (and sets) 9-11, 13-14, 15, 16, (and women) 11-12;

Radcliffe-Brown, A.R., 1, 30 n1
Rees, A., 12
Rendille, 161, 198, 205 n6
Richards, A.I., 30 n8
Rift Valley, 208
Ruel, M., 38
rules problems of, 4-5, 133
Rwanda, 10

Sahlins, M., 26, 96, 128, 129 n9
Sakuyye, 183
Salviac, Martial de., 258, 259
Samburu, 3, 6, 9, 10, 13, 15-16, 22, 31 n9, 69, 113, 136-7, 139, 142, 147, 148 n3 183
Sangree, W., 24
Sebei, 19-20
Seligman, C.G., 151
set-boundaries, difficulties of definitions of, 6-7, 22
sets and political functions, 18, 21, 152-5
sharing of wives, hardships etc., 15-18
Shekh Hussen, 24
Shoa Galla, 28-9, 245-267; Amhara (system of classification), 264; brothers, (relations between) 247, 251, (inequalities between) 252, (roles in *gada*) 265; *abba biya*, 259ff; *abba lafa*, 259 ff; blessings (by folle) 252, (by Galan) 254, (by *luba*) 254; *daballe*, 248, 249; *doroma*, 248, 249, 263; *dori*, 259; father/son relationship, 247, (and *gada*) 265; firstborn (*angaffa*) 248, 254; *folle gada*-grade, 248, 249, 251, (obscene songs) 250, (*sigaba*) 250, (in transition

Shoa Galla, *cont.*,
 ceremony 252-55, (military role) 263; *gada* functions, (political and judicial) 257, (military) 260, (religious) 261ff, (decline of) 261, 264; *gada* officers and councils, 255-6, (*hiyu*) 256, (*abba boku*) 256, 258, (*abba chaffe*) 257, (*abba dubbi*) 257, *abba sera*, 257, *abba dula*, 260; *gada* organisation, (grades) 248ff, (operational grades) 249, (recruitment to) 248, 265, 266; *gada* (leaders tribute to) 259, (effects of conquest) 257, 263, (myth of origin) 262; *gada* transition ceremony, 251ff, (symbols) 254, 265, (timing of) 255; hamlets, 247, 251, (as setting for *gada*) 264; households, 246, 266; *itimako* 248, 249; *kalacha*, 262; last-born (*kutisu*) 253; *luba* 248, 249, 253, 254, 255, (ceremonial role) 251, 253, (tribal leaders) 255, 256, 258, 259, 263; marriage, 246; Oda Nabbi, 257, 261; rinderpest, 262; seniority, 254, 255, 265; Tulama, as for Shoa Galla (definition of) 246, (settlement in Shoa) 255
Shoa, Amhara Kingdom of, 258, 260, 261, 262
Shoa Province, 245
Sidamo, 152
Sidamo Province, 207
slip mechanisms, *see* Jie
social generation, 6-8, 159-60
Somali, 22, 27, 160-1, 203, 183
Somalia, 9
Southall, A., 32 n16
Spencer, P., 1, 6, 10, 15, 19, 26, 69, 103-4, 113, 130 n19, 148 n2
Stahl, M., 179 n3
Stanley, S., 152
Stewart, F., 4, 5, 30 n1, 135-8, 145, 180 n8
Suri, 96

Tablino, Rev. P., 163
Tait, D., 19
Teso, 20, 38

Thomas, E.M., 38
Tignor, R.L., 20
Tiriki, 24
Tirmaga, 96
Toposa, 38
Torry, W., 1, 7, 28, 180 n11, 188
Tucker, A.N., 128 n5
Turbi, 161
Turkana, 17, 25, 38-9, 45, 48, 50, 54-9, 69, 82, 135, 136, 146, 183
Turner, V.W., 217
Turton, D., 26, 92 n15, 128 n3
Tutschek, C., 181 n16

under-aging and over-aging, 21, 135-6, 139-41, 143, 145-7

Vice-Lords, 3, 4, 11, 14, 31 n9

Waarta, 172, 176
Wayland, E.J., 48, 64
Welsh youth group, 12
Wiawer district, 48, 55, 64
Wilson, Monica, 12, 20, 30 n7
Wingfield, Alys, 156, 180 n13
The Winters Tale, 1
Wolof, 31 n9

Yavello, 162

Zanaki, 38
Zilmamu, 128 n4
Zulu, 17